For Sue,
Michael

Jenny's Journey
The Reality of Living the Dream

David A Schramm

Second Edition
Copyright © 2009, 2019 David A Schramm
All rights reserved.
ISBN-13:
978-1072694038

A journey is a person in itself; no two are alike. And all plans, safeguards, policing, and coercion are fruitless. We find that after years of struggle that we do not take a trip; a trip takes us.

John Steinbeck
Travels with Charley, 1962

Contents

Preface	xviii
The Dream	1
Book 1 – The Beautiful Pacific Northwest	4
Sunday, December 14, 2003	5
Monday, December 15, 2003	5
January 5th to March 15th, 2004	7
Monday, March 15, 2004	8
Monday, April 26, 2004	10
Saturday, May 01, 2004	13
Sunday, May 02, 2004	13
Monday, May 03, 2004	15
Tuesday, May 04, 2004	15
Wednesday, May 05, 2004	15
Friday, May 07, 2004	16
Monday, July 26, 2004	17
Tuesday, July 27, 2004	19
Thursday, July 29, 2004	20
Saturday, July 31, 2004	22
BOOK 2 – Passage to San Francisco	25
Thursday, September 9, 2004	25
Friday, September 10, 2004	26
Saturday, September 11, 2004	27
Sunday, September 12, 2004	27
Monday, September 13, 2004	29
Tuesday, September 14, 2004	29
Wednesday, September 15, 2004	32
Thursday, September 16, 2004	32
Friday, September 17, 2004	33
Saturday, September 18, 2004	34

Book 3: Working in San Francisco	36
October 2004	37
November 2004	38
December 2004	39
February 2005	39
March 2005	40
April 2005	41
May 2005	42
June 2005	43
July 2005	43
August 2005	45
Friday, September 02, 2005	45
Saturday, September 03, 2005	46
Sunday, September 11, 2005	47
Saturday, October 01, 2005	47
Tuesday, November 08, 2005	48
Saturday, December 03, 2005	48
Wednesday, December 28, 2005	48
Sunday, January 01, 2006	49
Passage: Bay Marine for haul out	49
Friday, March 17, 2006 6:59:54 PM	49
Sunday, March 19, 2006 11:25:12 AM	50
Saturday, March 25, 2006	51
Sunday, May 28, 2006 9:54:19 AM	51
Saturday, June 03, 2006 6:35:42 PM	52
Saturday and Sunday, June 17 and 18, 2006	52
Friday, July 14, 2006 9:07:10 PM	53
Saturday, July 15, 2006 12:02:00 PM	53
Passage: To Pillar Point for Vacation	54
Sunday, July 16, 2006 5:09:30 PM	54

Passage: To Monterey Bay	55
Monday, July 17, 2006 7:25:52 PM	55
Tuesday, July 18, 2006 7:16:01 PM	57
Wednesday, July 19, 2006 5:26:44 PM	57
Thursday, July 20, 2006 5:44:39 PM	58
Sunday, July 23, 2006 7:23:19 AM	58
Sunday, July 23, 2006 7:15:18 PM	59
Passage: To Pillar Point	60
Tuesday, July 25, 2006 12:49:19 PM	60
Passage: Pillar Point to Drakes Bay via Farallon Islands	61
Thursday, July 27, 2006 5:43:52 PM	61
Passage: Back to Emeryville	62
Saturday, July 29, 2006 8:47:26 AM	62
Passage: Napa Valley	63
Sunday, May 27, 2007 1:01:32 PM	63
Monday, May 28, 2007 9:01:32 PM	65
Tuesday, August 21, 2007 6:44:42 PM	66
Tuesday, September 04, 2007 6:05:29 PM	67
Thursday, September 06, 2007 5:09:10 PM	68
Sunday, September 16, 2007 12:23:33 PM	69
Monday, September 17, 2007 03:01:23 PM	70
Wednesday, September 19, 2007 10:42:21 AM	71
Friday, September 28, 2007 2:42:54 PM	72
Book 4: California Cruising	74
Passage: Emeryville to Pillar Point	74
Sunday, September 30, 2007 3:03:42 PM	74
Wednesday, October 03, 2007 2:52:29 PM	76
Passage: Pillar Point to Santa Cruz Harbor	77
Saturday, October 06, 2007 5:37:14 PM	78
Passage: Santa Cruz Harbor to Monterey	79

Tuesday, October 09, 2007 8:48:17 AM	79
Thursday, October 11, 2007 10:51:09 AM	80
Passage: Monterey Bay to San Simeon	81
Saturday, October 13, 2007 7:10:02 PM	81
Passage: San Luis Obispo to Cojo	82
Monday, October 15, 2007 10:55:04 PM	83
Thursday, October 18, 2007 12:26:57 AM	84
Tuesday, October 23, 2007 2:38:05 AM	86
Passage: Santa Barbara to Pelican Bay	87
Wednesday, October 24, 2007 9:52:18 PM	87
Passage: Smuggler's Cove to Marina Del Rey	88
Sunday, October 28, 2007 12:22:11 AM	89
Passage: Marina Del Rey to Newport	90
Wednesday, October 31, 2007 3:57:22 AM	90
Thursday, November 01, 2007 7:16:03 PM	92
Passage: Newport to Mission Bay	93
Sunday, November 04, 2007 1:04:30 AM	93
Passage: San Diego to Ensenada	94
Wednesday, November 14, 2007 12:26:15 AM	94
Book 5: Meandering through Mexico	**96**
Wednesday, November 14, 2007 12:26:15 AM	96
Passage: From Ensenada to Colonet	97
Friday, November 16, 2007 11:40:09 AM	98
Saturday, November 17, 2007 8:53:04 AM	99
Passage: Turtle Bay to Magdalena Bay	101
Monday, November 19, 2007 2:19:18 PM	101
Tuesday, November 20, 2007 12:25:58 PM	103
Thursday, November 22, 2007 1:38:40 PM	104
Passage: Magdalena Bay to San Jose	106
Sunday, November 25, 2007 8:12:03 AM	107

Sunday, November 25, 2007 6:51:41 PM	108
Monday, December 03, 2007 10:41:51 AM	110
Passage: Los Muertos to La Paz	112
Friday, December 07, 2007 6:31:14 PM	112
Sunday, December 16, 2007 3:05:36 PM	115
Friday, December 21, 2007 4:00:45 PM	116
Passage: La Paz to Partida	118
Thursday, December 27, 2007 1:12:09 PM	118
Friday, December 28, 2007 2:53:22 PM	118
Passage: Isla Partida to La Paz	120
Friday, January 04, 2008 1:57:54 PM	121
Passage: La Paz to Muertos	122
Saturday, January 05, 2008 5:23:15 PM	122
Passage: Muertos to Mazatlan	123
Monday, January 07, 2008 9:59:13 AM	124
Wednesday, January 09, 2008 6:37:50 PM	126
Wednesday, January 09, 2008 7:09:41 PM	126
Passage: Mazatlan to Isla Isabella	128
Monday, January 14, 2008 4:41:00 PM	128
Tuesday, January 15, 2008 11:46:17 AM	130
Wednesday, January 16, 2008 4:04:15 PM	131
Wednesday, January 16, 2008 5:07:29 PM	132
Passage: Isla Isabela to La Cruz	133
Thursday, January 17, 2008 8:24:23 PM	133
Friday, January 18, 2008 8:30:18 PM	134
Monday, January 21, 2008 5:48:43 PM	136
Sunday, January 27, 2008 4:34:49 PM	137
Sunday, January 27, 2008 4:50:59 PM	139
Passage: La Cruz to Ipala	140
Passage: Ypala to Chamela	141

Wednesday, February 06, 2008 3:38:13 PM	143
Passage: Ipala to Tenacatita	143
Friday, February 08, 2008 9:40:05 PM	144
Passage: Tenacatita to Barra de Navidad	145
Saturday, February 16, 2008 12:33:41 PM	145
Passage: Barra to Manzanillo	146
Wednesday, February 20, 2008 2:25:14 PM	146
Passage: Las Hadas to Santiago Bay	148
Passage: From Santiago Bay to Zihuatanejo	148
Monday, February 25, 2008 4:00:52 PM	148
Saturday, March 01, 2008 6:26:03 PM	150
Passage: Zihuatanejo to Papona	152
Passage: Papanoa to Acapulco	152
Thursday, March 06, 2008 5:44:53 PM	154
Saturday, March 08, 2008 11:56:58 AM	155
Thursday, March 13, 2008 3:31:52 PM	157
Passage: Acapulco to Puerto Marques	158
Passage: Puerto Marques to Jicaral	158
Saturday, March 15, 2008 12:01:19 PM	159
Sunday, March 16, 2008 10:34:07 PM	160
Passage: Jacaral to Marina Chahué	162
Wednesday, March 19, 2008 1:30:57 PM	162
Passage: Marina Chahué to Barillas, El Salvador	163
Sunday, March 23, 2008 11:16:45 AM	163
Sunday, March 23, 2008 9:50:49 PM	164
Monday, March 24, 2008 1:41:11 AM	166
Book 5: Central America Wilderness	168
Tuesday, March 25, 2008 8:08:08 AM	168
Passage: Acajutla toward Barillas	170
Passage: Acajutla toward Barillas	170

Wednesday, March 26, 2008 9:32:23 AM	170
Friday, March 28, 2008 5:43:37 PM	172
Thursday, April 10, 2008 3:31:01 PM	175
Friday, April 25, 2008 1:20:34 PM	178
Thursday, May 01, 2008 9:53:08 AM	179
Friday, May 02, 2008 2:57:30 PM	180
Thursday, May 08, 2008 1:00:54 PM	181
Passage: Barillas to Isla Meanquera	182
Saturday, May 10, 2008 6:10:01 PM	182
Sunday, May 11, 2008 6:50:42 AM	183
Passage: Isla Meanguera to Puesta del Sol	184
Sunday, May 11, 2008 1:58:38 PM	185
Wednesday, May 14, 2008 6:06:57 PM	186
Sunday, May 18, 2008 8:54:58 PM	187
Passage: Puesta del Sol to Bahía Santa Elena	188
Thursday, May 22, 2008 7:39:04 AM	190
Friday, May 23, 2008 6:43:40 AM	191
Saturday, May 24, 2008 6:50:54 AM	192
Monday, May 26, 2008 7:54:12 AM	192
Passage: Bahia Santa Elena to Playa de Panama	193
Monday, May 26, 2008 7:23:06 PM	193
Wednesday, May 28, 2008 8:20:07 AM	193
Wednesday, May 28, 2008 11:35:25 AM	195
Friday, May 30, 2008 7:15:48 AM	196
Passage: Playa Panama to Potrero	198
Sunday, June 01, 2008 7:36:13 AM	198
Passage: Potrero to Carrillo	199
Passage: Carrillo to Ballena Bay	200
Passage: Ballena Bay to Naranjo	200
Thursday, June 05, 2008 11:30:29 AM	200

Thursday, June 05, 2008 5:39:12 PM	201
Passage: Playa Naranjo to Los Sueños	202
Passage: Los Suenos to Quepos	202
Monday, June 09, 2008 10:18:25 AM	202
Passage: Quepos to Drake Bay	204
Passage: Drake Bay to Gulfito	205
Tuesday, June 17, 2008 6:56:49 AM	208
Wednesday, June 18, 2008 6:48:56 AM	209
Monday, June 23, 2008 11:47:08 AM	210
Tuesday, July 01, 2008 12:30:37 PM	211
Tuesday, July 04, 2008 9:30:01 PM	212
Passage: Gulfito to Isla Partida	212
Passage: Isla Parida to Bahia Honda	213
Tuesday, July 08, 2008 7:28:58 PM	213
Passage: Bahia Honda to Isla Catalina	214
Thursday, July 10, 2008 1:34:35 PM	215
Passage: Isla Santa Catalina to Bahía Naranjo	222
Friday, July 11, 2008 6:05:14 PM	222
Passage: Naranjo Cove to Flamenco Amador Anchorage	222
Saturday, July 12, 2008 8:29:44 PM	223
Sunday, July 13, 2008 1:41:55 PM	225
Thursday, July 17, 2008 4:00:52 PM	225
Tuesday, July 22, 2008 8:50:23 AM	226
Wednesday, July 23, 2008 3:59:35 PM	227
Monday, July 28, 2008 3:20:20 PM	228
Tuesday, July 29, 2008 7:15:14 AM	229
Passage: Towing *Ketching Up* to Balboa	230
Sunday, August 03, 2008 8:55:57 AM	231
Thursday, August 07, 2008 8:42:32 AM	232
Friday, August 08, 2008 5:12:07 PM	233

Passage: Panama Canal Transit	234
Monday, August 11, 2008 1:22:02 PM	234
Wednesday, August 13, 2008 8:50:07 PM	238
Book 5: Romantic Panama and Colombia	240
Passage: Shelter Bay to Chagres River	240
Sunday, August 17, 2008 1:20:18 PM	240
Monday, August 18, 2008 11:17:27 AM	241
Passage: Chagres River to Portobello	242
Tuesday, August 19, 2008 12:19:08 PM	242
Tuesday, August 19, 2008 10:05:19 PM	243
Passage: Portobello to Isla Grande	243
Friday, August 22, 2008 3:34:02 PM	244
Sunday, August 24, 2008 8:45:35 AM	245
Tuesday, August 26, 2008 11:18:26 AM	246
Friday, August 29, 2008 12:00:43 PM	247
Sunday, August 31, 2008 10:14:08 AM	248
Passage: Isla Grande to Chichime Cay	248
Monday, September 01, 2008 5:00:54 PM	249
Tuesday, September Cays02, 2008 1:03:04 PM	250
Thursday, September 04, 2008 12:16:52 PM	251
Passage: Chichime Cays to Isla Grande	251
Saturday, September 06, 2008 1:50:53 PM	252
Passage: Isla Grande to Shelter Bay Marina	253
Thursday, September 11, 2008 8:23:53 PM	253
Passage: Shelter Bay to Isla Grande	254
Saturday, September 20, 2008 1:24:59 PM	254
Passage: Isla Grande to Chichime	255
Sunday, September 21, 2008 7:15:14 PM	255
Passage: Chichime to Coco Bandero	256
Monday, September 22, 2008 6:22:49 PM	257

Tuesday, September 23, 2008 11:47:55 AM	257
Thursday, September 25, 2008 9:42:36 AM	259
Friday, September 26, 2008 9:29:04 PM	260
Sunday, September 28, 2008 1:27:29 PM	261
Passage: Coco Bandero to Isla Fuerte, Colombia	262
Monday, September 29, 2008 12:26:33 PM	262
Tuesday, September 30, 2008 11:25:52 AM	263
Passage: Isla Bandalero to Islas Rosarios	264
Thursday, October 02, 2008 7:22:20 AM	264
Saturday, October 04, 2008 1:10:44 PM	265
Sunday, October 05, 2008 8:30:05 PM	266
Thursday, October 09, 2008 5:46:39 PM	267
Wednesday, October 15, 2008 6:50:05 PM	269
Thursday, October 16, 2008 9:30:55 AM	270
Saturday, October 18, 2008 6:50:05 PM	270
Wednesday, October 15, 2008 7:02:12 PM	271
Wednesday, October 22, 2008 9:30:55 PM	272
Saturday, October 25, 2008 5:04:43 PM	274
Thursday, October 30, 2008 9:19:30 PM	275
Friday, October 31, 2008 10:35:35 PM	276
Saturday, November 01, 2008 5:04:35 PM	276
Friday, November 07, 2008 10:27:21 AM	277
Sunday, November 09, 2008 11:34:44 PM	278
Sunday, November 09, 2008 11:49:54 PM	279
Monday, November 10, 2008 8:44:53 PM	280
Saturday, November 15, 2008 3:39:38 PM	281
Friday, November 21, 2008 6:50:44 PM	281
Saturday, December 13, 2008 5:56:23 PM	283
Monday, January 12, 2009 11:45:56 PM	285
Monday, January 19, 2009 6:16:30 PM	287

Monday, January 19, 2009 7:31:48 PM	287
Wednesday, January 21, 2009 4:04:03 PM	288
Thursday, January 22, 2009 11:17:11 PM	289
Saturday, January 24, 2009 10:23:43 AM	289
Sunday, January 25, 2009 1:53:13 PM	290
Monday, January 26, 2009 8:06:35 PM	290
Tuesday, January 27, 2009 5:52:59 PM	291
Wednesday, January 28, 2009 6:23:42 PM	292
Book 7: Crossing the Caribbean	294
Passage: Cartagena to Punta Hermosa	294
Sunday, February 01, 2009 6:22:09 PM	294
Monday, February 02, 2009 1:33:21 PM	295
Passage: Punta Hermosa to Rodadero	296
Tuesday, February 03, 2009 6:10:16 PM	297
Wednesday, February 04, 2009 11:47:01 AM	298
Passage: Rodadero to Bahia Guayraca	300
Thursday, February 05, 2009 12:08:36 PM	300
Friday, February 06, 2009 10:23:50 AM	301
Saturday, February 07, 2009 7:31:34 AM	302
Sunday, February 08, 2009 9:01:11 AM	302
Passage: Bahía Guayraca to Puerto Bolivar	303
Tuesday, February 10, 2009 8:05:04 PM	304
Wednesday, February 11, 2009 7:02:57 PM	306
Passage: Puerto Bolivar to Bahia Honda	306
Thursday, February 12, 2009 3:00:38 PM	307
Friday, February 13, 2009 12:52:34 PM	308
Sunday, February 15, 2009 8:05:03 AM	308
Passage: Bahia Honda to Boca Chica DR	310
Monday, February 16, 2009 2:33:14 PM	310
Tuesday, February 17, 2009 2:40:20 PM	312

Wednesday, February 18, 2009 5:57:59 PM	313
Wednesday, February 18, 2009 7:42:20 PM	314
Tuesday, February 24, 2009 8:20:42 AM	314
Passage: Boca Chica to Samana DR	315
Thursday, February 26, 2009 7:09:37 AM	315
Thursday, February 26, 2009 2:54:45 PM	316
Passage: Isla Saona to Samana Bay	317
Saturday, February 28, 2009 5:59:34 PM	317
Tuesday, March 03, 2009 1:28:30 PM	318
Wednesday, March 04, 2009 6:00:46 PM	320
Passage: Samana Bay to Las Haities Park	321
Sunday, March 08, 2009 3:33:14 PM	322
Passage: Whale Watching	323
Monday, March 09, 2009 6:54:35 PM	323
Wednesday, March 11, 2009 9:12:49 AM	324
Saturday, March 14, 2009 8:36:01 AM	326
Monday, March 16, 2009 8:31:15 AM	327
Friday, March 20, 2009 7:20:10 AM	327
Saturday, March 21, 2009 2:26:30 PM	328
Wednesday, March 25, 2009 4:31:52 PM	329
Saturday, March 28, 2009 8:05:58 AM	330
Tuesday, March 31, 2009 12:37:07 PM	331
Thursday, April 02, 2009 1:04:17 PM	332
Thursday, April 09, 2009 5:22:16 PM	332
Friday, April 17, 2009 11:15:56 AM	333
Sunday, April 19, 2009 1:21:28 PM	335
Tuesday, April 21, 2009 3:37:40 PM	337
Book 8: Heading Home	339
Passage: Dominican Republic to Turks	339
Thursday, April 23, 2009 6:03:37 AM	340

Passage: French Cay to Mayaguana	342
Friday, April 24, 2009 6:16:04 PM	344
Sunday, April 26, 2009 7:14:53 AM	345
Sunday, April 26, 2009 5:39:49 PM	346
Monday, April 27, 2009 6:33:25 PM	347
Tuesday, April 28, 2009 7:08:16 PM	348
Wednesday, April 29, 2009 1:03:32 PM	349
Passage: Mayaguana to Georgetown	350
Friday, May 01, 2009 2:44:38 PM	350
Saturday, May 02, 2009 12:20:33 PM	351
Thursday, May 07, 2009 10:06:26 AM	352
Passage: Georgetown to Staniel Cay	353
Friday, May 08, 2009 5:40:17 PM	353
Passage: Staniel Cay to Highborne Cay	354
Sunday, May 10, 2009 3:07:35 PM	355
Monday, May 11, 2009 8:24:09 AM	355
Tuesday, May 12, 2009 11:43:20 AM	356
Passage: Highborne Cay to Nassau	357
Thursday, May 14, 2009 6:28:57 PM	357
Passage: Nassau to Chub Cay	359
Friday, May 15, 2009 6:02:39 PM	359
Passage: Chub Cay to St Marys	360
Monday, May 18, 2009 5:36:09 PM	362
Wednesday, May 20, 2009 11:37:43 AM	364
Wednesday, May 20, 2009 11:51:43 AM	365
Thursday, May 21, 2009 11:26:29 AM	368
Wednesday, May 27, 2009 9:33:02 AM	368
Cruise Totals	369

Preface

Around the world, thousands of wonderful vessels patiently wait for someone to become their caregiver and release them from the land into their natural element of the sea. They are incredible works of art and engineering born to be both vehicle and home. Their purpose in life is to transport their caregivers to distant places, foreign cultures and to provide them shelter against Mother Nature's worst conditions. When fully engaged in the realization of dreams, vessel and caregivers bond souls. This bonding begins before the purchase and continues to build over years of care giving, safe arrivals and shared experiences. Just as there are many kinds of dreams, there are as many boats designed to realize them. Unfortunately for a thousand reasons the dreams often dim with passing years and bonds are broken. Sometimes this disappointment is because the vessel cannot fulfill its expected role. However, mostly the dream is lost along the way by dreamers who take an easier path, leaving their charge tied to the earth, slowly decaying in great sadness.

I dedicate this book to the dreamers who are still engaged; still dreaming, planning, and getting ready. I know it takes more courage than the majority of dreamers have to actually step beyond the rim of their daily lives and leave for distant shores. My hope is to substitute dock folklore and TV fearcasts with real information gained from actually going.

I created this book from *Jenny's* log that started the day I bought her in La Conner Washington and kept all the way to St. Marys Georgia five years later. It reveals an evolution from novice passagemaker to experienced passagemaker and an evolution of a great passagemaking boat to a perfect passagemaking boat, at least for me. I experienced wonderful weather, nature, seas, people, and emotions and unpleasant weather, nature, seas, people and emotions.

You know the old adage, "The older you get, the quicker time flies." When I turned sixty it seemed like my fifties had flown by in a flash. And, for each of these years I was only able to count my memorable moments on one hand. To me, this was unacceptable. I determined to change. Since time is compressed as we get older, then we must also accelerate our experiences just to break even. So, I asked myself how I wanted to spend the last fleeting days of my life in which I would be physically fit enough to take on serious challenges. I figured that after seventy you just could not count on your health and fitness. Larry and Lynn Pardee's words echoed in my head: "Go now!" So, I did. Over the nineteen months of continuous cruising from San Francisco to St. Marys Georgia, life experiences were delivered an order of magnitude faster than ever before. Some were incredibly good and others not so good. I was living fully.

Finally, if a life's success can be measured by the people you bring joy to and the stories you can tell at the end, then there is no better way to live than cruising to distant shores. There is no better way to wrap up an adventurous life. Let me introduce you to this experience.

I want to thank all the wonderful people I met along the way including the fellow cruisers on the boats:

M/V Beverly S	S/V Lovely Rita
S/V Sweet Loraine	S/V Monju
M/V Nexus	S/V Rhapsody
S/V Moody Blues	S/V Tropical Dance
M/V Wandering Star	M/V Diesel Duck
S/V Encore	S/V Ketching Up
S/V Spirit	S/V Pendragon
M/V Wahoo	S/V Delfin Solo
S/V Astor	S/V Dubhe

Special mention goes to Larry and Sue Tomback on the motor vessel *Beverly S* who gave Mary and me so much knowledge and support. They verbally offered the assurance I have tried to provide you here. We might not have stepped over the rim without them. And there are many others I hope to encounter again in some distant port. Special mention also goes to the wonderful people I met who were natives in the countries I visited and allowed me to briefly experience their lives, share their ideas, and learn their cultures. While fellow cruisers provided support and comfort in wild places, my time with these people expanded my mind immeasurably and made the experience meaningful.

The Dream

One of my first childhood memories is set on the beach of the New Jersey shore. I was six. I had let a helium balloon go flying and watched as it went out to sea. I asked Mom where it would go. She said Europe if it stayed in the air long enough. I stared in wonder. I wondered what the journey would be like and what Europe was. It has been a long time since then, and while I have been to Europe several times, that balloon is still pulling me out to sea.

My Dad grew up on the New Jersey coast and spent his summers kicking around in makeshift boats. He volunteered for the Army Air Corps just out of College in 1942. He became a B17 pilot and flew sixteen missions over Germany in WWII. The Germans shot him down twice but miraculously he lost no lives. After the war, money was dear, but the pull of saltwater was still strong in him. When I was seven, I remember going to the Sears Roebuck hardware store with him and Pappy. Together they bought their first outboard motor; a six horsepower Elgin. After that our vacations were usually to saltwater and the Elgin was always with us, clamped to the back of a rowboat. No one had money for a boat of his or her own, so you rented a rowboat along with the small seashore cottage. Our Elgin provided the power for us to go out to the Virginia barrier islands to fish and play in the surf. Eventually Dad saved enough money to buy a boat and I grew up with outboards in the family. I still have that Elgin motor to keep those memories alive.

As I grew older, my spirit of adventure pulled me toward sailboats. I read every book that existed on voyaging. My heroes were Magellan, Cook, Darwin, Chichester, Larry and Lynn Pardee, Sterling Hayden, Joe Richards and so many other pioneers. I had a family by the time I graduated from College so thoughts of cruising the world were put in the deep freeze. However, I did manage to buy a sailboat along the way. I had a Herreshoff Eagle named *Harmony* on the Chesapeake Bay for a couple of years. She was gaff rigged centerboard sloop, looking very much like *Princess* above the waterline. She was perfect for the bay and we went for weekend sails with an occasional overnight thrown in. The dream remained alive, but still submerged. Work and family life demanded my full attention and the kids found sailing boring.

The years passed and all of a sudden, the kids were grown and raising families of their own. I was divorced and remarried. My second wife Mary did not grow up with saltwater experiences and while I mentioned the idea of sailing now and again, I pretty much had given up the cruising dream. Mary and I vacationed in wonderful places for a couple of weeks at a time and enjoyed traveling and experiencing new cultures. In 2003 we decided to explore Alaska for a couple of weeks. We traveled this vast and incredible land on the Alaska railroad system. Then we experienced the Alaskan coast on the Alaska ferry system. It was a wonderful, magnificent trip. We had time on the ferry to talk about retirement and how much we were enjoying this trip. The parts that did not work on this trip were the inability to bring our new puppy Nicholas, the cost of traveling this way, the hassle of packing, unpacking, and living out of hotel rooms. We talked about RVs and other options, dismissing them all. We were in a quandary.

Then we stopped at Valdez Alaska. There was Nordhavn 40 on the hard. While I had never seen a yacht like this I instinctively knew what it was. Maybe, just maybe this was the answer. It was obviously a comfortable cruising boat with good range and it looked seaworthy. I took a zillion photos so I could find out more about this kind of boat. We talked about the possibility of cruising on a boat like this. It was August 2003.

In September, we did some research about Nordhavn, Cheoy Lee, Kaddy Krogen, DeFever and other trawler yachts. I found out the prices and began to learn about their designs and capabilities. Meanwhile, we signed up for USCG boating courses and took a "Close Quarters Maneuvering" hands on course offered at one of the local marinas on a 32-foot trawler. Mary took the helm for the first time and did very well. We talked some more.

Before taking the next step, I explained my lifelong dream of going to sea to Mary and that I had long ago closed the door on that dream because she did not share it. I cautioned her about reopening this door as I might not be able to close it again. We agreed to crack it a bit. We went to the San Francisco Trawler Feast that October, attended the seminars, visited the boats, and talked to cruisers. Mary became more comfortable about the concept so we took another step. We flew to San Diego to meet with a broker and see some boats.

The first boat we saw was *Brass Ring*, a 1997 Nordhavn 46. Mary fell in love with her and while we courteously saw the other boats, we were in love. Mary agreed that she could easily live on a boat like this. Unfortunately, *Brass Ring* was out of our price range. A couple of weeks later we flew to Seattle and met with another broker. He had a Nordhavn 40 and two 46's to show us. The 40 did not impress us and neither did one of the 46's. But *Viking*, a 1994 Nordhavn 46 had potential. Like *Brass Ring* it was owned by a pilot and so was fully decked out with electronics and well cared for. Pilots live by their instruments and aircraft maintenance so they know the importance of looking after their vessels.

Viking was still priced out of our range, but now it was November in the Pacific Northwest and we figured the owner would not see another offer before next June. After some discussion and trepidation we took the next step and made an offer we could afford. We expected it to be rejected. It was. We waited. In December, the owner came back with a counter. We countered the counter at $20,000 above our original offer. Then we were surprised by an acceptance. Wow! We were going to be the owners of a 60,000-pound yacht. What had we done?

We decided to rename her *Jenny*. There is no *Jenny* in our history. Subconsciously this name probably came from the movie Forest Gump. For me

Jenny was a dream come true; a quality, focused, comfortable seagoing vessel. We closed the deal on December 14th in Anacortes Washington. What had we done?

BOOK 1 – THE BEAUTIFUL PACIFIC NORTHWEST

"A good sailing vessel is a thousand boats in one. She is a different hull on every different course and in every degree of tilt as she heels over. Within a moment in a changing seaway she may present a score of different contours to the water."

Joe Richards
Princess 1956

Sunday, December 14, 2003

We closed the deal in Anacortes on December 14th, 2003 and *Viking* became *Jenny*. On the way back to *Jenny* we stopped at a general store and bought some towels and sheets so I could camp out on her for a day or two. In order to avoid Washington State sales and use tax, I had made plans through the broker to rent a slip at Canoe Cove, a marina near Sidney on Vancouver Island Canada. The plan was to take *Jenny* to Canoe Cove the next day. Our insurance company stipulated that I needed a licensed captain on board until he certified that I could handle *Jenny* safely. I fully agreed with this stipulation! *Jenny* was enormous compared to *Harmony* or any of the outboard boats my Dad had. During the purchase process, I had her surveyed by Captain Galen Tyler. I liked him so I hired Galen to be my captain as we crossed from La Conner to Canoe Cove.

Proud new owners David and Mary

Monday, December 15, 2003

The departure location was latitude 48 degrees 40.950 minutes north, longitude 123 degrees 24.078 minutes west.

The US Coast Guard was broadcasting gale warnings when Galen and I departed Shelter Bay at La Conner Washington at 05:50 AM. It was blowing 35 knots in Shelter Bay when we started. I had no idea what was in store! I am sure Galen did but he was not talking and neither was *Jenny*. Both wanted to see my stuff. *Jenny* stepped in time with the tides, riding with the current as it filled the canal from the south and emptied it to the north as we crossed the midpoint. In the protection of the canal, we easily made it to Anacortes. However, it got nasty as we moved into the Rosario Strait.

The wind built to over fifty knots and developed six to eight foot seas. Fortunately, most of the weather was coming from the southeast and quartering *Jenny's* stern. This was my first real experience with *Jenny* and such weather. Galen was determined not to interfere with our first date. Nice! Along with the weather, some barge got sick and disgorged its entire load of logs. They were all over the place just waiting to do violent harm in the choppy water. Here I was at *Jenny's* helm steering us through this nasty weather and logs. She was nervous. She sensed that I was untested.

Jenny has "towed passive stabilizers" to slow her rolling motion in rough water. She has two large aluminum outriggers about twenty feet long that run straight out from her sides when she is underway. This makes her about fifty-five feet wide. The forty-pound steel stabilizers called "birds" hang by chain at the ends of the outriggers. They are triangular steel plates designed to fly fifteen feet under the surface and dig in when they are pulled upward. As *Jenny* tries to roll she digs the plate into the water and uses the leverage of her outrigger to keep herself from rolling. It is a very simple and effective system used by thousands of fishing boats, including the swordfish boat Andrea Gail in "The Perfect Storm". Once her birds are in the water, *Jenny* is rock solid steady.

Unfortunately, I could not put *Jenny's* birds in the water because of the logs so she rolled like a rubber ducky. *Jenny's* bottom is completely round and for the first fifteen degrees to each side, very tender. She worked into a nice thirty to forty degree swing every six to seven seconds. Once at fifteen degrees though, she stiffened up rapidly and I never felt she was trying to throw us or was in any danger except from the logs. She was an old pro at this.

I was very busy at the helm and at the same time thrilled by *Jenny* and the grandeur that can only come from experiencing Mother Nature in her anger. I was also amazed how quietly and easily *Jenny* carried us. We could not even hear the wind until it went over fifty knots. Galen wanted me to learn and I was climbing a very steep curve! He did not even show me how *Jenny's* autopilot worked until we were out of Rosario Strait and into the more protected channels among the carpet of San Juan Islands. By the time we reached Sidney to check into Canada I knew *Jenny* was quite a lady. We cleared customs at Van Isle Marina in Sidney at 3:30 PM and loaded fuel to top off her tanks for the winter. We then took her up to Canoe Cove Marina and into her slip. We had her snuggled in by 4:30 PM. Whew! I was ready for some cold beer. Galen and I had dinner at the very nice marina restaurant and then he headed for Sidney to catch the ferry back to Anacortes. I came back to *Jenny* by myself and let her cradle me through the night. The next day I said farewell, headed for the airport and flew back home to San Francisco, work and Christmas.

The arrival location was latitude 48 degrees 40.948 minutes north, longitude 123 degrees 24.074 minutes west.

January 5th to March 15th, 2004

Like all women, *Jenny* needs constant care and attention. Thought distant, I would not neglect her. Marty Seaholm, the owner of *Viking* had hired a local Canadian to care for her when she was resting in Canada. His name was Kevin and he worked out of Sidney. I met him at *Jenny* before leaving her in December and hired him to do the same for me. Kevin visited her when he could between his other jobs and he documented the following care between January 5th and March 15th. I also contracted with Philbrooks, the premier boat yard in the area, to give *Jenny* all new cushions. Hers were original and well warn out.

Below is Kevin's log for which he charged us about $12,000 US.

- January 5
Checked boat and furnace operation, furnace cycling. Started and warmed main engine. Looked for missing charges, not found. Bridge locker lid had condensation on it. Replaced paper towels at fittings into bridge heater. They were damp but not wet. Ran bilge pump as there was 4" of water in the bilge.

- January 9
Checked *Jenny* and topped up antifreeze in the heating system

- February 4
Checked *Jenny* and topped up antifreeze in the heating system. Found leak at bridge heater. Added water to batteries. Pumped clear water from bilge.

- February 7
Checked boat. The starboard VHF antenna was lying on bridge top. Repositioned and tightened the mount pivot bolt. Drained coolant from heating system. Discovered aft water tank vent not functioning. Cleaned and treated battery connections on batteries under master bunk. Found bilge water to be a combination of fresh water coming down the stack, PSS shaft seal and antifreeze from the heating system. Forward head needs overhaul. It is internally bypassing from discharge to suction.

- February 11
Took Lane from Philbrooks over to *Jenny* to estimate the upholstery work.

- March 4
Checked boat.

- March 10
Checked bilge, some water level increase in past thirty days. Battery lid on top of engine has less than 1/2 inch of water in it. Ran water system to freshen water in tanks. Turned on fridge and hot water heater. Checked watch berth - dry again as usual. Checked and changed forward GFI. Checked alternator operation - no output. Changed louver on heater vent in master suite. Checked skiff inflation.

- March 13
Reviewed systems and operations with owner.

- Equipment:
    Battery for EPIRB
    Hydrostatic release for EPIRB
    Liquid filled pressure gauge for pressure water tank.
    GFI outlet
    Fuel biocide
    Heat duct louver
    Delo 400 fifteen/forty oil (16 liters)
    Bronze elbows for forward holding tank.

Monday, March 15, 2004

Ladies do not like to reveal their secrets. They believe it is part of the allure and mystique that keeps their men interested. I flew up to see how *Jenny* had survived the winter, to begin giving her some personal care and getting her ready for Mary and I to begin our first cruising adventures with her. When I left *Jenny* in December I took all her maintenance records with me back home to San Francisco. I was fortunate that they were detailed and complete. I guess that was the pilot coming out in Marty. By April, I had read them thoroughly and discovered something interesting. It was to be the first of *Jenny's* many secrets. I noticed that Marty had maintained a normal motor oil watch and change schedule initially. However in the last several months of use, his focus on oil consumption gradually increased until it became an obsession. Hmmmm??? When I went on the sea trial, I did not see any smoke coming from *Jenny's* dry stack exhaust. However, I did notice some small black Cheetos on her upper deck.

Jenny's motor is a Lugger, a John Deere six cylinder 6.8 liter naturally aspirated diesel. I named it JD for short. JD is *Jenny's* heart of steel. JD produces 105 horsepower at a very low RPM and once started does not need anything but fuel and air to keep running. Electricity is not required. JD is rated for 20,000 hours of continuous duty and only had 2,600 hours to date. JD will be alive and beating long after I have been plowed under, probably by another John Deere.

The first thing Kevin and I did when I arrived in March was to change JD's oil. I knew that JD's specification was for it to hold 17 liters of oil. I had a hunch about what might be happening so we measured the old oil as it came out. We got to 17 liters and kept on going; 18, 19, 20, 21. Just as I suspected, JD was drowning in its own oil. While this is not a problem unless the oil got so high it froths and stops lubricating, it certainly was causing JD to choke some down and blow it up the stack as soot and black Cheetos. I asked Kevin about this and he said he had been filling it to JD's level indicated by its dipstick marks. We refilled JD with 17 liters of oil and I looked at the dipstick. Sure enough, it showed that the oil was below LOW. I had already noticed that JD was mounted at a slight tilt with the stern end down and the forward end up. With the dipstick located at JD's front, I wondered if it was designed to measure a level motor.

As I pondered this, I happened to turn it over. Barely visible, but definitely there, were another set of marks. The John Deere factory had not made them. Someone added them sometime later. Better yet, the oil was exactly on the top mark. Perfect. I had uncovered *Jenny's* first secret. Since then, I have found that JD does not burn a drop of oil between its 200-hour change intervals. I suspect that part of the reason we got a good price for *Jenny* was the fact that Marty believed he had a motor problem. *Jenny* just did not reveal her secret to Marty or Kevin. Just me. She had given me a kiss. We changed the oil in her generator and took her out for a run. Released from her slip, she smiled the whole time. I got a few more hours experience at her helm. This time it was in calm wind and water! Trust was building between us. Then I had to leave her alone again and head back to work in San Francisco. I promised to be back soon.

The following care was documented by Kevin between March 16 and April 25. Kevin charged me about $15,000 for the work and equipment. This included the new cushions. I budgeted generously for *Jenny's* spring debut, but it was now becoming clear to me that I could not afford to keep her so far away and have to rely on hired caregivers.

- March 28
Checked the boat and the CO alarm going off because the AA batteries were low.

- April 5
Assisted in the removal of the life raft for complete checkout. Installed repaired alternator, check fluid levels, started engine, removed bridge window covers, cast off, moved boat to Canoe Cove boat lift for bottom paint. Strung retrieval lines for the fish.

- April 16
Pressure tested genset cooling system and it would not hold pressure. Furnace not operating. Check fuses (thirty amp Buss Fuse under master bed was loose).

- April 20
Topped up cooling system in Gen Set and pressure tested again. It held this time but there are indications there might be a leak.

- April 21
Removed sound cover from genset and dried drip pan on left side of engine. Pressurized the cooling system. Water pump inlet hose connection leaking. Tightened hose clamps and checked the rest of the system - OK. Reinstalled

sound shield, tested furnace power circuit. Fuse holder no good. Replaced fuse holder under master bed and circuit now energized.

- April 22
Launched boat and returned to the slip. Assisted R&R upholstery. Tried several attachment points for the block on the stabilizer retrieval line. Deployed starboard stabilizing boom and removed bolt from starboard stabilizing boom base. Quick pressure wash of entire vessel. Removed battery from skiff and put battery on charger. Rigged new foot bump for the dinghy. Checked flare kits and started watermaker. Added coolant to the furnace system, circulating pump is leaking. Removed prop from the dinghy outboard. Figured out wiring route for 12 volt accessory plugs for new navigation computer.

- April 23
Loaded and mounted life raft. Moused shackles, installed starboard eye nut for additional retrieval line block. Mounted fire extinguishers, reinstalled pump mount and belt guard. Installed repaired prop on dinghy. Lubricated dinghy steering shift and throttle.

- April 24
Installed new battery in dinghy. Tested starting - ok. Pumped up dinghy and installed cover. Waxed life raft canister and secured lanyard. Installed port eye nut for stabilizer retrieval line clock. Washed overflow antifreeze from heating system off decks. Installed new bracket on belt guard. Replaced oil pads under engine and furnace. Temporarily wired in power supply cord for new navigation computer.

-Equipment
    12 1 liter Delo 400 fifteen/forty oil
    Dinghy inflator pump
    3" heater bent
    Groco head service kit.
    #4 single swivel block
    Dinghy start battery
    flare gun shells
    Flare gun in bag
    Amp connector components
    Life raft service and certification
    repaired aluminum prop for dinghy
    Alternator repairs

Monday, April 26, 2004

Mary and I are onboard *Jenny* again! This is the first time Mary has been onboard since we purchased her in December. *Jenny* was an empty vessel with no bedding, no plates, no kitchen stuff, etc. We needed to move in. We packed

Mary's Audi to the gills and drove all the way from Concord, California to Canada Saturday. After a long day of driving, we almost caught the last Ferry from Vancouver to Swartz Bay at 9:00 PM but were stalled for 45 minutes clearing customs into Canada. Fortunately, they did not ask to go thought all our stuff! We would have been there all night. There were no more ferries until morning and we were dog tired. We stopped at the first motel and crashed. We smuggled Nicholas in, got a bit to eat and fell into bed!

Nicholas is only eighteen months old and just had his first long trip in the car. He is a Havanese and weighs in at a whopping twelve pounds. His face is cute like a sea otter's and he is all puppy energy and happiness. He has not seen another dog since we got him and lives with our cat Samantha back home. He thinks he is a person, but has picked up some feline behaviors. We made the mistake of letting him sleep with us when he was a baby and he does so to this day. It is not a problem in our king size bed at home, but it might get interesting in *Jenny*'s queen size bed.

Nicholas standing watch

Sunday morning we were up early and caught the 09:00 AM ferry to Swartz Bay. It was wonderful to see the water and islands from the ferry. It was beautiful out, a perfect day and we were to *Jenny* by 11:00 AM. The rest of Sunday and all day today we unloaded the car and set up home. Since we had the car, we were able to go to Sidney where there are many places to shop.

Marc, our next-door neighbor stopped by Sunday and we chatted a bit. He is a live aboard and asked if I had an annual lease on my slip. I replied affirmative and he was perturbed since he had told the Marina that he wanted to switch from his slip (78 with a starboard gang way) to mine (80 with a port gang way). I then told him I had trouble backing *Jenny* in to 80 (she must dock starboard side to the gangway) and had asked them to look out for another slip for me! Well, we decided to swap during the week.

Jenny's navigation computer was a tower PC, taking up a lot of space in her pilothouse locker. I wanted to use this locker to store life jackets. It also had a nice but very large monitor that required one of the folding tables in the pilothouse to be set up, blocking the port pilothouse door. I extracted her old navigation computer equipment on Monday and the got her new laptop set up. This change opened up a tremendous amount of space in the pilothouse. The Bluetooth com port connection to the GPS works fine and I will have to test the autopilot when we go out.

On Tuesday, I set up the rear view camera. Visibility aft from the pilothouse is zero. I set up a color security camera and it seems to work fine. I mounted it on the starboard side, amidships looking aft. That should help!

Nicholas has been a constant companion. All the running around has him wiped out by end of day and he is nestled next to me in the pilothouse right now, snoozing while I type. Today he was running wild down the dock as usual and playing with our neighbors. Suddenly there was a splash and he was in the freezing water paddling like crazy. I quickly pulled him out and took him to a hot shower. From now on, he will be wearing his life jacket when running free on the dock!

On Thursday, April 29, 2004 around 3:00 PM we left the slip for the first time for close quarters maneuvering with Captain Galen Tyler. I learned how to back up straight by holding ten degrees of port rudder to counteract *Jenny's* prop-walk. We also practiced back-and-fill turns and I found that *Jenny* pirouettes really well.

We took a small spin down to Van Isle Marina and filled *Jenny's* dinghy gas tank. We filled up with 17.9 liters of gas, but could only put 44 cc of oil in. I need to take 1 liter of gas out of the tank and put the rest of the 442 cc of oil in to get to the necessary sixty to one gas / oil blend. Then we came back up to Canoe Cove around 6:00 PM and backed into the slip without a hitch. The rear view video camera works super. I need to extend the bracket to a total of twelve inches so that it looks down *Jenny* side though. We settled in around 6:30 PM.

On Friday, April 30, 2004 at 10:26 AM we took *Jenny* out of her slip for our first small passage down to Victoria. She stepped out into the channel like model going down the runway. It was another beautiful day, and a perfect start to our cruising life. Galen was with us to give us more instruction and satisfy our insurance restriction. He spent most of his time with Mary, helping her understand charting, piloting, the instruments, etc. He gave her a feeling of safety and built her confidence. We were in our slip in Victoria Harbour by 1:30 PM right in front of the famous Fairmont Empress Hotel.

The arrival location was latitude 48 degrees 25.299 minutes north, longitude 123 degrees 22.164 minutes west.

We stayed in Victoria for a couple of days, sightseeing and enjoying the restaurants. It is a marvelous town, very quant and British. Then we were off to learn more about *Jenny* with Captain Galen. We were at a side tie finger with a boat across from us on the port side, and another behind us. Galen talked Mary into taking *Jenny's* helm and she backed her out of the slip!

Saturday, May 01, 2004

Jenny anchored in Prevost Harbor on Stuart Island for the evening. There were quite a few boats here already, so we found a spot south of the crowd. It took a couple of tries for us to get it right, but *Jenny* was patient. With no wind at all *Jenny* was swinging all around her anchor chain that was pointing straight down. I hope that we have all used the same scope. One of the vessels here is a canoe stern trawler and looks Dutch built. Galen and I launched *Jenny's* dinghy from the roof. Mary and I went out for a spin. She was at the helm and very nervous but all went well. Then I took Nicholas for a spin. It was his first ride and he loved it! He was unsure at first but trusting. Soon he had his head into the wind, ears flapping and nose going full bore in the breeze. We then went ashore and took a walk. The island is very narrow at the middle and there is a trail that leads to a harbor on the other side. The other side is like a fjord with tall hills on both sides. Many more vessels were resting on their anchors there plus a couple in slips.

We had a nice dinner of shrimp that Mary picked up at Friday Harbor. This is very nice! What a life!

Sunday, May 02, 2004

I got up and took Nicolas for a walk in the park at Prevost harbor. After breakfast, we raised *Jenny's* dinghy to the upper deck and weighed anchor. A nice Dungeness crab was hooked on the anchor chain by its claw. It did not drop off when we raised it up to the deck and Galen grabbed it for lunch. Yumm.

Jenny's Sport Dingy, David and Nicholas

We then motored over to Patos Island for lunch and another lesson from Galen. Because the anchorage is deep and rises sharply to the shore, you cannot just drop the hook. You have to put the anchor down on one of the sides of the underwater arroyo and set it as you pull it up the side toward the shore. Naturally, if *Jenny* swings out over the anchor and away from the underwater cliff, she will easily pull it out and she will float free. Galen showed us the method used here in the Pacific Northwest. We dropped anchor deep and set it as we backed toward the shore. Then we launched the dinghy to take an aft line to shore. We tied the aft line to a mooring ring on the shore to keep *Jenny* from drifting over her anchor. Once tied off, Mary, Nicholas and I went for a walk on the island. When we returned to *Jenny* and tried to raise the dinghy, her winch would not pull it up. It seemed that her winch was not getting enough power. Galen and I wrestled the 350-pound dinghy up to the top deck and I put the mystery on the project list.

We then went down to Echo Harbor on Sucia Island, picked up a mooring buoy and tried to figure out the problem with *Jenny's* winches. She was not talking and it remained another of her secrets. Then we went around to the south end of the island and anchored in Echo Bay. Galen and I took one of her winches apart and found there was no grease in the gears or bearings. Even after greasing it up, it still did not work. Maybe *Jenny* needs new winches.

Monday, May 03, 2004

After a lazy morning, we departed Echo Harbor to head over to Anacortes. It was beautiful, with calm seas and little wind. Mary did some man-overboard exercises and some practice maneuvering *Jenny*. We arrived around 1:30 PM and took a slip. Galen told us that we were now qualified to keep *Jenny* out of harm's way and departed. He called our insurance company, so we were now free to take *Jenny* out by ourselves! We spend that day shopping in Anacortes for some necessary items and getting ourselves ready for our first solo passage back to Sidney. Mary was a wreck with worry. I felt comfortable with everything except the docking. Maneuvering *Jenny* close to hard things always worries me! She is a creature of the sea.

Tuesday, May 04, 2004

We left Anacortes in a light drizzle and *Jenny* took us quietly over to Sidney. We docked at the customs dock just fine and then had to do a hard 180 to come around into the transient slip. We did that with aplomb too! Mary was nervous all day over docking. I hope that more practice like this will build her confidence. Our first solo the trip covered 36.20 nautical miles in four hours and five minutes with an average speed of 7.40 knots.

Last night I started to investigate the mystery with the alternator not charging the house batteries. I called Kevin to find out more about a mysterious timer. As it turns out, *Jenny* has a timer that delays a solenoid that connects the start battery with the house batteries. At first start, the alternator only charges the start battery. The timer is right behind the same panel as the Battery Override button. It begins timing based upon getting current from the engine hour meter. So, x seconds after the meter starts running, the timer fires the solenoid and connects the alternator and start battery with the house batteries.

What failed was the installation. The person who wired it up did a crappy job. The timer was on the loose behind the panel, rolling around with *Jenny's* motion, and all the wires frayed or disconnected from the abuse. I will fix it tonight.

Wednesday, May 05, 2004

We stayed in Sidney and worked on *Jenny* all day. I started by tracking down the secret of the dinghy winches and Mary started cleaning the galley. By noon I found an electrical problem that probably solves the dinghy issue. There was plenty of power going to the master panel, but not enough ground circuit to produce voltage at high amp loads. It turned out that one of the two master ground wires was disconnected. That took quite a bit of time and luck to uncover. The end that was undone was hiding under the master bed and some other wires. UGH! Kevin admits it was his error. I am beginning to worry about his capabilities. I have uncovered two electrical problems on *Jenny* and they were two disconnected wires. This is not a positive endorsement of the maintenance crew.

Mary cleaned all the cabinet doors in the galley and salon. They were ugly dirty. After lunch, I took all the rugs out of *Jenny* and swabbed the floors. Mary continued cleaning. I also took apart the other winch that raises and lowers the dinghy boom to grease it. This was a dirty job, but it was dry just like the other. It is now all back together and running. Tomorrow we will anchor out and I will test to see if they work under load.

Mary continued to clean.

My next job was to see if I could get *Jenny's* new navigation computer to hook up with her autopilot. I had been steering by putting her autopilot in Auto mode that asks her to hold a particular heading. *Jenny* does so but wanders from a course line because of wind and currents. I wanted her to follow a course line. I plugged her computer into a test serial cable, adjusted the Nobeltec software and it all worked! Thus, the problem was in her Bluetooth serial port. Unfortunately, I could not figure out how to configure or otherwise manage the Bluetooth device. Since I could not use it, I had to trace *Jenny's* wiring from the closet where the old tower PC was and move the wire from the closet to the console where her new navigation computer was. After much searching, I found the wire! Now *Jenny's* navigation computer is fully functional and hard wired to her GPS and Autopilot. I will do more testing of the Bluetooth device at home. I am not so sure it is a good idea to use it though.

Tomorrow *Jenny* takes us to Bedwell Harbor.

Friday, May 07, 2004

We departed Sidney Harbor for Bedwell Harbor in the morning around 10:00. *Jenny* took the helm the whole way with her new navigation computer telling her autopilot to hold the course! Also, her small radar received the waypoint information and showed it on its screen! Too cool!

I ran with JD taking diesel from *Jenny's* starboard aft tank and returning it to her forward port tank. I monitored the transfer to make sure the port tank did not overfill. No need to worry. The transfer was minimal to non-existent. We arrived at Bedwell around noon. There is not much here except a new resort they are building. There were about five other boats anchored and we briefly met Jerry Mitchell on his Nordhavn 46 as he and his wife were heading out.

Their 1999 was in pristine condition and I took some photos. We launched *Jenny's* dinghy and went on shore for a walk.

After lunch, I waxed *Jenny's* hull to make her sparkle. It was about a six-hour job, but she really needed it. After dinner, we took her dinghy back up. I started JD to make sure we had plenty of power, and the winches worked just fine. I stopped her dinghy at rail level and connected the fresh water line to the outboard to clear the saltwater from the engine. I now know why Marty took the dinghy up on the port side since you can reach the dinghy key much easier to start and stop the motor.

Friday morning *Jenny* weighed anchor and headed back to her slip in Canoe Cove slightly depressed. She does not like being tied up. Based upon what the folks there saw when Mary and I left, there was a crowd of people at the dock ready to help guide us in and protect *Jenny*. Well, they were very surprised when Mary and I came in like professional captains without the slightest problem! We had big smiles on our faces for sure.

Jenny is now snug in her slip and we are packing and preparing her for our absence. I pickled the water maker, so it should be fine. The two weeks went too fast! There is no joy in going back to work.

To do next time up:
- Clean the rest of the lockers.
- Replace the burner on the barbeque.
- Change the starter on the stove.
- Wax the showers.
- Clean the dinghy.
- Fix the dinghy steering.
- Throw the old rugs out and clean the salon floor.
- Fix windowsills.
- Put rails under dinghy.
- Inventory and store spares under salon table.

Monday, July 26, 2004

Mary and I returned to *Jenny* last night after a twelve-hour road trip from Redding CA, our overnight rest stop. She woke from her slumber and welcomed us back. We were so tired we did not unpack much from the car; just the bare minimum. She cradled us to sleep in the security of her berth. We both slept like rocks except for real estate battles with Nicholas. He wanted to sleep between us by our heads and there just is not enough room for it. Eventually he settled somewhere near Mary's feet.

We woke with the sun as usual and cuddled a little bit. Even though it was not too cool out, I switched the furnace on so we would have very hot showers. *Jenny's* shower is very nice. It has a seat that is good when *Jenny* is moving, but also when you just want to luxuriate in a gentle hot shower.

I have been using aquarium sealer to mount hooks, toothbrush holders, etc in the bathrooms. I found a bunch of these things that either had double sided tape or suction cups to mount them on the fiberglass. However, none held. This sealer seems to be strong enough to do the job, but should come off easily when the time comes. The rule is no more holes in *Jenny*!

We spent the day getting *Jenny* ready for two weeks of cruising. I brought up her new teak navigation table and spent the morning fitting it. Got it to about a 90% level of perfection and then locked it in. I will do the fine-tuning when *Jenny* is in San Francisco. Amazing enough, the teak is a perfect color match to the rest of *Jenny's* interior. I used just varnish, no color additives. Mary got the galley in order with all the stuff we brought up and then went shopping in Sydney. Sydney is a beautiful town and is nearly perfect. There is one main street with enough shopping traffic from tourists to keep it healthy and stocked with nice stuff. You can walk from one end to the other in about ½ hour and have everything you need for a quality life. It is the ideal setup for elderly since they do not need a car for anything.

Mary with Nicholas wearing his vest and doggles

I checked all *Jenny's* fluids and stuff to make sure we were ok to go. I also took the water maker out of hibernation so we will have good water and will not need to stop anywhere unless we want to. I am concerned that all the marinas and harbors will be packed. We will see.

Tomorrow we head for Friday Harbor to check back into the States. We need to do this to stop the Canadian tax clock and to reset the US tax clock. It is a funny game, but the rewards are very substantial. So far we have paid no taxes at all. We will then anchor out in Prevost Harbor on Stuart Island, which is part of Washington State.

Tuesday, July 27, 2004

Well, today was an adventure! *Jenny* took us through Dodd Narrows and arrived at Port Nanaimo! Dodd Narrows is a narrow channel about ½ miles long where a tremendous (over nine knots peak) current runs. You have to time getting there just right. I did my calculations and we weighed anchor around 07:30 AM. Fortunately, the tide was coming in and the current was flowing north the whole way. At times, *Jenny* gained a couple of knots, Speed-Over-Ground (SOG). Up here, you cannot really assume which way the current will run on a flood or ebb tide as the water comes in from both ends of Vancouver Island. At a point somewhere up around Desolation Sound, it all comes together. North of there the flood tide runs south, south of there it runs north! This is true for many of the long narrow passages everywhere up here.

Slack water is the only time to go through Dodd Narrows. Today it was at 1:37 PM. Because of the current, I had to reduce JD's beat to 1400 RPM, so we would arrive at 1:00 PM. I wanted to catch about two knots of current flowing north through the pass and make sure we got through before it turned. About five miles from the narrows, we began to have considerable company. Power and sail boats all heading for the same place at the same time.

As we got closer, we saw a thirty-two foot sailboat with five people on board run aground on a reef with a lighthouse on it! What were they thinking? Some boats tried to help them but were afraid to get close. Eventually the tide lifted them clear and they motored on.

About 300 yards from the narrows, it was pandemonium. *Jenny* was nose to tail with about forty boats of all kinds. Just before 1:00 PM, the first boat made a break for it and everyone else jumped. A lot of wind was blowing through from the other side causing a small chop. Some other boats were also going through heading south. Boiling water and rapids awaited us at the north end. It was too cool, sort of like running river rapids in a 60,000-pound raft! *Jenny* wanted blinders on as she passed close by the boulders on each side.

On the north end of the Narrows the wind continued and four-foot seas built up. It was Mary and Nicholas' first "rough water". Mary vocalized a lot and Nicholas threw up on the pilot seat. On the plus side, Mary did not get sick! One more trial down! Sometime I must tell you about our first date canoeing down an alligator infested river in Florida. I had to see if the girl from Brooklyn had the right stuff!

Our trials were not quite over though. Mary wanted to dock at Naniamo for a night or two, and after what we just went through, I was not going to argue. Here we come into a very small marina with the wind blowing us in at about twenty knots and very little space to maneuver. Considering our vast experience with *Jenny*, it was a sphincter tightening moment. Mary is on the VHF with the harbor master, sea planes are taking off over our heads drowning out the radio, some guy in a thirty-two foot Bayliner is hovering in the middle of the channel trying to get gas, we are lost and being blown toward the closed end of the harbor. Hmmmm...

Then Mary connects with our man on the dock and locates him directly behind us. I swing *Jenny* a 180 and head over. There is a trawler behind where she is supposed to tie up and the end of the pier ahead. Because the wind is blowing us back toward the trawler, I bring *Jenny* in HOT. I get her nose close, throw her into reverse, her nose comes to a stop over of one of the dockhands and her stern swings in three feet ahead of the trawler. Could not ever do it again! BIG kudos from the trawler owner and dockhands! Mary is smiling for the first time in many hours. *Jenny* is proud of us. Its 7:01 PM and life is good!

Thursday, July 29, 2004

Location: Garden Bay, Pender Harbor
Latitude is 49 degrees 37.82 minutes north.
Longitude is 124 degrees 1.459 minutes west.

We stayed two days in Nanaimo, mostly because the Georgia Strait was blowing twenty to twenty-five knots. In the harbor, it was blowing twenty most of the day making it difficult to pull away from the dock. Mary wanted a rest too. It was hot even though we were in Canada and on the water. I worked on *Jenny's* salon table. The original is huge. If you added chairs around the outside, it could serve a family of eight and it overwhelms *Jenny's* salon. In addition, I could not lower it below the top of the seat cushions to make up a berth. When I had the new cushions made, I also asked them to make a cushion to fit between the salon seats so, given a table that would drop all the way down, it would make a double bed.

Between visits, I used the new cushion as a rough model and one-inch plywood to create a rough new tabletop. I brought it up this trip along with a saber saw, drill, bits, etc. Since we were on shore power and not going anywhere, I decided to tackle the job. We carried the old top to the forward berth and I lowered the pedestal down so that the new top was touching the wood edging around the salon seats. Mary served to hold it in place by sitting on it while I scribed the bottom for the cut. A few hours and a pile of sweat later I fitted and screwed it in place then cleaned up, put the salon back together, lowered the new table down and put the berth cushion in place. It all worked! Too cool! Mary and Nicholas tried it out for a nap and gave it the seal of approval.

This morning the winds were still ten knots out of the northwest pushing us against the pier. Getting out was going to be a chore. I was up off and on all night with the sound of twenty-knot winds and rehearsing in my mind various strategies for getting off the dock ok.

After a poor night's sleep, we dragged ourselves out of bed in an attempt to get out before the early morning lull was over. Mary got *Jenny* ready and walked Nicholas. I disconnected the shore power and shortened up the dock lines. Our first attempt was going to be to try to push *Jenny*'s nose through the wind. *Jenny* was pointed north, and the wind was northwest at eleven knots. I did not think her bow thruster was going to be able to push us around so I called the marina to line up some dockhands. Yesterday they proved their value as several boats slammed into the pier in twenty plus knot winds, with some coming very close to *Jenny*!

I set a line from the stern hawse to the dock to take the load with a release from inside. Then I started JD and took in all the other lines. When Mary returned, I tried to set her up with our headsets and FRS radios. They did not work. It seems like the noise from *Jenny* caused her mike to lock open. I have to read the manual again. I walked her thought the plan and went to the bridge to try the bow thruster. It worked. *Jenny* swung her bow through the wind and started to swing west. Mary was having some difficulty with the stern line so I could not put JD in gear!!! Panic! I ran back and released *Jenny* then ran up to the bridge again and put her in gear for a perfect launch. I let the marina know we were away. We had a perfect landing and departure. Big smiles!

Our next adventure was crossing the Georgia Strait and Mary did not want me setting the stabilizers. *Jenny* had the helm, but Mary was afraid to be on watch alone in a busy area and afraid I would fall overboard. She had too much fear and not enough self-confidence. I knew three hours in the Strait would be too much motion for her and Nicholas without the stabilizers down. I had to ask her to trust me and let me do my job. She was not happy, especially when she got a five-blast danger horn from one of the ferries. I zoomed down and got us out of the way.

The new clam cleat blocks made all the difference! It is now an easy single-handed job. Just follow the steps and 1, 2, 3 they are set. With the clam cleat blocks, I put *Jenny's* port bird just skimming the water and then put her other side to the same state. Then I dropped her port bird and set it, then her starboard. This way, *Jenny* is balanced for all but a very short time.

As soon as *Jenny's* first bird was in the water, she settled right down. We were in just a light chop but you could tell the difference. As we headed into the strait, it was as expected with the worst being three to four foot chop. With her birds down, there was barely any roll. In fact, as we turned further north changing from a beam sea to quartering the bow, *Jenny's* motion increased because of her pitching!

The three-hour crossing was very comfortable, lunch included. *Jenny* is quite the vessel! We were building a lot of mutual trust now. I have no worries about the ocean passage coming up. We got to Pender Harbor, Garden Bay and anchored without any trouble at all.

Mary took a nap. I worked on the dinghy. The controls are all stiff from disuse and lack of care. The arm connecting the steering to the motor was positioned wrong so that you could turn like crazy clockwise, but barely at all counter clockwise. The combination was deadly. The last trip up I crashed into everything I got near. I tried using motorcycle chain lube on the steering arm this time. It worked great. It goes on thin and penetrating but dries into grease. Everything got a dose!

The dinghy went over hard. It sits on *Jenny's* starboard side and I have been launching it on that side too. However this time *Jenny* is listing to port and when the dinghy came up out of its cradle, it swung the boom to port with a vengeance. It took both Mary and I too much work to muscle it back over *Jenny's* starboard side. I have to think about how to avoid this the next time.

I have to go now. We have Halibut on the grill tonight. It is still too hot but absolutely gorgeous!!!

Saturday, July 31, 2004

Location: Princess Louisa fjord
Latitude is 50 degrees 12.12 minutes north.
Longitude is 124 degrees 46.5 minutes west.

Every day we do something new and our learning curve is still steep. Princess Louisa Inlet is a fjord a couple of miles long, 700 feet deep and the tide is normally about twelve feet. All the water in the fjord tries to go through the Malibu Rapids entrance to keep pace with the tide level outside. The rapids form in a curving channel only fifty yards wide and thirty to forty feet deep. The result is an enormous amount of thrashing water trying to get through this narrow twisting pass without hope of keeping up with gravity's demand for equilibrium. Even at slack tide the levels are out of balance and the water inside is still waging war on the water outside. These rapids are notorious for their ferocity and our spring low tide made it even more challenging.

I checked the tide tables yesterday in order to time our arrival. I wanted to make absolutely sure we would not miss the slack. Unfortunately, my two tide programs predicted ebb tide slack with a two-hour difference. I went to one of the local marinas in Pender Harbor to see what they said. They were using one of the two programs I was using! I assumed it was the accurate one and slack was supposed to be at 11:30 AM, six hours from where we were. In order to catch the Malibu Rapids, we had to get up at 05:00 AM and be under way by 05:30. UGH. This is work!

The trip down was peaceful and beautiful. *Jenny* had the helm and carried us through the pristine wilderness on a magic carpet. We marveled at the snow-covered mountaintops and waved to the few other boats we encountered. We got to the rapids at 11:00 AM and a torrent of water was still gushing out. At noon, some powerful boats went in and we watched them be thrown about in the narrow channel. It was too soon for us to try. A seventy-foot yacht was also trying to get in but waiting as we were.

I made a couple of close passes between noon and 12:30 PM but did not feel it was good yet. Finally, I worked up my courage and headed in at 12:45 PM. *Jenny* felt the nervous energy like a thoroughbred in the starting gates. I was sweating bullets. Mary was wide-eyed and mute.

The tide nearly finished, but the water still boiled with confused currents trying to decide which way to go. The walls of this pass are granite boulders that you play chicken with as you navigate around the curves. People looking for the excitement of close encounters with disaster line the pass. Vessels are expected to go through slowly so they do not create standing waves for the next contestants. In the middle of our run, someone in the bleachers yelled we were going too fast! We could not have been going more than six knots through the water and needed every bit of propeller thrust on the rudder to keep *Jenny* from harm. We finally made it through to smooth, deep water and breathed a sigh of relief.

The fjord made it all worthwhile. It is narrow and gorgeous with vertical cliffs towering thousands of feet above the water. The deep blue water drops off to hundreds of feet below the surface just as steeply, making the head of the inlet the only place to anchor. We steamed all the way to the end and I released *Jenny's* anchor in 100 feet of water. Like everyone else, I backed her toward the shore until we were about 150 feet off, in about sixty feet of water. Then I ran a line to a tree on shore to keep *Jenny* from heading for deep water. More importantly, I found out that as the sun set, a breeze dropped right down the cliff behind us and pushed *Jenny* offshore. If I had not tied her, she would have swung around, dragged her anchor free into 600 feet of water and been on the loose!

Princess Louisa Inlet is a wonderful place to visit and the crown of our vacation. That evening a seal and its baby visited us. The next day we went to the shore and walked up to the waterfalls. Floatplanes, one of the major means of transportation up here, flew in and out during the day, bringing in tourists like an Indiana Jones movie. There are about eight other yachts here, almost all trawlers due to the potential for cold wet weather and total lack of wind.

Then way too soon, it was time to go. Princess Louisa Inlet was the northern most point in our plans, so we had to start heading back on a schedule. *Jenny* hauled anchor Sunday, August 1st and went back to Garden Cove in Pender Harbor. The outbound passage through Malibu Rapids was another thriller and fortunately uneventful.

We left Pender Harbor on Monday, August 02, 2004 and headed for Ganges Harbor. The trip covered 59.30 nautical miles in 8 hours with an average speed of 7.20 knots. Then we worked our way back down to Canoe Cove.

The vacation was a success. Apart from some of Mary's early trepidations, we really enjoyed our cruise and became much more self-assured about our abilities. We also realized we could not afford to leave *Jenny* in Canada. I had to find a slip in San Francisco and plan to bring *Jenny* down the coast. We left her with her blinders on and she was resting peacefully at her slip. She was happy being with us and with the care we were giving her. She knew we would be back soon.

BOOK 2 – PASSAGE TO SAN FRANCISCO

"*Princess* surged to the trough, lifted to kiss the comber, and ran the slope of sea, curling a silver bow wave into the trail of tress. To any water man watching her, it would have been the old story of Dante and his beloved Beatrice. *Princess* was still heading southeast true and sailing herself. There was no sense buttin in. She knew her business. Better than Lennie the bearded philosopher. Better than I.

The sea grew from ripples to waves and from waves to combers. Then the waves blossomed with spume. By the time this white flower of the sea brushed and broke along our quarter, we were far and gone out of sight of land."

Joe Richards
Princess 1956

Thursday, September 9, 2004

I found a slip for *Jenny* at the Emeryville Marina in San Francisco near our work. They had just added over 100 new slips in June and we had our pick. The price was right too. *Jenny's* slip cost $475 per month plus electricity. I also lined up a crew to bring *Jenny* down the coast. My cousin Chris Schramm from Atlanta and his friend Don Taylor had signed up, as well as my buddy David Cork from Truckee California. David Cork was a seasoned salt, but had never been on a yacht on the ocean. My cousin was also a seasoned boater, but mostly small coastal boats except for his huge houseboat on Lake Lanier. One of the reasons he came was for an adventure. He was hoping we would have a little more excitement than just a lake water cruise down the coast. His friend Don Taylor had a boat on the Tennessee-Tombigbee Waterway and was studying for his Captain's license. He needed some ocean time and experience. All in all, it was a good crew of dependable guys. However, we were all novices when it came to ocean passages. That was soon to change!

That was the good news. However, having volunteer crew almost always means you are on a schedule as a reflection of their work and family schedules. One of the primary principles of safe cruising is you must have the luxury of time to wait for good weather windows. Compounding the problem were my first grade weather skills. I had been watching the weather using the tools I knew at the time and as our target departure date drew close, I believed we would have a good weather window. We all boarded our planes and headed for the Victoria International airport only a couple of miles from Canoe Cove marina. Our flights were coordinated so that we all arrived at the airport within thirty minutes and all actually made it on time. Everyone was pumped! We got to *Jenny* around 9:00 PM Thursday night. We just had time for dinner up at the very nice restaurant at the marina and then crashed. What a good start!

Friday, September 10, 2004

Location: Canoe Cove, Vancouver Island, Canada
Latitude 48 degrees 40.951 minutes north
Longitude 123 degrees 24.079 minutes west

Friday morning my crew went for breakfast up at the local restaurant while I readied *Jenny* for the short run to Friday Harbor. I wanted to clear in to the US there and to provision *Jenny* for the trip. She had no idea what we were up to but sensed a big adventure was afoot. Four guys do not just show up every day.

We allowed ten days for the trip and bought food with that in mind. I walked the crew through *Jenny's* safety procedures and equipment. Chris thought I was overdoing it. Then I introduced *Jenny* to them. I went through how we were going to get her out of her slip and how we were going to get her docked when we arrived in Friday harbor. Around 09:00 AM we untied *Jenny* from Canada and headed out. It was only a twenty-one mile trip and I had each of them take her helm so they could get a feel for her. The weather was very nice and it was a piece of cake getting there. Everyone was happy and enthusiastic.

Location: Friday Harbor USA
Latitude 48 degrees 32.249 minutes north
Longitude 123 degrees 0.830 minutes west
Customs check in was US 3014 2004 0910 1506 47
The trip covered 21.00 nautical miles with an average speed of 6.70 knots

Jenny arrived at Friday Harbor around noon and we cleared customs. They took pictures of David Cork and his green card since he was a British citizen. We then took *Jenny* to a side-tie at the southern end of the marina and David and Don went food shopping while Chris and I prepared *Jenny* for offshore running. By now, she knew she was going to sea for the first time in years. She was used to it, seasoned by many passages up and down the west coast. Only once had a crew gotten her in trouble and that was on the San Francisco bar. She got them out of it but still had some fear of bars. I was the only one she knew but that gave her some piece of mind. We trusted each other.

Chris and I rigged up Jack lines, rigged *Jenny's* dinghy boom over her starboard side so we could haul someone in if necessary, and battened down her hatches, etc. I checked her water, oil, fuel, etc. We had lunch and dinner on shore and turned in around 10:00 PM. A front was moving through and the night stormed with wind and rain. Fortunately, we had a mega yacht on *Jenny's* windward side that sheltered us well. We were hopeful that the front would blow through by morning. It mostly did and I got some sleep.

Saturday, September 11, 2004

We left Friday Harbor at 07:00 AM and headed south for the Strait of Juan de Fuca. *Jenny* took the helm and kept it for the next five days confident in her capabilities. It was overcast and windy, but the weather cleared by the time we reached the strait. The islands were providing good shelter from waves and just to be safe, we put *Jenny's* birds (stabilizers) in the water while it was still flat.

We steamed by Victoria in the bright autumn sun and headed for Cape Flattery. It was good running. As we neared the Cape, we had a strong ebb current hitting some hefty incoming swells. This stacked the swells up into steep twenty-one foot swells that we had to climb up, up and over. It was our first taste of big water. *Jenny* was unperturbed. She had done all this before. We marveled at the power of these waves as they struck the rocky cliffs of Oregon on the south side of the strait that transformed them into plums of water shooting up fifty feet in the air. It certainly was not a somewhere we wanted to be anywhere near! *Jenny* rounded the cape and started heading south and the ocean settled down. She started steaming down the Washington coast.

Saturday night was a rude introduction to what would become routine this trip. Saturday night was overcast with some rain so we did not have stars above. We had no moon the entire trip so it was pitch black all night. There was absolutely no horizon. The fine salmon dinner that David Cork made for us was weighing heavy as we took our watches. Mine was from 02:00 AM to 04:00 AM and as soon as I came up, I knew I was in trouble. *Jenny* was throwing off big seas as they relentlessly beat against her bow and tried to make her submit to their will. She kept a strong hand on the helm and was not giving an inch.

I opened her starboard pilothouse door just far enough to get my head and shoulders outside into the cold wind, teaming rain and salt spray. I barfed my guts out. And that is how I spent most of that watch, trying to get some bearing on up from down by watching the blowing sea and rain. I was also wishing I had something else but salmon for dinner! Poor David Cork was also barfing.

Sometime during the night, Chris took watch and sat on the pilot's bench. Chris is a big guy and *Jenny* was moving about a lot. Pow! The weld on the bench broke. The bench was not much, but now we literally had to stand our watches.

Sunday, September 12, 2004

Sunday morning came with the front still moving into the coast. It was a rough day and by nightfall we were in a gale. The worst was on David Cork's watch from Midnight to 02:00 AM off Point Lookout, Oregon. When I came up to relieve him, all you could see was white water streaking by the windows at what looked like 100 MPH and *Jenny's* bow as she plunged into the sea after sea. It was brutal.

The noise was deafening. The 600 feet of anchor chain in the locker was being tossed in the air and slammed into *Jenny's* hull as she dropped off one comber and dove into the next. Pots and pans thrashed each other in a nonstop fight for stability in the galley. Glassware added to the cacophony breaking free in the cabinets and shattering. Three-hundred gallons of fresh water pounded *Jenny's* tanks like kettledrums. Wind howled through he rigging and water made a continuous wail as it beat against her windows. Through all this JD beat a constant chorus of reassurance. *Jenny* held her course and kept the water at bay. She did not bend or flex in the onslaught. She was solid, and unflappable.

During the night, we heard a sailboat calling a mayday somewhere nearby. A man and two women were aboard and they wanted off their vessel. The Coast Guard sent a helicopter out, dropped a diver and lowered a basket. The Coast Guard plucked them from their boat and whisked to shore. It all took about two hours from start to finish and reminded me of the situation on the Westsail 32 in the book "Perfect Storm". While the motion onboard *Jenny* was uncomfortable, we felt she was in full control of the situation and never felt in any danger. Don called her a small ship.

Jenny has a full displacement hull with a top speed of 8.2 knots. That is all the faster she can go no matter how hard you spank her. However, I saw *Jenny's* speed through the water hit ten knots several times as we slid down the big waves. This was a cause for concern. If *Jenny's* stern got too high, she could fall sideways and broach. Then the waves would kick her in her side and we would be in trouble. I did not have storm windows for the salon and if we got sideways, big waves could have broken the windows, allowing *Jenny* to fill with water and sink. A big wave can easily be as big as *Jenny* and represent 100,000 pounds of water slamming into her at ten to fifteen knots. The sea has tremendous force. However, with her birds in the water, not only were we tracking down these waves as if we were on rails, but we never had to help *Jenny* at the helm. Being dragged from the ends of her outriggers, her birds act like drogues with extra turning leverage. They helped to keep *Jenny's* stern to the oncoming waves and from veering off her course. She is a marvel of engineering developed over decades of fishing and sailing boat experience!

Still, the motion on *Jenny* was like being on a mechanical bull. Chris tried to sleep in the forward cabin for a while, but he was becoming airborne at the same time the sea tossed the 1000 pounds of anchor chain. To add to his problem, occasionally *Jenny* would move her bow over just a little and Chris would come down on the floor, three feet below his berth. Maybe this was in retaliation for breaking her pilot bench. After the second time coming to his senses on the floor, he moved back to sleep in the salon. He later said the only fear he had was that *Jenny's* chain would break though her hull as it landed over and over again.

David Cork had taken up residence in the salon with the salon table lowered and the cushion in place. He had wedged himself in with all the pillows he could find. He was doing better than Chris, but he too occasionally found himself on the floor. After Chris moved in, taking up David's landing zone on the floor they had some up close and personal encounters in the dead of night!

Don decided he would be most comfortable in the pilot berth. This was a pretty good choice. At least he was never thrown out of bed. However, he had to put up with any noise made by the radios and person on watch. I made the unfortunate choice of showing him the pilot berth could be made wider by pulling out the bottom and using the back cushion from the seat to fill the gap. Well, when you extend the berth, you cannot sit at the table! And, the pilot bench was broken. I just did not have the heart to disturb Don, so the only option left was to stand the two hours of each watch.

Monday, September 13, 2004

By Monday morning, the rain gave up and the sun came out of hiding. The waves were still large, but manageable. The Coast Guard went out to look for the sailboat and found it. They declared it a hazard to navigation and put the word out. They also said a Zodiac had been lost over the side. Now that was worth looking for! We keep our eyes peeled! Then we saw a few humpback whales, went over and stopped *Jenny* to watch them. I shut down JD so I could check its oil level. I still had some residual concern that JD might burn oil and it now been running for thirty-six hours straight. Don was surprised. He was concerned that we might not get *Jenny's* heart started again. My thinking was that I never once had any concern about JD starting at a dock or at anchor, why would this be any different. JD had not burned a drop, and her heart fired right back up on a steady beat. It was a good day.

Tuesday, September 14, 2004

The bad weather came back and lingered with thirty-knot winds and fifteen-foot waves the whole day. If we wanted to head into one of the harbors along the way, we would have had to cross a river bar. This is normally a challenging endeavor even in good weather that requires careful timing with the tides. With the waves as big as they were, the Coast Guard was actually closing the bar entrances as we came to them. They were too dangerous to enter. We were out in it to stay. *Jenny* was just as happy not being asked to run a dangerous bar.

Then it appeared that we were out of fresh water. None of the faucets was working. I did not know how much four people needed on a daily basis, but it surprised me. *Jenny* has a 200-gallon water tank in her front and another 100-gallon tank in her middle. Did we use it all already? Was there a leak? Making things worse, I did not know any way to check the amount of water in the tanks. I checked the water maker and it was not making water. There was so much foam going under *Jenny* that the pump could not deliver the necessary 600 pounds of pressure to the membrane. Too much air was in the water and I needed to rig an air/water separator so we could make water. This meant working in the engine room, in the heat while *Jenny* swam in the wild sea. I spent about four hours on Tuesday and another four on Wednesday before I had it figured out and running again.

There is really only one thing I fear happening when underway and it is essentially impossible to do anything to prevent. It is running over fishing nets or lines and having them wrap up *Jenny's* propeller like bolas thrown around guanaco legs. The fix would require someone going over the side in whatever weather and cutting the trap loose. The rougher the conditions, the faster you need to get this done, the more dangerous and difficult it is. This is truly a nightmare scenario. Another similar, but clearly less dangerous situation is snagging something in stabilizers.

Toward the end of the day, we caught something in *Jenny's* starboard stabilizer. She swerved to starboard and then struggled to regain her heading. It was obvious we needed to stop and fix the situation. I brought JD down to idle and organized a response. Everyone was wearing our inflatable life vests, but only three had harnesses that allowed them to clip a lifeline to *Jenny*. I was wearing the one without the harness. I put Don at the wheel. We clipped Chris and David to *Jenny* and hauled the starboard bird to the surface. The way *Jenny* is rigged a bird can be positioned about four feet off her side at her stern. There I can work on a problem like taking kelp off, or whatever. This time it was a tree. Yes, a tree, twenty miles off shore. This tree was covered in lines and what looked like shredded sails. It appeared to have had quite a career snagging unwary vessels. There was no way to get at it and cut *Jenny* free. It was too heavy to pull up and *Jenny* was being thrown all over the place drifting in this wild sea without any stabilization.

Jenny off the coast of Oregon

Chris and David clipped themselves into her cockpit and I was at her cockpit door giving instructions to them and up to Don on the helm. I figured we needed to use the dinghy winch to pull the tree up and at least partially into the cockpit where we could attack it with knives, hatchets, and saws. Fortunately, we had already rigged her for action. We had clipped the winch line to *Jenny's* hull right where we were working. I instructed Don to turn slowly to port. This brought the tree to *Jenny's* side where we clipped it to the winch line by one of the many ropes entwined in the tree's branches. My big fear was that some trailing lines might become caught in *Jenny's* propeller! After we got the tree hooked up, we had to bring *Jenny* to a full stop. It was now pitch black and we had her cockpit lights on.

On the pitching deck, I worked the winch while David and Chris got the tree up and the first eight feet of the trunk over the rail into the cockpit. The tree was big and heavy. It was alive and dangerous with the waves moving it one way while *Jenny* moved another. *Jenny* was glad she had these three big men with her for sure. We hacked at the lines until we could get to the chain holding the bird to the tree. Then we unraveled the bird from the tree and dumped it over the side. We had cut a ton of polypropylene line off (which floats) and hoped that the tree would now sink to the bottom of the ocean.

All this time *Jenny's* port bird had been hanging around going nuts in circles, tying itself into a ball. We spent the next thirty minutes getting her port side stabilizer untangled. Finally, we had it all sorted out and put JD back in gear, let the birds out and gave *Jenny* the helm again to take us south. She never tossed Chris or David out of their berths again.

Wednesday, September 15, 2004

Wednesday was just like Tuesday. More wind, more big waves. We got into a working rhythm and kept on steaming south. I expected we had made enough water by Wednesday afternoon to begin using it for showers. We were getting stinky. Don was the first to go. Initially he had water but then said it went out again right after he was all suds up! I knew the pump was working and I knew we had water. Now I suspected that the screens in the faucets and showerheads were the culprit. And, they were. All along, we had plenty of water! UGH!

Before turning in for the night I asked to be woken when *Jenny* got to Point Reyes near San Francisco Bay. This area of water was going to be even rougher than what we were in because the land was in the way. Big wind and waves do not like being pushed around by land. Then I headed down to sleep as best I could. The sea was still tossing us about pretty well, so sleeping was still a challenge. During the night, I could sense that the seas were getting steeper and they were changing direction. We were getting near land!

Thursday, September 16, 2004

Location: Point Reyes, California

We arrived at Point Reyes at 01:00 AM, just before my watch. The waves were very steep now and I was wedged into a corner of my berth trying to catch some sleep. *Jenny* has the master cabin amidships rather than forward. If you lie in this queen size bed with your head at the foot of the bed, your head is at the center of all twisting motion on *Jenny*. You only feel lateral and vertical motion. So normally, this is a very comfortable spot. However, the waves were slamming *Jenny* from all directions and even here it was difficult to be comfortable.

Once you have been living in a vessel for a period, you become part of her nervous system. You are wired into her synapses. Any change in sound, smell, touch, or motion instantly registers in your brain. I could tell things were getting worse and we would have difficulty making our turn east, toward the shelter of Drake's Bay.

I had asked the crew to call me to the helm when we got to the turning waypoint. I wanted to keep the big seas behind us by gradually turning *Jenny* east as the waves naturally curved around the point. Suddenly *Jenny* threw me against her port side as she requested and received permission to turn at the waypoint. We were sideways to the rough water and it was not good at all. I was up in the pilothouse in a flash, tired and not concealing my emotions very well. "Why was not I called up? Why did you give the go ahead to turn? Weren't my directions clear?" UGH. *Jenny* had turned now. She was not happy but making the best of it. We were gradually gaining shelter afforded by the Point. The 600-foot high bluffs were at first accelerating the wind and contributing to the size and steepness of the waves. However, as we worked further under its lee, they began to block the wind and waves from reaching us.

It was still pitch black and I was navigating in a new place using *Jenny's* extra senses: depth sounder, GPS and radar. As the wind and water began to calm down, we gradually were able to pick out the buoy that marked the rocky reef at the northwest corner of the bay entrance. When I was sure we had identified it correctly, I became confident that we were safely where we expected to be.

I opted to stop in Drake's Bay if we came around the point at night because it is a broad, open bay extremely easy to enter even in terrible conditions. Once in the bay, the waves were only three feet and life was good. We had to take *Jenny's* birds up because this bay is too shallow for them. By 02:40 AM, *Jenny* had dug here claws into the bottom and for the first time in five days, we could relax and rest! It was still blowing twenty-five to thirty knots over the hills, so I stayed up until the end of my watch at 04:00 AM to make sure we were not dragging. Then I collapsed and slept until 10:00 AM.

Friday, September 17, 2004

Location: Drake's Bay
Latitude 37 degrees 59.833 minutes north
Longitude 122 degrees 57.895 minutes west

The trip down from Friday Harbor covered 749 nautical miles in 6 days, 2 hours, 10 minutes with an average speed of 6.60 knots and a maximum speed of 8.20 knots.

It is hard to describe how exhausted we were. While we were in the thick of it all, our adrenalin kept us going and we really did not feel very tired. However, this morning the wind had died, the bay was calm, the sun was out and we could relax. It hit us like a freight train. The only thing that sparked us to action was the thrill of taking *Jenny* under the Golden Gate Bridge. The feeling of accomplishment was incredible and something few people get to experience. *Jenny* did all the work getting us here using her autopilot, navigation computer, charting software, and GPS. All the way down the coast, we only took the helm from her for a few hours' whale watching, tree trimming and coming into Drake's Bay. She was so precise she got us to the narrow entrance to the channel leading to Emeryville Marina and steered us right down the fifty-foot wide channel. Amazing!

David, Chris, Don coming into San Francisco Bay

Jenny was secure in her new slip by 3:00 PM. We took all our personal gear off, drove Chris and Don to the airport, and David Cork back to our house. David's wife Kathy came down from Truckee and we went out to dinner to celebrate the voyage.

Saturday, September 18, 2004

Location: Emeryville Marina

I learned a lot from this trip in a hurry. First, I needed to know much more about weather forecasting before heading offshore. I was woefully unprepared. Second, I did not know my vessel. I was learning about her systems, their use, and their state of operational readiness while underway. This is not a good place for this kind of discovery.

Not all dreamers have ocean passages in mind. They dream of rivers, waterways, and island protected straits. They choose their vessels to perfectly match their need and both are happy. Passages in the open sea are a step beyond and require additional consideration.

The open sea is a place of lithe, powerful creatures. A dense medium few air breathers comprehend. In repose, it lifts and sets *Jenny's* 60,000 pounds as if she were a feather. Agitated it plays her like a tambourine. Angry, *Jenny* is merely an irritating green fly it tries to swat. *Jenny* is a muscular athlete, agile, lithe, and graceful in a fight like a Jujitsu Master. In the face of danger, she has the calmness of a black belt in competition.

Regardless of how skilled you become in weather forecasting, even the most experienced cruisers know there is always the possibility of encountering an angry sea. *Jenny's* fitness does not excuse her captain and crew from also being creatures of the sea. Nor does she coddle them. She reflects her adversary's mood in her motion. You are her indispensable partner and she needs you to be equally lithe and athletic. Otherwise, you chance injury and open yourself to fear. Incapacitated by injury or fear you are longer an effective part of the symbiotic whole. You become a ward instead of a soldier and she is left to fend for herself like that sailboat off the coast of Oregon.

Some choose to hire a captain and crew for potentially dangerous crossings so they can become passengers for a time. However, if you intend to be a participant, you must be as mentally and physically ready as any athlete before a match. You must be able to see your toes from a standing position, run a mile, and swim a ½ mile. Stay up for 24 hours. Pushups, pull-ups please so you can lift yourself to a dock four feet above, so you can navigate a vessel with thirty degrees of motion in any direction, so you can lower yourself into a dinghy in a three foot chop without falling in, so you can help haul a tree into the cockpit. We were ready.

Jenny took good care of us in spite of our novice seamanship. I had let her down, but she did not let us down. The bond strengthened. I vowed not to get her into this kind of trouble again.

BOOK 3: WORKING IN SAN FRANCISCO

The fever that drives a man to rebuild a sixty-year-old vessel can make him lose sight of the reason for doing it. The surge of the tide down along the water's edge was lost on me. The clean westerly tugged at the shrouds and I heard nothing. A new part added to the vessel made the old parts look worse. The accomplishment of one day became a command for the next. I fell into a panic lest the cycle would take so long that I would have to start on the first again by the time the last job was done.

Joe Richards
Princess, 1956

Mary and I were still working for a living and having *Jenny* with us in the Emeryville Marina enabled me to be working on her most weekends. Jeep exploring and motorcycle riding in the Sierra experienced a sharp decline. *Jenny* was in very good shape when I bought her, but there were a ton of things I needed to learn about and give care to. Our plan was to voyage to distant lands and based upon this last encounter with Mother Nature I wanted *Jenny* to be fit as a fiddle. I have compressed the following entries to remove some of the tedium, but left enough substance to give you a feel for the reality of owning a ten-year-old cruising boat. If you are to cruise to distant lands, either you need a very big wallet, or you need to perform almost all maintenance on your own.

If you are not interested in this tedium, you can skip ahead. Moreover, some people might conclude that buying a new boat would eliminate this work. It does in a way. If you can afford a new boat, then these discoveries or ones like them happen throughout the first year or two of ownership. The builder generally picks up the tab and performs the corrections. Sometimes they fix it right, and sometimes it requires a few tries. The activities and timeframe are the same; it is just whether you choose sweat equity or payments. The bottom line is that the boating market is incredibly efficient. You get what you pay for. Rarely do you get a "deal". Here is a sample of the broad range of skills and projects that are typical for a ten-year-old boat.

October 2004

Location: Emeryville

- I found that the furnace coolant is leaking within the furnace itself. It leaked about a quart the week we were off *Jenny* through the water trap at the bottom elbow of the exhaust. I have to call Sure Marine, the installers, to find out what the problem might be.
- I set up three of the fenders with snap hooks so Mary will not have to deal with knots when pulling them in and setting them out.
- We did our first pump out today. Since the valve on the hose barely worked, I suspect that few people actually do pump outs. I have not seen a single other boat over at the pump out dock.
- I got some really large aluminum snap hooks from Home Depot that seem to be perfect for setting up the dinghy boom. This will be next week's project.
- Tomorrow we will take our first sail on the bay. That should be fun. Mary is a little scared, it has been a while since she was last on the water and this water is new to her.
- Replaced the lines running to the dinghy boom and added 3 part block system to enable the dinghy to be controlled better.
- Sanded and painted the dinghy winch motors.

- Checked the furnace for water. There was about a pint of brown coolant in the catch pan. I think there is still a bunch of fluid in the exhaust system due to the clogged up water catch. It seems to have backed up into the exhaust system and created a bunch of rust.
- I replaced the water catch copper pipe with a proper loop of tubing.
- I took the furnace apart and found that I need to replace the burn tube and heat exchanger. The burn tube had melted and caused the whole heat exchanger to rust through. I contacted s Sure Marine and the cost for a new one is. $664. Ugh.
- Changed oil in the Windlass, greased main bearing.
- Took Cathy and David on tour of SFO Bay.

November 2004

Location: Emeryville

- Replaced the furnace heat exchanger and burn tube.
- Installed new Perry water filter and fuel filter on furnace. I did not have to bleed the fuel system. I just over filled the new filter, and then screwed it in. There is a bleed bolt on top. I took it off and filled the hole with diesel. This seemed to do it since it fired right up.
- I am not sure about the fuel filter, but the water filter definitely needs to be changed at least annually since it contains a dissolvable slug. The slug is supposed to keep the coolant at 8 to 9 ph (very basic) to avoid acid eating away at the metal in the system. I got a pool PH test kit and will try it out tomorrow.
- I found rain water running down the stacks and landing on the engine. I opened the port side stack louver and found that the run out tube at the top of the stack was connected to what remained of a plastic water tube leading down and aft to the stock exit. The tubing had completely melted and turned black. Looks like it was close to burning. I replaced it with fire proof rubber fuel line and created a new exit fitting on the port side so the water would have a clear path over the side. The grill was glued in with caulking and very difficult to remove. Since there is no reason to make this grill completely waterproof and it should be easy to remove if access to the inside is needed, I did not use caulking when I reinstalled it. Instead, I hammered it straight and put in some backing wood for the screws to grab hold on.
- Installed the water filter after the fresh water pressure tank and before *Jenny*'s plumbing last weekend. This should keep the faucet and shower head screens from loading up. Checked the furnace and the new plumbing today and all are ok. It rained last week and the new drain tube in the faux stack solved the water on the engine problem. Now I need to figure out how to remove the rust spots and repaint the engine.

- We are going over to Sausalito this afternoon. It's a beautiful day out.
- Got to look over *Jenny* to-do list now and see what is next.

December 2004

Location: Emeryville

- I nearly finished re-plumbing the water maker today. I moved all the valves and support equipment to a new mounting board. The board contains the pump filter, lift pump, air / water separator and fine filter and from there supplies the high-pressure pump. The made water comes back to the board for distribution to the forward or aft tank or a sampling line used to sample the made water before sending it off to the tanks.

February 2005

Location: Emeryville

- We have been taking short trips in SFO Bay as well as doing a bunch of maintenance items. Today I reinstalled the furnace after having the burner part completely reconditioned.
- Completed the new dining table top.
- Moved and wired the backup TV Camera
- Completed the new navigation table.
- Finished the wiring for the navigation computer.
- Had the pilothouse bench seat welded
- Here is the ongoing saga about the Coastal Explorer software etc. The Coastal Explorer software was not hooking up properly with the AP20 autopilot. I figured it was about the NMEA network not working properly, so bought a NMEA multiplexer and installed it. That proved to be a challenge in itself. The old wiring was just a junction pad with various components being hard wired together. Needless to say, there was no mechanism to keep one component from talking over the other. After studying and drawing the existing wiring, I unconnected it all and started wiring the new multiplexer in. The instructions were very brief, and assumed you knew the answer before reading them. Once you had it figured out, they made perfect sense. I wired the outputs from the GPS, depth finder and AP20 as inputs to the multiplexer, the navigation computer as the talker.
- Autopilot Trials. When I began working on the NMEA multiplexer, I decided to tune up the autopilot. The big mistake I made was to run the

sea trial without first recording the original steering parameters. Now it is all wrong and I am groping my way back. Today is not ideal for running another sea trial, so it will have to wait for another day. Last time I did not know you were supposed to run at 1/2 speed. I hope it will correct itself this time. It is a beautiful morning, but the day is supposed to cloud up and rain tonight.
- I installed the reconditioned furnace this morning and it is running just fine now. Mary will be pleased since she will have the hot water she craves again.
- I designed and built an air / water separator based upon our experience coming down the coast. It is all finished and installed. I completed it before Christmas and it seems to be working according to design. I will not really know until we go out of the bay and need to use the water maker again. I need to re-pickle it today if possible. But, I need to see what Mary wants to do when she arrives.
- There are probably other items that I have forgotten about over the past two months and should record. Oh well.
- I re-ran the Sea Trial auto tuning on the AP20 to get better parameters. This time *Jenny* ran at 3 knots and ended up with much better results. This was close but she was not holding the line. It was running on the Low Speed setting, so I set the Low Speed Rudder up to .50 and that was much better. It ran the line and turned just fine. Later I reduced the Rudder to .45 and it reduced the rudder engagement.

March 2005

Location: Emeryville

- Mary and I took *Jenny* out to see a ship come in under the Golden Gate Bridge carrying a pair of massive ship loading and unloading cranes for the Oakland port. There were quite a few boats in the water, lots of Coast Guard too. People lined the Golden Gate Bridge to see it pass under.
- I re-pickled the water maker too. So it should be good for another 6 months.
- I have taken the long brush and wiped some of the algae off the bottom. I need to call a diver to finish that task and check the zincs.
- I worked on the windlass yesterday. The clutch on the windlass was not working. The chain wheel should be able to run free or be clutched in at various degrees of pulling strength. I finally got the top screw undone and found a mess. First, it was nearly impossible to get the drum off because the bronze key was jammed into the drum slot and would not come free. After a significant amount of grunt and 6 foot pry bars, I finally pried it off. Next I found the outer (top) clutch hub frozen to the chain wheel but disconnected from the shaft. It had a

broken key and the break chewed up the inside of the clutch hub. Got the clutch hub off and the chain wheel, but the broken key was holding the lower clutch and it would not come free. More serious levering and it finally came off. I will order the parts tomorrow.
- I also waxed the port side hull and outside white parts.
- Today is Good Friday so I took most of the day off. I installed the new top clutch and shaft keys on the windlass. Also waxed the white on the foredeck.
- The autopilot worked perfectly with the Nobeltec software today. The settings are: AAM, APB, BWC, RMC, VTG, XTE. The talker ID is EC - Electronic Chart Display, update Interval = 1 sec, bearing = Magnetic, Send bearing from boat to waypoint is checked, Arrival distance = .05, Sound once. The precision was set to: Bearings = 2, Range = 3, XTE = 2
- The Coastal Explorer software did not drive *Jenny* as well. The precision was set to auto, so that may have been it. I will try again next time.
- Note that I have set the AP20 to dial in 2 degrees port rudder to hold a straight course and that may also have contributed to the good run.
- Too cold to wax today. I cleaned the forward hatches.
- Found the master shower pump screen clogged but good. I need to replace it because it is not standard with the rest of *Jenny*.

April 2005

Location: Emeryville

We stocked up *Jenny* for a week of fun on the bay. Our plan is to go to Angel Island early tomorrow and get a place at the dock. Then we will tour the island. Poor Nicholas will have to stay onboard. The Park has rules.

I did some miscellaneous maintenance today. There was a safety recall on the burner tubes in the furnace because they were melting. Nice of them to catch up! Sure Marine sent me another new one. I was not sure whether my other new one was a good one or another bad one. Once again, I went down into the engine room. Fortunately, it is only a ten-minute job to replace the tube. The old new one was ok, but the tube was noticeably thinner than the newest one. I checked the coolant level and it was fine. Now, all is well there.

I bought a new Webber grill. The Force 10 was just not to my liking. The new one fits just right on the fish-cleaning table in the back and makes the cockpit look like a patio. The question now is what to do with all the stuff I have taken out of or replaced on *Jenny*. Fenders, BBQ, video players, small TV, etc???

We docked at Alaya Cove today and hiked up to the top of the island. It was pretty and good exercise. The wind was picking up and *Jenny* was not at ease, tugging at the lines that tethered her to land. We departed around 1:00 PM without lunch.

We went over to Chuck McGrath's Yacht Brokerage next. Chuck offered us a slip to use for a couple of days free. It was a good thing we left Alaya Cove early. The slip Chuck gave us is shared with another boat and our finger was on *Jenny's* port side bow in. The wind was blowing out of the west, toward our neighbor's boat. After two attempts to back in, I gave up a starboard side approach and pulled in port side. Mary had to undo the vinyl curtains on the port aft to get the dock door open. We did a good job coming in and the guy on the neighboring boat helped with the lines a little. Mary did the hard work. Then the rain came in, and it poured.

We enjoyed a couple of days in Sausalito, walking along the docks and town lanes, having dinner in the fine restaurants. It was short but very nice visit. Next, we took a short thirty-mile passage up to Drake's Bay, stayed two nights and returned to our marina without incident. It was good for all of us to get a little time in the ocean. *Jenny* needed the exercise and we needed to reassure ourselves that we could survive it without trauma.

May 2005

Location: Emeryville

Over Memorial Day weekend, David and Kathy Cork came onboard. *Jenny* took us all out to Drake's bay and down to the Farallon Islands for the weekend. We left after a very nice English breakfast that David Cork made and leisurely getting ready. I checked JD's oil and thought to check its transmission with the JD running. Good thing I did. It was down 1.5 quarts. *Jenny* had a beam sea going out, so we put her birds down. We stayed overnight in Drake's Bay and then left the next morning for the islands. Six sailboats accompanied *Jenny* on her way out of Drakes bay, all heading for the Farallon Islands. I found them chatting on VHF channel 72. Their plan was to round the southeast island and then continue down to Half Moon bay. It sounded like a good weekend plan, but this time we were returning to Drakes bay. Poor Nicholas got seasick.

As we approached the first island, we heard about whales and dolphins from the sailboat ahead. Sure enough, we saw about four grays, a pod of Pacific white sided dolphins and a bunch of sea lions. The sea lions were heading for shore like speed boats racing for the finish line. They were out of the water more than in, white spray flying from their flanks and froth through their teeth. It was a strange sight and after some thought we concluded they were frantically rocketing to shore to avoid being eaten by the Great White sharks that lurk in the depths of these waters.

Memorial Day weekend is now winding down. We had a great day coming back from Drake's Bay to the Emeryville Marina. The weather was perfect, and the water calm except where the currents stirred things up. *Jenny* had the helm and we luxuriated in the ambiance. The long weekend went by too quickly again. I am beginning to realize cruising takes time. You cannot be on a schedule. Maybe a good ratio of moving and sitting is about one to five. For every day / hour of moving you need five days / hours of enjoying where you are. Schedules cannot be important, just destinations.

We saw some lazy black backed porpoise, fishing boats, sailboats and sea lions clogging SFO bay. Coming into SFO bay against the current from the north is not all bad if you do what the fishing boats do. Just hug the northern coast, dive into the shallow bay just past the lighthouse and you will catch a counter current. Then shoot across to the other side when you get near the bridge. The last quarter mile is dead against the current with many swirls. Once inside it calms right down and you have light currents as you steam along the San Francisco waterfront.

June 2005

Location: Emeryville

We made a couple of day trips out to Alcatraz Island on nice days just to get out on the bay.

July 2005

Location: Emeryville

We came to *Jenny* this afternoon after work to begin our three day July 4th weekend. It was hot in Concord and typically cool at *Jenny*.

I have read that some boats use wire rope (cable) between the ends of the stabilizer outriggers and the birds. I do not like the chain that *Jenny* has. It is difficult to control when raising or lowering the birds and if it hits *Jenny's* sides, it can easily damage the gel coat. I also do not like how much drag it presents in the water. It slows *Jenny* down and causes her birds to drag toward the surface behind her. This also reduces their effectiveness. My initial measurements show a 10% loss of speed with the chain and birds in the water. The chain has a breaking strength around 2000 pounds. I am thinking that a 1/8 inch wire with roughly the same breaking strength will present no danger to *Jenny* when it is loose at her sides, will drag considerably less than the chain and possibly cut through kelp. I am making an experimental change from chain to wire. After I left work, I made the obligatory stop at West Marine to pick up the last parts for the wire rope replacements to *Jenny's* chains. Perhaps this weekend I will give it a try. I want to try a wire on one side and a chain on the other so I can get a very good look at the difference in drag if any.

Tomorrow we will be heading out to Drake's Bay again for some peaceful R&R. Bob on the Californian next door told me he got diesel fuel at Bodega Bay for $2.10 last weekend. If we feel like it, perhaps we will head up that way tomorrow afternoon. He said it was a Chevron station. Second best price was a Chevron station over in Sausalito.

However, the wind and waves were not cooperating. We stayed at the slip and I did miscellaneous maintenance items. *Jenny* did not mind. She had her caregivers onboard. *Jenny's* cap rails are natural teak. She wears no lipstick. No one has ever varnished them. She is a beautiful vessel, built for go instead of show. Her cap rails are working surfaces as our encounter with the tree testified. She had developed some cracks in her rails along the way and they needed some care. I filled them with black sanding sealer like the one you would use between teak boards on deck. I like the look of tan and black and I wanted to keep any more water out. In 24 hours, I will sand it down and *Jenny* will be looking good. She is not all Tomboy.

Next, I tackled the NMEA feeds to the instruments. While her instruments were receiving the GPS data from the Out port on the multiplexer, they were not receiving navigation data. I put the radars and depth finder on the Talker out port and they started picking up waypoint and other navigation data. The only thing I did not see was the waypoint mark on the radar screen. Perhaps *Jenny* needs to be moving.

July 3rd was a busy day. We cleaned *Jenny* top to bottom. I ran a signal cable from the Auto Helm Multi in the master cabin to the pilothouse. I could get wind information on Nobeltec but not on Coastal Explorer. I could get water temperature that seemed more like air temperature (74 degrees) on the Coastal Explorer, but nothing on Nobeltec. I plan to take a log tomorrow and look at the data.

I still cannot get the waypoint lollypop to show on the radars. I do get a GPS reading, so the wires are ok. I need to go to radio shack and get some terminal strip blocks. Then I plan to try wiring the radars to the auto pilot output. Maybe that will work.

Mary and I are having a different 4th this year. We are with *Jenny* having salmon for dinner. It is Monday and we are planning to watch the fireworks from the top of her pilothouse and going to work from her in the morning. This will be a first for Mary. Our neighbors in *Carpe Diem* went out to anchor somewhere with twelve on board. *Susan B*, the Nordhavn 47 left this morning for parts unknown. I suspect they were on their way home, in Oregon. There are plenty of people having picnics in the local park by the marina. This is a nice spot.

I spent the morning rewiring the NMEA signal wires one more time. This time I got it right. The secret was to wire the talker (PC) output only to the Autopilot input. Then wire the Autopilot output to the depth sounder and both radars. The lollypops now show up on both radars. The secret to the big radar was the menu setting to show all navigation data. I did not connect the depth sounder output because it is redundant with the Auto Helm data.

The final secret was to slow down *Jenny's* navigation PC output to two seconds. At one second, it was overloading the Multiplexer. The remaining mystery is why the charting software is not showing the Auto Helm depth and speed through water. I briefly saw it in Nobeltec last night, but nothing in either today. I took a log and sent it to Coastal Explorer today.

August 2005

Location: Emeryville

We just discovered Clipper Cove, ten miles from *Jenny's* slip and the best-protected anchorage in the bay. We went over for a couple of overnights. We also wanted to take on some fuel for the winter. The best price was down at the San Leandro Marina, south of the Oakland airport. We had not been that far down the bay before. It was an eighteen-mile trip and we picked up 300 gallons.

Friday, September 02, 2005

Location: Half Moon Bay

We decided we needed to go back out on the ocean before winter set in. I took *Jenny's* blinders off, got her saddled up and departed the Emeryville marina around 07:30 AM. I gave her the helm and we headed out for our first trip down the coast toward LA. This time we only went as far as Half Moon Bay, but it is a start. The trip down went very well except *Jenny's* Coastal Explorer chart software was not picking up the GPS information and thus could not tell *Jenny* where she was. She sounded her alarm asking for help. I took the wheel from her and as we reached the Golden Gate Bridge and switched back to Nobeltec. All seemed to be ok so I gave *Jenny* the wheel again.

Mary did very well in the ocean as usual. She is far more worried about a freighter running us down in SFO bay! On the other hand, Nicholas is not much of a sea dog yet. More like a seasick dog. He barfed several times on the way down.

Half Moon Bay has a nice protected harbor with a good anchorage, some good restaurants and places to visit at Pillar Point. I further investigated the GPS problem. At first, I thought it was the Coastal Explorer software. But once we got to Half Moon Bay, I discovered it was *Jenny's* Furuno GPS. I had noticed that it was taking longer and longer for it to synchronize with the satellites. This trip it took all the way to the Golden Gate Bridge. This morning it would not pick them up at all. Fortunately I had set *Jenny* up so I could easily plug our hand held Garmin GPS in lieu of the Furuno. I switched back to Coastal Explorer again and used that setup to get home. I find Coastal Explorer to superior to Nobeltec in many ways, so will retire Nobeltec as soon as I am sure Coastal Explorer is running flawlessly.

Saturday, September 03, 2005

Location: Half Moon Bay

I ran *Jenny*'s generator last night and this morning to charge her batteries. Funny thing, it is not surging now. The fuel tanks are full and I switched the source from the aft starboard tank to the forward port tank. That is the only difference. Also, in Marty's notes, he suggested that there was a problem with the fuel feed from the forward port tank to the generator's diesel manifold. Either that is wrong, or that problem is lower in the tank.

During the last fueling, I marked *Jenny*'s starboard tanks in fifty-gallon increments. The marks are slightly off since with all the remaining fuel in the forward port tank, *Jenny* was listing to port. The starboard aft tank took 255 gallons. The starboard forward tank took 180. Thursday, I transferred fifty gallons to the port aft tank to balance *Jenny*. With 380 gallons in the starboard tanks, fifty gallons in the aft port and unknown gallons in the forward port tank *Jenny* sits level.

The experiment for the weekend was to try *Jenny's* new wire rigging. I replaced her port side chain with 1/8 inch wire rope. My expectations were that it would run with less drag, deeper, and cut through kelp better than the chain. I had been warned that the wire would hum and it did, around 100 Hz. The vibration would probably aid cutting through kelp but was too punishing on the rigging. I have to solve this problem. I made the wire rig so the bird would fly twenty feet down instead of fifteen with the chain. Even so, the wire side runs significantly further forward of the chain.

Sunday, September 11, 2005

Location: Emeryville

I went down to *Jenny* this afternoon to work on her stabilizers. I replaced her starboard side ratchet block and cam cleat with a new ratchet block; no cam cleat. The old one was mashed during the summer and while I hammered it straight again, I prefer not to use it. I then took the cam cleat off her Port side stabilizer. The combination block and clam cleat was just not working.

I figured out that the ratchet part of the block, which heretofore I have not used, really improved my control of the line while dropping *Jenny's* birds into the water. Its wheel becomes a friction break because it does not rotate on the way out, only on the way in. I spent some time thinking about how to quickly snub the line and finally decided on railing mounted cleats. After several trips to West Marine, I found one and put it on *Jenny's* starboard side. West Marine stores rarely seem to have what I need. Today I started shopping through their web site. They provide free shipping with orders over $50. All mine are more than $50!

Saturday, October 01, 2005

Location: Benicia

Jenny took Mary and me on a very nice trip from Emeryville to Benicia today. The weather started out foggy so I ran for a while relying on *Jenny's* extra sensory perception: GPS, radar, depth sounder and the electronic charts. There were many sailboats out that appeared and disappeared in the fog for a while. Then the fog lifted all at once. We ran under sunny skies and clear weather, running with the tide all the way up. The further west we went, the warmer it became. We were both pleased to be in short sleeves when we arrived. The marina has condominium's surrounding the slips and is a very nice place to live and own a boat. We checked out the prices of the condominiums, but were not seriously looking.

I tested *Jenny's* new wire rope stabilizer design again on the way up. I installed a rubber dock snubber in the line to quench the vibration and it worked!!! Now all I need to do is to build the 5/8 inch line part again. The ones I made the first time were too short. The old lines were 11.5 feet long. I am going to make the new ones at least twelve so I can reach the shackle from the upper deck in case I need to change out the wire while under way.

Tuesday, November 08, 2005

Location: Emeryville Marina

I visited Jock MacLean at KKMI to get an estimate for winter work. I want to have *Jenny's* bottom stripped, a preventative barrier coat applied and switch from CSC to Trinidad SR. Jock agreed with the choice of Trinidad. He said a barrier coat might not be necessary, but we will find out when we get working. I also want them to drop *Jenny's* keel cooler for cleaning and change the coolant.

The second task will be to make the generator quieter. I suspect the mounting. Jock is coming over to *Jenny* next week to look at that item and the counter tops. We want to replace the counter tops with new Corian. The current tops are some kind of plastic, but not to our liking. We also want a drop locker added aft of the oven to reclaim some useless space. His swag estimate is about $12,500 for the mechanical work and another $12,500 for the Corian swap out throughout *Jenny*. With that revelation, I am now considering a different plan.

Saturday, December 03, 2005

Location: Emeryville Marina

Jenny sits at the end of the dock close to the fishing pier and promenade. She is not at all shy and likes having people come by and look her over. She knows many dream of distant shores and lust for her. She is not unfaithful, just a big flirt. This year she wanted some accessories for Christmas so she could show off a little festive sparkle. I went to Home Depot and bought materials to make two sunlight activated plug boxes and a few sets of "icicle" lights for her. With her railings lit up like Rockefeller Center, she is now the belle of the dock. I also put a decorated mini Christmas tree and Santa in her salon window. It all lights up automatically when the sun sets and *Jenny* brings Christmas cheer to her daily audience. Even the children stop to look her over now.

Wednesday, December 28, 2005

Location: Emeryville Marina

We had a nice afternoon with sun peeking through all the rain we have had this week. I undressed *Jenny*. She was not happy at all. I took down her lights and decorations. I stored everything but the tree in a tub and put the tub under the guest bunk in the forward cabin. The new finish on the salon table looks good.

I like it glossy, although I do not think Mary does. So, I was not in the ladies' good graces today.

Sunday, January 01, 2006

Location: Home in Concord

The major items that *Jenny* needs at this point are:
1. New Corian or Zodiac counter tops in the galley.
2. New carpet throughout.
3. Sound blanket for the generator.
4. Hull strip, barrier coat and Trinidad SR

That is it. I plan to get those things done in 2006. Everything else is extra. We are getting real close!

Passage: Bay Marine for haul out

Departed Friday, March 17, 2006 at 10:05 AM local time from Emeryville Marina.

Arrived Friday, March 17, 2006 at 12:05 AM local time at Bay Marine Boatyard. The trip covered 10.40 nautical miles in 0d 1h 51m with an average speed of 5.60 knots and a maximum speed of 7.10 knots.

Friday, March 17, 2006 6:59:54 PM

Location: Bay Marine Boatyard Richmond CA

Jenny and I went solo to Bay Marine Boatyard to have her hauled and a bunch of maintenance done. I decided to take her there for the work after getting their quote. They are right next to KKMI and their yard is full of commercial boats and yachts. I figured for this work they had the skill and expertise necessary. This was not something fancy, just routine work. Their price was right.

At KKMI for Bottom Paint

The bottom looked good but the CSC Micron paint was chipping off as I expected. The work order includes;

- Remove the Micron CSC completely down to the gel coat being careful not to damage it. Use solvent. Do not remove existing gel coat.
- Repair any blisters.
- Apply InterProtect 3000 Barrier coat to correct depth.
- Apply two coats of Petit Trinidad SR
- Replace coolant in keel coolers (Engine and Generator) with CAT Extended Life, John Deere, Detroit Diesel Powercool SCA, or Fleet Guard as recommended by Lugger. Pressure test for leaks.
- Polish propeller
- Check the zincs

Sunday, March 19, 2006 11:25:12 AM

Location: Home

I went down to visit *Jenny* yesterday to remove the water speed sensors so they would not be painted. Until *Jenny* was hauled, I did not know there were two water speed sensors, one on each side. I do not know which is connected to the

Auto Helm or what the other is connected to yet. It might be connected to the Furuno depth finder. I did discover that the sensor under the master bed is an AirMar ST600 and the one under the floor near the fuel manifolds is an AirMar ST650.

I am glad I did not attempt to pull either sensor while *Jenny* was in the water because they use very different fittings. Removal of the ST600 requires you unscrew the cap collar and pull the sensor out. A flap springs into the hole and reduces the amount of water that pours in. Even so, you have to be quick about putting the plug in. However, if you do the same on the ST650, you pull the tube with the flap out and you end up with a 1.5-inch hole and a ton of water flooding in. The ST650 requires that you pull out a pin its side and then pull out the sensor. The flap is inside an inner collar.

Saturday, March 25, 2006

Location: Home

Final inspection of the work Bay Marine revealed a nice big fat Oyster masquerading as part of the bow thruster housing. The yard manager and I spied the hitchhiker about the same time. It was dripping seawater and dying after being out of water three days. The water was the giveaway. Otherwise, it looked just like part of the thruster. After we chiseled it out and the passageway was considerably more open. Bay Marine did a very good job as far as I can tell. *Jenny*'s bottom was very smooth and uniform with a new barrier coat, a primer coat and two coats of Petit Trinidad SR bottom paint. She liked it when I rubbed my hand down her side. I could hear her giggle. My only complaint at the moment was how dirty the rest of her was. The lady had spent the last four days in the factory setting of the yard with all the dust and junk settling on her.

We got her back in the water. *Jenny* had new underwear and a new dress. It was all underwater, but she skipped along in her new duds back to her slip in Emeryville. I saw 8.7 at one point with JD beating at 1600 RPM. Sure current was helping, but we were both smiling. There was more work to do though. After months of solid rain, the topsides really need to be polished and waxed. Some bottom paint spray from the boat next to *Jenny* at the yard has coated part of the Starboard topsides. UGH.

Sunday, May 28, 2006 9:54:19 AM

Location: Emeryville Marina
Latitude is 37 degrees 50.519 minutes north.

Longitude is 122 degrees 18.749 minutes west.

It is Memorial Day Weekend. The Indy race is on the TV, Mary is grocery shopping and the kids (my son Derek, his wife Heather and two children David and Marina) are on their way down for a day with *Jenny*. I have been working on my BoatExec software heavily over the past couple of months getting it ready for release. That, coupled with keeping *Jenny* in top condition, working a real job and keeping Mary happy has been a challenge. I feel that BoatExec is coming together now and there are only minor things to polish up, so that is good. On the other hand, I get a new boss at Kaiser in a week and that will probably reduce the amount of time I have for focusing on this. Oh well.

We will probably ask *Jenny* to take us all down to Jack London Square today. I think grandson David will get a thrill out of seeing the big container ships! The weather is very nice but we wish it were warmer.

Saturday, June 03, 2006 6:35:42 PM

Location: Emeryville Marina

It was another nice day on *Jenny*. Mary and I came aboard last night and are spending the weekend as usual. The wind was low, sun high, warm and nice. We did not go anywhere, which bothers me. I guess its ok since we are investing in our escape by getting everything ship shape on *Jenny*. But, another nice day at the dock instead of underway is disappointing. Nicholas had a tough day visiting four stores and greeting all the customers. He sure likes all the attention.

Saturday and Sunday, June 17 and 18, 2006

Location: Clipper Cove

We released *Jenny* from her slip and she took Mary and me over to Clipper Cove at Treasure Island yesterday afternoon. We came in at close to low tide, so had little trouble getting through the shallow entrance. I have been watching boats go out this morning to see where the deep water is. It looks like you skirt the northern edge of the pier to be safe. Mary is out back in the sun, reading magazines, enjoying the warm weather.

Wild Eagle, a 55' (approximately) sport fishing boat from Alaska is anchored in front of us. It is a nice boat, and from the looks of all the antenna, well equipped. They have very large front deck upon which sits a large dinghy

(dinghy envy). *Jenny* keeps swinging over that way to get closer. I think she has a crush.

It is father's day and a good day to be on *Jenny*. Mary and I plan to spend the week on *Jenny* and go to work from Emeryville. I have been thinking about how to depart the working world. If BoatExec works out, then I will stay on the job until next year. Then I will take five weeks of vacation. Then maybe I will be able to take a one-year sabbatical. That leaves the option open to return.

Friday, July 14, 2006 9:07:10 PM

Location: Home

I am at home on Friday before our first long trip since 2004. It has been far too long since our last long vacation with *Jenny*. We had planned to go all the way down to Catalina, but Mary could only take two weeks off, I would have had some trouble finding a crew, and I wanted to take a week to finish up, polish up BoatExec. We will go from here to Pillar Point (Half Moon Bay), then to Monterey for the rest of the week. My daughter Laura will be flying in next Saturday to join us. Her son Alex may or may not be with her. She needs a break and he has been difficult lately.

Mary has the jitters as usual before departing on *Jenny*. She builds up high anxiety while on shore, but once we are underway, she seems to be fine. We both have just not had enough time with *Jenny* lately. I hope that will change through the rest of the summer. *Jenny* has been patient with all the attention I have been giving her, but is ready to go too. All dressed, polished and very fit. I am too. We should be onboard by 1:00 PM after finishing our shopping in the morning.

Saturday, July 15, 2006 12:02:00 PM

Location: Emeryville Marina
Latitude is 37 degrees 50.522 minutes north.
Longitude is 122 degrees 18.749 minutes west.

We just stored a second wave of provisions. The freezer is now packed, and I do not have to fire up the big one. I brushed the slime off *Jenny's* hull and checked her tanks. She hates it when I let her get slimy. All seems just fine for a good start. Mary is on her way down with the final wave of supplies and then off to get her nails done.

Passage: To Pillar Point for Vacation

Departed Sunday, July 16, 2006 at 7:50 AM local time from Emeryville Marina. The departure location was latitude 37 degrees 50.519 minutes north, longitude 122 degrees 18.748 minutes west.

This weather observation was taken on Sunday, July 16, 2006 10:06:26 AM local time.
Observation location: Off of SFO peninsula.
Latitude is 37 degrees 43.427 minutes north.
Longitude is 122 degrees 32.274 minutes west.
The air temperature is 54, and water temperature is 68 degrees Fahrenheit.
The forecast is Haze then sun.
The current weather is Dry.
The sky is Overcast (more than 90% clouds).
The wind is 10 knots from the South.
The visibility is 5 nautical miles.
The wave height is 2 feet with 4 foot swells.
The barometer is 1027 millibar and Steady.

Arrived Sunday, July 16, 2006 at 1:25 PM local time. The arrival location was latitude 37 degrees 29.788 minutes north, longitude 122 degrees 29.505 minutes west. The trip covered 34.24 nautical miles in 0d 5h 33m with an average speed of 6.15 knots.

Sunday, July 16, 2006 5:09:30 PM

Location: Pillar Point Harbor
Latitude is 37 degrees 29.786 minutes north.
Longitude is 122 degrees 29.505 minutes west.

It was a lumpy start. Swells build during their long journey from Japan and then come against the headlands of the Golden Gate only to be thrown back on one another like bowling pins. The scattered swells become dissonant waves hurled in all directions. Locals call it the Potato Patch. Today we had six to seven foot swells coming in to make things interesting. *Jenny's* birds were down which helped a lot. Still, Nicholas was seasick as usual. Once we got down the coast a bit *Jenny* got to the unbroken swell that was much more bearable.

We had planned to stay here tomorrow, but since the wind is up, we cannot put *Jenny's* dinghy down and there is not much point in staying. I called the harbormaster in Monterey Harbor and he said there was a good chance for getting a 45-foot slip there. No reservations though. We huddled and decided to head down there in the morning.

The wire on *Jenny's* stabilizers worked well today, but the dock snubber on her port side broke at the ends. I am going to try to rig it up a different way and see if that works. In any case, it looks like I need to use a one-inch size snubber instead of the 5/8 inch.

Passage: To Monterey Bay

Departed Monday, July 17, 2006 at 6:31 AM local time from Pillar Point. The departure location was latitude 37 degrees 29.789 minutes north, longitude 122 degrees 29.518 minutes west.

This weather observation was taken on Monday, July 17, 2006 9:05:13 AM local time.
Observation location: Pigeon Point.
Latitude is 37 degrees 16.086 minutes north.
Longitude is 122 degrees 27.478 minutes west.
The air temperature is 52 degrees Fahrenheit.
The forecast is Sunny.
The current weather is Dry.
The sky is Clear or a few clouds.
The wind is 8 knots from the South.
The visibility is 10 nautical miles.
The wave height is 2 feet with 4 foot swells.
The barometer is 1013 millibar and Steady.

Arrived Monday, July 17, 2006 at 4:36 PM local time at Monterey Municipal Harbor slip A7. The arrival location was latitude 36 degrees 36.195 minutes north, longitude 121 degrees 53.386 minutes west. The trip covered 63.67 nautical miles in 0d 10h 4m with an average speed of 6.32 knots and a maximum speed of 7.32 knots.

Monday, July 17, 2006 7:25:52 PM

Location: Monterey Municipal Harbor
Latitude is 36 degrees 36.197 minutes north.
Longitude is 121 degrees 53.384 minutes west.

We started out at 06:30 to a perfectly calm, sunny morning. We needed an early start for the sixty-mile journey down the coast. The water was much better all day, with only a little chop and fog as we went over Monterey canyon. The canyon is 2,400 feet deep and the cold current welling up at the coast creates the fog and chop. Mostly, there were a few small wind waves and the swells were soft. I dropped *Jenny's* birds for an even more comfortable ride. We ran the radar occasionally when in the fog and only saw one boat, a nice new sixty foot trawler yacht going on a reverse course north.

As *Jenny* approached Monterey Harbor, we came out of the fog and all was sunny and warm. It was a nice 77 degrees Fahrenheit when we arrived. We saw lots of seals and sea lions on the way in and even had a sea otter greet us as *Jenny* crept down the fairway to her slip. It hung around *Jenny's* stern cute as a button as we tied up and washed the salt off *Jenny*. Later we found it alongside a boat a couple of slips up, snoozing on its back while floating in the water. It was too cool and a good start to the week here.

Our friendly Monterey sea otter at *Jenny's* stern.

I had to make a repair to *Jenny's* port stabilizer rig. The dock snubber broke apart on the way to Pillar point. I rigged it back up a little differently and it worked better than the old way. Tomorrow I will fix her starboard one the same way. As we approached the harbor, I had the opportunity to compare *Jenny's* speed with her birds down and with them up. She is now rigged with wire instead of chain and her speed dropped just .4 knots instead of .7 with the chain. Most Excellent!

We are tired after two days at sea, so will sleep long and hard tonight. Tomorrow we will explore the town and see if the bikers are beginning to arrive for the Laguna Sea Moto GP race this coming weekend.

Tuesday, July 18, 2006 7:16:01 PM

Location: Monterey Harbor
Latitude is 36 degrees 36.196 minutes north.
Longitude is 121 degrees 53.386 minutes west.

We were busy today. We got up around 06:30 as usual. It is hard to break old habits. I discovered a problem with how BoatExec connects to send email and was up early figuring out what to do. The old way was to ask Internet Explorer to invoke the user's default mail program. It seems a weak and error prone approach. I spent the day working out a new, more direct way. Tonight is the test. I will send this to myself, and then distribute it.

Around 10:00 AM, we started with a walk to Cannery Row, and stopped in the coffee shop we know. We took Nicholas and he was good all the way down Cannery Row and most of the way back. Then he got tired and just plopped on the walkway. We had to take turns carrying him back.

Our Sea Otter friend came back after lunch and played around. There are a lot of them in the harbor here. After lunch, we left Nicholas with *Jenny* and went for another walk and some shopping. I got a hat (big surprise) with Sea Otters on the front to replace the one I bought in 1998 and lost. It was the same hat, only a different color. Then I worked on my software while Mary read the local newspaper. Life is a struggle. Maybe tomorrow we will sleep in.

Wednesday, July 19, 2006 5:26:44 PM

Location: Monterey Harbor

We were up at 07:30 this morning instead of 06:30, so we are making progress. Today is a light duty day. We took our morning walk, but Nicholas stopped before we even got to Cannery Row. His legs are just too short for long walks. Poor baby! The folks in the sailboat next to us took off today for Santa Cruz. The weather is just great. Mary did laundry using the marina machines. I tried to nap, but fishing boats were coming and going making a lot of racket. Our friendly sea otter showed up on schedule this afternoon and I got some good photos. He looks about the size of Nicholas when in the water, but he hauled out on the slip next to us and is really about twice his size. I estimate about forty or fifty pounds. He is a healthy little devil.

There is a fresh seafood place at the end of the pier and we have been shopping there for dinner. Tonight is shrimp. After dinner, we will take Nicholas out for an evening walk. The bikers are starting to show up for the Moto GP races at Laguna Sea this weekend. We saw part of the Yamaha team eating at a nearby restaurant. Mary checked out the riders and logistics for watching the race. We do not have tickets or a way to get to the Laguna Seca racetrack, but a big tent is being set up in the town square for big-screen viewing of the race. How convenient!

I cleaned one of *Jenny's* water speed and temperature sensors today, the one in the engine room. I was hoping that it was the one hooked up to the Auto Helm instruments we use when underway, but it was not. It's the one hooked up to the depth sounder. The other one is under the master bed and inconvenient to reach or service. Good thing neither are very important to our running.

Thursday, July 20, 2006 5:44:39 PM

Location: Monterey Harbor
Latitude is 36 degrees 36.198 minutes north.
Longitude is 121 degrees 53.383 minutes west.

It is another day in paradise and Margarita time to boot. The locals say this is the best weather they have had in a long time. It is nice to be warm again after a very cool and wet spring in Oakland. Since it is warm here, it must be boiling at the house in Concord. We have very good luck like this. In 2004, we spent two weeks in Alaska interior and at sea along the coast and had nothing but beautiful weather. The sea was like glass from Seward to Valdez, Yakutat, and Juneau. Maybe it is Mary's luck of the Irish.

Mary hit the outlets in town today and I bought some new snubbers for *Jenny's* stabilizers. I doubt the original 5/8 inch Taylor ones will last. The guy at the ships' store confirmed they are not industrial strength. I bought some 3/4 inch ones made by Tempo. I have not decided whether to wait until the others break, or go ahead and put these up. So far, the design is working very well.

The weather was so good we took a walk on the beach this afternoon. The water is very cold, but it was nice. It has been too long since we strolled on a beach. This vacation is starting to sink in. Our friend the otter did not show this evening. In fact, we suspect we have been seeing two; one tagged with pink and the other blue. We saw a pair vigorously mating around noon and it might have been them. They might be off somewhere on honeymoon...

Sunday, July 23, 2006 7:23:19 AM

Location: Monterey Harbor
Latitude is 36 degrees 36.202 minutes north.
Longitude is 121 degrees 53.383 minutes west.

Yesterday was filled with meeting and welcoming people. Larry and Sue Tombach arrived from San Simeon aboard *Beverley S* the day before and anchored out. They brought *Beverley S* into a slip yesterday and we went over to meet them. They are wonderful people. As we stepped on board and were shaking hands, Mary drew back. She asked, "Is this *Brass Ring*!" Larry confirmed it was. "Oh! You took my first love so I do not think we can be friends." We all had a good laugh as we explained our encounter with *Brass Ring*. As it turns out, they were shopping for their 46 at the very same time we were.

Their *Beverly S* was born in 1997 and *Jenny* was born in 1994. You would think they would be similar. Not so. *Beverly S* has a forward master cabin and a very nice layout. I think the forward cabin boats have more storage and a better use of space than the mid cabin boats but I am not sure they are as comfortable for sleeping when in motion. We exchanged tours and picked up some new ideas.

Master mariners Susan, Larry with Mary

Laura and Alex (my daughter and grandson) arrived around 6:00 PM last night. They are out for the week and looking forward to ecotourism and fishing. They flew in from Florida, so were up at the crack of dawn today. UGH.

Sunday, July 23, 2006 7:15:18 PM

Location: Monterey Harbor
Latitude is 36 degrees 36.195 minutes north.
Longitude is 121 degrees 53.385 minutes west.

We met up with Larry and Sue for cocktails and dinner. They are bringing the garlic bread and wine. We are fixing the spaghetti. We had a great cocktail hour reliving boating experiences and dreaming about customizing our 46's. They have a lot more sailing experience than we do. Larry and I figured out the best place for the deck boxes and the life raft that will allow better deployment and allow us to put a nice patio canopy up top for deck chairs and a nice evening chat. Larry's setup on *Beverly S* convinced us that we need to get rid of *Jenny's* cockpit ladder to the top deck. It is a useless hatch and doing this gains a lot of space above and below. So, that is now on the to-do list. Our local otter even put in a guest appearance. Our next rendezvous with them is set for Drake's Bay. We are leaving tomorrow morning for Pillar Point and they are going to stay in Monterey and visit the aquarium.

The next day we spent the morning doing a little fishing just outside the harbor. Somehow, I lost an entire fishing rod and reel between the slip and the channel out of the marina. It was sitting in the stern rod holder when we started and not there moments later. It is the second one I lost that way. Then a poor baby Halibut decided to ingest the whole squid I had on as bait, hook and all. Poor thing; there was no way to get the hook out. We have to pick on bigger fish next time. Laura and Alex went to the beach to look for sand dollars and shells.

Great gobs of warm weather have been our friend since arriving. We hope it will continue at our next two anchorages. It was another great day.

Passage: To Pillar Point

Departed Monday, July 24, 2006 at 8:15 AM local time from Monterey Harbor. The departure location was latitude 36 degrees 36.196 minutes north, longitude 121 degrees 53.382 minutes west.

Arrived Monday, July 24, 2006 at 7:11 PM local time at Pillar Point. The arrival location was latitude 37 degrees 29.813 minutes north, longitude 122 degrees 29.552 minutes west. The trip covered 64.36 nautical miles in 0d 10h 55m with an average speed of 5.89 knots and a maximum speed of 7.65 knots.

Tuesday, July 25, 2006 12:49:19 PM

Location: Pillar Point
Latitude is 37 degrees 29.824 minutes north.
Longitude is 122 degrees 29.553 minutes west.

Jenny beat her way north yesterday. The seas were ok but she had a twenty-knot wind on her bow. She also found some fog. Otherwise, it was sunny and cool. She snagged a crab pot about thirty minutes out from the Pillar Point harbor. The marker was covered with sea moss and nearly invisible. It was not her fault. I did manage free it, but not until *Jenny* had dragged it about a mile. While I was trying, to free it my fingers became tangled in the wires and I nearly lost a couple. These crab pots weigh two hundred or so pounds and I learned they are not something to be messed with. Next time I will cut it free.

The rubber stabilizer snubber on *Jenny's* port side broke just as we were starting, so we listened to her wire play a monotonous tone all the way up. I bought some new ones in Monterey; bigger and look better quality. This morning I put them up and used a better knot to tie them in. I hope this knot will put less cutting stress on the rubber. We will see. The whole rig is proving out pretty good but still needs a lot of fine-tuning. *Jenny* managed two miles per gallon on the way up, fighting the southerly current that runs down the coast and averaged only 6.3 knots running JD at 1650 RPM.

We got *Jenny's* dinghy down at first light and set it up. Its battery was dead for some reason, but after a short charge, the Tohatsu motor started with a manual pull. The battery is a couple of years old now, so I might need to replace it. It is a simple lawn mower battery, so a trip to Kmart is the plan. Once I got the dinghy running I took Laura and Alex to the beach and Mary to the small town here. Then I worked on *Jenny*'s stabilizers, did a round of water taxi pickups and then lunch. I feel like a soccer mom with a dinghy! We are all going to the beach in a few minutes, except Nicholas.

Passage: Pillar Point to Drakes Bay via Farallon Islands

Departed Wednesday, July 26, 2006 at 7:57 AM local time from Pillar Point. The departure location was latitude 37 degrees 29.835 minutes north, longitude 122 degrees 29.569 minutes west.

Arrived Wednesday, July 26, 2006 at 4:43 PM local time at Drake's Bay. The arrival location was latitude 38 degrees 0.087 minutes north, longitude 122 degrees 58.000 minutes west. The trip covered 48.97 nautical miles in 0d 8h 46m with an average speed of 5.59 knots and a maximum speed of 7.46 knots.

Thursday, July 27, 2006 5:43:52 PM

Location: Drake's Bay

The trip up to Drake's Bay was nice. The sea calmed down especially after *Jenny* rounded the Farallon Islands. We did not see any whales and not many marine mammals. It was overcast and has been since leaving Pillar Point. Drake's Bay is empty other than some local fishermen. There is no electricity on shore and there are no cell phone connections or TV. It is very quiet, and with no moon or fog, and is very dark at night. The sea elephants we expected to see are not here this time. There are many seals, dolphins, birds in the water though and deer and cows on the shore. Laura and Alex walked the beach this morning and found all sorts of small wild things. They took a walk on the hills this afternoon and saw the deer and the ocean on the other side of them.

There was a commercial boat anchored with a couple of guys onboard over by the fish cabin this morning. I asked them about anchoring there and it sounds like a better place than we have been using out toward the middle of this area. We have decided to pull anchor in the morning and head back to civilization. On Saturday, we can motor down the Oakland channel and show Alex the big ships, and maybe do some fishing out in the bay.

I have a crab net down, and have caught two female Dungeness crabs so far. I threw them back, but now know that crabs are about. It seems like the males either are fished out, or are somewhere else.

Passage: Back to Emeryville

Departed Friday, July 28, 2006 at 8:47 AM local time from Drake's Bay. The departure location was latitude 38 degrees 0.391 minutes north, longitude 122 degrees 58.546 minutes west.

Arrived Friday, July 28, 2006 at 2:32 PM local time at Emeryville Marina. The arrival location was latitude 37 degrees 50.522 minutes north, longitude 122 degrees 18.751 minutes west. The trip covered 35.53 nautical miles in 0d 5h 44m with an average speed of 6.19 knots and a maximum speed of 10.58 knots.

Saturday, July 29, 2006 8:47:26 AM

Location: Emeryville Marina
Latitude is 37 degrees 50.519 minutes north.
Longitude is 122 degrees 18.748 minutes west.

Laura and Alex explored the beach and hills around Drake's bay all day yesterday. We found out that one of the buildings on the bay is a Coast Guard museum. It is now being restored so we could not go in. There is a boat ramp that makes a nice dinghy landing though. The kids saw deer on their walks up the hills. We decided to come back into SFO Bay yesterday, after a rolling night. The wind was pushing *Jenny* broadside to the small waves that enter Drake's Bay. We were anchored in fairly shallow water so could not put her birds down to dampen the roll. We need some flopper stoppers that do not need more than ten feet of water. We weighed anchor around 09:00 AM to catch the incoming tide. On the way down the coast into the bay, we were treated by a whale doing acrobatics. As we got closer, the display became more and more subdued, but still a treat. There were several boats out fishing.

I timed the tide right and *Jenny* flew at eleven knots over ground as we came under the Golden Gate. I got her birds up; stabilizer gear stowed and she is now in her slip. One thing of note is that the four of us were using water from *Jenny's* tanks from Monday through now and still have plenty left. We are working off her forward 200-gallon tank and I think it has about forty gallons left. The aft 100-gallon tank is still full. I did not have to fire up the water maker and with some husbandry of water, could have four people last maybe two weeks on the tanks.

It was a great two-week cruise with the highlights being Monterey and meeting Larry and Sue Tomback. We are now washing down *Jenny* and starting the cleanup. I learned some ways to further improve her stabilizer rigging, but the wire works and works well. I also want to add a cleat to the dinghy's foredeck for convenience. Nothing major though and our confidence grows that *Jenny* is ready for continuous cruising. We just need to retire!!!

Passage: Napa Valley

Departed Saturday, May 26, 2007 at 9:53 AM local time from Emeryville Marina. The departure location was latitude 37 degrees 50.520 minutes north, longitude 122 degrees 18.750 minutes west.

Arrived Saturday, May 26, 2007 at 6:04 PM local time at Napa River. The arrival location was latitude 38 degrees 13.917 minutes north, longitude 122 degrees 17.690 minutes west. The trip covered 38.74 nautical miles in 0d 8h 7m with an average speed of 4.76 knots and a maximum speed of 7.05 knots.

Sunday, May 27, 2007 1:01:32 PM

Location: Napa River
Latitude is 38 degrees 13.906 minutes north.
Longitude is 122 degrees 17.683 minutes west.

It is Memorial Day weekend and *Jenny* tagged along with four sailboats to take her first cruise up the Napa River. Being a very close cousin to sailboats, she does not mind at all being with them. PAE made Mason sailboats before transitioning to long-range trawlers and the Nordhavn 46 was their first trawler model. So *Jenny* has a lot of sailboat blood and soul left in her. She is a creature of the sea, naturally blending with it rather than a machine trying to defeat it with size and power.

Originally, we were all going to Drakes Bay, but the weather showed gale force winds building over the weekend. We headed up here seeking sun and warmth. *Jenny* is not really a Napa kind of gal, but Mary definitely is.

The trip up was our first use of *Jenny's* new AIS system. This system shows commercial vessels on *Jenny's* chart plotter, their name, speed, course, etc. It is sort of like watching the Marauders' Map on Harry Potter. Vessels show up and are moving about the chart on their own. It turned out to be very useful. At a manageable distance, we could see the real hazards of the bay: the ferries hurling along at thirty-five knots. *Jenny's* AIS system told us instantly how close they were going to come to and whether she needed to run for cover. I even saw one on the chart up the river before I could even see the river.

It was strange gliding by homes and farms as we navigated up the river. Once to our anchoring spot, *Jenny* struggled settling in. She had not done this before and last night she sat with her anchor in the middle of the river (about 100 yards wide) and a stern line tied to a tree on the bank. I was up at midnight to watch the tidal current change and all was well. However, I was worried that *Jenny* presented too large a target for riverboat traffic. So this morning (06:30) I moved *Jenny* to the inside of the bend and just set her anchor. *Jenny* is now swinging free, with the wind pushing her up stream and the tide and current pulling her down. The good news is that there is plenty of room on both sides for other boats to pass.

Nicholas and I took Elizabeth, an eight year old, for a ride on *Jenny's* fast sport dinghy this morning. I am not sure who enjoyed the ride more. Nicholas loves going fast. Now Elizabeth is a speed freak and her Mom already said no-way...

At 02:00 AM *Jenny's* carbon monoxide alarm in the master cabin came to life with a wail! Initially I thought it must be broken, since no motors were running. However, after procrastinating too long I rolled out of bed and shuffled into the guest cabin to do a sniff test. *Jenny* has two big 4D batteries located under the settee up there. They supply the electricity to her bow thruster. About a month ago one of these five-year-old batteries shorted out. The electricity going through the short got the battery so hot, it boiled the acid and that set off the CO sensor. The reaction only stopped after it had boiled itself dry. I found the same thing going on again. I should have replaced them together. Lesson learned. Here I am in my underwear, 02:00 in the morning, hauling a 125-pound boiling battery through *Jenny* to get it outside. UGH.

Later in the morning, the four sailboat crews took their dinghies on a ride to visit Napa and check it out. They are much slower than *Jenny's* fast sport dinghy, so I gave them a forty-five minute head start. The way up the river was down wind and calm water. We caught up with them at Napa in no time. They said the dinghy dock in town had washed out during last winter's storms and we could not land. They were heading back. We also found one of them with a broken motor and offered to tow it back. Meanwhile the wind had picked up and was building a nice set of wind waves up the river. We pounded our way slowly back, becoming soaked and cold from the constant splash. The woman we were towing fell asleep in the bottom of her dinghy and had a nice nap. Ugh!

Jenny's dinghy is a pretty, sporty thing. It looks like a little sport car with a foredeck, windshield, seats, and steering wheel. Strangers stop to admire it. On flat calm water, it goes like stink. I used to race superbikes for fun and this creature makes me nervous at speed! Its flat bottom tracks like it is on casters. It has a hound mentality running after the slightest distraction without the slightest impulse control. It seemingly goes in random directions when you try to approach something and always ends up plowing into it with a thump. Its forehead impacts first rendering it even more stupid. In anything but flat water it throws water all over everything and everyone onboard. It is athletic like a bull but all that speed and strength makes it heavy and unsuitable as a tender. It is a beast.

Monday, May 28, 2007 9:01:32 PM

Location: Emeryville Marina
Latitude is 37 degrees 50.519 minutes north.
Longitude is 122 degrees 18.757 minutes west.

That was not the end of it by a long shot. After drinks and dinner with our sailing buddies last night, I woke up with a terrible headache and sick as a dog. We set up our chairs in the cockpit for three sunny quiet hours while I tried to recover. Then we released *Jenny* from the river bottom and she floated back down to the Bay. She left the Napa River around noon to catch the outgoing tide and was doing fine until she got to the middle of the bay. Remember the gale warning… The wind was blowing thirty knots, creating a nasty four to five foot chop. Since the east side of the bay is too shallow to drop her stabilizers she just got pitched and rolled about with spray coming up over her pilothouse. If Mary could have found a way off, she would have jumped ship.

With the wind this strong, and having no bow thruster because the battery had cooked itself out, we dared not take *Jenny* back to her slip. We headed for Clipper Cove, nicely sheltered and easy to get into in a blow. Here we are for dinner. If the winds die out, we will take *Jenny* back to her slip tonight. Otherwise, we will make an early start in the morning.

After dinner Mary and I decided to try getting *Jenny* back to her slip in the Emeryville marina. The winds had died down. When we got inside the breakwater we determined we could get *Jenny* safely back into her slip. But, to end this horrible weekend, we slid *Jenny's* starboard stainless steel rub rail along the cement piling on the way in. I could not hold her off because of her disabled bow thruster and Mary could not get a fender in place in time. I promised *Jenny* no more trips to Napa.

Tuesday, August 21, 2007 6:44:42 PM

Location: Emeryville Marina
Latitude is 37 degrees 50.519 minutes north.
Longitude is 122 degrees 18.757 minutes west.

I have now finished working for Kaiser and in the beginning of August, Mary and I moved aboard *Jenny* full time. We are anticipating beginning our full time cruising life in October. No one told us it would be this much work leaving our old life. It is work; real work. A month ago, we started taking STUFF to Goodwill, having garage sales, and throwing STUFF away. We have been constantly moving stuff out of the house since then. Two weeks ago, we packed up the remaining STUFF and loaded it onto the biggest Penske rental truck I could rent. I drove east with stops in Nashville TN, Riverview FL, and finally Deland FL to drop STUFF off with Derek and family, Laura and family, and storage. My back was not the same for weeks! We still have about five times more STUFF than will fit in *Jenny*. This STUFF is loaded in plastic tubs and located on *Jenny*, in Mary's Audi, and in my Jeep. We are far from complete.

Meanwhile, for the past four months, I have been working steadily to prepare *Jenny*. New carpet, new fresh water pump, new master cabin toilet, and finally fixing the furnace that supplies our hot water and never has been quite predictable or dependable. I installed a Port Networks high gain Wi-Fi antenna and transmitter after finding out that *Jenny's* laptop was not capable of a reliable internet connection with an access point only 200 yards away. It works great, and has been the easiest project to date. I am not even going to mention the toilet project that after a month, I hope to have wrapped up soon.

We are on track to leave the San Francisco Bay area during the first week in October. I hope that our task lists will dwindle and we will have nothing else to do but leave when the time comes. Meanwhile, we fall asleep exhausted.

My latest project is installing and testing a Pactor modem that will enable us to communicate via Email while we are voyaging. It was easy enough to hook up, but as with all things marine, has proven to be quite a challenge to make work.

Tuesday, September 04, 2007 6:05:29 PM

Location: Emeryville Marina
Latitude is 37 degrees 50.519 minutes north.
Longitude is 122 degrees 18.75 minutes west.

I am overdue on a report. *Jenny's* new Wi-Fi antenna and amplifier went in without a problem and I am connecting easily to the internet now. This is a sweet little Port Networks box. The next project was to get the SSB Radio modem installed and working. Well, actually it went in just about as easily as the Wi-Fi box. I had it up and running in a couple of hours. While it was receiving a lot of valuable information (weather faxes and bulletins), I was not able to connect to a mailbox station. Further investigation revealed that the SSB radio was not really working as well as it could. I kind of knew this for a while because when I tried to use it to reach Larry on *Beverly S* only about thirty miles from here in Drake's bay, I could not. Something was wrong.

Well, I started by taking the Shakespeare antenna apart to discover that the top part was not electrically connected to the bottom part any more. The connection had corroded. Even if the top part was connected, the wiring inside the antenna was completely inadequate for reliable use at sea. So began a week of work. First, I visited the local HAM radio store and talked to one of the experts there. He recommended running special High Frequency antenna wire from the top of the antenna tube to the bottom. It was a flat fine wire braided cable folded in half to be ½ inch wide. I bought the wire, went back to *Jenny*, tore the guts out of the old antenna, drilled a 1/2 inch hole from the top section to the bottom and ran the wire. Cool, except that the antenna tuner was now in the wrong place. It needs to be as close to the base of the antenna as possible and it was up above the instruments by the radio. I moved it to another compartment right at the base of the antenna.

Then I went to work on the ground plane. You are supposed to run flat copper tape down to the hull and then to water tanks and through-hulls. Gordon West says, "An ideal counterpoise for all frequency single side band work should consist of up to 100 square feet of metal surface area directly below the feed point." *Jenny* had a round ground cable to a single strip of copper tape that ran along the ceiling in the master cabin: about two square feet. That was it.

I got fifty feet of the High Frequency wire, this time folded in half to a one inch width. I ran it down to a forward through-hull and then back along the hull to another. When I fired up the modem again I was able to connect to Portland (500 miles away) on half power. Big smiles! This means I will be able to send and receive email from almost anywhere in the world. Too cool! However, before I could savor that moment of success, another project presented itself. I was vacuuming up the mess while the soldering iron was still plugged in. With this load the onboard power inverter/charger decided those twelve years of service were quite enough and had a meltdown. It is time for a Corona!

Fortunately, most of *Jenny's* equipment runs through the batteries at 12 volts, with only the refrigerator and microwave being needy 120-volt AC devices. Since *Jenny* is plugged into the grid a quick bypass of some circuit breakers got them running. On the web, surfing for the right replacement at the right price produced a hit (a Xantrex) and a purchase that was delivered last Wednesday, 8/29. In the meantime, I recharged the batteries by running JD.

I was facing a potentially beastly job installing the new inverter/charger. Maybe the new unit would fit in the same place, maybe not. Maybe it would use the same wiring, maybe not. A NOT on either would mean a terrible challenge which kept me awake a couple of nights. Harry Potter has nothing over the suspense delivered by a simple question: What will it take to fix *Jenny*!

After a couple of days of worry, I picked up the new Xantrex from the UPS store. I found that the new one would indeed fit in the same space, and had a hypothesis about how to wire it. I called the manufacturer support line, confirmed my hypothesis and I had it running by the end of the day. Not installed, but running. Whew!!!

Now, the Pactor modem needs just a little work, the power supply installation is just about done, and I have got three of the six storm windows (the last of the planned big projects) mounted and finished. Yes, while *Jenny* came with the mounting points for the salon storm windows, she did not have them. The idea is to put sheets of strong plastic over the outside of the salon windows so that if a wall of water slams *Jenny* on her beam, the water will not break through the windows and sink her. This is the sort of scenario that took down the *Andrea Gail*. I ordered 3/8 inch Lexan sheets to size and have been finishing them into storm windows. These things are bullet proof!

Next week I will take *Jenny* up to KKMI to get her bottom painted again and some other minor maintenance done. The plan is to be in cleanup mode by September 15th!!! Then we are planning to have an open house for Bay Area friends on 9/29. Then we shall be going. The only date on our calendar is Paradise Village Marina, Puerto Vallarta Mexico for Christmas. It sounds very good to me.

Thursday, September 06, 2007 5:09:10 PM

Location: Emeryville Marina
Latitude is 37 degrees 50.516 minutes north.
Longitude is 122 degrees 18.75 minutes west.

Now it is a matter of cleaning *Jenny* up and packing things away. I found a new location for the thirty fuel filters we will be carrying. That opened up some other storage for other spare parts and repair stuff. Big smile!

We are carrying a lot of dog food since we are not sure about getting the right brand in Mexico or other countries south of the border. The big storage challenge right now is where to store the working forty-pound bag of dog food for Nicholas. I reserved a spot for the spare bag, but not the open one. Should I put it into a tall plastic bin and put that in the spot the vacuum cleaner is in? Should I get rid of the vacuum cleaner since it is only uniquely effective on the stairs? I wrestle with these questions daily.

I have been able to send and receive email now through the SSB radio. It is SLOW (200 bps) but reliable and effective. The system is neat in that it keeps track of the land stations you connect with and ships mail to those stations for a while, then retires them as you move on. It is a kind of a follow-me system. Right now, I am connecting to San Diego (300+ miles away) and will do so until Panama becomes a better connection. Who needs expensive satellites?

Another Cerveza please...

Jenny is just an awesome vessel. While some of the workers who have installed stuff on her since her birth might have been idiots, most were geniuses as was the original owner, designer and builder. I am continually amazed at how well designed and built she is for the task at hand with such comfort and conveniences for Mary and me. She is a perfect vessel for this adventure. She is all smiles about us being with her all the time and all the attention she is getting.

Mary flies east on Sunday to take care of East Coast business and family activities. Monday I take *Jenny* up to the KKMI boat yard for her anti-fouling paint and some other final projects I cannot do. Nicholas is a happy boy now that I am with him all day and the family is here with him at night. He is curled up beside me as usual when I am on the computer. He is always overseeing my activities, although mostly through closed lids.

Ahhh well. All systems are pretty well up and running. I am starting to relax a bit. Our good friends on *Beverly S* are on their return trip from Canada now. They will be visiting on Saturday by renting a car and driving down from Urekia while they wait out a spell of challenging weather. It will be good to see them again and catch up on their summer in the Pacific Northwest.

Sunday, September 16, 2007 12:23:33 PM

Location: KKMI Boat Yard, Richmond CA
Latitude is 37 degrees 55.468 minutes north.
Longitude is 122 degrees 22.505 minutes west.

It has been a very busy week. You would think it was 1805, and we were setting sail for the new world... The good news is apparently Mary did not find a job back in Florida and is on the plane back to Oakland as I write. Whew... She almost stayed back in Florida when I came out for the job with Kaiser. She has some strong ties there.

Nicholas and I spent the week in a tree house since *Jenny*'s deck is a story up when she is on the hard. Boat yards are very dirty places with all the bottom paint being sanded, fiberglass being ground to powder and being mixed anew. Noisy too with metal being drilled, pounded and ground into new shapes. Good clean girl-next-door boats like *Jenny* get a real bad case of just plain dirty. Boots come aboard with all sorts of nasty stuff that stick to her deck. I had her blinders on the entire time (cover across the pilothouse windows) so she would not get too frightened by all the hard land around her and embarrassed by having her naked bottom exposed to the sun.

Nicholas just had to be with me as much as possible. He did not like the tree house and got very anxious each time I climbed down the ladder without him. Every time we climbed back up into *Jenny*, Nicholas had to have a footbath to get rid of the gunk he collected from the ground and to keep him on *Jenny*'s good side.

Monday, September 17, 2007 03:01:23 PM

Location: KKMI Boat Yard, Richmond CA
Latitude is 37 degrees 55.468 minutes north.
Longitude is 122 degrees 22.505 minutes west.

Now we are back in the water, *Jenny*'s blinders are off and she is in the gate ready to go. Nicholas is happier too and will be even more so when Mary returns this evening! We are still at KKMI since they could not complete one last project last week. That item should be finished on Tuesday, the hourly money tap should be closed, and we will be steaming back to the Emeryville marina Tuesday morning.

What did they do? Well, first the periodic bottom painting and zinc replacements. KKMI did that under a package priced by the foot. I think I did well on that deal since few boats this length weigh 60,000-pounds. *Jenny* used a few more gallons of bottom paint than the amount they calculated into the price. Big smile!

Next, they replaced almost all the rubber hoses on JD. JD's cooling hoses looked original (thirteen years old now) and were definitely ready. I put diesel coolant in the AC Generator since I suspected automobile antifreeze was in it. That job went well and I am satisfied.

Next, I asked them to put a small adapter on the bowsprit so that I could lock down the new Rocna anchor with a ¾-inch diameter pin the keeps it in place and from swinging while we are underway. The guy doing this work was fun and did very good work. He also replaced the wires that connected the railing sides on the upper deck behind the dinghy with new stainless steel railing. Not only does this provide a much safer guard, but also it really finishes the deck off much better. It looks like a deck that is part of *Jenny* now. Big smiles.

Finally, they tackled *Jenny's* stabilizer chain plates that hold the mast and provide strength to her stabilizer system. The more we took that part of *Jenny* apart, the more things we found to fix. I do not know if this was original PAE work, or work done later. However, whoever did it had no clue about how to do it right. KKMI has corrected most of this already, and the rest should be finished on Monday.

Nicholas is curled up beside me as I write this. He is a constant buddy and companion. *Jenny* is supper strong and complete now and Mary is on her way home. We just have to sell the cars, clean and polish *Jenny* so she sparkles and off we go. We have decided not to party until we anchor in Half Moon bay, our first stop since then the surreal future we now face will actually be real.

I am going to try to send this out via the SSB radio to check that system out.

Wednesday, September 19, 2007 10:42:21 AM

Location: Emeryville Marina

With a weather system heading in today, and the wind finally dying down a bit at 5:00 last night, I decided to bring *Jenny* back to Emeryville this morning. The wind in the Golden Gate Bridge slot was about seventeen knots, but as I came into the marina, it died down quite a bit. I called Mary to alert her of the move and she was at the marina trying to get through the locked gate since her key was onboard.

Jenny was doing quite well as she approached her slip. The approach is tight and she must cut very close to a big catamaran as she turns the corner into the fairway. That is where the collision occurred. Yup, collision! All I saw was a glimpse of a small wooden rowboat, a flash of international orange on *Jenny's* port bow, and then it all disappeared under her bow. There was some frantic yelling and people started coming out of everywhere to see what was going on.

JD was in neutral anyway, so there was very little I could do except put JD into reverse and slow *Jenny* down even more. *Jenny* had to keep some forward movement to maintain steerage in the light wind and tight fairway. She missed her slip and headed on up the fairway. The other people and boat were ok and now I had to get *Jenny* back to her slip. One option was to take her back out and come back in. The other was to back her into her slip, a tricky maneuver with quite an audience now. UGH

Well, *Jenny* and I did our thing and she backed right into her slip like a thoroughbred backing into the starting gates. The guy in the rowboat assisted and was all apologetic. No harm was done except the extra dose of adrenalin for all. He and his wife were in their fourteen-foot rowboat with a six-horsepower motor on the back. They were just cruising the docks looking at the beautiful vessels. This is sort of like running a golf cart around Oakland's runways. There are many interesting things to see, but it is not a benign environment. His motor drowned out any sound from *Jenny*. She is super quiet anyway. He hugged one side of the fairway and was just under the big catamaran's bow and suddenly they came face to face with *Jenny's* bow. I can only imagine their surprise...

That is all the news. *Jenny* has now backed into her stall, blinders off, full of energy and waiting for the gun.

Jenny in Emeryville

Friday, September 28, 2007 2:42:54 PM

Location: Emeryville Marina
Latitude is 37 degrees 50.52 minutes north.
Longitude is 122 degrees 18.747 minutes west.

It's Friday afternoon, Mary's last day of work, and less than two days to our tentative departure. It is very scary. Both of us are wound tighter than a drum. Yet, if we could just consider the next few weeks as another vacation trip down to Monterey Bay it would change our whole perspective. Just take one-step at a time!

We have been having wonderful little parties with our friends and have an open house scheduled for tomorrow afternoon. I guess one real difference this time is leaving the friends we have made here over the past six years and moving on to make new ones. Both of us recognize that going under the Golden Gate this time will have a completely different significance than in the past. This is what has put us on edge more than anything has. We have sold the cars and that is the final proof that we have forsaken the land for the sea. We are now without keys and are free to roam. The realization is assaulting or minds.

Nicholas is curled up beside me as usual. He needs a bath. I have neglected him while getting *Jenny* all spruced up for her debut as our cruising home. He does not seem to mind though since he dislikes baths and Mary and I have been with him more and more. He lives for that and is our model of what we should consider important.

I have finished everything I can think of. We have at least six weeks before we cross the border into Mexico. I have put together the routes from here to San Diego and created a float plan using BoatExec. We will be taking our time getting to San Diego since we have not been along any of the California coast south of Monterey Bay. I planned stops in Half Moon Bay, Monterey Bay, Pebble Beach, San Simeon, Morro Bay, San Luis Obispo, Santa Barbara, Santa Cruz Island, Marina Del Rey, Avalon on Catalina Island, Newport Beach, Mission Bay and finally San Diego. Sounds pretty cool huh... That is what keeps us moving forward on this journey. Our experience is that you meet many other boaters on the way and you make lasting friendships that have very loose geographic parameters. It is sort of like visiting family when friends afloat converge on the same place at the same time; good family that is.

The weather is nasty now, but it looks like there will be a nice window on Sunday that will allow us to depart in the morning. If not, then the next window looks like Wednesday. Weather and tides rule our travel plans as opposed to the calendar. Life is already a bit different.

BOOK 4: CALIFORNIA CRUISING

"The hatch cover was shoved forward, and the sea bags went down to sleep like portly pigs on the port bunk. I lit the running lights, hooked them on the port and starboard shrouds, and cast off her lines. She drifted out clear of the dock and picked up the urge of a west wind in her staysail without a sound or a sigh. We were underway.

This was the dream. This was the target of all my years, the end that lay buried in the endless prosecution of the means. My boat was standing out to sea. I had to believe it. There was a pile of evidence. The deck was certainly solid under my feet. The shifty wind was hard to pin down, but caught in the tightly woven net of canvas its testimony was strong in the pinch of the sheet lines."

Joe Richards
Princess, 1956

Passage: Emeryville to Pillar Point

Departed Sunday, September 30, 2007 at 8:06 AM local time from Emeryville Marina. The departure location was latitude 37 degrees 50.519 minutes north, longitude 122 degrees 18.748 minutes west.

Arrived Sunday, September 30, 2007 at 1:39 PM local time at Pillar Point Harbor. The arrival location was latitude 37 degrees 29.775 minutes north, longitude 122 degrees 29.482 minutes west. The trip covered 34.22 nautical miles in 0d 5h 32m with an average speed of 6.17 knots and a maximum speed of 7.67 knots.

Sunday, September 30, 2007 3:03:42 PM

Location: Pillar Point Harbor
Latitude is 37 degrees 29.776 minutes north.
Longitude is 122 degrees 29.484 minutes west.

Yesterday I returned the rental car and walked back to *Jenny*. I caught up with Mary as she was hiking back from Harry and David's with some nice dry packed soups and some other goodies. We then had an open house from noon to 6:00 PM and had quite a few friends stop by, see *Jenny* and wish us well. Mary was well pleased with all the party fun and it took her mind off her departure fears.

Mary's coworkers at open house party.

We cast off *Jenny's* Emeryville tethers for the last time and left at 08:00 to face a flat calm bay. Our friends in the Emeryville Marina got up early to wave us off. We laughed about our getting-ready adventures. All were envious that we were actually living the dream we all shared. Most knew in their heart they never would. *Jenny* bade a sad farewell to all the lovely lonely boats that had not seen their caretakers in months. She was Cinderella leaving a town of relatives tied to the ground and left to fend for themselves. *Jenny* had the helm heading for the Golden Gate Bridge and caught a little of the outgoing tide. I took several photos of San Francisco and the Golden Gate Bridge as we left them for good in *Jenny's* smooth wake. We have been snacking on the leftover goodies all day.

As usual, the water just outside of the Gate was very lumpy and I put down *Jenny's* stabilizers to quite her motion. Once a few miles down the coast, the water was very nice, we started playing some CDs and relaxing. Mary first stretched out on the pilot seat, and then migrating up to the pilot birth to snooze. I do not think she actually slept, but at least she was feeling much better and more relaxed. Nicholas heaved a small amount as we came through the water around the Gate, but then settled down for a snooze.

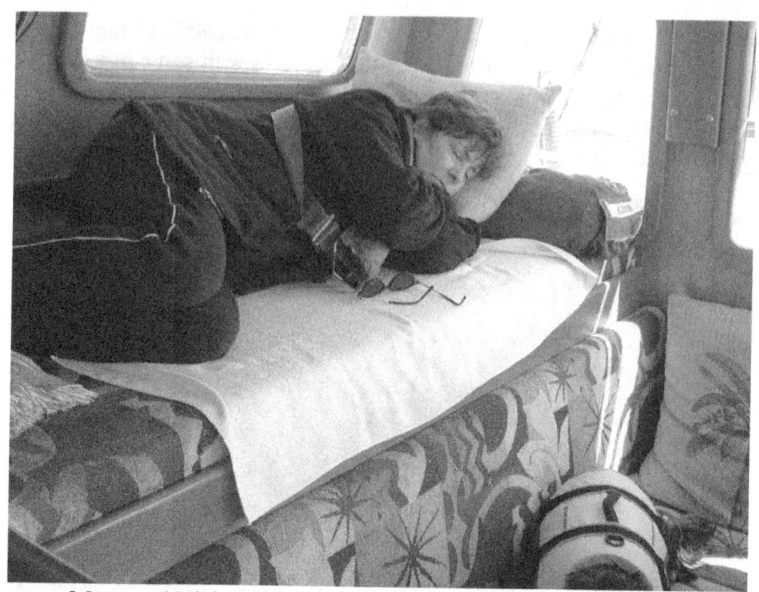
Mary and Nicholas snoozing on the way to Half Moon Bay

When we arrived at Pillar Point Harbor, *Jenny* dug her new anchor into the harbor floor. It stuck instantly. I tidied up her stabilizer rigging and then we took a nap until Mary's dad called. He is excited about our trip and being a former submariner envious too. We hope he visits us in the spring. The weather here is supposed to degrade as a small front moves through tonight and tomorrow. I had planned to stay here a few days anyway so all is good. Steak and champagne tonight!

Thanks to all who helped send us off yesterday and are standing by in case we need some assistance. We will miss seeing all of you.

Wednesday, October 03, 2007 2:52:29 PM

Location: Pillar Point Harbor
Latitude is 37 degrees 29.819 minutes north.
Longitude is 122 degrees 29.429 minutes west.

Originally, we were going to depart Pillar Point Harbor today and head down to Monterey Bay. However, a small front will come in this afternoon and we decided to wait it out. Fortunately, we really like staying here. The anchorage is very good, the dinghy dock is handy, and there are the essential amenities ashore. This afternoon, we took a walk around the bay to an area of protected beach. Off his leash, Nicholas went nuts in the small surf, running like a crazy dog up and down the beach. A couple of times he laid down right at the edge of the high water mark and then was startled as the water crept under him. We are so happy he likes the beach because he will be spending a lot of time there in the future.

Yesterday when we decided to stay here, I also decided to load up on some diesel fuel. I called our friends Larry and Sue who just came down the coast and they recommended I call Ventura Fuel docks to see what their price was since they were usually among the lowest cost on the coast. I did and their price was $2.94 with a price break at 1,000 gallons. Since *Jenny* only holds 1,000 gallons that would not be attainable. With a $2.90 price break at 500 gallons here, we loaded 520 gallons, filling *Jenny's* aft tanks. We now have about 750 gallons and we will probably burn about 250 gallons getting to Ensenada. The plan is to burn the older fuel from now on and load up another 500 gallons in either LA or Ensenada.

The only problem I have is the new Tecma head (toilet) decided to stop working again. A call to Larry and Sue who also have a Tecma returned a service number and I talked to the service rep. He suggested that using the original wiring was the problem. However, I tested that theory by jumping the head directly from the engine starting battery while the engine was running. There were plenty of amps there, but no joy on the problem. I put another call in. We will see. That head has it in for me! Fortunately, we have the old mechanical head in the guest cabin we can use.

The weather looks like it might break again on Sunday, so our current plan is to head for Monterey Bay on Sunday, get a slip and stay over on Monday. If the weather looks good for the following week, we will do the laundry, wash *Jenny*, load the water tanks and boogie south on Tuesday. If I need anything for the head, I can pick it up there too.

Passage: Pillar Point to Santa Cruz Harbor

Departed Saturday, October 06, 2007 at 7:07 AM local time from Pillar Point. The departure location was latitude 37 degrees 29.791 minutes north, longitude 122 degrees 29.445 minutes west.

Arrived Saturday, October 06, 2007 at 3:49 PM local time at Santa Cruz Harbor. The arrival location was latitude 36 degrees 57.661 minutes north, longitude 122 degrees 0.970 minutes west. The trip covered 52.58 nautical miles in 0d 8h 41m with an average speed of 6.05 knots and a maximum speed of 7.70 knots.

Saturday, October 06, 2007 5:37:14 PM

Location: Santa Cruz Harbor
Latitude is 36 degrees 57.661 minutes north.
Longitude is 122 degrees 0.97 minutes west.

Jenny broke us out of Pillar Point this morning, but not without some difficulties. Before we left the protection of the harbor, I readied her stabilizers for deployment, but did not put her outriggers out because the entrance is narrow. If we encountered another large boat going through we might become tangled. We headed out into the bay with them up. This was a big mistake! The swell was medium large at six to nine feet and was being refracted by Pillar Point into a disorganized lumpy sea. By the time I got up to the top deck to put the outriggers out, the wild motion had tangled the rigging into a rat's nest.

We turned back for the harbor where it was calm. I untangled the mess and put the outriggers out. That worked much better because it only takes seconds to drop them in from this position. Mary was awesome during this whole thing. While unhappy about all the rolling around, she agreed that we should try again. She is incredibly brave in the face of her departure jitters.

Once *Jenny* made it out away from land, the seas returned to their natural large but slow swell comfortable for all of us. We decided to head for Santa Cruz Harbor rather than Monterey since it was about four hours closer. Tomorrow we will head across Monterey Bay and get a slip for the rest of Sunday and Monday. Then we will see what the weather is going to let us do next.

As usual, the bane of *Jenny's* stabilizers is kelp. When uprooted, it floats to the surface in large fields that are unavoidable. As we pass through, we pick up the stuff on *Jenny's* stabilizers and her speed drops from more than seven knots to the mid sixes. In addition, the effectiveness of her stabilizers is seriously impaired. I noticed this time that the floating kelp is thickest when the water is less than 200 feet deep. We got a lot of practice slowing to idle and cleaning the accumulated kelp off. My tree trimmer was effective, but needed modification. I took the blade from the end of the trimmer and turned it around so that the blade was the hook. Instead of hooking the kelp stems and pulling a cord to cut them like a branch, I just hooked them and the blade sliced through them. This setup was much more efficient and was lesson two of the trip.

We are learning several small things very quickly and are tuning our game. By the time we reach Mexico, we should be pro's.

Mary is in the galley, putting our dinner together with *Jenny* anchored off the beach here in Santa Cruz. Behind us is an amusement park complete with Ferris wheel, roller coaster, etc. The pier off to *Jenny's* starboard has a herd of sea lions that are barking and she is rocking a little since this anchorage is open to the south. This new life is challenging and good and we are making progress on our quest for turquoise water, white sandy beaches, coconut palm trees and Pina Colotas. The Gators are beating LSU on the TV...

Passage: Santa Cruz Harbor to Monterey

Departed Sunday, October 07, 2007 at 7:33 AM local time from Santa Cruz Harbor. The departure location was latitude 36 degrees 57.239 minutes north, longitude 122 degrees 0.828 minutes west.

Arrived Sunday, October 07, 2007 at 11:44 AM local time at Monterey Harbor. The arrival location was latitude 36 degrees 36.224 minutes north, longitude 121 degrees 53.394 minutes west. The trip covered 23.02 nautical miles in 0d 4h 10m with an average speed of 5.51 knots and a maximum speed of 6.88 knots.

Tuesday, October 09, 2007 8:48:17 AM

Location: Monterey Bay
Latitude is 36 degrees 36.221 minutes north.
Longitude is 121 degrees 53.404 minutes west.

Jenny gave us a nice and short four-hour ride from Santa Cruz to Monterey on Saturday. The weather here on Sunday and Monday was very nice with highs in the 70's. Sea Lions and Otters visit *Jenny's* stern every day as they cruise the marina for food and protection. It is nice to have the wildlife so close. The sea lions are trying to use the docks to bask on, but the locals have erected barriers that keep them off for the most part. One got up on one two slips up yesterday and as we returned from a walk, Nicholas went nuts. Fortunately, we still had him on the leash because he was delivering his full brave and mean routine. The sea lion was easily 300 lbs, but became nervous enough he bailed into the water. Good boy!

We had a weather window to get down to Morro Bay last night, but it would have been Mary's first overnight trip and I decided not to push it. We are here holding for good weather at least through Friday as a storm and cold front make their way on shore. It seems like the whole weather system in the US has stalled and these storms are finding it difficult to make landing. Maybe this is connected to the record high temperatures across the country. The downside is that they are slow to clear and give us a window.

Nicholas is on the pilot berth at my shoulder, helping me write this and watching the action around the harbor. He really loves this. He finally got his bath on Sunday, looks and smells a lot better now. He is quite the dapper dog! I will give him another before we leave. It is nice to have endless electricity and water, plugged into the grid.

The Tecma problem took a lot to diagnose but was simple to fix and is now working well. *Jenny* is loosing a little bit of coolant from the engine and I am working on that project as we go. I am tightening up the hose clamps and putting new clamps on some. I will eventually get it nailed. Otherwise, all is working very well. While I can get an internet connection through one of the local restaurants, it is blocking our ability to send email. While we are receiving emails, we have a big outbound queue waiting for transmission.

Our day usually begins around 07:00 AM when I switch on the furnace. The water for our showers is ready about fifteen to twenty minutes later and I am out of bed by 07:30. Mary and Nicholas snuggle in the bed until about 08:00. Right now Mary is off to the Longs drug store and we plan to walk down to the outlet mall here this afternoon. Life is a struggle.

Thursday, October 11, 2007 10:51:09 AM

Location: Monterey Bay
Latitude is 36 degrees 36.23 minutes north.
Longitude is 121 degrees 53.395 minutes west.

A couple of vessels down the dock left yesterday and headed north for SFO Bay. They are going the wrong way! In their absence, a pack of Sea Lions came in and claimed the slip fingers. The alpha male is about 600 or more pounds. He is a big brute and not impressed by Nicholas' routine. Their barking is very annoying. I found out that the harbor has hired a couple of guys to keep them off the docks. Our entertainment was watching this cat and mouse game of the guy in a boat shoeing them off one dock and them diving until he left. Then they sneak back on the dock and begin barking again. This barking was not too clever though, since it alerted the guy to come back and shoe them again.

The guys use a water gun to get the Sea Lions to move if their arrival alone does not work. I suppose this is California Kind, but it really does not teach the Sea Lions to fear humans. I would go for a paint ball gun and then escalate to rubber bullets. That way, they would learn a valuable lesson, and stay away. But, that's just me...

This morning I noticed seals that bask on the boulders when the tide goes down. It was funny to watch them staking out their rocks while the tide still covered them. It reminded me of people in a parking lot circulating for a parking space.

Since we have not really lived and cruised on *Jenny* full time before, I am uncovering small projects that need done to improve the quality of our days. For example, *Jenny's* dock lines are a mess on deck if they are not properly stowed, but it is a hassle to put them away in the deck boxes. Also, her stabilizer lines need to be coiled and hung too. This would also be a good solution for her dock lines, but there is not a very good commercial solution to hanging them easily and securely. I have tried a couple. Yesterday I bought 80 feet of 1/4 inch line and made my own hangers. So far, they work great. I also hooked up the trip line on *Jenny's* anchor so that I can retrieve it when it becomes fully stuck on something on the bottom. I attack the list daily and it grows overnight as I mull things over.

Except for one night of rain, the weather here has been beautiful, with highs in the 70's every day. While we like it here, we must be heading south soon. A three-day weather window is opening up beginning Saturday so we are going to use it to try to get around Point Conception. That means a very early start on Saturday morning and a run to San Simeon. We will be passing by Pebble Beach, but we have spent too much time here in Monterey. Sunday morning we plan to run down to San Louise Obispo and then round Point Conception on Monday. All the weather sources are converging on a good forecast for this.

Passage: Monterey Bay to San Simeon

Departed Saturday, October 13, 2007 at 6:23 AM local time from Monterey Bay. The departure location was latitude 36 degrees 36.115 minutes north, longitude 121 degrees 58.998 minutes west.

Arrived Saturday, October 13, 2007 at 5:46 PM local time at San Simeon Bay. The arrival location was latitude 35 degrees 38.266 minutes north, longitude 121 degrees 11.416 minutes west. The trip covered 75.81 nautical miles in 0d 11h 23m with an average speed of 6.66 knots and a maximum speed of 8.04 knots.

Saturday, October 13, 2007 7:10:02 PM

Location: San Simeon Bay
Latitude is 35 degrees 38 minutes north.
Longitude is 121 degrees 11 minutes west.

Somehow, our departures are never as smooth as we wish. Mary and I moved *Jenny* from her slip in Monterey to the mooring area just outside the marina last night. We did this so we could put the fenders away, set up the stabilizers, and get her ready for a smooth early departure. The waves in the anchorage were rolling *Jenny* a little, but as soon as we put her birds in the water, things calmed down considerably. Still, neither of us slept very well.

The trip from Monterey takes twelve hours and the longest passage we have done together. We had to get an early start to get there in daylight. So, when the alarm went off at 05:00 AM, we both groaned in the dark. I awoke first and got *Jenny* up for getting underway while Mary took care of Nicholas. She also started nailing loose stuff down to keep it from moving about as we steamed down the coast. Everything was going quite smoothly. I put *Jenny's* birds in their shoes up on the outriggers with their wires looped down, trailing in the water. While still dark out, *Jenny* released her hold on the sandy bottom and we were off at idle.

This mooring field has several private buoys spread about, and some of them even have lights. Well, suddenly a white pole appeared right off *Jenny's* bow. I made an aggressive turn to avoid it, but Mary saw it go into the trailing stabilizer wire on her starboard side. She thought we had hooked it and came quickly in with the news. I put JD in neutral and went out to look. As far as I could tell, the buoy slid under the wire and we were not entangled. At least that is what I thought.

I got back into the pilothouse and moved the throttle forward to increase *Jenny's* speed as now we were in the harbor channel and some fishing boats were coming out. *Jenny's* speed did not increase. I pushed the throttle forward a little more. No forward speed! I figured we must have snagged that buoy after all in some way. Back to idle and I walked around *Jenny*. I ran *Jenny* boathook as far down as I could reach off her stern. Nothing! Hmmm.... I ran back to the pilothouse to run another test. It sure helped when I put JD in gear! You know, sometimes things just conspire to give you heart failure. Fortunately, that was the extent of the excitement for the day.

As forecast, the seas and weather got better all day. By 3:00 PM, the seas were almost flat, and the temperature in the sun hit 80 degrees. We went out on *Jenny's* bow, watched the California Big Sur roll on by, and were disappointed by the lack of whale sightings and other boats heading south. In fact, we saw three boats heading north, and none heading south. How strange?

The anchorage here at San Simeon is marginal. Luckily, the wind and waves are out of the Northwest, so we are pretty well sheltered. Nevertheless, it will be another uncomfortable night with *Jenny* rolling about in the waves. Tomorrow we head for San Luis Obispo. It is only forty miles away, so we should be there in six hours. The weather is supposed to be good again, so it should be a good, short day.

Passage: San Luis Obispo to Cojo

Departed Monday, October 15, 2007 at 1:48 PM local time from San Luis Obispo. The departure location was latitude 35 degrees 10.223 minutes north, longitude 120 degrees 44.319 minutes west.

Arrived Monday, October 15, 2007 at 9:01 PM local time at Cojo Anchorage. The arrival location was latitude 34 degrees 26.900 minutes north, longitude 120 degrees 26.426 minutes west. The trip covered 52.24 nautical miles in 0d 7h 12m with an average speed of 7.25 knots and a maximum speed of 8.40 knots.

Monday, October 15, 2007 10:55:04 PM

Location: Cojo Anchorage
Latitude is 24 degrees 26 minutes north.
Longitude is 120 degrees 26 minutes west.

Mary barely slept a wink last night in anticipation of our rounding the infamous Point Conception. We were both up at 01:30 AM for some reason and watched a nearby sailboat haul anchor and head off south. He probably got to Point Conception around dawn and had a very smooth rounding. We went back to bed. Our alarm went off at 06:00 AM and I got up and going. Mary was sleeping in the salon to avoid the sound of the water slosh in *Jenny's* tanks as we rocked and rolled. I tried to be quiet and let her sleep through our departure, but no dice. She began going about, getting ready.

Jenny's anchor trip line is proving both useful and a challenge. It shows me exactly where her anchor is. As the wind died last night, *Jenny* could have picked anywhere in the bay to come to rest. But she decided to place one of her birds right on top of her anchor. I knew this because in spite of my best efforts, she tangled the trip line and its small buoy up in her stabilizer wires. I got it all untangled, started JD and backed *Jenny* away from her anchor. Well, in the morning I discovered that she must have done a few laps around her anchor during the night because she had now wrapped the trip line around her anchor chain. I fixed this easily once I raised her anchor. She was definitely showing her displeasure with the trip line for some reason and uses these little mischievous tricks to let me know.

Our trip from San Luis Obispo to Cojo was very easy with smooth following seas and light wind. It only kicked up a bit when we got close to Point Conception, and then it was not bad at all. We have been in worse in San Francisco Bay. We saw several seals swimming and jumping, and even saw a whale today. We made it around Point Conception! We are in Southern California for sure dude!

The anchorage here is a beach on the backside of the point. It is fairly well sheltered from Northwest wind and waves, but is open to everything else. The wind is supposed to pick up tonight, so I put down some extra chain just to be secure. I do need to get a longer trip line. I figured forty feet would be enough, but it is proving to be too short. Right now, it is bobbing a foot or two under the surface.

Mary and I took hot showers and are in the salon watching the water and relaxing. The sailboat that left ahead of us is anchored here too. At least I think it is the same one and there is an oil industry ship here too named *Mr. Clean*. Tomorrow we head for the Santa Barbara Marina, will get *Jenny* into a slip and visit the town. I feel more relaxed now that we have successfully gotten down the coast and away from the northern California nasty winter weather. The water in Santa Barbara Channel is supposed to be like lake water.

Thursday, October 18, 2007 12:26:57 AM

Location: Santa Barbara Harbor
Latitude is 34 degrees 24.339 minutes north.
Longitude is 119 degrees 41.331 minutes west.

While we were hoping that the water would be friendly once we past Point Conception, it had just a little surprise for us yesterday and a hard day it was. We got up and listened to the weather forecast that said strong winds would be out of the northwest but little else. We decided that Cojo was not a good place to spend a lot of time since it was open to the south, east, and west. We hauled *Jenny's* anchor around 07:00 AM and headed for Santa Barbara. First, I had a good fight with the giant kelp here. I had a huge pile come up with her anchor and it took the good part of thirty minutes to get it off. This should have told us something.

Once free of weeds, our plan was to hug the coastline on the north side of us, believing that it would protect us from the northwest winds. This worked ok until we got into water less than 200 feet deep where we encountered more weed and the much dreaded crab pot. *Jenny's* birds run about twenty feet under the water and about twenty-five feet out from her sides. There is a wire that runs from the end of her outriggers to the bird and another rope that runs off the back end of each bird that I use to drop it into the water and haul it back to *Jenny's* outriggers.

When the kelp breaks free, it floats to the surface and forms mats of floating weed. The kelp itself is like a long vine with long broad leaves. If we hit a single piece of kelp with *Jenny's* wires and are going fast enough (over seven knots), the front wire will slice right through the vine and we are good to go. However, if we hit a floating mat of it, the mat slides down the wires and becomes entangled on her birds. It adds tremendous drag to that side and throws *Jenny* off balance. *Jenny* first turns toward the trouble. Then she adjusts the helm to get back on course. With the mat of kelp in tow off one side, *Jenny* slows down by about one knot and that is a lot.

Once we know we have a problem, we have to bring JD's beat down to idle, haul the birds one at a time to the surface and cut the kelp off with the tree trimmer. This subjects us to extra motion since the stabilizers are not running at speed, and is a lot of work. We have now honed this dance to a fifteen-minute quick step. So, it is manageable. On this trip, we needed to dance with the weeds twice.

Then *Jenny* had a close encounter with a dreaded crab pot. We discovered that this area is laced with crab pots wherever the water is less than 200 feet. Crab pots are very heavy and have a line running to the surface with small floats attached. The lines are used to drag the pots to the surface to empty and bait them. Getting into a crab pot field is our most stressful situation to date. Many of the floats are old and have a lot of marine growth on them, making them very difficult to see and distinguish from floating kelp. When *Jenny* hooks one of them in her stabilizer wires we have to quickly bring JD to idle and put it in neutral since the pot line could foul *Jenny's* propeller and then we would be in a pickle.

Once a crab pot is on the wires, it acts just like an anchor. If wind is blowing or current running, then *Jenny* pulls away from the pot as she floats down wind and / or down current. We need to do a dance with the *(#$$) thing to get it safely along *Jenny's* side. On the two previous occasions we have snagged one of these hazards to navigation, I have spent the time to untangle it and set it free. However, the last time my fingers almost became tangled in the wires and could have suffered serious damage given the amount of pressure there is on all this gear.

Well, this time we snagged one in choppy seas and windy conditions. It took us nearly forty minutes to get the crab pot floats along *Jenny's* side and hooked on the tree trimmer. After the fingers experience, I now just cut the devils loose. Sorry Mr. Crabber, it is just too dangerous to play with these things. Needless to say, Mary was very stressed while helping maneuver *Jenny* and with me working over the railing. I always wear a life vest and clip onto *Jenny* when something like this is going on, but it still is more dangerous than just motoring along. As soon as I cut the thing free, we headed back out to deeper water.

On top of all this, the forecast was not exactly on target either. The wind shifted around to the west and even a little south so that it could work the long fetch up the Santa Barbara channel and build up nice steep choppy wind waves as the afternoon progressed. Mary was already strung out from our crab pot exploits, and this was icing on the cake. Again, I was amazed at her fighting back her fears, and remaining calm at least on the surface.

When we got to the harbor, there was little in the way of protected water space for us to take *Jenny's* birds and outriggers up, put out her fenders, etc. *Jenny* had to play around in a small area with moored sailboats, kayakers, small sailboats playing in the wind, etc. Mary manned the helm while I worked the rigging. After another forty minutes, we entered the harbor and sought out the dock they wanted us to go first. I made two passes at landing and ended up backing into the side tie without too much trauma and no damage. The marina assigned *Jenny* to an end tie on one of the new docks. It is very nice.

What a day! We walked up to the farmers market in town, bought some veggies, treated ourselves to a restaurant dinner and crashed early. While it is still windy, it is warm and sunny out and we are enjoying the area. We are going to stay here until the wind and weather become much friendlier, and then take our next step. Today I worked on improving some of *Jenny's* rigging, and Mary walked into town to do some shopping. I have not been able to latch onto a free internet connection, so tomorrow we will take the laptop to town and seek out a free hot spot.

Tuesday, October 23, 2007 2:38:05 AM

Location: Santa Barbara Harbor

The adventure continues. We happened to arrive in Southern California just in time to catch the highest and longest lasting Santa Anna winds in over twenty years. These winds (some over 100 mph) first lift tons of ash from the summer's fires and then dump them all over the counties down here. I begin every morning by washing the black ash from *Jenny*. Over last weekend it came down so fast that in one hour *Jenny* was visibly covered again. The sky has been brown with dust and ash so dense that we could not see the hills of Santa Barbara from *Jenny*.

Saturday night was the worst. We had been thinking about heading over to Santa Cruz Island that day, but our friends Larry and Sue urged us to stay put. The winds steadily increased all afternoon and by evening were blowing forty knots through the well protected marina. As we ate dinner, Mary noticed a boat out in the anchorage drifting down wind. I first thought was someone who was trying to anchor. However, the binoculars revealed no one onboard. I radioed the harbor patrol about telling them there was a boat (about forty feet long) dragging its anchor through the anchorage and heading out to sea. They already knew it. The recovery mission unfolded in front of us, but both the rescue boat and the boat adrift disappeared in the haze and we have not seen either since.

Now there are over ten major fires burning the nearby hills, filling the air with smoke. The fires extend form San Luis Obispo to San Diego and the smoke is visible from space. Thousands of families have been evacuated from their homes, and the wind is expected to continue for another two days. Hot ash is now falling on *Jenny*. One burned a small hole in her stern awning.

The good news is that we are enjoying Santa Barbara even with all of this. For example, we have found Yoda. He is alive and well in Santa Barbara. We have seen him several times now walking the town streets. I even think we have spotted his spacecraft cleverly disguised as a trimaran here in the harbor. At close inspection, the trimaran is very different from any I have seen. The center module is obviously designed to provide a vacuum seal, and is fully aerodynamic. I think the outriggers are the fuel pods. Yoda is about five feet tall, wears a white smock, is barefoot, pure white long flowing hair, beard and mustache with a Japanese Zen master look about him. You would recognize him in a heartbeat. I think he is getting ready to head back out to space though. We saw him at a Bank of America cash machine today, using some kind of sophisticated electronic device to extract earth money so he could fuel his ship. We will keep you posted.

The main drag in Santa Barbara is like downtown Walnut Creek, with all the high-end stores lining the street. It is very trendy. The beach area sports surfer dudes, with a regular flow of joggers, bladers, and skate boarders flowing up and down the beachfront path. Young kayakers paddle by *Jenny* in droves in the morning heading out to the kelp fields hoping to catch a glimpse of some fauna and kids take the yacht club sail boats out for a spin in the afternoon. Maybe it is part of their physical education class. College kids play volleyball on the beach and guys work out with weights in the sand. How nice.

On the other hand, we have seen more mentally ill folks on the loose here than any place we can remember. Today Mary had to skirt around a guy in the middle of the main drag who was in a full rage about his shopping cart stuff being in disarray and we saw a homeless family (three kids) selling trinkets while camping out on the sidewalk. What a contrast!

Nicholas has trained us to take him out for his long walk together. He is such a clever dog.

I hope the Santa Anna winds will die on Wednesday and we can take off for Marina Del Rey to visit our friends Larry and Sue on *Beverly S* then continue our trip south.

Passage: Santa Barbara to Pelican Bay

Departed Wednesday, October 24, 2007 at 2:58 PM local time from Santa Barbara Harbor. The departure location was latitude 34 degrees 24.341 minutes north, longitude 119 degrees 41.328 minutes west.

Arrived Wednesday, October 24, 2007 at 6:45 PM local time at Pelican Cove, Santa Cruz Island. The arrival location was latitude 34 degrees 2.065 minutes north, longitude 119 degrees 42.139 minutes west. The trip covered 23.15 nautical miles in 0d 3h 47m with an average speed of 6.11 knots and a maximum speed of 7.81 knots.

Wednesday, October 24, 2007 9:52:18 PM

Location: Santa Cruz Island, Pelican Cove
Latitude is 34 degrees 2.063 minutes north.
Longitude is 119 degrees 42.144 minutes west.

When we got up this morning, the sea was like glass and it still is at 2:30 PM. We washed down *Jenny*, organized all the stuff and by 08:00 AM we were underway. Our destination of Pelican Cove was just three hours away. While I rigged *Jenny's* stabilizers for deployment, I never launched them. It was that glassy smooth.

On the way over, we encountered three pods of dolphin and two decided to play on *Jenny's* bow and stern waves. For the second encounter, I went up to *Jenny's* bow and looked straight down at four of them playing side to side in *Jenny's* bow pressure wave. They seemed near enough to touch. You could see every detail of their skin, the teeth marks from fights or mating, their nostrils and how they breathed, and the position and use of their fins as they darted about. Every now and then, one would turn on its side and look up at me. I am sure they were as curious about us as we were of them. This was the first time Mary had seen them do this and it was a real treat.

Pelican cove is a shallow cove protected on the south and west sides from wind and waves. Right now, there is not much of either and that is the forecast for the next three days. We have the anchor down, and it is delightful. I decided it was time to be barefoot! Prior to now, it has always been too cold to go about *Jenny* without shoes. What a treat!

We did some dusting and wiping *Jenny* down from all the soot and ash that has been falling. It will probably take another week or two before she is clean again. I even have to wash down her engine room since it is vented to the outside and tons of soot blew in. Now, Mary is up on the pilot berth reading a magazine. Nicholas is napping at her feet and I am typing.

We plan to go to another cove tomorrow and then on Friday head for Marina Del Rey. There is no phone or Wi-Fi on the island, but the radio is working very well. I have started sending *Jenny's* position to a web site that will map out where we are. Once I confirm it is working, I will publish how to access the info.

The first game of the World Series is on tonight and we may be able to receive it. The beer is cold and popcorn is ready for the microwave. Chicken is defrosting for the Weber. Life is good.

Passage: Smuggler's Cove to Marina Del Rey

Departed Friday, October 26, 2007 at 2:50 PM local time from Smuggler's Cove. The departure location was latitude 34 degrees 0.985 minutes north, longitude 119 degrees 31.759 minutes west.

Arrived Saturday, October 27, 2007 at 12:15 AM local time at Marina Del Rey, CA. The arrival location was latitude 33 degrees 59.005 minutes north, longitude 118 degrees 26.872 minutes west. The trip covered 55.41 nautical miles in 0d 9h 24m with an average speed of 5.89 knots and a maximum speed of 7.61 knots.

Sunday, October 28, 2007 12:22:11 AM

Location: Marine Del Rey
Latitude is 33 degrees 59.003 minutes north.
Longitude is 118 degrees 26.874 minutes west.

On Friday, *Jenny* took us around from Pelican Bay to the south side of Santa Cruz Island to Smuggler's cove. The trip was only twelve miles and very pleasant. We did not need her stabilizers, so they were up and stored. This is the way this water is supposed to be.

Smuggler's cove was very nice and well sheltered from the northwest winds and waves. By nightfall, there were five other boats here with plenty of space. The cove had a gentle rise from a sand beach up to hills covered with olive trees and was very pretty. We settled into some light chores and then watched the World Series game. This was the best anchorage we have stayed in so far.

We hauled anchor on Saturday and *Jenny* made a beeline over to Marina Del Rey to visit her girlfriend *Beverly S*. The trip was easy with her stabilizers up most of the way. Her only challenge this time was fog and an active missile firing range we found ourselves in. "Ah, hello Fleet Control! Can you give me the coordinates of that target zone again?" Yup, we were in it. After giving Fleet Control *Jenny's* position, speed and heading, they cleared us to continue and exit the zone. Thank you!

Then the fog rolled in. A guy on a forty foot Sport Fisherman called the Coast Guard. The following is a fairly accurate rendition of the conversation.

Man: "Hello Coast Guard. If I could only see the land, I'd know just where I am. But, the fog rolled in and now I do not know where I am. I know if I could just see the land, I would be ok.
Coast Guard: "Can you tell us your position?"
Man: "If I could see the land, I could. But now I am completely lost."
Coast Guard: "Do you have a GPS on board?"
Man: "Errrr... Yes"
Coast Guard: "Can you give us your latitude and longitude?"
Man: "Ummm I am afraid I do not know how to use it."
Coast Guard: "Can you turn it on?"
Man: "Ummm let me see."
Silence
Man: "I have turned it on."
Coast Guard: "Can you read your position to us?"
Man: "Errrrr I do not know how to read it. I feel really embarrassed."
Coast Guard: "Do you have a depth finder?"
Man: "Yes, but I do not know how to use that either. I know the land should be somewhere North of me. If I could only see it, I would know where I am."
Coast Guard: "What is your heading?"
Man: "North"

Coast Guard: "Sir! Please turn around and head South immediately!" We do not want you to be near land!"
Man: "Oh... ok, I can understand that."

This went on for a while until they triangulated the guy's position by his radio and then they sent the local harbor patrol folks out to get him. This is an absolutely true story.

Marina Del Rey is very large and nice. *Jenny* wanted to snuggle up next to *Beverly S*, but had to take a slip behind her. I think they talked anyway. Larry and Sue have been wonderful, taking us all over to get stuff and introducing us to the soft life of Yacht Club living. Sue has been comforting and encouraging to Mary. Larry has been showing us around to stores and we are meeting them and a Mexico Cruise expert tonight to chat about cruising in Mexico. Tomorrow we are meeting another couple who are heading down in their powerboat *Midnight Voyage*.

I will extract some pictures from the camera and send them out tomorrow. I am afraid I have not been very diligent on the camera front.

Passage: Marina Del Rey to Newport

Departed Tuesday, October 30, 2007 at 3:00 PM local time from Marina Del Rey. The departure location was latitude 33 degrees 58.879 minutes north, longitude 118 degrees 26.918 minutes west.

Arrived Tuesday, October 30, 2007 at 11:40 PM local time at . The arrival location was latitude 33 degrees 36.020 minutes north, longitude 117 degrees 52.918 minutes west. The trip covered 49.56 nautical miles in 0d 8h 38m with an average speed of 5.73 knots and a maximum speed of 7.07 knots.

Wednesday, October 31, 2007 3:57:22 AM

Location: Newport
Latitude is 33 degrees 36.023 minutes north.
Longitude is 117 degrees 52.924 minutes west.

Jenny is now sitting in Newport Harbor, just south of LA. It is about 8:30 PM and the shore is filled with lights shining out from the expensive homes that line the hills and harbor. The water is like a sheet of glass gently undulating. It is so quiet that the fan on the PC is the only sound I hear. *Jenny* is hooked up to one of the harbor's mooring balls at a cost of $5.00 per night. Tomorrow we will lower the dinghy and explore the miles of waterways that lace the town. There are a dozen public docks to tie up to that provide access to various places in town.

Jenny's forty-five-mile ride down started out in choppy water, but as the day went on the water grew smoother. She had to cross the big ship channels that enter and exit Long Beach and LA Harbor. She seemed used to this and kept out of the way of an ocean tug headed up to Coos Bay, OR pulling a huge barge, and Warship 91 heading in from San Diego. Once she was out of the channels and into the quite water, Mary and I did not feel the need to keep a constant eye on her and we took turns napping. Napping is our most prevalent daytime activity underway. The ocean is empty most of the time and as long as you are avoiding bad weather, there is not much to do. I have a couple of books waiting for me and I am getting close to cracking them open. That is a good indication that my project list is down to a nice-to-have-fixed level as opposed to a must-fix situation.

Speaking of projects, my main project in Marina Del Rey was to replace the blocks in *Jenny's* stabilizer rigging. While most of her stabilizer design and rigging is wonderful, the blocks at the end of her outriggers rub against lines and each other. They are also very old now and low quality to begin with. I found three of the four nice roller bearing blocks I needed at the local West Marine store and with the help of our good friend Larry, we hunted down the fourth and got them installed. This was not a simple job, since two of them had to be placed at the end of the outriggers. With a little ingenuity, I positioned *Jenny* so that her outriggers could be let down over the walkway alongside of *Jenny's* slip. I used the stabilizers today and it was much easier to both let them out and retrieve them with the new blocks in place.

The only problem I found is that I ran one of the lines through one of the blocks backwards. It did not interfere too much with their operation, but I have to re-rig it tomorrow or the next day.

Speaking of friends, Larry and Sue have been just wonderful. They took me all over town hunting down the block I needed, and took Mary on a tour of Hollywood. We even had a sumptuous brunch (one of the best I have been to) at their yacht club. Sue did all this while she had a broken foot in a cast. We worked hard on them to cast off and head to Mexico with us to no avail.

Our plan is to stay here three more days, then head to Mission Bay near San Diego on the 3rd. We will be in Mission Bay the 4th, 5th and 6th. On November 7th we will head into San Diego harbor and anchor in Glorietta Bay for the 7th and 8th. On the 9th we will move over to anchor in La Playa Cove behind Shelter Island. We are looking forward to seeing some of our San Diego friends while we are there. We sail for Ensenada on the 11th!!!

Thursday, November 01, 2007 7:16:03 PM

Location: Newport Beach
Latitude is 33 degrees 36.033 minutes north.
Longitude is 117 degrees 52.926 minutes west.

This is a very boat oriented city and very wealthy too. If I had endless money, I would have a waterfront home here to visit now and again. There are miles of waterfront with one mansion after another. Each mansion has a yacht or mega yacht out front. Full time staff works in the house, on the garden, and on the yacht. Many homes also have a Duffy electric launch to get them from house to house and then take the party to a restaurant. How nice.

A small white bird with black eyes just landed on *Jenny's* pennant pole on the bow and is surveying the water for small fishes.

We took the dinghy around about ¼ of the harbor yesterday and used three of the nine public dinghy docks scattered around. This is the first place we have been in that actually recognizes dinghies as modes of transportation around town. It is sort of like being in Venice I guess.

Last night I showed Mary something she had never seen. After dark, I asked her out to *Jenny's* starboard side to look down into the water. As she did, she saw the photo luminescent plankton drifting by in swirls of light. Too cool!

This morning I decided to fix *Jenny's* rigging on her starboard stabilizer. When I put the new block on, I ran the trip line through it backwards. It needed to be fixed. The problem is that the block is very high at the end of the outrigger when they are stowed vertically and high off the water when they are out at her sides. In Marina Del Rey I lowered her outrigger over the shore walkway at low tide and reached them easily. Over the last couple of nights, I figured out a scheme to get it done and this morning was the time to test the plan. I lowered her outrigger over the water and looped a long line over the end. I parked the dinghy under the end of the outrigger then attached a block and tackle (a four-part mainsheet block and tackle with a jam cleat) to one end and hauled it up to the end of the outrigger. I attached a boson's chair to the block and tackle and hauled myself up to the end of the outrigger. I chose this morning because there was no wind or waves. Once up, I just pulled the line through the block and put it back the right way. Not bad.

This Mary is now food shopping, and this afternoon we will do laundry, etc.

Passage: Newport to Mission Bay

Departed Saturday, November 03, 2007 at 2:28 PM local time from Newport mooring. The departure location was latitude 33 degrees 35.581 minutes north, longitude 117 degrees 52.797 minutes west.

Arrived Saturday, November 03, 2007 at 11:11 PM local time at Mission Bay, CA. The arrival location was latitude 32 degrees 45.979 minutes north, longitude 117 degrees 14.849 minutes west. The trip covered 61.16 nautical miles in 0d 8h 41m with an average speed of 7.03 knots and a maximum speed of 8.28 knots.

Sunday, November 04, 2007 1:04:30 AM

Location: Mission Bay, CA
Latitude is 32 degrees 45.975 minutes north.
Longitude is 117 degrees 14.848 minutes west.

Well, we are starting to get the hang of this passage-making thing. Today *Jenny* took us south fifty miles and it was as if we were on a cruise ship. While we stood watch in turns, we also did stuff other than nap. The water was perfect and we felt comfortable enough to read, do some computer work, and make a real lunch. It was very nice.

The water changed color today. Further north it had a greenish color. Today was indigo blue. A few dolphins came over and played with us again. I tried to get some pictures, but they were definitely camera shy. I will get them though.

Some folks have asked, "Where on earth are you?" Well, I have figured out how to report *Jenny's* position to the Winlink organization and they have it hooked up to Google Maps to show you! Add the following link to your Favorites and you will have us located.

http://www.winlink.org/positions/PosReportsDetail.aspx?callsign=KI6CEL

Tomorrow morning we will be putting *Jenny's* dinghy down again to go exploring Mission Bay. This is the home of San Diego Sea World among other attractions. Right now, we are in a very quiet anchorage. Life is good.

Passage: San Diego to Ensenada

Departed Monday, November 12, 2007 at 6:20 AM local time from A1. The departure location was latitude 32 degrees 42.934 minutes north, longitude 117 degrees 13.913 minutes west.

Arrived Monday, November 12, 2007 at 4:56 PM local time at Marina Coral.

Wednesday, November 14, 2007 12:26:15 AM

Location: Ensenada, Mexico
Latitude is 31 degrees 51.77 minutes north.
Longitude is 116 degrees 39.77 minutes west.

First a few words about our San Diego visit. We stayed at two anchorages, A5 that is by Coronado, and A1 that is closer to the sea and downtown. A5 is also by the Amphibious Naval station, which hosts the Navy Seals, and a bunch of very strange looking fast stealth boats. When we moved from A5 to A1, *Jenny* was met by one of their more conventional and fast small boats (about *Jenny's* size) and asked us to follow it through a team of swimmers that were out for their morning swim in the very cold water of the bay. *Jenny* was all too eager to follow that Navy boat lusting after all that steel, muscle and speed. I have to keep my eye on her. Mary was interested in the swimmers who looked like Seals, no wetsuits, swimming between one island to another, pushing and pulling large bundles of stuff. Brrrrrr...

We enjoyed both anchorages, except for the cold, overcast weather we had until the last day. The highlights were catching up with the *Paloma* crew and having dinner with them and having the *Beverly S* master mariners drive all the way down from Marina Del Rey to take us around on a last minute provisioning excursion. We surely hope we cross their paths again on our journey east.

My friend Rob who I worked with at Kaiser invited us to dinner and provided us with a nice memory for our last night in the USA for a while. With *Jenny* fully provisioned (except for the customs restricted items) we were ready to go the next morning.

You know how some things just seep into your consciousness unexpectedly? Well, I had been chatting with some other sailors about our passage into Ensenada, and they all said that the charts for Mexico are estimates at best. Then at dinner with Rob, he related their story about arriving in Ensenada at midnight, and finding the way into Marina Coral the dark difficult at best. Then hearing some conversation about how the days are growing shorter... Well, sometime during the night I realized our ten-hour trip had the potential to deliver us in Ensenada in the dark. That would not be a good thing at all. So... At 05:00 in the morning, I was UP. Better to leave a known place that has good charts in the dark than to arrive in a new place with marginal charts in the dark. Mary was not exactly pleased. She had worried her night away with little or no sleep.

For *Jenny*, crossing into Mexico was old hat. She had been there before with other caregivers. She took the wheel while we were still in San Diego harbor and went her way south like a trail horse that has followed the same path too many times. The ocean threw her a small chop at the start and soothed her with smooth water at the end. I had her birds in the water anyway. She put up with my anxiety without a word. We arrived in Marina Coral at about 4:00 PM on Sunday. No one at the marina answered my VHF calls. After several attempts to raise someone, anyone, I just laid *Jenny* up against the end of one of the piers and settled in. While it was old hat to *Jenny* and the marina, Mary and I had just accomplished a major milestone in our lives, crossing the border to Mexico. To our surprise, no one cared! Monday morning we connected with the marina, took *Jenny* to her slip, and all was well.

BOOK 5: MEANDERING THROUGH MEXICO

In time of peace in the modern world, if one is thoughtful and careful, it is rather more difficult to be killed or maimed in the outland places of the globe than it is in the streets of our great cities, but the atavistic urge toward danger persists and its satisfaction is called adventure. However, your adventurer feels no gratification in crossing Market Street in San Francisco against the traffic. Instead he will go to a good deal of trouble and expense to get himself killed in the South Seas. In reputedly rough water, he will go in a canoe; he will invade deserts without adequate food and he will expose his tolerant and un-inoculated blood to strange viruses. This is adventure. It is possible that his ancestor, wearying of the humdrum attacks of the saber-tooth, longed for the good old days of pterodactyl and triceratops.

John Steinbeck
Log from the Sea of Cortez, 1941

Wednesday, November 14, 2007 12:26:15 AM

Location: Ensenada, Mexico
Latitude is 31 degrees 51.77 minutes north.
Longitude is 116 degrees 39.77 minutes west.

Our timing for entering Mexico was not good. Today is the start of the big, really big, Baja off road race. This must be the biggest event in Ensenada all year. People from all over the world are pouring in. The cab driver thought we were part of the race, and took us to where all the cars, trucks, and other vehicles of all shapes and sizes were lined up for tech inspection along with all the media, crew and crowds. We had to walk back to the government building, arriving around 10:00 AM. At 2:00 PM we finally were done. The place where you get your Visa and other papers was mobbed. While standing in line after line we met a very nice couple, Carl and Mei on *Monju*. After hours of confusion and boredom, it was way past lunchtime. Margarita's and enchiladas were all we were thinking about by the time we were done. So, that's what we did.

We went to a local open-air restaurant with Carl and Mei and heard each other's stories. They quit work and went to live with an aluminum boat builder in the Pacific Northwest. Three years later, they were in Ensenada. Carl and Mei are spirits from another planet. Very funny, intelligent, fearless and nice.

The weather for our first day in Mexico was a wonderful break from the San Diego gloom; sunny and warm! The people are all friendly and we have met two other couples on sailboats going our way with the same attitude about taking our time. We hope to see more of them. Life is good and getting better!

Passage: From Ensenada to Colonet

Departed Thursday, November 15, 2007 at 6:10 AM local time from Marina Coral. The departure location was latitude 31 degrees 51.760 minutes north, longitude 116 degrees 39.719 minutes west.

Thursday, November 15, 2007 10:47:35 AM
Location: At sea off Punta San Jose
Latitude is 31 degrees 25.974 minutes north.
Longitude is 116 degrees 39.549 minutes west.

This weather observation was taken on Thursday, November 15, 2007 10:29:49 AM local time.
Observation location: Punta San Jose.
Latitude is 31 degrees 26.169 minutes north.
Longitude is 116 degrees 39.665 minutes west.
The air temperature is 63, and water temperature is 66 degrees Fahrenheit.
The forecast is Sunny.
The current weather is dry.
The sky is clear or a few clouds.
The wind is 7 knots from the south.
The visibility is 20 nautical miles.
The wave height is 1 feet with 3 foot swells.
The barometer is 1011 millibar and steady.

Jenny is took us out of Ensenada this morning after fueling up. She is full of energy and underway again. She left Ensenada at dawn to make sure she would reach her anchorage before dark this evening. It is a seventy-mile passage and the water and weather are wonderful. Mary is reading a book and I am writing.

Ensenada was about what I expected. A cruise and commercial ship port force certain characteristics. The main harbor is industrial with cargo cranes, tugs, and industrial buildings. The town near the harbor is full of small shops and other tourist traps for the cruise ships. The infrastructure is poor, so sidewalks are broken and the streets rough. However, the people are very friendly and helpful and for the most part seem to be happy. Marina Coral is about four miles outside of the harbor, is new and caters to North Americans, our culture and money. There is nothing wrong with that.

The marina itself is very nice, but the warnings about arrival in daylight were accurate. The entry to Marina Coral is very narrow and lined with cut boulders. It is not straight, and there are no markers on shore to line up with. It would be very dangerous to enter at night! The fairways are narrow, requiring very good close quarter maneuvering, and there is a constant surge back and forth under the docks as the Pacific swells flow through. The slips are doubled up so you can only tie off on one side. This causes the boats to be pushed and pulled against their lines and fenders all the time. The heavier the boat, the harder it is on the gear. Many of the cleats on the docks are already loose. I did not like the strain on *Jenny* putting up with this. One Nordhavn 47 behind *Jenny* had a string of fenders mounted at the height of its neighbors rub rail. Smart move, since the lines in this Marina probably have short lives. One was caved in across the middle. Hmmm...

Jenny is completely full of energy. I tanked her up with fuel (400 gallons), water (300 gallons), and propane (11 liters). When full, she has a port list of a couple of degrees because she holds more fuel and house batteries on that side. She is now heavy and that makes her ride even smoother. I have started her water maker and we will have plenty of water clear through La Paz. We also stocked up her refrigerator, deep freeze and pantry. We are an eco-system of our own and good to go for a month or two.

Jenny is in her element on the ocean and now heading to our next anchorage, Punta Colonet. It is so nice we get to be passengers again. I had planned to go from Colonet to another anchorage and then take an overnight to Turtle bay. However, this weather is supposed to last through Saturday so I am thinking about telling *Jenny* to go directly there from Colonet. Mary and I would have to do an overnight anyway, and this way we can take advantage of the weather and maximize our distance covered. We might even get to catch up with Carl and Mei on *Monju*. That would be fun.

I still have not made SSB contact with our friends on *Paloma*. The SSB is a strange radio, influenced by atmospheric conditions. That makes its performance dependent upon a mixture of Mother Nature's whims and electronics. This presents a challenge to mechanically minded folks. I will give it another shot today. I will also try to connect to the mail system and send this out.

Friday, November 16, 2007 11:40:09 AM

Location: Cabo San Quentin
Latitude is thirty degrees 24.714 minutes north.
Longitude is 116 degrees 10.908 minutes west.

This weather observation was taken on Saturday, November 17, 2007 8:39:08 AM local time.
Observation location: Cedros Island at Sea.
Latitude is 28 degrees 8.125 minutes north.
Longitude is 115 degrees 7.019 minutes west.
The air temperature is 63, and water temperature is 73 degrees Fahrenheit.
The forecast is Sunny.
The current weather is dry.
The sky is clear or a few clouds.
The wind is 10 knots from the southwest.
The visibility is 10 nautical miles.
The wave height is 1 feet with 2 foot swells.
The barometer is 1015 millibar and rising.

Here we are again on a beautiful flat sea heading southeast. *Jenny* is our magic carpet and we are passengers. Last night *Jenny* anchored below a high bluff on her north side and open to the south in company with a sailboat and a Mexican fishing boat. As our guidebook said it would be, the small swell that reached around the corner of the point rolled *Jenny* a lot and made the anchorage uncomfortable. I think this convinced us to avoid such anchorages going forward. Today we are taking a big step. We decided to take our first overnight passage together, and tell *Jenny* to move 220 nautical miles further southeast, directly into Turtle bay. If this sea and weather persists, it should be an awesome passage.

This morning we saw a herd of dolphin racing out to the west, with many leaping in the air and doing back flips. It seemed like a very happy and prosperous community. With *Jenny* carrying us so gently south, we are doing some cleaning and other odd chores, reading our books and magazines. Other than a sailboat on the horizon heading west on a close reach, no one is in sight. Turtle Bay is supposed to be a nice anchorage with a small town.

Saturday, November 17, 2007 8:53:04 AM

Location: Off of Ceros Island
Latitude is 28 degrees 7.91 minutes north.
Longitude is 115 degrees 7.009 minutes west.

This weather observation was taken on Saturday, November 17, 2007 8:39:08 AM local time.
Observation location: Ceros Island at Sea.
Latitude is 28 degrees 8.125 minutes north.
Longitude is 115 degrees 7.019 minutes west.
The air temperature is 63, and water temperature is 73 degrees Fahrenheit.
The forecast is Sunny.

The current weather is dry.
The sky is clear or a few clouds.
The wind is 10 knots from the southwest.
The visibility is 10 nautical miles.
The wave height is 1 feet with 2 foot swells.
The barometer is 1015 millibar and rising.

Our first night at sea together was good with a couple of interesting events. We are now about fifty miles from Turtle Bay where *Jenny* will rest for a day or two. Based upon an email exchange, our friends on *Monju* will be there, and we are looking forward to a movie night together.

The night started clear, with nearly a half moon and plenty of stars to light *Jenny's* way. Mary went down to the main cabin after dinner to read and rest while I stood watch. At 9:00 PM she came up for her first watch and I climbed into the pilot berth. Although, the pilot berth is comfortable for naps, it is a little short and cramped for me as a bed. But, I promised Mary I'd sleep here so I would be right at hand if she needs me. First watch went quietly with a couple of other vessels passing by, heading north. *Jenny* ignored them and steamed on south.

I took over the watch at midnight and by then, a cloud cover had moved in, making it very dark out. When this happens, basically all you can see is the glow of the running lights shining off *Jenny's* foredeck and nothing else unless it has lights on. Radar helps, but so far I can see navigation lights before *Jenny's* radar picks up the target. *Jenny* had one boat come right at her on a course north, so she had to jog slightly to starboard to let it go by. It was lit up like a New York City skyscraper at 5:30 PM in the dead of winter. It was going fast (relative to *Jenny*) and probably a cruise ship. After it passed, *Jenny* steered back to her course line. So far so good. Then, I saw a flash of birds taking off and a big floating kelp mat as it went down *Jenny's* port side. UGH! I knew *Jenny* was going to snag it and she did. It was about 01:00 AM.

Reluctantly, I went down and woke Mary. There was no avoiding it. *Jenny* snagged it on both her bird and trip line. So much kelp was on her trip line that her bird was skimming along the surface behind us. We have this drill down to a science now and had the mess cleared in about fifteen minutes. Mary returned to our cabin, and I went back on watch.

At 03:00 Mary came up for her watch. All was well, and Ceros Island showed us its north end lighthouse just before dawn and *Jenny's* radar confirmed our approach. It was back to the pilot berth for me, then BAM. *Jenny's* port bird struck something heavy. Mary knew something was wrong immediately and turned to wake me up. I had heard it in that part of my mind now wired to *Jenny*'s synapses and was already returning to full awake.

After a quick checkup of *Jenny's* health I discovered three pieces of good news; only the bird's main wire broke and the bird was trailing behind her on her trip line; whatever it was did not strike her hull; and the wire broke at its connection point to the bird. Since I designated this wire to be the weak link in stabilizer system, the break happened just as it was supposed to. And, because the wire broke at the end, I can easily fix it when we stop in Turtle Bay.

With only one bird, and some waves about, I slowed *Jenny* down to five knots for the next hour and got her down to the lee side of Ceros Island where the water is much calmer. There we pulled her port bird up and she has been cruising along at about seven knots with a headwind of about eight knots since. In spite of her injury she will still get us settled into Turtle Bay this evening.

Mary went back to bed once we had both birds up, and just came up (09:00 AM) declaring that it was the first time she had a drool worthy sleep since we started.

Arrived Saturday, November 17, 2007 at 2:08 PM local time at Turtle Bay. The trip covered 217.00 nautical miles in 1d 10h 18m with an average speed of 5.60 knots and a maximum speed of 7.20 knots.

Passage: Turtle Bay to Magdalena Bay

Departed Monday, November 19, 2007 at 6:48 AM local time from Turtle Bay. The departure location was latitude 27 degrees 41.014 minutes north, longitude 114 degrees 53.152 minutes west.

Monday, November 19, 2007 2:19:18 PM

Location: Pita San Hipolito at sea
Latitude is 26 degrees 59.739 minutes north.
Longitude is 114 degrees 23.817 minutes west.

This weather observation was taken on Tuesday, November 20, 2007 12:01:21 PM local time.
Observation location: Cabo San Lazario at sea.
Latitude is 25 degrees 0.229 minutes north.
Longitude is 112 degrees 36.588 minutes west.
The air temperature is 74, and water temperature is 82 degrees Fahrenheit.
The forecast is unknown.
The current weather is dry.
The sky is broken clouds (60 - 90% clouds).
The wind is 7 knots from the northwest.
The visibility is 5 nautical miles.
The wave height is 0 feet with 4 foot swells.
The barometer is 1011 millibar and rising.

Turtle Bay is a quiet and poor small Mexican outpost on the coast. It has a very well protected anchorage, one of the few on this coast so almost all the sailing and motor yachts stop there for a day or two to rest up and get fuel. I was hoping the water in the bay would be clear, but it was brown, so I decided not to go for a swim. Even so, it was teaming with dolphins, seals, sea lions, pelicans and many other birds. The weather was good and warm enough that we spent some time in our lounge chairs in the cockpit soaking up the sun.

Repairing *Jenny's* wounded bird was an easy task and first on my to-do list. Next came climbing the mast to re-attach the top of the generator stack to the mast. During the trip down to Turtle Bay, I noticed that the hose clamp was undone. Next was creating a shim for one of the stabilizer struts so it would not bang as it shifted under varying loads. Finally, I tried to figure out why the reverse polarity light came on when the generator was running. On this task, I was and still am stumped. It is time to read up on AC wiring. You see, life on board is a constant set of challenges coupled with exotic scenery, people, and wildlife.

We caught up with *Monju* just as they were heading south again. We should meet up again in Magdalena bay. We also made radio contact with a couple from Canada in a forty-nine-foot aluminum trawler called *Mystic Michael*. *Mystic Michael* was being created in the same yard at the same time as *Monju* and they are good buddies. We made a plan to visit each other in Magdalena bay. They are about a day behind us and paired up with another sailboat from the same yard. I also tested *Jenny's* sideband radio with the Larry and Susan on *Midnight Voyage*. They left yesterday around noon and as they went down the coast our last contact with them was around 6:00 PM. I will try to re-establish contact his afternoon since they should be stopped now and we should be closing on their location. So far, only *Midnight Voyage* seems to be on a similar schedule and plan as we are, but nonetheless, we are building up a set of nice boating buddies as we go.

We left Turtle Bay at daybreak to get a good start on our 250-mile journey to Magdalena Bay. It should take about thirty-six hours if *Jenny* can keep a good seven-knot average. If we are running out of daylight, we can stop in a nice cove called Bahia San Maria. It is only thirty miles north of the entrance to Magdalena bay, about five hours for us.

There is a sport fishing boat on the horizon toward shore passing us. We had a sailboat behind us this morning, but he dropped out of sight, and we passed a couple of sailboats heading north. Its 85 degrees Fahrenheit in the sun and Mary is sitting outside on the foredeck soaking up the rays with Nicholas. Nicholas seems to have found his sea legs since he is now quite actively going around *Jenny* when we are underway. He is also eating better.

That is about all from onboard *Jenny* for now. Tonight is an overnight passage so we will have more to report in the morning. It is nice to be able to send email while at sea!

Tuesday, November 20, 2007 12:25:58 PM

Location: Cabo San Lazario at sea
Latitude is 25 degrees 0.012 minutes north.
Longitude is 112 degrees 36.403 minutes west.

This weather observation was taken on Tuesday, November 20, 2007 12:01:21 PM local time.
Observation location: Cabo San Lazario at sea.
Latitude is 25 degrees 0.229 minutes north.
Longitude is 112 degrees 36.588 minutes west.
The air temperature is 74, and water temperature is 82 degrees Fahrenheit.
The forecast is unknown.
The current weather is dry.
The sky is broken clouds (60 - 90% clouds).
The wind is 7 knots from the northwest.
The visibility is 5 nautical miles.
The wave height is 0 feet with 4 foot swells.
The barometer is 1011 millibar and rising.

What is it like being sixty miles off the coast of Mexico at night? Well, for the most part, dull and boring. This is a good thing. The night started out clear and bright with a ½ moon shining above and stars glowing. I have *Jenny's* birds in the water since the wind at thirteen knots is stirring up a lumpy sea. By 03:00 in the morning, the moon had set and it was dark as a cloak closet at midnight. A few stars shined through the thin layer of ice clouds above. The radars were on and were our only source of comfort that the way ahead was clear. As the night went on, the wind died down and dawn began to break around 06:00. By 07:00, I had *Jenny's* birds up and she was steaming along at seven knots. I still have not decided whether to go all the way into Magdalena bay, or stop at the Bahia San Maria cove around 3:00 PM. Looking at the charts, this is probably the longest passage we will need to make in quite a while.

Jenny keeps purring along. JD, her heart of steel, is rock solid and strong. In the middle of the night, you just know it can go on beating forever. I adjusted JD's ventilation system last night and this morning that has made its room cooler and better for everything down there. I plan to install another ventilation fan while we are in Magdalena bay.

The water is getting close to eighty degrees! I have forsaken shoes and socks now and am running around barefoot on *Jenny*, as it should be. We will even be able to set up our deck chairs in Magdalena Bay and spend the evening outside. Because of the cold water north of here, this is impossible without bundling up in a sweater and jacket. We finally put our fleece away!

One of the difficulties in leaving the States is also leaving the excellent NOAA weather forecasts that are reliably accurate and local. The problem is that NOAA stops at our boarders. However, one of the weather models others and I have been using to understand wind, wave and swell models is the US Navy

WW3 model that covers the world in sections. I have been trying to see how I could get the WW3 model while remote from the internet. I have now succeeded using *Jenny's* SSB email system. This is so important because otherwise you are really left with low quality guesses, including your own, regarding what the sea and wind conditions will be over the span of a passage. Make no mistake; the weather dominates all plans and experiences!

A few dolphins came over to play this morning. The sea is exceptionally clear out here, and they were fun to watch. These were kind of green and brown on top with white bellies about the size of a German Sheppard. Nicholas stands watch with us but sleeps through most of it. He is catching up on whatever sleep he lost last night. I want his job.

I have not been able to raise *Midnight Voyage* or *Paloma* on the SSB so far today. With *Paloma* in La Paz, I should be within radio range when we get to Magdalena Bay. We are still exchanging emails to set this up. The last time we talked was in San Diego.

We are now fifteen miles from seeing land again.

Arrived Wednesday, November 21, 2007 at 7:12 AM local time at Magdalena Bay, Man of War Cove. The trip covered 256.50 nautical miles in 1d 14h 011m with an average speed of 6.70 knots and a maximum speed of 9.80 knots.

Thursday, November 22, 2007 1:38:40 PM

Location: Magdalena Bay Man of War Cove
Latitude is 24 degrees 38.45 minutes north.
Longitude is 112 degrees 8.148 minutes west.

After 37 hours at sea, we arrived at our anchorage in the dark. With the help of *Monju* and *Midnight Voyage*, we got a good spot in about thirty feet of water. They shined lights at us to guide us and walked us in on the VHF radio. We then had a small dinner and went to sleep.

A typical Panga

The next day, *Midnight Voyage* had arranged for a panga to take some folks to the small town north of this anchorage by about fifteen miles. A panga is an open boat like a combination of a dory and a rowboat about twenty feet long with high sides and outboard powered up to 250 HP. They are the pickup trucks of these ports and serve all functions from fishing to transportation. They always seem to be going full speed. That morning *Jenny* was flirting with a panga screaming by. She had the devoted attention of the poor panga as she coyly bobbed in the bay. It did not even notice the red buoy on her anchor trip line as it ran right smack over it. The panga severed the buoy from the line and hog-tied its outboard motor. I swear she did it on purpose. She just hates my trip line setup. Needless to say, the poor panga came to an abrupt stop. Fortunately, the only damage was to the buoy. UGH.

Town was interesting. First, there was no dock. The panga got close to shore and then a pickup truck backed into the water to meet it. We clambered from the panga into the back of the pickup truck for the ride into town.

Town had some paved streets, but because there is no rain here, blown dirt covered the pavement. Shopkeepers on Boardwalk Street go out each morning to sweep off the dirt in front of their shops. This was the only clue that there was actually pavement beneath. The houses were all open. Open to the air, and people, dogs, kids and visitors. We stopped at one on the main drag, thinking it was a store since it was all open with a nice patio out front. It turned out is the home of a woman who moved down here from Arizona thirty years ago. She gave us all the info on where to find shops and lunch.

Lunch was across the street in a nice open cafe. It had a thatched roof and some half-high stonework around the perimeter. We were with the *Midnight Voyage* crew of three and we ordered some Cerveza, enchiladas, shrimp tacos, etc. All the food was prepared fresh as we drank our beers and chatted. It was delicious and we must have spent a good two hours just enjoying the meal and company. I think that lunch was our real introduction to Mexico and cruising enjoyment.

Last night *Midnight Voyage* hosted a pre-Thanksgiving party and about fifteen cruisers were there. It was a great time talking to all these folks with such interesting stories. It was both fun and very enriching.

Today is Thanksgiving. We began the morning by visiting the local village and checking in with the port captain. We were supposed to do that yesterday, but were carried away by all the activity. We took the dinghy in and pulled the beast up on the beach. The village has about 140 adults with over fifty children according to their sign. I would say their livelihood is just above subsistence fishing, except for the port captain and the restaurant owner. The port captain was very nice, we signed his entry log and then went for a walk in the village. There is a school on one of the hills, filled with happy children. The people may be poor, but I do not think they spend any time thinking about it. We also stopped in the local Catholic Church. It was as you would expect in this setting: small, clean, door open and kind of really spiritual. One can only imagine what stories the walls could tell.

Then we picked up Nicholas and went to a deserted beach nearby. The approach to the beach gradually became very shallow, so we anchored the dinghy well off shore in about 18 inches of water and walked in. Once on shore, Nicholas went nuts running around like a wild thing! He loves the beach. We took a walk up the beach and discovered two dead Humboldt squid about four feet long from beak to tail. Then, we found a third, bigger than the other two. It had dug a pool for itself in an attempt to live through the low tide. Its fins were about sixteen inches across and it was at least four feet long with short one-foot arms. It watched us as we watched it. Nicholas studied the strange being. Deep water was about 300 yards away, with nothing but sand in between. We could do nothing for it.

Mary's making a sumptuous dinner for us. Champagne is in the ice box. Fresh bread! Yum!

Happy Thanksgiving

Passage: Magdalena Bay to San Jose

Departed Sunday, November 25, 2007 at 6:53 AM local time from Man of War Cove. The departure location was latitude 24 degrees 38.351 minutes north, longitude 112 degrees 7.555 minutes west.

Sunday, November 25, 2007 8:12:03 AM

Location: At sea Magdalena Bay Entrance
Latitude is 24 degrees 34.728 minutes north.
Longitude is 112 degrees 2.78 minutes west.

This weather observation was taken on Sunday, November 25, 2007 7:48:39 AM local time.
Observation location: Magdalena Bay Entrance.
Latitude is 24 degrees 34.881 minutes north.
Longitude is 112 degrees 2.871 minutes west.
The air temperature is 61, and water temperature is 71 degrees Fahrenheit.
The forecast is Sunny, low wind, low waves.
The current weather is dry.
The sky is clear or a few clouds.
The wind is 8 knots from the west.
The visibility is 20 nautical miles.
The wave height is 0 feet with 0 foot swells.
The barometer is 1014 millibar and steady.

Well, we are saying goodbye to Magdalena Bay today. It is a beautiful place with nice people, both Mexican and cruisers. Last night I was conferring with another team on the sailboat *Serenity* about leaving today. The wind was howling down the bay the entire day, making dinghy travel wet and wild. The report from boats coming into the bay was large seas and bad conditions outside. None of this showed on any of the forecasts. I suspected it was a local thing. Bob on *Serenity* was going to depart at 01:00 AM, but decided to wait another day. Last night I said I would wait until dawn to decide.

The forecast was for very calm seas all the way down to Cabo San Lucas. By nightfall, the bay fell dead still and calm. This morning there is some wind from the west as predicted.

Two days ago, I caught some sort of stomach bug that gave me a fever and the runs. It seems like a 24 hour thing, because by mid yesterday, I was pretty much back to normal. This morning Mary has the chills and is in bed below. If the forecast were anything but very nice weather, we would have stayed. But, with the weather that I expect, she would be no better sleeping it off in the bay than underway. *Jenny* is now carrying us south again.

Jenny has yet another secret. Something is very strange in the AC wiring. Bob from *Serenity* is a marine electrician and he braved yesterday's waves to come over and look at it. He had no clue. At first, I thought it was a generator problem. Next, I thought it was an inverter problem. Now, I think it is the refrigerator. One of my activities for today is to break out the refrigerator manual and see how it is supposed to be wired. When we get to our next stop, I will track down the actual wiring and see what is up. The list never ends.

While in Magdalena Bay, I pulled down the engine room exhaust fan ducts and reseated them. They had fallen loose over the years and were not providing all the exhaust power they should have. These fans keep the engine room and exhaust stacks cool. As we go south, I think I will need additional air-cooling for the engine room. I was going to install a new four-inch fan to blow cool air into the engine room from the starboard side vent. However, I found that I could not wire it as I wanted. The existing fans only run when JD is running, so there is no way to cool the engine room down once I stop JD. After several hours of tracing wires, I found out why. The fans are hooked up to the engine room shutdown system in case of a fire below. The system shuts JD down and then deploys Halon. The fans must be off while this is happening. The new fan gets hooked up the same way, when I get to it again.

Unfortunately, I was not able to satisfy my desire to go swimming here. While my water temperature gauge read 70's, a thermometer in the water showed low sixty's. UGH. While sunny and pleasant, the air temperature combined with the wind kept a slight chill in the air. I hear that it finally starts to get warm once you get to Cabo San Lucas. Well, that is the rumor.

Jenny is right at the entrance to Mag bay now, heading out against a flood tide. Somehow, I got that wrong. Oh well, it is not much of a current and it is only in *Jenny's* teeth for 1.4 miles. Then I hope she will pick up the normal southerly pacific coast current and glide south. The ocean looks flat. I will hang a line out to do some fishing on the way down. Perhaps, we will catch something! The word is that my thirty-five pound tackle is much too light though. The recommended line is eighty or ninety lbs. Hmmm...

Sunday, November 25, 2007 6:51:41 PM

Location: Pacific Ocean
Latitude is 23 degrees 41.356 minutes north.
Longitude is 111 degrees 2.297 minutes west.

This weather observation was taken on Sunday, November 25, 2007 7:48:39 AM local time.
Observation location: Magdalena Bay Entrance.
Latitude is 24 degrees 34.881 minutes north.
Longitude is 112 degrees 2.871 minutes west.
The air temperature is 61, and water temperature is 71 degrees Fahrenheit.
The forecast is Sunny, low wind, low waves.
The current weather is dry.
The sky is clear or a few clouds.
The wind is 8 knots from the west.
The visibility is 20 nautical miles.
The wave height is 0 feet with 0 foot swells.
The barometer is 1014 millibar and steady.

Few days on the ocean are better than this one. The wind was at *Jenny's* back as well as the slow lazy swell. We have been running with *Jenny's* birds up all day, JD beating at 1400 RPM and still averaged 7.2 knots so far. *Jenny's* water speed should be about 6.5 knots at this beat, so wind, swell, current has added about .7 knots. At this speed, we will be in Cabo San Jose by 08:00 AM.

I made an awesome discovery this morning as I broke out the refrigerator manual to see if it might be the cause of my mysterious 120-volt AC problem. As it turns out, this refrigerator is set up to run on either 120 volts AC or 12 volts DC. If it does not have AC, it uses DC. I have always been running it on 120 volts AC. Well, that is just pure waste of good energy. First, JD makes 12 volts DC, then *Jenny* uses her inverter to make 120 volts AC then her refrigerator uses more energy to transform it back to 12 volts DC! UGH! I located the AC plug and unplugged it to see if it was wired up properly for 12 volts and voila, it kept running!!! It automatically switched over to DC. Why does the refrigerator keep running even though I flip the circuit breaker off and why are there two circuit breakers? Duh... I had uncovered yet another of *Jenny's* secrets!

This makes *Jenny* purely 12 volt DC for all essential items. The refrigerator was the only appliance that we absolutely needed to run on 120 volts AC, or so I thought. This is such good news because now dear friends I can turn the inverter off. Yup. I can turn the inverter off all day and night and save gobs of energy just going to waste keeping the refrigerator running. We were consuming 100 amp hours each night. The next time we are at anchor, I will see what the new figure is with no inverter and no refrigerator transformer loss.

Now for the fun part! Imagine a perfect summer day, about 76 degrees in the sun, soft gentle swell of the ocean, fishing rod in a holder on the teak rail with a jig running out about 100 yards behind *Jenny*. Me in a recliner chair in the cockpit, soaking up the rays, listening for the line to go whizzing out with a strike, and watching the clear blue sea unfold from beneath her stern. Ah yes, that was my afternoon today. Life is getting better and better.

The reel did go nuts with a strike, but the hook did not sink home. I reeled the line in to find a serious set of teeth scars across my plastic lure. However, my jury-rigged lure did not bite back. I added more hooks. What else! It went back in the water, but no more action for the day. I will keep working on it though. I think I am getting the hang of this trolling thing. Nicholas was watching all the action. Wait until I get a big one and he sees it! That will be fun.

Right now, there is a full moon rising on *Jenny's* port side, and two small boats just passed by on *Jenny's* dark starboard side going north. Starboard to starboard, green to green in a most friendly and silent way. Their blips are dropping down and off the green glowing radar screens, receding into memory. Mary is below, resting up for her watch with Nicholas. The sea is empty again with only a faint line of moonlight separating water from air.

Arrived Wednesday, November 28, 2007 at 6:39 AM local time. The arrival location was latitude 23 degrees 3.760 minutes north, longitude 109 degrees 40.626 minutes west. The trip covered 186.00 nautical miles in 1d 8h 7m with an average speed of 5.80 knots and a maximum speed of 8.40 knots.

Monday, December 03, 2007 10:41:51 AM

Location: Los Muertos Cove
Latitude is 23 degrees 59.34 minutes north.
Longitude is 109 degrees 49.618 minutes west.

Well, it has been a while so this might be a long entry to catch up. We left the very nice marina at Puerto Los Cabos on Wednesday to start heading up the inside of the Baja Peninsula toward La Paz. We enjoyed the town, and found a brand new Mega food store located and designed to supply the gringos buying condominiums and time-shares along the coast. We did a major resupply and now have the pantry, refrigerator and freezer full of food again. The store was bigger and better than any Safeway we have been in. The produce was excellent. The old stories about food in Mexico seem to be outdated now.

Since leaving the marina on the southern tip of the Baja, the weather has not been kind to us. Our first stop was Los Frailes, fortunately only thirty miles up the inside coast. As soon as we turned the corner to head north, *Jenny* ran into wind (ten to fourteen knots) and a wicked chop. She bashed her way up the coast into the cove protected from the north and thankfully dropped her anchor. Los Frailes had about five vessels already there, and more came in after we did. Since we were well protected from the wind and seas, we had a good night's sleep. Thursday, we woke to less wind and dying seas. The forecast was for the wind and waves to die in the afternoon and then shift to come from the south during the night. The crews in Los Frailes got on the radio and we discussed options. I was for heading up to Los Muertos that day and if there was bad weather from the south, go around to the other side of the peninsula and anchor there. However, the consensus was to stay put and go to the other side of the Frailes peninsula, an area with uncharted reefs, if the weather turned bad. We decided to stay with the crowd. Bad decision.

Group consensus does not always result in good choices. In the evening I moved *Jenny* further off the beach since the wind already shifted and we were too close and too shallow. I dropped her hook in sixty feet of water and put out 300 feet of chain. I knew we were safe. *Jenny* has a compass, depth and wind gauges right over our heads in the main cabin bed. I could check on our situation all night without having to get out of bed. I highly recommend this setup. It blew all night and the waves kept building. I had *Jenny's* birds hanging out, but they are not as effective at anchor as when we are going.

It was an ugly night. The seas built into a four to six foot chop with a very short period. *Jenny* was a wild thing on a tether. I had let her down again. *Jenny's* water tanks were not full so as the seas threw her about, her fresh water slammed the tank sides like a drum. Pots and pans in the galley were playing their own cacophony as they flew about in the cupboards. The wind wailed through *Jenny's* rigging. Wild nature was tossing us about in all directions. No one in the anchorage got much sleep and some dragged very close to the rocky shore.

Friday morning we were all hell bent on leaving that place. One by one, the cadre of weary vessels took off, some heading north and some heading south. Anywhere but there! The trip from there up to Los Muertos was good, with some following seas out of the south, dying out and then as the wind shifted back north, building again. By the time we got to Los Muertos around 3:00 PM there was a good chop building from the north, we were glad to gain the protection of a cove once again and drop *Jenny's* anchor.

One of the smaller sailboats had fuel problems. They left Los Frailes two hours after the rest of us, and had to fix their fuel supply several times on the way up. At about 7:00 PM, they called in to make sure they were on the right track and to alert us of their troubles. They were about six miles out and the chop was bad again. They could not keep their motor running for more than an hour or two at a time. When it stopped, they were at the mercy of the seas. Fortunately the couple on board was seasoned, world experienced sailors. We lit up *Jenny's* lights to give them a visual, confirmed their heading and distance and kept a vigil. They made it in, the last of the Los Frailes group.

Saturday, I received the weather and it called for strong winds out of the north for three or four more days. It seems that the weather in the Sea of Cortez is heavily influenced by the weather over the Four Corners area of the USA. In this case, a massive high was building over Denver. Who would have thought? There is a good weather forecaster, Don Anderson, on the SSB radio and a lot of communication among the boats regarding what is going on. Do not leave home without a well functioning SSB radio!!!

There is a nice restaurant and bar here with a very large thatch covered porch. Yesterday we gathered there to watch US football, tell stories and drink beer. Nice. Those that were at Los Frailes all voted for getting tee shirts, "We survived Frailes". Everyone was well beaten up that night. One of the vessels here named *Adios* has a couple in their third year of cruising the area and we picked their brains for where to go.

Last night the wind picked up again out of the north and has been blowing hard ever since. This anchorage is good though, and *Jenny* is snuggly attached to the bottom. A big sport fishing boat came in late yesterday and parked too close for my comfort, but did not drag. They went out this morning to go north and were back here about an hour later. We are probably going to be here until Wednesday morning.

Projects: I got the new engine room blower installed. I put a new more easily accessible light switch on the compass in the master cabin. At Los Frailes, I put on my wetsuit (for the first time) and dove on *Jenny* to check out the zincs and propeller. I found the bolt holding the propeller zinc was backing out and tightened it up.

Then I decided to figure out why I have not been able to contact *Paloma* and other boats using the SSB. Before parting we pick a channel to use for connecting on but I could never hear or talk to them. So, I did some checking in the SSB books about channels and frequencies. It turned out that some of the channels were programmed to the wrong frequencies. I do not know why they were wrong, but it has caused much head scratching. I reprogrammed the bad channels and hope that fixes the problem! Now I have to tackle the generator reverse polarity problem and hope to figure that out today too.

We all took a walk on the nice beach here yesterday and Nicholas went wild again. He really loves to run when he gets the chance. Unfortunately, he has sensitive skin and his belly turns bright pink after being in saltwater. We have to hose him down really well when we get back to *Jenny*. And that's about it. La Paz on Wednesday. Until then, projects, beach, beer, buddies. Hmmmm. I can do that.

Passage: Los Muertos to La Paz

Departed Wednesday, December 05, 2007 at 7:48 AM local time from Los Muertos Cove. The departure location was latitude 23 degrees 59.037 minutes north, longitude 109 degrees 49.158 minutes west.

Arrived Wednesday, December 05, 2007 at 3:42 PM local time at Marina Costa Baja. The arrival location was latitude 24 degrees 13.034 minutes north, longitude 110 degrees 17.977 minutes west.

Friday, December 07, 2007 6:31:14 PM

Location: La Paz, Mx
Latitude is 24 degrees 13.035 minutes north.
Longitude is 110 degrees 17.975 minutes west.

We are now in La Paz, Mexico. The air is warm and the water is all shades of blue. It is wonderful. We pulled into Marina Costa Baja two evenings ago and got a slip for a week. The cost is about $30 per night and includes satellite TV, cable Internet, a shuttle to and from the city, and other nice extras. Wow! The next morning we discovered that *Midnight Voyage* is on the same dock, a few boats down. How much fun is that?

Marina Costa Baja is the only marina we have been in truly serious about not pumping waste overboard. Other marinas have their obligatory pump out stations. However, the use is optional and rarely employed. Here, each dock has a pump-out system with a hose that can reach every boat on that dock. When you check in, you sign up for a pump-out schedule. We were on a three-day schedule. Every three days, two guys show up and pump out *Jenny's* holding tanks. The result is crystal-clear water in the marina.

When you get to a marina after being remote for a while, the first things you do are washing the salt off your vessel, laundry, more laundry and even more laundry. All the while, you are loading water when you trust the source. Many cruisers in Mexico do not trust the local water and prefer to use their water makers. However, you cannot trust the bacteria level in the saltwater near towns either. In La Paz, some head out to a nearby gorgeous island, throw down the hook for a day, make water, swim, fish, and generally suffer through the day.

Speaking of fishing, I caught my first fish while we were in Los Muertos. I used my light, freshwater spinning reel, put a small bass sized Rapala lure on and started casting off *Jenny's* stern. Down here, there are fish everywhere. At night they surround your boat and splash about in swarms because they are drawn to the light. In the day, you see small fish shoals trying to jump out of the water to escape larger fish, larger fish doing the same, and bat rays leaping out of the water, flapping their wings, attempting to fly. It truly is amazing.

Well, here I was casting away, aiming at small shoals going nuts on the surface, and WHAM, something took the lure. Whoaaa it was big. Line was running off the spool and I had to tighten the drag. After a good fight, I got it along side *Jenny* and hauled it into the cockpit. It was about eighteen inches long, maybe a bit more, shiny silver with gold spots. My first guess was that it was a mackerel and it later proved to be so. I clubbed it, skinned it and the next night ate one side (the other is in the deep freezer). It was sooooo good. Just like swordfish.

The fish here are so plentiful it is easy to catch them while running at *Jenny's* normal six to seven knots. I have seen other boats come in with yellow fin tuna and (yum) Dorado. My attempts at trolling have yet to yield our first fish though. This is primarily because I am running tackle far too light at thirty-five pounds. I also did not have the right lures. Twice I lost the only large lures I had, with the fish biting right through thirty-five pound wire leader. UGH. I fixed that today. I got ninety-pound stuff and big lures.

There are two ways to fish, one for pleasure and one for food. Pleasure fishing consists of rod, reel, reasonably light tackle, etc. The sport is to land a large fish on light tackle, and enjoy the fight. Most motor boaters are sport fishermen. But, dedicated sailboat cruisers are fishing for food. They run 80-100 pound line and leader off the back of their boats hooked to the boat with bungee cords. No rod, no reel. When a fish is hooked, it has no chance. The bungee keeps the shock load low and alerts the crew to haul in the meat. That's the tackle I just got and need to set up. I will use my spinning reels and rods for casting from *Jenny* while at anchor.

We went into La Paz last night with some friends to have dinner at La Boehme restaurant. We heard that they had fantastic pizza, something you do not find too much of down here. The restaurant was a work of art. Really! The whole thing was as though it came off some Parisian 3D canvas. I am going back to take a ton of photos. You will not believe it. The Pizza was exquisite, with a 1 mm crust that was a pastry. Yum.

La Boehme, La Paz

We went into La Paz today to do some shopping and look around. This town is booming, as are most in Baja Sur California. The people are wonderful and put up with our attempts at Spanish. The setting is spectacular. It is easy to see why USA citizens come and stay. We found what we needed, saw some other boating friends that had anchored in the bay downtown. We had a great lunch for $24.

We are due to leave the Marina on the 12th and we will tank up on the way out. I expect that we have used 250 gallons since Ensenada. We will see. If so, we have used less fuel over the past month than most of you readers have used in your cars.

Life is good.

Sunday, December 16, 2007 3:05:36 PM

Season's Greetings to all from La Paz, Mexico.

Mary:

We hope this finds everyone enjoying the beauty of the season. We are well and very blessed. As many of you may know 2007 has been quite a year for us in many ways. We retired in September and left San Francisco on September 30th on our boat *Jenny*. We went under the Golden Gate Bridge turned left and headed south. It was after a summer filled with moving out of the house, getting rid of many things and putting stuff in storage for our return to land. We moved on *Jenny* at the end of July. We sold the cars right before we departed. That was a very stressful and emotional period.

Mary, Nicholas and David, Christmas in La Paz

Thus far our trip has been an adventure, full of learning and seeing beautiful places. The seas have been good to us and I am most thankful for that. We had encountered a few rough passages but overall pretty good. We have met many wonderful people doing a similar adventure as we are. It is a completely new way of living and has taken us time to adjust. We are planning to cruise for about a couple of years if all continues to go smoothly. We are taking our time, which allows us to stay in places that we like and get a real feel for the lifestyle of the area.

We are lucky as many folks have a schedule to keep. We wait until the conditions are the best they can be before we complete the next passage. We have completed three overnight passages which are quit the feat for me as I said I was not sure I could complete one. Our longest overnight passage thus far was

250 miles and it took us 37 hours. Wow, I was happy when that was over. During the night we each do three hour watches and then sleep for three hours. Of course once you get to your destination the first thing is a shower and sleep. Nicholas our dog is doing really well. He had to get his sea legs and overcome being seasick. He is getting much too much love from all the people we meet. Spoiled is not the word!!!!!

We will stay in La Paz until after Christmas and then when the weather permits head across the Sea of Cortez to Mazatlan. It is a twenty-eight hour passage and since there is no place to stop, we will complete another overnight passage. According to what we have heard the water should be warm enough to swim, snorkel and David is looking forward to some diving.

Our families are both doing well and the grandchildren are growing and thriving. This has been a tough year especially for me as my Mom past away in April. We have wonderful memories and her love lives in our hearts. My Dad is doing really well and took a trip to Europe in the fall. He cared for Mom for many years and we are all glad he is able to do what he wants to do and enjoy the activities he was not able to enjoy while care giving to Mom.

Our goal for 2008 is to continue heading south looking for white sandy beaches, turquoise water, coconut palms and drinking pina coladas!!!!

Happy Holidays and wishing for peace, love, health and happiness to all in 2008!

Feliz Navidad,
Mary, David and our furry companion Nicholas

Mary

Friday, December 21, 2007 4:00:45 PM

Location: La Paz, Mexico

We are starting our third week in La Paz. Our current plan is to stay here through Christmas and then head out to the nearby Isla Espiritu Santo (Holy Ghost) for a couple of weeks, enjoy a nice anchorage, do some fishing and a little diving. After that, we will head back to La Paz to pick up some marine stuff we are having delivered from the States. Here is the story.

After talking to some folks here who have been south, I realized that we had forgotten how hot and humid it is in Florida, let alone the tropics. Sure, we will be on the water, but still, I have become anxious about trying to get a good night's sleep when we go further south. After much research, I settled on getting a water-cooled, 120-volt Cruisair air conditioner for *Jenny's* master cabin. It has a 6,000 BTU capacity and that should be sufficient for that room. It is self-contained, so in theory all I need to do is plug it in and run the water lines. However, there is a lot more work to it and it will be a major project over the next few months. I am going to take the small closet above our bed and put it there, so I need to find new storage space for all the stuff in there. If we have the money and need, we will put another unit in the guest cabin. The downside to all this is that we will need to run the generator or have *Jenny* plugged into the grid when using them. Oh well. We will try one first. I hope that night breezes from the water will keep us cool enough most nights.

As we were told, getting anything from the States into Mexico is very expensive. If you go through the normal channels, you pay 17% import duty and 15% sales tax. That makes any purchase through the normal channels prohibitively expensive. After considerable discussion with the Cruisair dealer in San Diego, the one in La Paz, and the one in Puerto Vallarta I decided to use the back door. The dealer in San Diego is up the street from Downwind Marine and Downwind Marine has a system whereby people going to Mexico can voluntarily take shipments to the various ports they are going. I had the Cruisair dealer walk the boxes down the street to Downwind, and they are holding them for someone heading to La Paz. Obviously, there is no firm date for delivery, but the price is right.

Now on to the cool stuff! Last night we stepped outside and looked up at the ¾ moon. We saw an awesome sight. There were very high ice clouds streaking across the sky. A perfectly round black hole of clear night sky devoid of stars formed around the full moon. A shining bright halo of ice crystals marked the boundary between the cloud and the beyond. It was spooky because the clouds should have been moving through the hole and over the moon too. But they weren't! It was as if the moon had burned a hole in the sky. This lasted about twenty minutes before streaks of high clouds pulled the halo apart and entered the inner circle. No one had ever seen such a thing before and several people commented about it during the morning radio net.

We are all stocked up for Christmas and Mary is organizing a Christmas dinner with a few other boats. She may have oversubscribed *Jenny's* accommodations because at last count there were twelve coming... I suggested we use the nearby palapa instead of *Jenny*, but Mary wants to decorate and be the host. I am good as long as the Tequila holds out.

Contrary to some of the stories we have heard about food shopping down here, we have found everything we could possibly want in the large food stores. The only thing I have not been able to find is real Maple Syrup. I have not found it anywhere. I am not sure they know there is such a thing. Oh well.

Passage: La Paz to Partida

Departed Thursday, December 27, 2007 at 9:34 AM local time from Marina Costa Baja. The departure location was latitude 24 degrees 18.784 minutes north, longitude 110 degrees 21.983 minutes west.

Arrived Thursday, December 27, 2007 at 12:00 PM local time at El Cardonal. The arrival location was latitude 24 degrees 33.012 minutes north, longitude 110 degrees 23.282 minutes west. The trip covered 22.97 nautical miles in 0d 3h 37m with an average speed of 6.32 knots and a maximum speed of 7.35 knots.

Thursday, December 27, 2007 1:12:09 PM

Location: El Cardonal, Isla Partida
Latitude is 24 degrees 33.005 minutes north.
Longitude is 110 degrees 23.308 minutes west.

Just a quick note to let everyone know we moved to one of the islands near La Paz to get back to nature for a while and save some money. I have posted a new position on the net. This is a stunning desert island with water clear enough to see bottom at thirty feet with many shades of blue as the depth changes. It is well protected from the winds that are supposed to crank back up tonight.

Our trip was only twenty-three miles and we had two to three foot wind waves and ten knots of wind following us up. It was pleasant enough, given the high winds that have been haunting La Paz for the past few weeks. The natives say it is very unusual for them to get so much wind for so long. Maybe folks in the States are getting similar peculiarities in their weather too. Tonight and tomorrow morning it is supposed to blow like stink again and then gradually get a little better. We chose this cove because it is surrounded by high bluffs on all sides except the west. While we will get strong down drafts and gusts, we should not get much of any wave action.

Friday, December 28, 2007 2:53:22 PM

Location: El Cardonal, Isla Partida

Our friends Larry and Susan on *Midnight Voyage* left this cove just as we were arriving. The forecast was for the winds and waves to build throughout the afternoon and they did. I chatted on the SSB this morning and they made it across to the north of La Paz but paid the price in a scary ride. They saw winds hit forty and took water into their fly bridge, twenty feet above the water. The problem with this sea is there is no swell to keep the wind waves from becoming a very nasty chop. This can result in six to nine foot wind waves with five to six second periods very quickly. Unless you are over 100 feet long, that kind of sea results and a heavy pounding.

Here is an excerpt from their email.

"We have been carefully exploring the spots around the various islands and resorts here. Then we headed out to Loreto about 100 miles north just before January 1, 2008. There it got magical, especially around Isla Danzante. I proposed to Susan in Honeymoon Cove that, was a photographers dream. By the way, she said yes! We took my good friends Elliott and Elisa there for a week. They actually flew into Loreto and went "out island" with us from the anchorage to protected areas called "Escondido". David Balfour made wonderful crew and great support as we headed back down south from Loreto.

Larry cracked a rib on the trip North to Loreto. Powerful northerly winds; green water and very high winds with bright sunny skies attacked us with minimal warning. Large waves with maximum winds of forty knots bashed us pretty well as we headed north. We had to really hide from these windy elements for a few days when heading northbound to see our friends.

Susan looks wonderful, is relaxed, and the best damn cook in the southern seas of Baja. What a perfect life partner."

Several very large motor yachts arrived in our cove just after we did and threw down their anchors. A couple of vessels relocated and reset their anchors in anticipation of a windy night. This morning I could see that only one of the boats dragged, and since they had several hundred yards of open space behind them did no harm. *Jenny* was exactly were she was at sundown. The winds came in gusts that reached over thirty knots, but because this is a closed cove there are no waves. This wind is supposed to let up by the 31st and we should have a couple of good days for the New Year.

The cove has remains of Indian dwellings and you can clearly see fish traps in the shallows and a cave up one of the bluffs. Mary and I will explore as soon as we feel comfortable putting the dinghy down. There are also two nice beaches and a trail that leads to the other side of the island. Nicholas is bored and wants to go for a dinghy ride and romp on the beach. He has been following me around all day while I take care of some routine maintenance.

Mary and I went exploring the beach with Nicholas. It is a desert with cactus and shrubs. The only animals we saw were rabbits, pelicans and seagulls. Nicholas ran wild again chasing birds and just generally going nuts in the water.

I have been working on repacking stuff in *Jenny* because we will loose a precious closet to the air conditioner when it arrives. I made some progress this morning, taking stuff out of some places and putting new stuff in that either fits better or is more appropriate for the space. Then I hunted for another spot to put the stuff I just took out. It is sort of like musical chairs. I suspect the stuff at the end of this exercise might have to go in the dumpster since all storage space is pretty much consumed.

Nicholas on the beach

I now have a good setup now for audio books. I have downloaded several from the US Government's Gutenberg Project web site in text format. There are over twenty thousand books on the site and about 160 just regarding historic voyages! Then I found a free text to speech reader that works pretty well. Now I plug in my earphones and listen to books when I want to kick back. Not bad huh! The software is called DSpeech if you are interested. I can tell this will also be very good for night watches!

That's all for now!

Passage: Isla Partida to La Paz

Departed Wednesday, January 02, 2008 at 6:33 PM local time from Cardonal Cove. The departure location was latitude 24 degrees 32.421 minutes north, longitude 110 degrees 24.138 minutes west.

Arrived Friday, January 04, 2008 at 1:28 PM local time at La Paz anchorage near Marina La Paz. The arrival location was latitude 24 degrees 9.266 minutes north, longitude 110 degrees 19.926 minutes west. The trip covered 26.90 nautical miles in 0d 4h 36m with an average speed of 5.80 knots and a maximum speed of 7.41 knots.

Friday, January 04, 2008 1:57:54 PM

Location: At anchor in La Paz

Jenny came in from the Isla Partida the day before yesterday and dropped her anchor outside the La Paz Marina in town. This is a good anchorage until strong winds blow out of the north. The bay here gets real choppy and uncomfortable in a north wind. Right now it is very nice.

I have been doing projects as usual. One of the real discoveries on the cruise so far is how much you depend on the HF SSB radio. It is like having long distance telephone service at home, coupled with email, and a weather radio. Tons of information is sent and received via the SSB radio. Since many of the folks you meet along the way become spread out as we move around, it is the only way to stay in touch with your community of friends. Every morning and evening there are set times and frequencies that the "network" of cruisers uses to keep each other updated.

One of my projects was to see if I could improve the transmission distance of ours. I knew some of the people could hear us on the morning net, but I did not know just how far I was reaching. When trying to reach other boats on a one-on-one basis, I was not very successful. I had a feeling that I could further improve *Jenny's* installation. With these sets, there are basically three pieces, the radio, the antenna and the grounding system that enables huge voltage differences to be achieved between the end of the antenna and the radio. The radio and the antenna are as good as I can make them. I removed the old separate radio grounding system and connected it to the new grounding system. Then I connected the new grounding system to the forward water tank to give it more surface area to work with.

My first test was to connect to our email post office in San Diego. The results were good. For the first time I had a complete set of transmissions at 1400 characters per second. Smokin! Then I got on one of the informal nets at 6:00 PM and called a boat I knew would be listening now located in Chacala, about 250 miles south of here. We connected well, with weak but clear signals. I know I can now reach at least that far. Good work David!

My next project was to grease the two electric winches that we use to raise and lower the dinghy. Since we will probably be raising the dinghy every night from here on out to make sure it will not be stolen, these winches will get a workout. I already reduced the load on the up haul winch by replacing the wire with 3/16 high strength rope and adding a two part block. This cut the load on the winch in half. The next item was to grease the gearboxes. I did this once in 2004, and not since. It is a messy job. I decided it would be better to install grease fittings on the gearbox housings. Then I can just use a grease gun to lube them more frequently. An easy job is less likely to be avoided!

I called on the local VHF net to see if anyone had the right tap to cut the threads I would drill into the gear box and met Bob on *Zig Zag*. He did have one but it was broken, so we set out in his car to find new ones. A short time later, I was armed with the right drill bit and tap. An hour later, the grease fittings were installed and greased!

Meanwhile, Mary was hiking around town, shopping and getting her hair done. Nicholas was helping me and going on every dinghy ride he could hop aboard. We plan to stay on the hook here until our stuff from Downwind arrives, and / or the weather forces us into a marina. Life is good. And, life on the hook is quite cost effective!!!

Passage: La Paz to Muertos

Departed Saturday, January 05, 2008 at 3:00 PM local time from La Paz anchorage. The departure location was latitude 24 degrees 9.910 minutes north, longitude 110 degrees 19.166 minutes west.

Arrived Saturday, January 05, 2008 at 4:33 PM local time at Muertos Bay. The arrival location was latitude 23 degrees 59.221 minutes north, longitude 109 degrees 49.693 minutes west. The trip covered 56.74 nautical miles in 0d 8h 32m with an average speed of 6.64 knots and a maximum speed of 7.47 knots.

Saturday, January 05, 2008 5:23:15 PM

Location: Muertos Cove
Latitude is 23 degrees 59.225 minutes north.
Longitude is 109 degrees 49.698 minutes west.

I could not resist the weather window we now have to cross in the Sea of Cortez to Mazatlan. I canceled our Downwind and Cruisair orders and we left La Paz this morning. It was too calm for the sailboats to move, but is wonderful weather for us. We had a very comfortable ride down to Muertos Cove, the place we last stopped on our way up to La Paz. Tomorrow we will set off on a thirty-hour trip across the sea of Cortez to get to Muertos sometime on Monday. The forecast is for no wind, which also means no waves all of tomorrow and I am hoping for a great trip across.

I rigged the new "meat hook" fishing rig this morning. Tuna cord did not work for me. I spooled out about 100 yards of my ninety-pound test line with a nice lure on it then put a loop at the boat end. I ran the loop forward so that it came up outside of the pilothouse doors and hooked it to two bungee cords attached to one of *Jenny's* cleats. I hung a reindeer bell from the bungee where it connected to the fishing line loop. This is a nice effortless way to catch meat. And, low and behold, just before we got here I hooked a small Dorado!!! The dinner bell rang! I dropped JD to idle and hauled it in. I am grilling it tonight for our dinner. Yum!

That's all for now. Oh by the way it was ninety degrees Fahrenheit on our way down today... I know, salt in the wounds.

Passage: Muertos to Mazatlan

Departed Sunday, January 06, 2008 at 2:36 PM local time from Muertos cove. The departure location was latitude 23 degrees 59.239 minutes north, longitude 109 degrees 49.321 minutes west.

Sunday, January 06, 2008 1:24:59 PM
Location: Sea of Cortez
Latitude is 23 degrees 51.479 minutes north.
Longitude is 109 degrees 11.52 minutes west.

This weather observation was taken on Monday, January 07, 2008 9:49:16 AM local time.
Observation location: Sea of Cortez.
Latitude is 23 degrees 18.816 minutes north.
Longitude is 106 degrees 43.538 minutes west.
The air temperature is 73, and water temperature is 70 degrees Fahrenheit.
The forecast is Clear, Sunny.
The current weather is dry.
The sky is clear or a few clouds.
The wind is 4 knots from the east.
The visibility is 10 nautical miles.
The wave height is 0 feet with 1 foot swells.
The barometer is 1016 millibar and steady.

Jenny weighed anchor and was underway by 08:00 this morning. I checked into the Amigo Net, the one we listen to and join the most, to let the net know we were underway. As a surprise, and probably due to my work on the radio, *Jenny's* autopilot now goes nuts with voice transmissions as well as email. Just as I was getting out the word, her autopilot promptly started turning us in circles. With one hand disengaging her autopilot and taking over her helm, and the other holding the microphone, I completed the broadcast. It was not as smoothly as I would have liked. In any case, the word went out.

The forecast for today was for light and variable winds all day, small wind waves, and a three foot swell coming from the south. And that is what we have. *Jenny's* birds are up and she's making 6.7 knots at 1400 rpm. So far so good.

I have the meat hook out and heard one jingle on our jingle bell alarm (now called the dinner bell), but alas it was a false alarm. We have both been reading and taking watches. I am reading *Typee*, by Herman Melville about Tahiti in 1842. I downloaded it from the Gutenberg Project site and am reading it from this laptop. Mary is reading another Danielle Steel book that gives me a few good moments when she comes over, all mushy. Nicholas is snoozing next to us. Another fish or two and I think he will figure out what the dinner bell means and will get into the fish-catching thing. He watched with great interest yesterday as I hauled in the Mahi Mahi and killed it.

There is very little mammal sea life here, just a couple of sea lions every now and again and a few dolphins. The dolphins are a different kind than we had been seeing in the Pacific, all dark black or blue and less playful. This morning thought I did see flying fish for the first time. They come out of the front of small waves and flutter for about 100 feet before falling back. I think they must have evolved this capability to avoid being eaten. You see shoals of other small fish jumping around on the surface now and again with birds going after them from above and obviously some carnivorous fish attacking from below. It was a good thing we saw the Humboldt squid we did in Magdalena Bay, because there is no sign of them down here.

In a few hours we will be out of sight of land and tonight will be a new moon so we should have complete darkness around us. You just cannot believe the star shine. Because we have absolutely no light pollution and are in the desert, the stars are so plentiful and bright we actually see the light from them on *Jenny* and the water. When you hold binoculars up you can see a 100 stars in the background of each star you can see without them. It is lovely.

Mary woke me during her watch around midnight. She saw some lights on the horizon and could not figure them out. She was pretty sure it was another boat coming our way, but... I cleared my bleary eyes and looked where she was pointing. I saw them too. They were bright and in fact there were lots of them on the horizon. Compounding the problem, it was not clear exactly where the horizon really was because the lights were being reflected in the water. I grabbed the binoculars and after a few moments began to understand the problem. The air was so crystal-clear and sky so dark we were looking at stars shining brightly right down to the horizon! I never saw such a thing in my life.

Monday, January 07, 2008 9:59:13 AM

Location: Sea of Cortez near Mazatlan
Latitude is 23 degrees 18.783 minutes north.
Longitude is 106 degrees 43.334 minutes west.

This weather observation was taken on Monday, January 07, 2008 9:49:16 AM local time.

Observation location: Sea of Cortez.
Latitude is 23 degrees 18.816 minutes north.
Longitude is 106 degrees 43.538 minutes west.
The air temperature is 73, and water temperature is 70 degrees Fahrenheit.
The forecast is Clear, Sunny.
The current weather is dry.
The sky is clear or a few clouds.
The wind is 4 knots from the east.
The visibility is 10 nautical miles.
The wave height is 0 feet with 1 foot swells.
The barometer is 1016 millibar and steady.

We made it through the night just fine. The wind went from north at 5:00 PM to west by 11:00 PM and then back to north through the night and now is out of the east. This is good because it keeps wind waves from forming. And now we have no wind at all. We are about fifteen miles from the Marina Mazatlan breakwater and should be in the basin by noon.

Yesterday the dinner bell kept ringing briefly in the afternoon and I finally saw that a seagull was diving on it. It was a pretty stupid thing to do and sure enough it finally got it, right through the beak. By the time I pulled the line in it was very dead, drown. I gave some sea lion an easy meal.

The only excitement through the night was dodging the ferryboats that run from Mazatlan to La Paz on a nearly identical course to *Jenny's*. Around 9:00 PM one was headed right for *Jenny* and I had to adjust her course. The captain was very nice and called us to verify that we were going to pass port-to-port and wanted to know what we were. There was no moon so we were invisible to him other than *Jenny's* running lights. He was broadcasting on his AIS so I knew exactly what he was and where he was going. In fact I changed course slightly before he saw us since he showed up on *Jenny's* chart plotter about thirty miles away. Boy I am glad I got the AIS receiver! Then about 03:00 AM another one going from La Paz to Mazatlan overtook us. This time we passed about three miles apart without having to change *Jenny's* course.

We hope to get a slip at Marina Mazatlan for a couple of days and then anchor out in their marina basin while we explore the town and shop.

P.S.

We arrived in Marina Mazatlan ok, but so far are very unimpressed by what we found. On the way into the area I started seeing garbage floating on the water. Coke bottles, paint cans, dishwashing gloves, etc. In the marina there is a pervasive sheen of diesel fuel and smell and the water is scummy with a couple of dead fish floating about. We might not stay long.

Arrived Monday, January 07, 2008 at 12:23 PM local time at Marina Mazatlan. The arrival location was latitude 23 degrees 16.256 minutes north, longitude 106 degrees 27.250 minutes west. The trip covered 190.12 nautical miles in 1d 4h 45m with an average speed of 6.61 knots and a maximum speed of 8.02 knots.

Wednesday, January 09, 2008 6:37:50 PM

Location: Mazatlan

We have had some inquiries about communications equipment from other cruisers and I thought it would be good to document our thoughts here.

I found that it is essential to keep communications going with the communities we are part of. The SSB is REALLY important if you are going to be an active cruiser. There are plenty of folks that use VHF, cell phones and local internet as their pipelines to the world. This works well in marinas. However if you are on the move, the order of importance becomes SSB with email, VHF and a very good Wi-Fi transponder. We use the Port Networks MWB 200 and it has connected with free APs over a mile away. I am now putting it together with a 12 dB gain antenna to really reach out (not legal in the US). With this and Skype + MS Messenger we have cheap phone and free video calls to friends and family on a regular basis. Keeping the communication lines open is very important to our mental health.

Before leaving San Francisco I installed the Militec Marine AIS receiver. *Jenny* has a very good radar profile so I figure we will be seen on that if anything and I would rather look a lot larger than I am then give away the family secrets with an AIS transponder. This has proven very useful on our journey. Big boats call us to work out our passing or overtaking arrangements rather than us having to call them and I can see them on AIS way before they can see us on radar. I know whom I am dealing with early in the encounter. I put up a separate six-foot VHF antenna for the AIS and it is good for about thirty miles.

I need to top off the fuel tanks here in Mazatlan and will know the price soon. *Jenny* has burned about 350 gallons since Ensenada so it is not a big expense item for us. I expect somewhere around $2.40 US per gallon.

Wednesday, January 09, 2008 7:09:41 PM

Location: Mazatlan

What is really important to get right on a boat? Good question. After a couple of months, I would now say:

1. The reliability and dependability of the stuff that keeps your vessel out of harm's way is at the top of the list. For *Jenny* it is her Lugger motor, transmission, drive gear, steering gear, and ground tackle. The first set is obvious, but do not shortchange your ground tackle. If you are actively cruising, expect that you and your vessel will depend on her ground tackle holding in a full gale if not worse to save your lives. Get her the biggest anchor that will she can hold. I chose a 55-kilogram Rocna and it has allowed us to sleep soundly in bad stuff. Many other boats we talk to have dragged and spent miserable nights full of fear.

2. Keeping in touch with the world around you and your communities of friends is essential to successful cruising life. If you are really on the move, your SSB with email is at the top of the list. Make sure it is a good set and is installed to really pump out the watts. Most powerboats do not have adequate installations. Their antennas and ground systems are completely inadequate. They also have too much RFI noise reaching their receivers. I have spent many hours improving *Jenny's* SSB capability and have installed over fifty RFI chokes to drive the noise down. Download and follow Gordon West's guide for good SSB installations. It is on the money. An easy way to find out if you have a good rig is to use your Pactor Modem and see how good your connections are to distant stations. When away from a field of sailboat masts (e.g. at anchor) I can easily get error free transmissions over 600 miles at 1400 characters per second. When I started working on this, I could not get any at fifty miles.

Wi-Fi APs are everywhere and some of them are open to leaches like us. I use a Port Networks MWB 200 and it has given us a good connection with an AP over a mile away. I have just ordered a 12-db gain antenna to get even greater range. Wi-Fi is our link to the wide world and with Skype is our phone system. This is very important to keep us connected with our world.

Jenny has two VHF sets and they are our local phone service with the boating community in the anchorages, towns, and marinas that we visit. On the west coast of Mexico the custom is to meet on Channel 22 at 08:00 AM each morning and go through a script about who has arrived, who has departed, emergency traffic, announcements, swaps and trades, local information, etc. It is the morning newspaper and news station. VHF Channel 22 is also the calling channel for stationary boats. Two sets let you monitor 16 on one, and 22 on the other and know which channel someone is calling on.

Jenny has an AIS receiver and that tells us what big boats are approaching long before radar picks them up, gives us all their details, and how close they will come to us. Priceless!

Jenny has short and long-range radars. When we are on an overnight passage, we have AIS, then radar, then visual to verify we are safe. In the fog, we have the first two. Do not leave home without them.

3. Food and water. Strange huh? Well, these are easy to come by and the absence of them takes a long time to kill you. So they are 3rd. We have a deep

freeze and a top / bottom refrigerator. Both are 12 volt. If at all possible, make all the food / water equipment 12 volt so you do not need to run an inverter or genset when at anchor. This saves many amps. We have a six GPH 12 volt watermaker and so far it is sufficient when we are in a desert. A twelve GPH 12 volt watermaker would be ideal. When we get to areas that actually have rain, we intend to catch it rather than make it.

Everything else is comfort, style, status.

Passage: Mazatlan to Isla Isabella

Departed Monday, January 14, 2008 at 7:05 PM local time from El Sid Fuel Dock. The departure location was latitude 23 degrees 12.552 minutes north, longitude 106 degrees 28.022 minutes west.

Monday, January 14, 2008 4:41:00 PM

Location: At sea
Latitude is 22 degrees 58.6279 minutes north.
Longitude is 106 degrees 21.4709 minutes west.

This weather observation was taken on Tuesday, January 15, 2008 11:38:33 AM local time.
Observation location: Isla Isabella.
Latitude is 21 degrees 50.696 minutes north.
Longitude is 105 degrees 52.667 minutes west.
The air temperature is 68, and water temperature is 68 degrees Fahrenheit.
The forecast is High clouds.
The current weather is dry.
The sky is scattered clouds (10 - 50% clouds).
The wind is 5 knots from the north.
The visibility is 20 nautical miles.
The wave height is 0 feet with 0 foot swells.
The barometer is 1013 millibar and rising.

I tanked *Jenny* up and we left Mazatlan this morning. Its official, we used 375 gallons from Ensenada to Mazatlan. I will have to add logic in BoatExec for a resettable odometer that adds up all the trip mileage and figures out the fuel consumption. In any case, before starting I expected to consume 500 gallons getting to La Paz, so all is very well in this regard. We paid 6.88 pesos per liter which I think works out to about $2.50 per gallon. Not bad. If I can get *Jenny's* propane tanks refilled in La Cruz, *Jenny* will be fully energized again. I have not had to crack either the oven/stove or the barbeque second tanks so far, having filled them up in Ensenada too.

I cannot say many good things about Mazatlan other than it has Home Depot, Sam's Club, Wal-Mart and Mega Food Stores. We re-provisioned well. I have been working on refinishing some of the interior teak and Home Depot came in real handy to restock sandpaper and brushes. Wal-Mart was a super store, food and the usual stuff, but we did not really need anything from there. Like La Paz, there is a bunch of condos, timeshare units, houses, etc. being built for the boomers and during the week the stores were at least 50% Canadians and Americans. Also like La Paz, the downtown had a large mercado that is like a flea market for produce, meats and fish. This one covered an entire indoor block. Mazatlan is a city and since it does not rain very much everything is covered in dust and dirt. Both Mary and I thought that La Paz was nicer and much more comfortable. We are not really going to miss Mazatlan that much.

We are going to Isla Isabella now, about 100 miles southeast of Mazatlan. It is supposed to be an excellent bird sanctuary and as far as we can tell everyone heading south from Mazatlan stops there to see the baby boobies, etc. A 100-mile passage is kind of annoying. It takes us about fifteen hours to go that far, more time than there is daylight. We do not like arriving or departing in the dark, so the only alternative is to head out in the afternoon and do the trip overnight. According to *Jenny's* navigation computer, we should arrive there around 06:00 AM tomorrow.

We will probably only spend a day or two there and then head for La Cruz. This is a small town on the outskirts of Puerto Vallarta. From what we can tell talking to folks and looking on the web, it seems like a nice place where you can anchor out and dinghy in.

Mary's dad is flying into Puerto Vallarta to join us for a month and we are looking forward to his visit. However, he did not know he was also signing up to be our mule for stuff we need from the States. I suspect he will have a few bags with him. The Puerto Vallarta airport is only ten miles from La Cruz so I will take a cab over and pick him up. The plan is to take him down the "Riviera" coast as far as Zihuatanejo where there is another international airport.

Right now the wind waves (swell?) are about four feet and every five seconds. *Jenny's* birds are down, and the waves are on her aft quarter. But still, she has more motion than was in the predictions. Oh well, we are heading south! Mazatlan had coconut palms, so we are getting closer!!! I will go on the Southbound Net tonight and check in for the first time in a while. SSB radios lose a lot of their range when surrounded by a forest of aluminum masts in a marina.

Arrived Tuesday, January 15, 2008 at 7:26 AM local time at Isla Isabella East Anchor. The arrival location was latitude 21 degrees 50.696 minutes north, longitude 105 degrees 52.671 minutes west. The trip covered 94.62 nautical miles in 0d 18h 46m with an average speed of 5.04 knots and a maximum speed of 5.59 knots.

Tuesday, January 15, 2008 11:46:17 AM

Location: Isla Isabella
Latitude is 21 degrees 50.696 minutes north.
Longitude is 105 degrees 52.67 minutes west.

Jenny's anchorage is pretty exposed so we will only be able to stay here as long as the weather permits. I hope it will be two or three more days. In spite of only turning JD at 1300 RPM last night *Jenny* arrived here before dawn and had to dawdle around until the sun came up. Then we went into the small cove where the fishing fleet anchors and decided not to stay. It was very small, enclosed on two sides with rocky cliffs and too crowded to be safe. We proceeded around to this east side anchorage. So far, it is very nice. We are tired from the overnight so we will wait until tomorrow to put the dinghy down and hike on the island. We hear the boobies are completely unafraid of humans and you can go right up to them.

We are now out of the heavy jet traffic lanes of North America and the sky is deep blue instead of milky blue. Ansel Adams called jet condensation trails "worms in the sky" and lamented that he had to wait for days to get a clear sky. This was back in the 1940's. We are now so accustomed to the mass of entangled worms overhead and subsequent milky blue sky that we take it for granted. We think it is natural. When 911 occurred and all the airports were shut down I marveled at a silent and truly blue sky for the first time since I was a small boy. It was probably the first time my children had ever seen such a sky. The sky here is that deep blue, the air is clear, and we are anchored off an island beach teaming with wildlife.

I feel clean again. I took a nice hot shower and washed the dust of Mazatlan down the drain. This place is drop dead gorgeous. There is a rock formation dead ahead that looks like an abstract sculpture. In four casts off the back of *Jenny* I caught a Sierra (Spanish mackerel) about eighteen inches long. A few minutes ago a BIG blue whale surfaced about 50 yards off *Jenny's* beam. Its exhale was so loud it sounded like it was inside *Jenny*. The smell of its breath was. Its back looked like it was about twenty-five feet wide! It must have been 100 feet long. My God!

My only problem is that all my AA rechargeable batteries are dead!!!! UGH. I am going to go back to the cockpit and try to catch some more fish... :-)

Wednesday, January 16, 2008 4:04:15 PM

Location: Isla Isabella
Latitude is 21 degrees 50.696 minutes north.
Longitude is 105 degrees 52.663 minutes west.

I went onshore today with Allen from *Charisma* and went hiking through the island taking pictures. Mary wanted to stay onboard with Nicholas. Wow, what an experience! This island is an extinct volcano with a salt and soda lake in the middle. Water enters below the surface of the ocean and evaporates out from the top. Since it rarely rains the water is more salty than the ocean and has a PH of 10, very alkaline.

Boobies

There must be thousands of green and blue-footed boobies, frigate birds, seagulls, etc. The boobies are so unafraid of humans that they are nesting everywhere on the ground, along and on the footpaths. They will not get out of the way when you approach. They just stare you down and if there is a nest involved, squawk at you too. The frigate birds are above in scrubby trees that are mostly only about six feet high. The birds and nests are at eye level. Apparently, this time of year is when they have their chicks because most did. There are iguanas here too and you can get within about three feet of them before they scoot away.

The frigate birds constantly soar above the island and the sea. Their flight is effortless and amazing to watch. Hundreds of them constantly ride the updrafts. They must land in a tree or on a cliff though because their wings are so big they cannot open them on the ground. Frigates are pure flight machines.
Unfortunately one frigate fell from a tree and become earth bound. It had the

canapé of the trees above to contend with and he was caught on flat land. They have virtually no legs so it kind of was hopping along the land, trying to find a way to get airborne. I took quite a few photos and will send the best ones out.

Wednesday, January 16, 2008 5:07:29 PM

Location: Isla Isabella
Latitude is 21 degrees 50.697 minutes north.
Longitude is 105 degrees 52.661 minutes west.

Water Makers

I recently got an inquiry regarding what size and make watermaker is best for the kind of journey we are on and the person asking was going through the same kind of thought process I did before leaving. I thought others might be interest in the reply I sent. My current thinking is quite different from what it was just a few months ago.

There are too schools of thought here. One is to get a high output 120-volt AC unit and expect to fill your tanks while your genset runs to charge the batteries. You have to run the genset a couple of hours a day anyway, so why not make water while doing so? A twenty-five to fifty GPH unit will give you a lot of water quickly. This is cool and if our budget had permitted I would have upgraded *Jenny's* six GPH 12-volt DC watermaker to one of these. But we did not, and now I am glad of it.

The second school of thought is to have a small 12-volt DC unit that produces between five and twelve GPH. This is what we have and being a powerboat, we run it whenever we are underway and are in clean water. *Jenny's* front tank holds 200 gallons and a 24-hour trip usually tops it off. With occasional stops at marinas we have had plenty of water for just the two of us and have not cracked the aft 100 gallon tank yet.

The problem with option #1 is that the water in most anchorages and all marinas is not sufficiently clean to use your watermaker. Therefore, the idea of filling up your tanks while running the generator at anchor does not really work. This is the first anchorage where I have run *Jenny's* watermaker while charging *Jenny's* batteries and it is at an island miles from shore. You have clean water and plenty of DC power while you are underway and that is when you make water. So, I now think a DC unit is the way to go. If you have two people on board and large water tanks, *Jenny's* little six GPH unit is sufficient. If I had the money, I would upgrade to a twelve GPH unit.

Sail boaters seem to have this pretty well figured out. Since they are low energy consumers and do a lot of motoring underway, they are universally using option 2. They also have orders of magnitude more watermaker hours under their belts.

What vendor do they use? My personal experience says they prefer Village Marine systems. That is what *Jenny* has. Ours must be at least ten years old now and is still working fine, probably with the original membrane.

I would like to be able to stay at anchor for extended periods when we get to a town or small city where we really like it. We cannot really afford to luxuriate in a marina and do not like them as much as a mooring or anchorage. What do you do then for water? Sailboats carry water jugs and transport water to the boat using their dinghies. We consume too much water for this option. Sailboats also catch rainwater. I like this way of thinking. When we get further south where it actually rains, I intend to catch water off the drains on the pilothouse roof and keep *Jenny's* tanks full that way. It is simple, with no energy usage and good water. I will let you know how it turns out.

Finally, if your boat is a twelve volt DC boat then keep as many things twelve volt as possible. Preferably all your must-have appliances are 12 volt. That way, you do not need to run the inverter and you save considerable amp/hours. If your boat runs on twenty-four volt DC, then make all replacements and additions twenty-four volt DC as well. I manually turn on *Jenny's* inverter now when we need the Microwave or hair dryer. Other than that, it is off. If you do not have a generator yet, then consider the new high output solar panels and a small genset or none at all. They are noisy and take up a lot of room. Solar panels now pump out many amps. If you use a sailboat mentality on a powerboat then you have the best of both worlds!

Passage: Isla Isabela to La Cruz

Departed Thursday, January 17, 2008 at 1:16 PM local time from East Anchorage. The departure location was latitude 21 degrees 50.648 minutes north, longitude 105 degrees 52.652 minutes west.

Arrived Thursday, January 17, 2008 at 5:48 PM local time at La Cruz. The arrival location was latitude 20 degrees 44.566 minutes north, longitude 105 degrees 22.670 minutes west. The customs checking was None. The trip covered 81.00 nautical miles in 0d 11h 15m with an average speed of 7.00 knots and a maximum speed of 7.71 knots.

Thursday, January 17, 2008 8:24:23 PM

Location: La Cruz
Latitude is 20 degrees 44.557 minutes north.
Longitude is 105 degrees 22.669 minutes west.

We are now in Banderas Bay the home of La Cruz and Puerto Vallarta and are at the northern edge of the "Mexican Riviera". *Jenny's* has her anchor imbedded in the sea bottom, her birds down and doors open. It is finally warm enough to be outside at night. We saw at least a dozen hump back whales on the way down, mostly just at the entrance to the bay. One pair was only about 100 feet from *Jenny's* starboard side. Other than the whales, there was not much excitement except JD's water temperature gauge going nuts again. I put a new one in just before leaving the States. So, another project is born.

On this trip, timing was everything. The trip was eighty miles and that translates to about the same number of hour's journey as there is daylight. We were up at 05:00 this morning and anchors away at 06:00, after daybreak but before sunrise. I dropped anchor about ten minutes before sunset. Being this far south it is dark out about fifteen minutes after sunset. Whew.

Tomorrow morning we will join the local Net and ask someone to call us after the net and give us the local lowdown. We want to stay at anchor for a while and then go into the marina just before Mary's dad arrives. We will take our garbage in, take on water, wash down *Jenny*, and do laundry. Then off again south to enjoy the Mexican Riviera.

I caught no fish today. I am beginning to suspect that our meat hook lure is unattractive. Hmmm. Our poor Rapala caught a couple of Sierra and is all chewed up with only one eyeball left. It may have lost its charm. I ordered a new one that Jim will be bringing down. We had chicken tonight. Tomorrow we will explore La Cruz.

Friday, January 18, 2008 8:30:18 PM

Location: La Cruz

Well, some days you eat the bear, and some days the bear eats you. Today was one of those days that the bear was burping. We got up and tuned into the local net to learn about the local information. Then we moved *Jenny* to get a spot closer in with less motion. Well, we found a spot in fifteen feet of water right by the beach and dropped her hook. But as we backed *Jenny* down on it, I discovered her anchor was skipping over a rock bottom. We moved a little and tried again. No joy. It was still a rock bottom. We moved back on the outside of the fleet and dropped her hook yet again, in an only slightly better spot.

Then we put the dinghy on *Jenny's* boom and after some struggling got the beast in the water. We went into the marina's basin and parked at the dinghy dock. As with other marina's we have stopped in, this one is new and unfinished, and the office was in a home near town. We hopped on the golf cart and were driven to the office. Luckily the Captain de Puerto's office was also nearby. I made reservations for a slip for the 23rd and Mary's dad flies in the evening of the 24th. All was good. I then checked in with the port captain, a government necessity.

I hate to be taken advantage of, and the marina has decided to charge $10 / day for the right to dock your dinghy. The normal fee we have encountered is about $3 per day. This guy is gouging us yachtsman. In protest, many in the fleet have chosen to land their dinghies on the beach near the marina rather than pay the fee. I dropped Mary off at the panga fishing dock, and attempted to land the dinghy on the beach. The beast is too heavy to land on the beaches here. I have worked out a process to drop a small anchor off its stern on the approach to the beach. When real close to the beach I hop out and drop a bow anchor on the beach. The dinghy is then anchored just off the beach. I dropped the stern anchor and all was well as I approached the beach here. Before I stepped off the dinghy, I tested the depth with the oar and found it only about one foot. I stepped out of the dinghy and fell into water up to my waist. The expression on my face was just like the cartoon. My shorts, wallet, etc were soaked. Apparently my sample was taken on the top of a rock.

After several attempts to anchor the Beast I gave up. Mary was dry and on the beach, but I could not land. I headed back to *Jenny* to get a shower and take care of some projects. Mary explored the beach, but did not find a way into town. What a bust. I later picked Mary up from the Panga docks and our shore adventure ended. Tomorrow I will pay the $10.

On the west coast of Mexico and Central America, almost all landings are on the beach. The sea generally has a tidal range of ten to twelve feet. If you have a light dinghy with a total weight around 120 pounds including motor, then you can drag it up the beach without too much difficulty. Most of these dinghies use DaNard wheels that bolt onto the transom to make this an easy activity. However, a 120-pound dinghy is so light that wind and waves easily have their way with it. There is a good possibly you will be dumped in the surf at some point of landing or getting off a beach. When you get dumped, the motor drowns and may never be right again. If you have a heavy dinghy with a more powerful motor you can muscle your way onto and off the beach with a smaller chance of being flipped over. However, once on the beach, you really have a problem. Dinghies over 200 pounds are too heavy for the wheels. You end up dragging the heavy monster up 100 feet of beach to get it above the tide line. There is no easy answer. We resorted to using rollers under *The Beast*. Even so, we really struggle.

Overall you have a fairly good chance of getting soaked landing on a beach on the west coast of North America. You need to protect your wallet, passport, cell phone, etc. I solved this problem by using a Pelican 1040 Micro Case as a wallet.

Back to the story. After bringing Mary back to *Jenny*, I was tying up *The Beast* and it broke free. It knew I hated it and was going off to find some new unsuspecting fool to care for it. I could not snag the line with the boat hook in time, so I was forced to dive over the side and go swim after it as it tried to scoot off with the wind as fast as it could. I caught it, and fortunately, it still had the key in the switch. *The Beast* was captured and tied up to *Jenny* again. I was soaked again and took another shower.

Lovely Rita just pulled in along side of us. What a surprise! We have heard them on the SSB nets many times and it will be good to tip a few margaritas with them. Just recently, John fell overboard and Debbie saved his life. Debbie was below in their Islander 41 and John was at the helm. He had a fishing line trailing from a rod and reel and got a strike. As he leaned back against the safety lines to grab the reel they gave way and he fell overboard. She came up into the cockpit just a few minutes later to discover John was gone. She had the presence of mind to throw a marker into the water and let the sheets go. She could not see him. She got *Lovely Rita* turned around and back-tracked their course. After about fifteen minutes she saw him and brought *Lovely Rita* alongside. She was a wreck and was still shaking when she got on the evening net to tell the story. We heard it and were also shaken.

These are the same kind of safety wires with pelican clips that *Jenny* had on the stern of her upper deck. Apparently the wire can become loose in the clip without any sign. I am glad I replaced them with stainless steel railings.

We are going to ask John and Debbie over tomorrow for drinks and also expect to see them at Philo's on Sunday to watch the NFL playoffs. As we were talking on the VHF, *Jenny* swung around. I looked out and she snagged her anchor buoy with one of her birds again. We were now anchored on the trip line and *Jenny's* outrigger. The anchor will trip and we will be dragging through the fleet before long. I cannot motor out of it because we will certainly drag her chain across other anchors or debris on the bottom. *Jenny* just will not put up with that trip line and buoy and I just cannot figure out what the issue is. This is a bad situation. *Jenny* is escalating the dispute.

I took *The Beast* out and tried to pull it all up to no avail. I then started JD and swung *Jenny* around to release the pressure on the outrigger. After a struggle, I got it all untangled. Just minutes later *Jenny* again snagged the trip line. This time it was between her hull and rudder and her starboard bird. This will not do. I took *The Beast* out again and removed the buoy. *Jenny* won. I surrendered. It was really no contest. She was gentle with her displeasure at the start, but was clearly escalating the situation. I was defeated. The trip line now lies on the sea floor. I need to figure out a better system.

Tomorrow, I pay our $10 and go to town.

Monday, January 21, 2008 5:48:43 PM

Location: La Cruz
Latitude is 20 degrees 44.656 minutes north.

Longitude is 105 degrees 22.408 minutes west.

Yesterday we went into town and watched the football games at Philo's, the local ex-pat bar. We expected a good turnout and a typical sports bar kind of fun time, but it was DEAD. We left at the end of the first quarter of the Giants / Packers game. This morning we heard it was an awesome game. RATS! Then we went down to Anna Bananas in the evening, and watched the old ex-pat farts rocking out to an over-the-hill ex-pat rock band. It was just like out of some surreal movie where all youth had aged overnight. I was waiting for someone to have a heart attack. Band or crowd, who was going to fall first? When the first band folded and they brought on the next one and we left. No one needed a defibrillator at that point.

Today was pretty good. In the early morning you could hear the whales singing to each other through *Jenny's* hull. As we rose, we could see them, humpbacks, surfacing and diving off *Jenny's* bow. We talked on the radio, had breakfast, watched the whales and then did some chores. I took Mary to shore in *The Beast*, and put down another coat of varnish on *Jenny's* window frames. It is not perfect, but it probably never will be. I declared that section of refinishing done. Then I worked on some other items that needed attention; little stuff. This afternoon we watched a school dolphin swim by.

I have a problem sending email through our internet mail servers, so no photos for now. As soon as I get that fixed, I will fire some off. I am checking out some new SSB nets now, the ones that extend down into Central America. I listened to the Pan Pacific Net that sounds like a good replacement to the Amigo Net and the Marine Mobile Service Net, a Ham net run from land based folks in the USA. I checked into that one, first time on a Ham net, and connected to a controller in Mobile Alabama. Cool.

The ever-present bubbling fish are under *Jenny* again. This time some smart-ass pelican figured out that he could sit on *Jenny's* bow and just drop in on them at will. Unfortunately he was pooping every time he launched an attack. I had to rig up some anti-bird lines to finally cure the problem.

It is almost 6:00 PM now, we still have *Jenny* open and we are in bare feet. Oh yea, we are definitely getting closer to heaven. Chicken on the Webber this evening and a movie on the big screen[1]. Hmmm... Does it get any better?

Sunday, January 27, 2008 4:34:49 PM

Location: La Cruz

---

[1] The "big screen" is a 40 inch flat screen TV that we store when not in use.

The last two days have been difficult. During the days I have been taking care of the usual list of small projects. I solved the internet email problem. As soon as we left the Baja Peninsula I could not send email. I could receive it, but not send it. I suspected there was some kind of international firewall stopping the traffic. I called my service provider for our email post office servers and asked if they had another port I could use. Normally email traffic operates on port 25. Most servers run a second port though. I found out that our server also ran on port 2525. I changed our Microsoft Outlook settings and we were back in business. The firewall was apparently only blocking port 25.

I took the starboard ladder rail off the top deck yesterday and gave it to Paul and Anne, a young couple from the Netherlands on *Free Spirit*. They are on a three year hiatus to circumnavigate. It is always refreshing to see young people breaking free and doing this. They allocated one month to fly to San Francisco, find, buy, and prepare a boat. San Francisco is a good place to find a seaworthy vessel at a reasonable cost. No vessel survives there long without being seaworthy even if she never leaves the bay. And, the Bay makes an excellent sea trial area. They found a wooden double ender, strong as a mule but needing some TLC as all vessels constantly do. They took two months to prepare her and continued to work on her on their way down to La Cruz. *Free Spirit* only has an icebox and a small gasoline motor. She is very basic but adequate and safe. They are in the process of painting the topsides and making her look pretty. This is important to a lady.

Removing the ladder railing cleared out the space on *Jenny*'s top deck by the hatch and removed a hazard on deck. Today I mixed up some gel coat repair plastic and filled in the holes and some other gel coat oowies. A little sanding and they will be invisible.

There is a first class marine store in Puerto Vallarta and I was able to buy the marine varnish I needed to continue my refinishing work. That was a nice find. I talked to a crew at a downtown marina and they said it was convenient but very busy day and night with the cruise ship and panga traffic. They moved out here to the La Cruz marina. This marina is new and very incomplete. One thing to be careful of if you are coming here is the shore power voltage. This place has voltage consistently in the 136 VAC range. *Sans Souci* burned out an AC motor in two days. My Zantrex inverter / charger has a feature that cuts off the shore power when it is more than 10% over or under. As a result, I have not used much shore power and I have had to run the generator to charge *Jenny's* batteries.

I am also tracking down a loose connection on the diesel furnace that keeps it from firing up. First, I had to hot wire the thermostat since it only went to 82 degrees and with the temperature now in the high eighties it would not trip. We could not make hot water. The control unit on the furnace looks like it survived WWII. It was mounted on the burner and was subject to a lot of vibration. That vibration cracked the solder joints on the circuit board. I have been mending these cracks repeatedly and eventually I get it back in running order. Someday I will get a new control unit and give up this line of insanity.

I just designed and contracted to have an awning made for *Jenny's* bow but more on that in a separate narrative.

Friday night we went to town with a party of nine to enjoy dinner and a couple from Europe playing guitars and singing Mexican and European songs. The boats *Lovely Rita*, *Toucan Play*, *Jenny*, and *Wandering Star* were represented. John and Debbie on *Lovely Rita's* were celebrating their 29th anniversary and had a lot to celebrate. It was a good time. *Lovely Rita* headed south yesterday and last night we had *Wandering Star*, *Wandern Star*, and *Toucan Play* over for margaritas and snacks. It was another good time. Mary's Dad is beginning to like it here! Little did I know at the time, but he was working on two of my bottles of twenty-year-old Scotch. Nicholas is enjoying the parties.

The weather here is warm and nice when there is a breeze, which there usually is. Life is good.

A 2009 update from Paul and Anne: "We sailed *Free Spirit* to New Zealand through the Marquesas, Tuamotous, Societies, Cooks, Niue and Tonga. Then we sold her there last March 2008. After that we flew home to the Netherlands via Borneo, where we had our last little break as a couple because last night, August 8, 2009 our beautiful daughter Lali was born!"

Sunday, January 27, 2008 4:50:59 PM

Location: La Cruz

For a while, I have been thinking about one idea I picked up from *Wind Horse* and another from a Blue Water Sailing article. *Wind Horse* has awnings over her decks that allow keeping their hatches open when it rains. The last thing you want to do when you are in the tropics is close up when the rain comes. The BWS article was a discussion about what size watermaker to have on board, written by an Australian sailor. The article recommended a minimum watermaker as long as you could catch water. I liked both but had not put 2 + 2 together until we got here.

Originally I was going to catch water off the pilothouse roof and had not really much about an awning for the foredeck. Then, the light bulb went on. If I ran a ridgeline from the front pennant holder to the front of the pilothouse top, I could have an awning that worked as a tent over the foredeck providing shade. The tent could be attached back along the foredeck railing to the Portuguese Bridge and then up along the pilothouse roof with snaps. The front of the pilothouse would also be in the shade. Wind could come under the railing providing cooling air and I could leave the hatches open in the rain. The coup de grâce is that the port side of the tent could be set up to catch water. Yummy.

I called on the net for canvas maker recommendations and hooked up with Full Sail Canvas who came out Saturday to discuss the design and take measurements. I liked their design and signed up. They agreed to deliver by next Saturday and the price was $1,300 US, which I thought, was very good for the size of the awning and the features. They are coming back on Tuesday to do the fitting while we are still at the dock. We are going back out on the hook on Wednesday, so I will pick them up with the dinghy for the delivery and final fitting.

Jenny with her new awning

Passage: La Cruz to Ipala

Departed Monday, February 04, 2008 at 2:34 PM local time from La Cruz anchorage. The departure location was latitude 20 degrees 44.550 minutes north, longitude 105 degrees 22.672 minutes west.

Arrived Monday, February 04, 2008 at 4:09 PM local time at Anchorage in Ipala. The arrival location was latitude 20 degrees 14.112 minutes north, longitude 105 degrees 34.371 minutes west. The customs checking was none. The trip covered 45.40 nautical miles in 0d 7h 33m with an average speed of 6.00 knots and a maximum speed of 7.10 knots.

Passage: Ypala to Chamela

Departed Tuesday, February 05, 2008 at 1:48 PM local time from Ypala anchorage. The departure location was latitude 20 degrees 13.566 minutes north, longitude 105 degrees 34.334 minutes west.

Tuesday, February 05, 2008 11:00:13 AM
Location: At Sea
Latitude is 19 degrees 58.238 minutes north.
Longitude is 105 degrees 32.751 minutes west.

This weather observation was taken on Tuesday, February 05, 2008 10:28:11 AM local time.
Observation location: At sea.
Latitude is 19 degrees 58.452 minutes north.
Longitude is 105 degrees 32.898 minutes west.
The air temperature is 75, and water temperature is 70 degrees Fahrenheit.
The forecast is Fair.
The current weather is dry.
The sky is broken clouds (60 - 90% clouds).
The wind is 5 knots from the southeast.
The visibility is 10 nautical miles.
The wave height is 2 feet with 3 foot swells.
The barometer is 1015 millibar and rising.

We stayed in La Cruz to watch the super bowl and glad we did. Mary and James, Mary's dad, are NY Giants fans and the last five minutes were spectacular. Unfortunately, it was too late to set up a Skype call to Mary's brothers to rub it in. Mark in New Hampshire is a BIG Patriots fan. Maybe we will pick up a Wi-Fi connection in Chamela, our next stop.

We are now on Central time, but failed to set the alarm clock forward, so we got started from La Cruz to Ipala an hour late. No problem though, it was only a forty mile trip and we had plenty of time. This was the first passage James made with us and it was nice because we saw several turtles, a couple of whales, and caught a thirty-five pound Jack on the meat hook.

Ipala used to be a nice snug little cove that you could duck into after rounding Cabo Corrientes, the last point we will be rounding for quite a while. However, fishermen have set up some kind of aquatic farming that now takes up most of the cove with lines, holding nets and buoys effectively closing the cove down. Some folks on shore made a business from the visiting yachts with a restaurant, and other amenities.

Jenny anchored in Ipala overnight, outside of most of the cove's protection and too close to the rocks for her comfort or mine. However, there was a Mexican Navy PT boat anchored behind her and she liked that. As she set her hook in the seabed, she snuggled her stern up to its bow. The slut! The PT boat was raising its anchor to get underway and inched even closer, perhaps to get a good sniff.

It was very nice about it. *Jenny* was getting excited. I motioned to the Navy crew I could move *Jenny* forward, and they waived it off indicating there would be no need. They were right and their hook came up about 100 feet behind us. These boats are former US Navy PT boats, still bearing the same numbers they did in the USN. We guess they are Vietnam era boats. They still are very well armed and fast. *Jenny* was sad to see it go. I have to keep an eye on her!

Last night I set an anchor watch on *Jenny's* GPS, a set of guard rings, the Watchman function on her small radar, and a depth alarm on her depth gauge. I was hoping all these alarms would give me some piece of mind through the night. Even so, I was up several times. It is funny how I sense when the smallest thing change on *Jenny*. Maybe its wind direction or speed, wave action, a different sound, anything that changes gets me up. Now our nervous systems are so intertwined that I immediately sense any change.

Mary and Jim did not get much sleep either because of the rocking, even with *Jenny's* birds down. As the sun came up, we were within forty feet of where we were the evening before and all was well. I really do not like anchoring near rock cliffs. This should be the last roadstead we have to anchor in.

Ever since we left San Francisco I have been concerned about JD's coolant temperature. It is supposed to run in the 180-190 degree Fahrenheit range and *Jenny's* gauge has been reading 190 - 200, and going over 200 when JD goes over 1500 RPM. I strapped a temperature sensor from my volt/ohm meter to JD's oil filter and a thermometer near JD's temperature sending unit. Today, both of these are reading in the 170's. This is driving me absolutely nuts! *Jenny* has yet another secret and she is holding onto it dearly. I already replaced her gauge, so will order a new sensor for JD and ask Laura to bring it when she comes down.

Nicholas just came up and is giving me kisses. He is sitting behind me on the pilothouse berth with Mary and has his front paws on my shoulder... and now his head resting on my shoulder. He is pure love and a gift from God.

In La Cruz I discovered a coupling in *Jenny's* exhaust system had come loose and consequently a chunk of gasket had broken away some time ago. This problem was all wrapped in a heat and sound blanket so was not readily apparent until I discovered heavy soot on the faux stack grill. Our good friends Larry and Sue on *Beverly S* are tracking down some new gasket material. In the meantime, I filled the gasket gap with high temperature gasket RTV, tightened up the coupling bolts and that seems to have stopped the leak. There is always another project.

Jenny is now on her way to Chamela, her first real stop on the Mexican Riviera. We are seeing some cumulus clouds for the first time in ages indicating we are slowly escaping from the desert and entering an area with some humidity. Maybe we will get some rain! We are in the company of two sailboats that were also at Ipala.

Life is good.

Arrived Tuesday, February 05, 2008 at 4:13 PM local time at . The arrival location was latitude 19 degrees 35.066 minutes north, longitude 105 degrees 7.794 minutes west. The trip covered 54.20 nautical miles in 0d 8h 36m with an average speed of 6.30 knots and a maximum speed of 6.55 knots.

Wednesday, February 06, 2008 3:38:13 PM

Location: Chamela, Mx
Latitude is 19 degrees 35.086 minutes north.
Longitude is 105 degrees 7.798 minutes west.

Man is it nice here. It is like a scene out of a movie with pangas, palapas, families playing on the beach, sailboats and motorboats anchored in the bay. We took *The Beast* in for a walk on the beach and lunch. All is very casual. The restaurants are placed right on the sand beach with either big tent tops (Corona logo, etc.) or thatched roofs, plastic chairs and tables. Mexican music is playing, but not obnoxiously loud. We are beginning to like it!

The Beast is too heavy to beach, and my anchoring scheme is not working. I will have to find another solution. I am thinking a two-person kayak for going to a beach might be the answer.

I donned my shorty wet suit and dive gear to brush down *Jenny's* bottom and remove things growing from the through hulls. Everything was good except for the propeller and the propeller zinc. The zinc dropped off somewhere along the line. I think I need a big washer to keep it on. The propeller was growing barnacles and all sorts of stuff that is very bad for *Jenny's* cruising speed and efficiency. I spent some time scraping and polishing the blades today with more to do tomorrow. This is where a hookah would be nice. Oh well, no place to put one anyway.

There is no Wi-Fi here so photos will be later when our regular email is up. We are also interested in the US presidential primary race results if anyone has them!

Passage: Ipala to Tenacatita

Departed Friday, February 08, 2008 at 1:57 PM local time from Ipala at anchor. The departure location was latitude 19 degrees 33.787 minutes north, longitude 105 degrees 7.524 minutes west.

Arrived Friday, February 08, 2008 at 12:50 PM local time at Tenacatita Anchorage. The arrival location was latitude 19 degrees 18.112 minutes north, longitude 104 degrees 50.098 minutes west. The customs checking was none. The trip covered 27.53 nautical miles in 0d 4h 24m with an average speed of 6.24 knots and a maximum speed of 7.26 knots.

Friday, February 08, 2008 9:40:05 PM

Location: Tenacatita, Mx
Latitude is 19 degrees 18.116 minutes north.
Longitude is 104 degrees 50.099 minutes west.

It was a picture perfect ride down to Tenacatita today, and only twenty-eight miles. The water turned deep indigo blue again and we saw a whale jump completely out of the water twice and another breach. We are also surprised by the number of turtles we see on the surface. We must have spotted ten of them today. There are flying fish in the bay here which are really festinating to see fly. They are tiny and their fins (wings?) go just about as fast as humming birds.

Tenacatita is a lovely bay with nice beaches and a big resort on the north shore where *Jenny* anchored along with about thirty-five other boats. I am listening to a live band in the resort play 'YMCA'. Earlier this afternoon, the weekly Mayor's raft up took place with twenty-eight dinghies. We passed around hors d'oeuvres and each told about their boat, journey, plans, and hobbies. We met a few crews we knew from other stops, and a bunch of new ones.

Cleaning *Jenny's* bottom, prop blades and intercooler made her happy, with a noticeable drop in the reported coolant temperature and better speed. While here I will dive on her bottom again and check out the prop zinc to make sure it is still there and tight. The last one fell off somewhere between Frailes and Chamela. I will also polish up her propeller blades, clean her intercoolers a bit more and do a couple of other projects. The Beach Boys song Surfing USA is now playing at the resort.

There is a large tidal stream that empties close by and is said to be a nice dinghy ride to a dock at the source. The mouth is filled with rocks, so it is tricky going in. I think we will wait until there are some more boats going in and then follow them. There are supposed to be some small saltwater crocs in there too. And, there is a group dinner at the palapa restaurant at the mouth tomorrow night that We will join.

Jim is still with us and I think he is getting to like Mexico and cruising. It is real hard to get used to this! Unfortunately he flies out on the 19th and we are already teasing him about the snow and cold he'll likely go back to in Saranac Lake, NY. UGH. Well, that's it for tonight.

Passage: Tenacatita to Barra de Navidad

Departed Tuesday, February 12, 2008 at 3:55 PM local time from Tenacatita at anchor. The departure location was latitude 19 degrees 11.913 minutes north, longitude 104 degrees 48.563 minutes west.

Arrived Tuesday, February 12, 2008 at 11:44 AM local time at Bara Lagoon. The arrival location was latitude 19 degrees 11.597 minutes north, longitude 104 degrees 40.815 minutes west. The trip covered fifteen.00 nautical miles in 0d 2h 45m with an average speed of 7.00 knots and a maximum speed of 7.80 knots.

Saturday, February 16, 2008 12:33:41 PM

Location: Barra de Navidad Lagoon
Latitude is 19 degrees 11.362 minutes north.
Longitude is 104 degrees 40.45 minutes west.

You know you are going to have a good day when the French Baker comes on the radio in the morning announcing his deliveries. The cruiser community here bows to his slightest needs. He has priority on the VHF network as he makes his rounds. Baguettes, croissants, pastries, pies... Mmmmm... Yummy!

Barra is a very nice place. The lagoon reflects this with about fifty boats packed in. This lagoon has a very narrow entry with mud flats around the major part of the lagoon and no markers. Yesterday I saw one big sailboat become stuck in the shallows that line the channel. Within minutes, dinghies and a big outboard motorboat surrounded it. They pulled her free. Then she anchored too close to another sailboat, but the other owner did not complain. I am just waiting for the two vessels to collide as the wind shifts around. In the evening a sailboat came in with no motor. As they came down the channel and got closer to the fleet, I could see her sails were all tangled up in her rigging. A couple of dinghies had already lashed to her sides providing power. As they got to the lagoon, another swarm of buzzing dinghies with little four horsepower motors surrounded it and herded it to a spot. Then they swarmed again to move it to another spot that had a little more space. The waterline of that sailboat revealed a buildup of algae, so maintenance does not seem to be a high priority for the caregivers.

The town is a nice size and very cruiser friendly. Pangas pickup and deliver laundry, Marie's Tienda goes to Costco once a week and takes orders, and restaurants are plentiful. Marie's even had a gallon of real maple syrup! The down side of the Barra Lagoon is that the water is fetid. Some mornings it frothed as it exploded with a bacteria bloom. Nasty stuff! I hope it killed all the growth on *Jenny's* bottom!!!

We had John and Gay from *Mainstay* over last evening. They just arrived from Ecuador and gave us a ton of great information about routes and stops in Central

America. El Salvador through Panama sounds very nice and I have started plotting our routes.

Jim will be going home on Monday back to Saranac Lake, to the cold and the snow. I think he has really enjoyed being on board. I gave Nicholas a bath yesterday. He builds up salt in his hair and starts to feel sticky. Now he is a good smelling happy dog again.

Mary is unhappy. The problem does not appear to be her fear of the sea since all our passages lately have been really calm and delightful. She just shows no enthusiasm for cruising life and feels she is not making a contribution to humanity here. Her career has been helping people who need social services, particularly respite care centers for Alzheimer's patients. She also has a band of sisters back in Orlando that she really misses. She wants to fly out of Acapulco.

Passage: Barra to Manzanillo

Departed Wednesday, February 20, 2008 at 2:32 PM local time from Barra Lagoon. The departure location was latitude 19 degrees 10.960 minutes north, longitude 104 degrees 43.177 minutes west.

Arrived Wednesday, February 20, 2008 at 12:47 PM local time at Las Hadas Anchorage. The arrival location was latitude 19 degrees 6.066 minutes north, longitude 104 degrees 20.702 minutes west. The customs check in was none. The trip covered 28.80 nautical miles in 0d 4h 47m with an average speed of 6.20 knots and a maximum speed of 6.90 knots.

Wednesday, February 20, 2008 2:25:14 PM

Location: Las Hadas Anchorage
Latitude is 19 degrees 6.067 minutes north.
Longitude is 104 degrees 20.703 minutes west.

Well this is nice. We are in the bay that includes Manzanillo. Las Hadas is where the movie '10' was filmed and it is gorgeous.

Jenny was glad to get out of the Barra toxic waste Lagoon. At daybreak I took her over to the fuel dock before they got busy with real customers. *Jenny* pounded down about 150 gallons of water.

The Barra Lagoon was most interesting because of the rescues that unfold each day. We had at least one grounding every day. Last evening was most exciting as a sailboat cut adrift in the wind and started charging through the lagoon on its own. She wanted out. Needless to say, the downwind vessels got excited pretty quickly. The alarm went out and instantly a swarm of buzzing dinghies converged on the wayward vessel. Before she crashed into another vessel, the dinghy brigade brought her under control. It is semi-pro and has lots of practice and very quick response times. Truly impressive.

There were other creatures there as well. One morning I woke up to hear great commotion emanating from the cockpit of a neighboring sailboat. There stood a woman beating the cushions in the cockpit with her dinghy paddle. How strange! Well it turned out she was cleaning up the cockpit from last night's party when she turned over a cushion and discovered a snake. Her husband quickly appeared from below to save the woman and the snake. He succeeded in getting the snake over the side safely twice. But each time, it climbed back up the self-steering gear and came back in. The third time the snaked entered the lagoon slightly damaged and swam off.

Then there is a story I heard second hand. The vessel was on its way from Barra to Manzanillo, the passage we just completed when her electronics started going crazy one by one. The crew could not figure out what was going on. Finally, her electronics were completely disabled and the guy had no choice but to start taking the electronics out of the console to see if he could discover what was happening. He peered into the dark opening and at first could not figure out what he was looking at. How did that strange looking wooden dowel get in there? He was pondering that riddle when he decided to reach in and pull it out. He touched it. It moved. He flew through the air about three feet as though he had just connected with a 220-volt circuit, screeching as he flew, and landing in a pile of sails. His wife thought he was dead.

After recovering, getting a flashlight and the biggest kitchen knife they had, he approached the electronics console again. After a more considered inspection, he was sure he was staring at a tail. He then moved to the other end of the console and removed the VHF radio. With some trepidation, he took the flashlight and approached the new opening. This time he discovered two beady eyes and a flicking forked tongue assessing him. He recognized it as the head of a very large iguana. Somehow, it had climbed aboard in Barra and decided the electronics console was a nice warm dry spot to spend some time. It took three hours to drag it out of the electronics console and set it free. It took another two weeks to get all the wiring reconnected!

Jenny's walk down here was a milk run of thirty miles. She had flat seas, and we saw several turtles floating by. The turtles are about eighteen inches wide and about two feet long. Mexico has had an active program to bring them back and is succeeding fabulously. I only plan to spend a few days here to get some stuff and then head down to Zihuatanejo. I wish Mary had chosen to bring her father here to spend a few days rather than Barra. Barra was nice, but this is very nice. You'll see.

Passage: Las Hadas to Santiago Bay

Departed Saturday, February 23, 2008 at 2:29 PM local time from Las Hadas Anchorage. The departure location was latitude 19 degrees 5.192 minutes north, longitude 104 degrees 21.222 minutes west.

Arrived Saturday, February 23, 2008 at 9:05 AM local time at Santiago Bay, Manzanillo. The arrival location was latitude 19 degrees 6.411 minutes north, longitude 104 degrees 23.548 minutes west. The trip covered 4.30 nautical miles in 0d 50h 35m with an average speed of 4.22 knots and a maximum speed of 6.80 knots.

Passage: From Santiago Bay to Zihuatanejo

Departed Monday, February 25, 2008 at 1:40 PM local time from Santiago Bay, Manzanillo. The departure location was latitude 19 degrees 6.606 minutes north, longitude 104 degrees 23.574 minutes west.

Monday, February 25, 2008 4:00:52 PM

Location: At Sea
Latitude is 18 degrees 25.971 minutes north.
Longitude is 103 degrees 46.544 minutes west.

This weather observation was taken on Monday, February 25, 2008 3:21:12 PM local time.
Observation location: At Sea.
Latitude is 18 degrees 26.155 minutes north.
Longitude is 103 degrees 46.727 minutes west.
The air temperature is 87, and water temperature is 70 degrees Fahrenheit.
The forecast is Sunny, calm.
The current weather is dry.
The sky is clear or a few clouds.
The wind is 5 knots from the south.
The visibility is 10 nautical miles.
The wave height is 1 feet with 3 foot swells.
The barometer is 1011 millibar and steady.

Jenny is in her element, at sea and heading southeast for Zihuatanejo. The ocean is gently lifting her and setting her down as if she is resting on the chest of a giant living creature. And, she is. The earth ocean is a living organism as truly as we are. Just as we are symbiotic hosts to millions of bacteria, yeasts, viruses, enzymes that keep us alive, the ocean is host to millions of creatures that keep her alive. Her health is a direct reflection of the health of the creatures that inhabit her. We need to be more careful how we treat these, our brother and sister creatures that all life depends on.

It has been this way all day and I hope all night too. *Jenny* is making excellent time at 7.5 knots with the JD beating 1400 RPM. We saw a couple of whales and several turtles and even though we have become accustom to this, it still gives us a thrill.

It is a shame we could not spend more time in Las Hadas. It was a very nice spot with plenty of amenities and easy access to the shore through the dinghy dock at the marina. We only spent two days there and walked to the Mega store, which is similar to one of the Wal-Mart Super Center's that includes a big grocery store, twice for provisions. Mary wanted to go around the small peninsula to the Santiago anchorage to visit friends, so we did not even go to a restaurant here. I did dive on *Jenny* to clean her prop and the keel cooler though. Brrrr. The water was colder than Tenacatita, about 68 degrees. The propeller was fairly clean this time and there were still some plants growing on the keel cooler and I had to brush them off with our stainless steel wire brush. I now believe that the cooler is the limiting factor on the engine temperature. When it is clean, the thermostats bring her up to 190 degrees and she says there. When they get covered with growth, the temperature edges up toward 200 degrees. The plan is to always keep them clean.

The Santiago anchorage is somewhat exposed to waves and wake from the large ships that go into and out of Manzanillo at the southeast end of the bay. Access to shore is by beach landing and we bummed rides in to go for walks, lunch, Bocce Ball and other fun activities organized by the cruisers. We played Pegs and Jokers onboard *Lovely Rita* with the couple from *Masquerade* and had a good time. The guys beat the gals, but I think the gals were much further smashed than the guys. One thing about cruisers so far is they are heavy drinkers. In the work-a-day world, one would go out and socialize maybe once a week or less. In this world, it is nearly every night. Consequently, you start drinking more and more unless you really watch yourself. I have backed off and now am a Coke drinker unless it is the weekend.

It also surprises me how many people have serious medical problems. Cancer here, a back problem there, heart bypass surgery... Some are disabled from one incident or another and drawing on Social Security. Go as soon as you can while you have your health. The years go by too fast.

It surprises me how many vessels are tethered to California. They go as far as Santiago Bay in the winter and then head back north. Some go back to California, most go up into the Sea of Cortez year after year. Some venture up to the Pacific Northwest and maybe even Alaska now and again. However, very few go beyond Manzanillo Bay even though they say they will be someday. We find ourselves among maybe five boats now in various places working further south toward Huatulco, the jump off point for leaving Mexico and going to El Salvador. When we left Santiago, we were leaving quite a few friends that we have met and enjoyed over the past few months.

Nicholas is thoroughly boat-dog now, not even getting the slightest bit worked up about a passage. He snoozes at my side and Mary is up in the Pilot Berth reading another Daniel Steel book.

We are picking up crew at Acapulco for the trip down to Huatulco and across to El Salvador. He is a former Nordhavn owner. He owned the 47 dropped from a travel lift and had the bottom crushed. He should be an excellent crewmember and we have set a date around March 12th to pick him up.

I have ordered a bunch of marine stuff to replace worn rigging, etc. on *Jenny*. One thing I did not really bring up to top condition before we left was her stabilizer and dinghy lift rigging. Lines, blocks, etc. have been shipped to my daughter Laura for her to collect and box for shipment to us. I was going to pick them up in Zihuatanejo, but heard that all DHL, etc. shipments go through Guadalajara customs and are exposed to theft and serious duties even though replacement parts should be duty free. I have decided to wait until we get to Barillas in El Salvador. El Salvador is US Dollar based and duty free.

The Beast, weighing in at over 300 lbs. is good for going ashore when there is a dock. However, more often now we beach land through small surf. In these situations it is too heavy to get up onto the beach and leave. Since beach landings will be an important part of our journey going forward, I have to solve this problem somehow. After surfing the internet, I have not found a great solution yet. Occasionally someone wants to sell their small dinghy and if we run across a deal, I will probably solve our problem that way. It is a shame that a boat builder has not specialized a boat for this use.

Arrived Tuesday, February 26, 2008 at 11:54 AM local time at Zihuatanejo Anchorage. The arrival location was latitude 17 degrees 40.851 minutes north, longitude 101 degrees 54.860 minutes west. The customs check in was none. The trip covered 196.00 nautical miles in 1d 3h 43m with an average speed of 7.00 knots and a maximum speed of 9.00 knots.

Saturday, March 01, 2008 6:26:03 PM

Location: Zihuatanejo
Latitude is 17 degrees 38.085 minutes north.
Longitude is 101 degrees 33.352 minutes west.

Zihuatanejo has been a disappointment. It is a nice enough place, but it is very busy and uncomfortable. The panga fishing fleet goes out at sunrise and sunset. The panga ferries go all day between the north shore and the south shore. Today a big Carnival cruise ship came in and their beef barges have been ferrying North American heifers back and forth all day. All this causes a ton of noise and chop. Add to this the large swells that pipeline in from the ocean, and the anchorage is anything but peaceful.

Because cruise ships stop here, the town is bars, restaurants and trinket shops. I am beginning to see why people like La Paz. So far it is the only Mexican town of any size that has not been completely spoiled by tourists. Every other town of any size is hell bent on becoming the next grand tourist stop or time-share resort. It is all very disappointing. Las Hadas is nice because it is mature and too small for the cruise boats. With nearby Santiago Bay, it seems to have it all. One could stay there all winter in comfort and many do.

I am hoping that El Salvador is less well developed from a tourist grazing ground point of view. It looks like it. I am afraid Costa Rica might be a lot like Mexico. However, there might be treasure in the Pacific islands of Panama. These islands look unspoiled and utterly gorgeous. We may in fact spend quite a bit of time down there before going through the canal. Many folks also go to Ecuador to escape the heat and rain.

I am beginning to become concerned about how developed and expensive the Caribbean is. I would really like to visit Cuba, and that may become possible again in another couple of years. In the meantime, Surinam, French Guiana might prove interesting. Then we might accelerate our trip up the Windward Islands and head for the northeast US and Canada. I am wondering and hoping that northeast Canada is like the Pacific Northwest. We will see.

On the projects front, the keyboard on this PC died two days ago. Fortunately, I can swap in the one from the navigation computer and am using that now. I had not thought of this before, but the keyboard is one of the weak spots on laptops. A singular benefit of the tablet PC we have is that the keyboard is a detachable module, and therefore replaceable without any problem other than the $300 it cost.

On the dinghy front, I am making progress in two areas. First, I bought two pieces of six-inch PVC pipe thirty inches long to use as rollers under *The Beast*. We put them down on the hard wet sand and it rolls on them with various degrees of effort but better than just dragging its belly through the sand. Next, after a whole day of searching, I found and bought an eight-foot pole to keep in the dinghy. It serves two purposes. First, I use it to pole off the beach when we leave. It is much more effective than trying to paddle. Second, I have rigged two lines to the lift eyes on *The Beast's* transom. When we get to the beach, we put down the rollers and put the pole through the two lift lines. Then we use the pole to lift and push *The Beast* up on the rollers. This lets us put its weight on our shoulders like a pair of draft steers rather than bending over and pulling on its handles. So far, this system is allowing us to land *The Beast* the beaches.

Second, I was chatting with another cruiser about his dinghy. If I had to buy a new dinghy, I would now get what he has: an aluminum bottom RIB. Aqua Pro makes them in New Zeeland and the ultra light nine-footer weighs only thirty kilograms. The ten-foot one weighs only 38 kilograms. This is the ticket for sure. They are very nicely made, have oarlocks and will plane with a small motor. When the time comes to bury *The Beast*, that is what we will get and will put DaNard wheels on the back. Maybe I will just leave it in the sun for the vultures to pick over.

Passage: Zihuatanejo to Papona

Departed Tuesday, March 04, 2008 at 1:53 PM local time from Zihuatanejo Bay. The departure location was latitude 17 degrees 37.431 minutes north, longitude 101 degrees 33.611 minutes west.

Arrived Tuesday, March 04, 2008 at 2:10 PM local time at Papanoa. The arrival location was latitude 17 degrees 16.590 minutes north, longitude 101 degrees 3.528 minutes west. The trip covered 38.82 nautical miles in 0d 6h 25m with an average speed of 6.00 knots and a maximum speed of 7.00 knots.

Passage: Papanoa to Acapulco

Departed Wednesday, March 05, 2008 at 1:20 PM local time from Papanoa Anchorage. The departure location was latitude 17 degrees 16.652 minutes north, longitude 101 degrees 4.710 minutes west.

Wednesday, March 05, 2008 9:33:49 AM
Location: At sea
Latitude is 17 degrees 10.556 minutes north.
Longitude is 100 degrees 56.618 minutes west.

This weather observation was taken on Wednesday, March 05, 2008 9:08:36 AM local time.
Observation location: At sea.
Latitude is 17 degrees 10.625 minutes north.
Longitude is 100 degrees 56.754 minutes west.
The air temperature is 70, and water temperature is 70 degrees Fahrenheit.
The forecast is Sunny.
The current weather is dry.
The sky is clear or a few clouds.
The wind is 1 knot from the east.
The visibility is 10 nautical miles.
The wave height is 2 feet with 5 foot swells.
The barometer is 1013 millibar and steady.

Jenny's trip down to Papanoa was another milk run. She has not had her birds in the water for quite a while. The Mexican Rivera is truly the peaceful part of the Pacific. Papanoa is a small isolated fishing village along the coast where the government built a breakwater to help protect the fishing fleet from hurricanes and storms. When we arrived, a thirty-foot Navy panga carrying about ten army kids greeted us. It pulled up to *Jenny's* stern, and we chatted a bit about where we had been and where we were going. They accommodated our limited Spanish and after a few minutes they went on their way without boarding. Mary was concerned about all their guns, but they were the good guys and quite nice.

The anchorage last night was quite peaceful after all the rolling *Jenny* did in Zihuatanejo. My only concern here was about the seabed. It did not embrace anchors well. The construction crew created this outer basin by blasting out the rocky cliffs above it. They used the boulders to make the seawall and the seabed seems to be solid rock. It took two tries to get the anchor to hook onto something. It was sliding across rock when it did. I said a prayer about being able to raise it and wished *Jenny* had not forced me to remove the trip line and buoy.

The other problem is you cannot trust the anchor to hold when it sets like this if the direction of pull changes. I was up all night listening to *Jenny's* anchor chain drag across the rock seabed, watching her depth and heading. While the wind was very light, and the water was calm, *Jenny* still moved around and pointed in all directions. Morning proved we never were in any danger, but you have to keep a watch anyway.

The alarm went off at 06:30 AM and *Jenny* was underway by 07:00. She is at sea now steaming along with virtually no wind with just a few lumps in the water. Mary and I are very spoiled now and I am wondering how we will adjust once we get back into real ocean conditions. We also are having our usual humpback whale and floating turtle sightings. We must have seen fifty turtles floating by yesterday. I do not know what they are doing on the surface like that. Maybe they are sleeping. Some pass within a few feet of *Jenny* and we can see them quite clearly.

We are losing contact with our HF nets lately. Maybe it is the location of the Net controllers or maybe it is that we have been moving so far east. I can hear some vessels checking in from way up in the Sea of Cortez, and some from way down in Costa Rica, but not the net controllers who are probably only a couple of hundred miles from us. Maybe this will clear up when we get the right distance from them and have a better skip.

We are going to get into Acapulco tonight, probably after dark. That will be interesting since it is a very busy port and we have never been there. We will anchor out tonight and then I hope pick up a mooring ball at one of the marina's tomorrow morning. With that will come privileges to use the dinghy dock, Wi-Fi, etc. There are no slips available, and the price for a slip is too high anyway. We will provision again in Acapulco and pick up Donald Perrine, the other

Nordhavn owner who will be joining us as crew for our passages to Huatulco and then on to El Salvador. That is right, only two more passages and we will be in El Salvador. The first is an overnight to Huatulco, where we will stay in a marina and wait for the right weather for crossing the Tehuantepec, and the second is a four or five night passage to the Barillas marina in El Salvador. This is getting exciting.

Arrived Wednesday, March 05, 2008 at 7:08 PM local time at Acapulco Anchorage. The arrival location was latitude 16 degrees 50.590 minutes north, longitude 99 degrees 54.316 minutes west. The trip covered 78.58 nautical miles in 0d 11h 55m with an average speed of 6.60 knots and a maximum speed of 8.00 knots.

Thursday, March 06, 2008 5:44:53 PM

Location: Acapulco, Mexico
Latitude is 16 degrees 50.471 minutes north.
Longitude is 99 degrees 54.301 minutes west.

Yup! We are less than 100 degrees west! Wow! And, just as we were approaching Acapulco, we had quite a thrill. We caught up with a herd of maybe 200 pilot whales. They were black on top with grey bellies, about ten or twelve feet long. This is big for a porpoise, small for a whale and they had blunt faces with no nose. Since our internet access has been more and more difficult to get as we head south, I have not been able to hook up to the net and determine what kind they were. In any case, they came over to play. How wonderful. Two or three at a time played on *Jenny's* bow wave, looked up at us and for twenty minutes entertained us. Nicholas loves to watch them too. He probably also hears their whistles better than we do. Yes, they were whistling all the while they were playing. Away from her bow they were jumping out of the water and splashing about. Nicholas demands to be held up so he can see them, or allowed on the bow so he can look over. I think our visitors really enjoy looking at him. I am not sure whether it is curiosity, or as a potential meal.

We got into Acapulco just as the sun set and dropped *Jenny's* anchor in 65 feet of water. This morning I saw a nearby empty mooring buoy and hooked up to it, assuming that it was part of the marina. Then I went in and paid for six days at $1.00 per ft for a mooring ball!

Jenny's VHF radios have been acting up again. Ever since La Paz, I have noticed they seem to switch channels randomly. On our way into Acapulco the big one was impossible to use. I was trying to talk to the marina on channel 68 and every second or two it switched to another channel. How annoying! I ordered a new ICOM 422 radio to replace the old small ICOM radio onboard. The old one did not have DSC and with the big one acting up, I needed a new reliable radio. Don is supposed to bring it down with him.

Acapulco is a big city and quite beautiful. It looks like it should be in the Mediterranean Sea. Homes dot the desert landscape on the hills. Nightly they shine like stars, surrounding the whole bay with their points of light. This morning a cruise ship arrived and disembarked a couple of thousand visitors. However, because the city is so large the cruise ship visitors do not disturb its character or culture much. I did not see any specific commerce targeted to them as we walked through Centro.

This evening Vincenté visited *Jenny*. *Maiestra* told us to contact him for a mooring ball when we arrived. I tried, but failed to contact him yesterday. Well, it turns out that the mooring ball I picked was his, and, I paid Club de Yates for the privilege. While I told Club de Yates the name on the buoy (Pez Azul), they gladly claimed it to be theirs and took our money. They wanted to charge $1.50 per foot per day and then backed down to $1.00 per foot. This amounts to $46 per day. Well, what a rip AND not even their buoy!!! Vincenté wants only $10 per day and went in with us today to straighten it out. The official was not there so, I hope we will straighten it out in the morning.

Three generations of anglers in Acapulco

Saturday, March 08, 2008 11:56:58 AM

Location: Acapulco
Latitude is 16 degrees 50.484 minutes north.
Longitude is 99 degrees 54.317 minutes west.

My daughter Laura wrote:

"Making good progress it seems, and having fun to boot! But, do you feel like you are seeing the things you thought you'd see as you travel? Other than coasts and ocean and islands, everything seems to be something you just drive by, like a road trip with minimal stops. Is this what you envisioned this trip to be?"

Good questions! Cruising can be like an extended road trip and *Jenny* has been more vehicle than home in an exotic location. We stayed a month in La Paz and began to get to know the place. Staying months in a place is more like what I have in mind. However, two things are driving us south. One is the hurricane season that begins in May. We need to be below the hurricane belt by then, which is in Costa Rica. If I knew which places in Mexico were really worthwhile staying in for an extended period, and if Mary were comfortable making multi-night passages, then we would have skipped a lot of the little stops and just headed for the ones we have since found worthwhile. The list includes La Paz, Isla Isabella and the Manzanillo area that includes Las Hadas and Santiago Bay. That is what our very experienced friends onboard *Lovely Rita* and *Adios* did and we should have followed them.

The other thing driving us south is our quest for an exotic, tropical location. Mexico is very nice but just not our cup of tea. It is desert and the water all the way down to Acapulco has been too cold to enjoy. So, south we go. When we get to El Salvador, we expect to stay in the Barillas marina for the month of April, then maybe another month in Nicaragua before getting to Costa Rica. Then a month or two in one spot in Costa Rica, and a month or two in Panama in the pacific side islands. The hope is less moving and more staying. We need the right combination of place, cost, water, etc. to make it happen.

Also, we really need to learn more Spanish now. It will be the only way we will be able to meet and enjoy the wonderful people in these countries.

Tuesday, March 11, 2008 10:02:02 PM
Location: Acapulco, MX

Well I got my exercise this morning. I rented a dive tank, buoyancy compensator and regulator for a grand total of $25 and dove on *Jenny*'s bottom to clean it. I would say it was less than 1% covered with dime-sized barnacles. Not bad, but still energy-robbing none the less. I used a sixteen-inch wide plastic squeegee on a broom handle that I bought at Wal-Mart yesterday to knock them off. Then I used a brush on another broom handle to brush off the soft growth. The propeller was good, but I polished it up with some emery cloth and now it is as smooth as a baby's butt. The keel coolers were clean, but with the tank, I spent additional time knocking off some calcium growth. They are as good as they are going to get. The bow thruster is a disaster and while I used the wire brush to get to some of it, before long the entire tube is going to be filled with growth. I will have to address it when I have *Jenny* hauled. We are now good to go to Huatulco and El Salvador!

I have been challenged getting timely US news and found the answer! I discovered the American Forces Radio Network on the sideband radio. At 5:00 PM CDT NPR comes on!!! We now have a way to stay current. To get the frequencies, eleven of them, just Google AFRN and you will get to their web site.

When you know your charts are not accurate, what do you do about it? You plot your course and then verify it with Google Earth. I used this method on our plots coming into Acapulco because the charts are known to be very inaccurate and you have to go through a channel about 1000 feet wide. *Jenny's* raster charts showed the channel one place, and *Jenny's* vector chart showed it in another. Which was right? Neither! I took each waypoint and found it on Google Earth, then relocated it to where Google Earth showed the point should be. These new waypoints were right on the money and both charts were wrong. So, if you have any doubt, use Google Earth as another source of information.

We went out to dinner with two other sailboats that just came in today and are also heading south. They are nice folks and roughly on the same schedule at least down to Costa Rica as we are. We will be seeing more of them. One vessel is from Canada and the other from San Diego, both with a ton of experience. One thing of note is that one of the vessels had the same observation as I did regarding Yamaha outboards being the dominate vendor at least on this coast of Mexico. They bought one before coming down this time. Well, they found out that the Yamaha motors you buy in the States are not the same as the ones down here and the parts are NOT interchangeable. Bummer!

Thursday, March 13, 2008 3:31:52 PM

Location: Acapulco
Latitude is 16 degrees 50.474 minutes north.
Longitude is 99 degrees 54.302 minutes west.

Donald Perrine joined *Jenny's* crew yesterday and has already been a great asset. He was the first owner, and had a hand in the design of his Nordhavn 47. He also has several decades of sailing experience, a captain's license and it shows. He has given us a wealth of knowledge already. Mary and Don are at Wal-Mart now doing some final provisioning and I hope recovering the credit card that Mary left there yesterday...

This morning *Jenny* dropped her mooring ball at about 08:00, went in to fuel up and check out. I also had *Jenny* washed down for the first time since La Cruz. She needed it badly and the team of two did it for 500 pesos; about $45 US. Now she looks nice and clean again. She did not get back to her mooring ball until noon because of the marina bureaucracy and a fuel pump breakdown. By the time she left the dock, there was quite a line of boats waiting to pull up. Nothing happens swiftly in Mexico. With a full load, *Jenny* is listing again to the port side and this means her hull above the bottom paint is now under water. Ugh... But, *Jenny* will be doing a lot of motoring over the next two weeks, so it should fix it self relatively quickly. The price this time included "propina" which means a tip and was $2.40 per gallon roughly because the transaction is in pesos per liter.

Since Ensenada we have loaded 375 gallons in Mazatlan and 258 gallons here for a total of 632 gallons. I still have not added up the mileage though. We are doing well. The price of diesel in El Salvador is $4.00 per gallon. Fortunately, I will not need to load any more until we get to Panama or Colombia. Don knows of several places in the Caribbean where fuel is cheap, so we are going to pick his brain some more.

Tomorrow we are going to drop *Jenny's* mooring and anchor out in a bay on the east side of Acapulco. There we will do the final prep for our overnight down to Huatulco, go through our processes and safety equipment with Don, and we will be an hour or two closer to our next stop. We will also test the Man Overboard Button (MOB) on *Jenny's* navigation computer and find out what it actually does. There is no documentation. We are expecting very calm seas and light winds all the way down. I hope also to be better able to pick up Don Anderson's weather in the anchorage and begin to listen for windows to cross the Tehuantepec. I would like first to spend a few days anchoring in the Huatulco area as I have heard that it is very nice there.

Passage: Acapulco to Puerto Marques

Departed Friday, March 14, 2008 at 7:17 PM local time from Acapulco Mooring. The departure location was latitude 16 degrees 48.410 minutes north, longitude 99 degrees 50.504 minutes west.

Arrived Friday, March 14, 2008 at 2:18 PM local time at . The arrival location was latitude 16 degrees 48.412 minutes north, longitude 99 degrees 50.510 minutes west. The trip covered 5.73 nautical miles in 0d 0h 58m with an average speed of 5.90 knots and a maximum speed of 7.10 knots.

Passage: Puerto Marques to Jicaral

Departed Saturday, March 15, 2008 at 12:50 PM local time from Puerto Marques Anchorage. The departure location was latitude 16 degrees 43.559 minutes north, longitude 99 degrees 52.661 minutes west.

Saturday, March 15, 2008 12:01:19 PM

Location: At Sea
Latitude is 16 degrees 27.429 minutes north.
Longitude is 99 degrees 35.392 minutes west.

This weather observation was taken on Saturday, March 15, 2008 11:44:11 AM local time.
Observation location: At Sea.
Latitude is 16 degrees 27.464 minutes north.
Longitude is 99 degrees 35.516 minutes west.
The air temperature is 78, and water temperature is 75 degrees Fahrenheit.
The forecast is Sunny.
The current weather is dry.
The sky is clear or a few clouds.
The wind is 1 knot from the east.
The visibility is 10 nautical miles.
The wave height is 0 feet with 2 foot swells.
The barometer is 1011 millibar and rising.

Yesterday we got *Jenny* ready for passage, dropped her mooring ball in Acapulco, and took a very short hop around a small headland to the next bay east called Puerto Marques. What a difference a small distance makes. Instead of all the energy associated with spring break kids, party boats, sport fishing boats, pangas, cruise ships, etc. in Acapulco, the bay is here is small with very expensive private homes and condos on the north and south shores with a long sandy beach down the eastern edge lined with beach restaurants and families enjoying the water. It is lovely.

We anchored off a small beach on the north shore backed by tall coconut and fan palms and was very well manicured like a golf course. It was picture perfect. Later in the afternoon, we noticed that a dinner was being set up on the lawn, followed by a small stage, speakers, and all the trappings of an evening event. After listening to the Acapulco party boats booming their best spring break energy music for several days, I was somewhat concerned about the amount of sleep we were going to get if we stayed off this beach. Our plan was to wake at 05:00 AM to pull the hook. After some discussion, we decided we could take naps today, and see what the event was all about.

A couple of crewed yachts came and went during the afternoon, but by sundown we were the only boat parked off the beach. The event was still being set up and there was no indication of when it might start eliciting more worries about what kind of event it was going to be and when it might end. At 8:00 PM people started to arrive.

Well, the event was a VERY upscale wedding. They treated us to a wonderful concert of Mexican and American music. Better than you could find anywhere else. We parked ourselves on *Jenny*'s bow with a great Merlot that Donald brought and just had the best front row seats to a very special evening of entertainment and cultural emersion. The quality of the singing was equal to any concert you could find in Las Vegas or NYC and all the songs were very romantic and wonderful. None was too loud. All were incredibly well done. At the close, there were fireworks. What good fortune. We told Don that we forgot to mention this in our advertisement for crew...

Nicholas, David and Mary waiting for the big show

We woke at 05:00 this morning and *Jenny* was underway by 06:00. Now, her navigation computer forecasts 1.2 days left on this passage. The water is flat and the weather is perfect. Wow, this part of Mexico is nice.

Arrived Sunday, March 16, 2008 at 6:05 PM local time at Jicaral Anchorage. The arrival location was latitude fifteen degrees 41.760 minutes north, longitude 96 degrees 13.481 minutes west. The trip covered 239.20 nautical miles in 1d 10h 14m with an average speed of 6.90 knots and a maximum speed of 7.10 knots.

Sunday, March 16, 2008 10:34:07 PM

Location: Jicaral Anchorage
Latitude is 15 degrees 41.76 minutes north.
Longitude is 96 degrees 13.489 minutes west.

We made another successful overnight passage. This one filled with delights and challenges as is usual. The delights were porpoises that decided to play with us in the dark. The first pack arrived just after sunset and individuals were jumping five to six feet out of the water just off *Jenny's* sides showing their stuff. When under water, they left a trail of trees woven in light from their disturbance of the bioluminescent critters in the water. You could see them zooming together, toward, in and away from *Jenny's* bow wave. They are so fast and agile it begs description. Other packs came to *Jenny* throughout the night and entertained whoever was on watch.

Jenny was challenged to keep out of the way of the tankers, freighters and cruise ships that came toward her from ahead and astern. For some reason, they all seemed to have the same waypoints. I had to alter her course several times to avoid getting too close to these 600-foot monsters. It kept each of us alert during our watches. I hope, the multi-night passage to El Salvador will be free of ship traffic and our course argues for this.

Jenny got to the Huatulco area on schedule. She had about ninety minutes to get into her anchorage and hooked up to the seabed. She is in a well-protected cove about 1000 feet in diameter with rocks protecting the entrance and a white sandy beach on the north end. She's the only vessel here so it is very quiet except for the sound of the surf. Once *Jenny* hooked up, we jumped into the water. It must be about eighty degrees Fahrenheit, clear and clean. This is the first time we have been able to enjoy a recreational swim and it was very, very good. Tomorrow we plan to spend the day swimming and snorkeling here. It is very pretty. An oddity is the description in the cruiser guide. First, you have to remember that the author is a Californian. She describes the shore as jungle. Yes, jungle! Now when I picture jungle, I see parrots, monkeys, lush green vegetation, etc. Well this shore is barren trees, cactus, and scrub bushes. Hmmm... a California Jungle?

I had very good net reception tonight and caught up with many of our friends' whereabouts. For those heading west, it seems now is the time they leave. Several boats are underway for the Marquises and several more plan to depart soon from Puerto Vallarta and nearby stops. The North - South commuting boats are underway north now for the summer. And finally, a few are on their way to El Salvador and points south. We still are the only power boat checking in to the Amigo and Southbound nets on a regular basis.

We started the evening with Margaritas and had barbeque pork chops, rice and broccoli in a totally wilderness setting. Wow! Tomorrow we will be snorkeling on the rock reefs, relaxing from the overnight and enjoying the elements of this time and place.

Love to all.

Passage: Jacaral to Marina Chahué

Departed Monday, March 17, 2008 at 5:04 PM local time from Jacaral Anchorage. The departure location was latitude fifteen degrees 40.666 minutes north, longitude 96 degrees 11.545 minutes west.

Arrived Monday, March 17, 2008 at 1:56 PM local time at Marina Chahué. The arrival location was latitude fifteen degrees 45.857 minutes north, longitude 96 degrees 7.317 minutes west. The trip covered 12.30 nautical miles in 0d 2h 6m with an average speed of 5.40 knots and a maximum speed of 7.20 knots.

Wednesday, March 19, 2008 1:30:57 PM

Location: Marina Chahué
Latitude is fifteen degrees 45.831 minutes north.
Longitude is 96 degrees 7.32 minutes west.

When I talked to Don about joining us for this crossing, I made it clear that he should allow at least three weeks in his schedule. However, as time goes on he is becoming more insistent that we get to El Salvador as quickly as possible. He has a house under construction back in the States, and the longer he goes without direct control over what is happening there the more nervous he gets. I wanted to stay in this anchorage for a few days, but to accommodate him we only spent one. I also wanted to spend a week or two in Huatulco enjoying that lovely town. This is why you really need to weight the benefits of crew against the inevitable conflict with schedules.

Jenny did not mind. She was going to a marina for the first time in months. She likes to flirt with the other vessels. I have to watch her constantly. She released her grip on the sandy bottom and took us from the wonderful anchorage to the marina on Monday. I went to see if we could clear out of Mexico and catch a nice window for crossing the Tehuantepec. This gulf is on the southwest side of a gorge that comes all the way from the Caribbean. It is notorious for sudden gales you really do not want to be caught in. Weather planning takes on even more importance here than usual.

Well, we arrived at the marina a little after noon. Enrique, the marina captain, did everything possible to clear us out by 4:00 PM. We did manage to clear with the port captain and emigration, but customs was tied up at the airport. Around 6:30 PM I told Don we were staying put until the next window. Customs showed up at *Jenny* Tuesday morning and stamped our papers. I then took a fully stamped copy back to the port captain and we are officially out of the country.

This area of Mexico is very nice. The port itself is very pretty, with amenities for the cruise ships that pull in for the day. Then there is a larger town a couple of miles away, bustling with vacationers and natives. It seems as though many Mexicans vacation here. We see them in the resort hotels and on the beach. The marina is very nice and charges $.60 US per foot per day in the fully constructed area and $.25 US per foot in the area that does not have power or water. The marina captain is super and will do anything for you. The area is wealthy with very good roads, lots of new buildings and cars running around, and a nice supermarket within walking distance from the marina. The climate, water and beaches remind me of Florida. Overall, I think it is the best place to visit in Mexico, at least on this side.

Short range cruising is great here too, with easy day trips to pristine coves for snorkeling and swimming. It is a mystery to me why most of the boats that commute to Mexico for the winter do not come down this far and stay here. Right now the weather is shaping up for an early Saturday morning departure, which is what we will do if things do not change. Our trip plan then puts us into the Barillas Marina in El Salvador on Tuesday. Given the opportunity, I would like to have spent much more time here in the Huatulco area. That said I am getting excited about seeing a new country!

Passage: Marina Chahué to Barillas, El Salvador

Departed Saturday, March 22, 2008 at 1:22 PM local time from Marina Chahué. The departure location was latitude fifteen degrees 44.845 minutes north, longitude 96 degrees 6.234 minutes west.

Sunday, March 23, 2008 11:16:45 AM

Location: At Sea
Latitude is fifteen degrees 40.261 minutes north.
Longitude is 93 degrees 35.052 minutes west.

This weather observation was taken on Sunday, March 23, 2008 11:04:47 AM local time.
Observation location: At sea.
Latitude is fifteen degrees 40.4 minutes north.
Longitude is 93 degrees 35.189 minutes west.
The air temperature is 80, and water temperature is 75 degrees Fahrenheit.
The forecast is Sunny.
The current weather is dry.
The sky is clear or a few clouds.
The wind is 4 knots from the southeast.
The visibility is 10 nautical miles.

The wave height is 1 feet with 3 foot swells.
The barometer is 1009 millibar and steady.

Jenny is on her way to El Salvador. She is now cruising down the last part of Mexico, heading for the Guatemala boarder 100 miles away. She should be there about 05:00 AM day after tomorrow.

The Gulf of the Tehuantepec is the last big body of water in Mexico and at its head is a gorge that extends all the way to the Caribbean. Mexico pumps the oil they get from the Caribbean across this gorge all the way to the pacific side. The city Salina Cruz lies at the Pacific side and holds a large refinery and tanker port. Mexico runs the tankers up its west coast to supply petroleum products to the cities on this side.

Any differential in pressure between the Caribbean Sea and the Pacific Ocean will cause gales and storms on this side. All vessels look seriously for weather windows to take across. We, along with *Astor*, the beautiful eighty-three foot 1926 schooner and a catamaran named *Southern Bell* from Louisiana chose a relatively small weather window.

Regardless of the forecast, it is wise to keep very close to shore to avoid the large, steep nasty wind waves that build quickly when the wind goes higher than twenty knots. Last night we saw a gust or two in the thirty-five knot range and except for the two times we were forced off the beach by bottom features, all was good. I put *Jenny's* birds down at about ten o'clock this morning and still have them down. We will probably pick them up soon since *Jenny's* speed is only 5.4 knots with this wind and an opposing current on her nose.

There is nothing to report about wildlife here except for the flock of Frigate birds that wanted to make *Jenny* their night roost. They are really large and persistent! I ended up throwing a coil of rope at them repeatedly. Boy, I wish I had my Benjamin pellet gun with me. I have looked for something to make a slingshot out of without success so far. But the quest is on.

With the tricky part of the crossing over, it is now just a matter of steaming down the remaining 370 miles to Marina Barillas. I am already looking forward to cracking open a bottle of champagne with our friends on *Southern Bell* when we get there.

Sunday, March 23, 2008 9:50:49 PM

Location: At Sea
Latitude is 14 degrees 52.6 minutes north.
Longitude is 92 degrees 48.15 minutes west.

This weather observation was taken on Sunday, March 23, 2008 11:04:47 AM local time.
Observation location: At sea.
Latitude is fifteen degrees 40.4 minutes north.
Longitude is 93 degrees 35.189 minutes west.
The air temperature is 80, and water temperature is 75 degrees Fahrenheit.
The forecast is Sunny.
The current weather is dry.
The sky is clear or a few clouds.
The wind is 4 knots from the southeast.
The visibility is 10 nautical miles.
The wave height is 1 feet with 3 foot swells.
The barometer is 1009 millibar and steady.

It was a busy day. Mary was making meals for Easter Sunday. I was busy washing *Jenny*, checking various pieces of equipment, and building a slingshot. Don was busy standing watches, reading and photographing the wonders around us.

Jenny is now cruising down the last leg of Mexico toward Puerto Madero in relatively smooth seas and calm winds. An orange moon just broke over the low clouds that are hugging the coast, and a fresh loaf of bread is cooling in the galley. Mary and Don are snoozing. I am on watch.

The battle with the birds continues. At the moment we are Frigate and Booby free, but with small white birds clinging to the stabilizer wires. The motion of *Jenny* causes them to be in a constant fight for equilibrium and I cannot quite figure out why they work so hard to stay. During this morning's huddle, Don suggested I use the hose to scare the big birds. I tried it but we do not have enough pressure to reach them. The Boobies just laughed at me. He also suggested a bright light, so I used the hand held 1,000,000 candlepower spotlight and the target Booby just stared into it. These are not bright birds. The construction of the slingshot continued. No more Mr. Nice Guy. I finally found a suitable base, and used elastic material and fire hose cloth to finish the weapon. Being Easter, we had some small jelly beans on board to use as our initial ammunition.

The Boobies lined up on *Jenny's* stabilizer wires not twenty feet away and made inviting targets. The Jelly Beans rolled onto the deck and I fired away. After fifteen or twenty, I was getting to be a pretty good shot. It was time to bring out the heavy artillery; fishing weights. Yup, one ounce of lead. These birds were going to learn a thing or two about messing with *Jenny*. I went to work. Shots flew over them. Shots flew by them. Shots flew under them. These Boobies are fearless. They hardly noticed at all that a war was on. I hit one in the foot and it took off. The other boobies looked at each other in puzzlement. I hit another in the chest. He looked at me in puzzlement. Nobody moved. But they did stop laughing.

I ran out of ammo just as I was getting qualified with the weapon system. I hate it when that happens! Well, there was always the coil of rope to throw at them but it was just a ton of work heaving it out and dragging it back, coiling it again for another throw. I dove into the garbage can and found one apple, a rotten green pepper, some chunks of potato, and best of all, some eggs. Yup, raw eggs!

By this time I had singled out the alpha Booby and he became the focus of my wrath. I figured if I got him off, the others would take heed and follow. The fruits and veggies flew by this Booby at pro baseball speeds. I was proud. But the alpha Booby would only glance up from preening his feathers as something sailed by. "Hmmmm, I wonder what that was?" Life is just not fair I'm telling you. However, I saved the best for last: the eggs. Somehow, the sight and perhaps smell of raw chicken eggs flying by this Booby at high speed rattled him to the core. By the time the third one flew by his beak he had had it. He took flight and the rest followed. That was it, at least for a while. That will teach those Boobies.

Monday, March 24, 2008 1:41:11 AM

Location: At Sea
Latitude is 14 degrees 32.775 minutes north.
Longitude is 92 degrees 28.723 minutes west.

This weather observation was taken on Sunday, March 23, 2008 11:04:47 AM local time.
Observation location: At sea.
Latitude is fifteen degrees 40.4 minutes north.
Longitude is 93 degrees 35.189 minutes west.
The air temperature is 80, and water temperature is 75 degrees Fahrenheit.
The forecast is Sunny.
The current weather is dry.
The sky is clear or a few clouds.
The wind is 4 knots from the southeast.
The visibility is 10 nautical miles.
The wave height is 1 feet with 3 foot swells.
The barometer is 1009 millibar and steady.

It is my watch again. The Frigate birds have returned and are circling high above *Jenny* waiting for an opportunity to land. The port side wire has a dozen little white birds and the moon is throwing a good shine on the ocean.

The sea has been dead calm with no wind. Our sailboat buddies on *Astor* and *Southern Bell* must be going mad. This is definitely a motor vessel coast with most sailboats under power eighty plus percent of the time. *Southern Bell* is concerned about how much fuel they have left to get to Barillas if they have to motor all the way. The good news is that we seem to be picking up the Pacific current again and are back up to 7.0 knots. At least that will help them. Another Tpecker (Tehuantepec storm) is forecast for later today and that might at least give them some wind too.

It is clear the Tehuantepec is the great divide between desert Mexico and the rainy, humid climates south. It is just after midnight and still 82 degrees out and the humidity is way up. *Jenny* heats up with JD running and becomes pretty warm below unless we can open the hatches and have some wind. We are running the small DC fans when below to help. It seems like the wind is picking up as I write this.

We are now very near the border of Guatemala and should cross in the next few hours. I will have to break out the Guatemala courtesy flag soon and pack up the Mexican one. I think I will mount all the courtesy flags we use on the wall of a future house.

Easter was somewhat of a non-event in spite of Mary's valiant efforts. We were all just too busy with *Jenny* to get into the groove. Mary is bummed. Our timing on this crossing would definitely have been very different without crew aboard. But, Don has been a great help and maybe this multi-day passage will result in Mary being more comfortable with making them with just the two of us.

Arrived Tuesday, March 25, 2008 at 7:24 AM local time at Acajutla El Salvador. The arrival location was latitude 13 degrees 41.647 minutes north, longitude 90 degrees 2.017 minutes west. The customs check in was None so far. The trip covered 434.00 nautical miles in 2d 18h 18m with an average speed of 6.50 knots and a maximum speed of 8.36 knots.

BOOK 5: CENTRAL AMERICA WILDERNESS

A land half tamed, a people not.
Families remote and isolated, tightly woven.
Families across borders power separated.
Nature across borders God imposed.
All beautiful, remote, endearing, captivating.
A world beyond and behind civilized possibilities.
A world not to be forgotten.

Tuesday, March 25, 2008 8:08:08 AM

Location: Acajutla, El Salvador
Latitude is 13 degrees 41.643 minutes north.
Longitude is 90 degrees 2.013 minutes west.

We are now six miles inside the El Salvador border, anchored in sixty feet of water off the beach. You might wonder how we got here. Well, it is another story of an area claimed to be very benign behaving very badly. As we crossed into Guatemala yesterday afternoon, we began to get weather reports about a strong wind coming out of Cuba that would cross over Central America and result in high winds last night and this morning. First we tried to outrun it by trying to find a favorable current. That took us about twenty miles offshore. We did not find anything. We humped down the coast at about 6.5 knots with JD at 1600 RPM and set a course to gradually close back in.

There is a small headland in El Salvador that has a small commercial port with a breakwater and some protection from the southwest swell that generally runs here. I used that as our goal to close with land. However, while we were still twelve miles offshore at about midnight, it struck. The wind went from zero to twenty-four knots out of the north in a flash. Since no waves had yet formed, I immediately brought *Jenny* to an idle and dropped her birds. Then I set a course directly upwind to land. Both radars were running and they gave us a good picture of our progress. We were 1.5 hours away from the shelter of the shore.

As we slogged our way in, the seas built up and the wind increased to a constant thirty knots with gusts to thirty-five. *Jenny* is just an awesome vessel. She takes rough seas pounding at her with barely any notice. Mary and I were up in the pilothouse while Don remained below in the front cabin. Every now and then we would hit a set of waves that were just placed right to get *Jenny* really pitching. We would pound into one wave after another with spray flying by at a high velocity. Don did not even see the need to abandon the front cabin and come up! I thought he must be airborne down there. Mary was concerned about the motion, but there was no danger.

Our timing for turning in was fortunate. The winds were coming across the continent from the north directly offshore. We were just offshore of some mountains that are pretty close to the beach. As we came in, both the wind and waves died down because they had less and less fetch and the mountains began to blanket the winds. After dodging several unlit fishing pangas, I decided on a spot. It is near the entrance to Rio Santiago. We found a nice sandy bottom in sixty feet about 1/2 mile off the beach and dropped the hook with 400 feet of chain. By this time the wind had was down to about ten knots and it was very peaceful. After tidying up and setting the birds up as flopper stoppers, we went to bed. I did not know we were just inside the El Salvador border. Good spot.

Beautiful ranch house on the El Salvador beach

Right now the wind is building again with gusts to twenty knots as predicted. It is supposed to blow for the next 24 hours off and on, so we will be just hanging here for a day. The shore is beautiful with brown sand, green palm trees, and some homes and palapas. Right in front of us there is a picture perfect home on the beach. I can see a road behind it running along the beach. Last night before the blow I was on watch and saw a volcano going off somewhere in Guatemala. What a show. It lit up the sky with red light and I could see the lava thrown in the air using the binoculars.

Life is good. I will exchange some email and call our buddies on the SSB this morning. *Southern Bell* was too far behind us to make El Salvador so they stopped into the port in Guatemala. This morning they will have to clear in and pay the $300 fee. But, they will also be able to pick up fuel. They will probably stay there for at least another 24 hours too.

Passage: Acajutla toward Barillas

Departed Tuesday, March 25, 2008 at 5:48 PM local time from Rio Santiago beach. The departure location was latitude 13 degrees 41.691 minutes north, longitude 90 degrees 1.991 minutes west.

Arrived Tuesday, March 25, 2008 at 6:38 PM local time at anchor off the beach. The arrival location was latitude 13 degrees 30.812 minutes north, longitude 89 degrees 37.816 minutes west. The customs check in was none. The trip covered 30.08 nautical miles in 0d 5h 50m with an average speed of 5.20 knots and a maximum speed of 6.70 knots.

Passage: Acajutla toward Barillas

Departed Wednesday, March 26, 2008 at 1:56 PM local time from Acajutla Anchorage 2. The departure location was latitude 13 degrees 28.483 minutes north, longitude 89 degrees 26.249 minutes west.

Wednesday, March 26, 2008 9:32:23 AM

Location: At Sea
Latitude is 13 degrees 27.765 minutes north.
Longitude is 89 degrees 22.875 minutes west.

This weather observation was taken on Wednesday, March 26, 2008 9:24:50 AM local time.

Observation location: At Sea.
Latitude is 13 degrees 27.823 minutes north.
Longitude is 89 degrees 23.031 minutes west.
The air temperature is 84, and water temperature is 80 degrees Fahrenheit.
The forecast is Sunny, windy.
The current weather is dry.
The sky is clear or a few clouds.
The wind is 4 knots from the southeast.
The visibility is 10 nautical miles.
The wave height is 2 feet with 3 foot swells.
The barometer is 1011 millibar and rising.

Who would have guessed? While still very dry this time of year, the coast of El Salvador is spectacular. There are small fishing towns on the beaches, and huge resorts or palatial estates on the cliffs. All is neat and clean and speaks of affluence even in the fishing villages. A few fishing pangas came out to see *Jenny* this morning. They seemed happy and friendly and we waved to them after we hauled anchor and passed them setting their gear on the way out. The lush green of the palms and trees extends about a mile inland even now, and there are sections of green in the mountain valleys. Clearly shaped volcanoes dot the landscape. Fortunately, Don has a super high-resolution camera and is taking scores of photos.

Jenny is about 77 miles from Marina Barillas this morning. Getting there has been a real slog. She hauled anchor around noon yesterday to get around the Acajutla headland and make some progress. As soon as she passed the headland though, she was again smacked with twenty to thirty knot winds coming off the land. It seems that her first anchorage was nearly perfect, hiding behind one of the really big inland mountains. She was headed toward a lower set of hills that came up close to the beach on the other side, but again she had to slog her way in. She finally broke free of the wind waves about ½ miles offshore in sixty feet of water and dropped the hook for the night. The wind blew in gusts above thirty knots all night, but *Jenny* had set her Rocna deep into the seabed and we slept very securely on 400 feet of chain.

By dawn, the wind had died and *Jenny* released herself from the seabed around 06:00 AM to get a good run to Barillas. While she will not get there by the time they close the entrance, she will be set up to go in tomorrow morning. Because the marina is behind a bar and up an estuary, they will send out a pilot boat to escort *Jenny* in. They only offer this between sunrise and 3:00 PM because they need enough light to see the channel. *Jenny* will spend another night at anchor off the nearby beach if necessary. I expect the winds will pick up again this afternoon, so I have her steaming along close to the beach to avoid the waves.

We saw *Astor* as we left our anchorage, about ten miles out and gave them a call. They were motoring with their sails up and looking pretty.

Arrived Wednesday, March 26, 2008 at 7:12 PM local time at Barillas Offshore Anchorage. The arrival location was latitude 13 degrees 7.193 minutes north, longitude 88 degrees 25.021 minutes west. The customs check in was none. The trip covered 78.67 nautical miles in 0d 12h 15m with an average speed of 6.40 knots and a maximum speed of 7.60 knots.

Friday, March 28, 2008 5:43:37 PM

Location: Barillas Marina
Latitude is 13 degrees fifteen.796 minutes north.
Longitude is 88 degrees 29.247 minutes west.

I am sitting in *Jenny's* pilothouse listening to a local radio station playing easy listening Latin (not Mexican) music drinking a fresh squeezed lemonada (lime) watching the sun set on the mangrove. *Jenny* has her awning up in the front and her screens on in the back. She is in full houseboat mode. It is warm and humid, with the sound of cicadas in the trees, very much like Florida in the spring. The trees are in bloom and as we came in yesterday, I smelled the rich scent of trees in bloom, grass and flowers instead of dust and dirt. Mojitos tonight! Life is good.

But, let me back up a bit. Barillas is a resort in a mangrove estuary. The marina provides a waypoint in the ocean where they will meet you with a panga to lead you in. Two days ago, we hugged the coast all day for 77 miles and arrived at the waypoint at 6:00 PM. I called the marina at 3:00 PM to let them know we were on our way. However, because they need sunlight to read the location of the ever-shifting bar, it closes at 3:00 PM. *Astor* heard our discussion and called us to coordinate our arrival. The marina instructed us to anchor at the waypoint overnight. *Astor* was still pretty far away, so they just slowed down. *Astor* draws eleven feet and high tide was at 05:30 AM. We were to meet the panga at 05:30 in the morning at sunrise and have *Astor* go first, behind the pilot panga, with us following closely. We anchored out in the ocean again to wait for the 05:30 AM rendezvous. The ocean is not the best place to anchor and get some sleep due to the constant motion of the water. I had another restless night.

Jenny entering Barillas at daybreak

It was still dark when I got up and found *Astor* right there with us. We prepared to get underway, raising *Jenny's* stabilizers all the way up, and hauling anchor. Because I did not know the depths we would be going through, we could not use her stabilizers. I rigged for a wild ride. The panga showed up on schedule just as the sun rose and off we went.

The bar entrance has several stages over a zigzag course of about four miles. This is not something you attempt on your own. Although some sections rolled *Jenny* thirty degrees, she was in good control the whole way in. Once past the bars and breakers, the rest of the ride was like cruising up a river. The marina does not have slips; just mooring balls that line both sides of the "river" and the panga helped us hook up after attending to *Astor*.

Now this is how checking in should be in all countries and was second only to Canada for ease and simplicity. The marina manager, port captain, immigration, and police pulled up in a panga to do their routine, which took about thirty minutes including showing the police officer a tour of *Jenny*. Then I went into the marina office, signed their papers, and went to customs to get our passports stamped and pay $10 per person. That was it. Bada bing, bada boom.

Meanwhile, Don quickly arranged for his trip to the airport and flight back to Tennessee. He was done and gone before we were even done with our passports. What a difference from Mexico! Things run on time here.

Mary and I went back to *Jenny* and started cleaning up from the long passage. By lunchtime I had her awning up and boy I am glad we have it. The sun is fierce here and it really makes a big difference. Do not go to the tropics without significant awning coverage. We then dropped *The Beast* and headed over to the palapa restaurant for lunch. They have a dinghy dock and *The Beast* was at home.

The "marina" here is a resort with bungalows. There is a pool, an open air palapa restaurant overlooking the boats and the water, tropical birds, humming birds, flowers, coconut palms, a runway for small planes, a nature preserve where you can interact with spider monkeys and see the more birds, and an area of tables and hammocks for hanging out. I feel like we are on vacation. Twice a week they have a bus that takes you into Usulután for shopping. And the charge for all this is a total of $11 / day.

Last night we had dinner at the restaurant, and then came back to *Jenny* to continue to clean up. I put up *Jenny's* cockpit screens for the first time since they were made in San Francisco to enclose the back. Surprisingly, we have not had any mosquito or no-see-um problems. Anyway, I dropped no-see-um nets over *Jenny's* forward hatches. I am also running a 120 V floor fan after sunset when the wind dies to drive cool evening air through *Jenny* while I run the generator to recharge the batteries.

Today we took the van to town of Usulután. A resort guard armed with a shotgun accompanied us. This seemed a little odd at first. But, El Salvador is the country with the most recent revolution. We went on dirt roads through an old cotton plantation to the paved highway. There were additional armed guards at the entrance to the resort property. The highway was new and smooth, bustling with buses, trucks and motorcycles.

As we entered the city, the intense chaotic energy overwhelmed me. Everything was in motion without any controls. The traffic crept along intermingled with carts, people, dogs, motorcycles, a few cars, more people each going their own ways. The street turned into a market, taking almost two lanes of highway out of circulation. The huge street market (mercado) fanned out on side streets beyond sight. The first-world stores, a grocery store, Pizza Hut and McDonalds, clustered together in defense of the concept of indoors shopping. Only the rich went inside. Most people here do not have the capital or the spending money to support that kind of infrastructure.

The weather permits the open market. As the town's prosperity improved, the stores that lined the streets just expanded into the streets. Except for occasional delivery trucks, the lanes are pedestrian only with booths that went on forever. The veggies and fruits were all fresh and beautiful. We picked up a pound of fresh tomatoes for fifty cents and two pounds of limes for a buck. We bought most of our fruit and veggies there, generally offering ½ the asking price and usually had the offer accepted. The people expect you to bargain for everything. I am finding that I am eating far more fresh fruit and veggies here than I would in the US. It is so good and fresh, you cannot resist. Tonight it will be jumbo shrimp (the fleet is here), mozzarella, tomato and cucumber salad, wine and a Cerveza for dinner.

After a few trips to the bazaar, we established some rapport with several of the local people, limited only by our Spanish. The people here are poor but they are happy and really enjoy life. As we walked through the Mercado streets they would talk to us, joke with us and generally made us feel very welcome. Everyone had a smile and we met no angry people. How refreshing.

The local agriculture economy looks to be primarily sugar cane. Hence, instead of cheap Tequila we have cheap Rum. A liter of Anjou Bacardi cost $11.00 while a half liter of Jose Quervo was over $16.00. I have officially replaced margaritas with Mojitos, which, if you have not tried one, are exceptional. Yum.

Our friends from New Orleans on *Southern Bell* arrive today and are decompressing as we did yesterday. Their trip over the bar was even more stressing since it was blowing about twenty knots and they had an ebb tide to go through. It was good to see them. We chatted while they lunched in the restaurant. Nicholas has quickly become the local chief pet and he makes the rounds from person to person sucking down all the attention he can.

Jenny's port aft tank is now empty and all the other tanks appear to be full, so I guess *Jenny* consumed 250 gallons on the 800-mile trip down here from Acapulco. It looks like we got 3.15 miles per gallon in spite of adverse winds and currents and JD beating between 1500 and 1600-RPM range the whole time. Awesome!

Tomorrow more cleaning, pickling the water maker, an afternoon at the pool, and perhaps a siesta in a hammock. We plan to stay here the month of April.

Thursday, April 10, 2008 3:31:01 PM

Location: Barillas Marina

Latitude is 13 degrees fifteen.793 minutes north.
Longitude is 88 degrees 29.25 minutes west.

Sorry for the blackout. I got a really awful computer virus on this machine that forced me to completely rebuild it. UGH! I believe this virus came in on a CD that I received *Jenny's* photos on. It replaced several system files, changed the registry so that I could not see its files, and started recording keyboard strokes. The only way I knew it was there was because Internet Explorer requested permission to run the script it initiated to send my keystrokes to a web site in the UK. UGLY! The lesson learned is to create a limited user account for all internet and external data exchanges. Limited users do not have permission to modify the system files. Most people run with administrator privileges. Do not do it.

That said; my last five days have been consumed by getting this machine back online. It is mostly there now, with only a couple of glitches. On top of all that, I got some food poisoning last night and barfed my guts out all night feeding the local fishes.

Each day the thunderstorms get closer and we have had a few nighttime ones come in on us. The front awning is working well as a rain catcher. The only thing I need is more rain.

Life is teaming here. We went on a hike with Richard, Lani, Byron and Susan from *Astor* to see the local family of spider monkeys, lizards, exotic birds and various fauna. Our guide from the marina described everything we saw, but we had to translate from Spanish. It was awesome to see all this nature in the wild. When not working on *Jenny* we spend our time by the pool socializing with our friends from the other vessels here. It is very comfortable and the local people here are delightful.

Laura has sent my box of boat parts and other goodies down the channel to get it delivered to me. I am still not completely sure how it all works, but she sent it to an address in Miami with my name and *Jenny* on the address. I think that everything that goes to that address ends up at the San Salvador airport, which is not in San Salvador at all. The marina manager must make the connection between the box and the marina somehow. It's magic. Then somehow, the box gets from the airport to the marina. There are no import duties for "boats in transit". I am sure there will be other fees though. I will let you know.

I think I am making progress on getting an air conditioner for *Jenny*. It's kind of hard to tell. But, so far I know the freight charge will be $250 because it contains compressed gas and I guess that means special handling. More to come.

Spider Monkey at Barillas

We are planning a trip back to the States in a few weeks and trying to line up the kids to make sure we will be able to spend some time with each of them. We are also going to get our annual health checkups. This is a very safe place to leave *Jenny* and many people make trips from here.

Mary made her first dinghy solo this morning to take Nicholas to shore for his morning walk since I was still sick. A swallow flew into the pilothouse and it took a little while for it to figure out how to escape. It has a pretty white body with metallic blue wings. I will take some photos to send in. We are also planning a trip down the river to the beach on Saturday with a couple of other crews. I will bring my pocket Garmin GPS to be sure I can find our way home!

When the box of goodies arrives from Laura, I will have a ton of boat projects to be done. Every day is packed with work! Well, I guess it is time to go to the pool and see how Mary is doing...

Friday, April 25, 2008 1:20:34 PM

Location: Laura's home in Florida
Latitude is 27 degrees 48.542 minutes north.
Longitude is 82 degrees 18.959 minutes west.

The flight back to Florida went well. We arrived in Miami with Nicholas and our luggage around 6:00 PM Florida time, picked up our rental car and drove north to get a start on Friday's drive to St. Marys. Friday morning we got an early start and finished the drive to our property in St. Marys. We needed to validate our decision to settle there after we finish cruising and were very pleased with what we found. Money Magazine recently voted St. Marys number one small town and the Travel Channel voted Cumberland Island number one national seashore.

Neighbors across from our lot are building a huge house with dock. It has convinced us that we probably will not build on our lot. We do not need or want a big house. We will either buy another property in Cumberland Harbour or in the town itself. The town is developing as a very nice tourist destination, with the ferry to Cumberland Island as one of the draws as well as the yacht anchorages and marinas. In another five years it will be quite the little Mecca of shops and restaurants.

We left St. Marys and drove up to Atlanta to visit my cousin Chris and his wife Rene. Chris is more like a brother than a cousin though. We are very much alike. Rene is wonderful and I hope will join us for a visit in Costa Rica. Their super nice and well-mannered children are growing like weeds. It was a real pleasure being with them for a couple of days.

Next, we drove up to Nolensville, TN to see my son Derek, his wife Heather and their children. We also had the pleasure of seeing Heather's parents again as they were in town too in their RV. Their kids are also growing and very nice. Marina, the only girl in all of our grandchildren, is a trip. At three she is fully in control of her environment and pushes every chance to expand her influence! Heather took the month off from her medical residency at Vanderbilt so we were able to see her too which was nice.

Then we drove down to Riverview yesterday to see Laura and family. That drive was ten hours. The kids are good. We are going to some soccer games tomorrow. Laura's home is our parts depot. *Jenny's* new air conditioner was waiting for us as well as a Hookah system and various other marine supplies. It will be very interesting getting all this on the plane and through customs in El Salvador. The box that I had shipped down cost over $300 in fees, and without customs duties. Hmmmm... It seems it would be cheaper to fly into Miami, go shopping and then fly back with whatever stuff you needed!

We are going to spend a couple of days with Laura now. Tomorrow we are going to celebrate grandson William's birthday and should see my son Terry, wife Alissa and their son Christopher. Then we will go on to Mom's and some final shopping. Wednesday we drive all day to get back to Miami and catch the morning plane back to El Salvador. There is nothing quite like a whirlwind tour of the Southeast.

Thursday, May 01, 2008 9:53:08 AM

Location: 37,000 ft over Florida Keys

Mary and I are now on our flight back to El Salvador after a very nice visit with our children, grandchildren and my Mom. We also had a successful shopping trip. The logistics getting our dog, luggage, and boat supplies into the airport system has been challenging and stressful. However, so far, all are onboard with no hassle and the only trial left will be when we land and go through customs. Below are miles of very inviting turquoise and green transparent water I hope to have under *Jenny* as soon as we leave the Barillas Marina Club estuary.

At each family we visited, we did a little shopping. In Georgia, Mary hit the salon and got a bunch of cosmetic supplies. In Tennessee I shopped Home Depot for various boat goods like home insulation to beef up the deep freeze's insulation, bungee cords, water filters, wire ends. I also bought supplies for making Mojitos and showed the kids how to make them. I got a car charger for the cell phone since I forgot the AC charger on *Jenny*. I also picked up a BIG duffle bag to start to fill with all our shopping stuff. I took the busted Taylor fender back to West Marine and they replaced it under warranty. They are guaranteed forever, and at a cost of $80 a pop, it is very nice to be able to swap them out! I took the eight-foot VHF antenna waiting at Laura's back and exchanged it for a three-foot stainless steel whip for the dinghy. After breaking two fiberglass antennas on *The Beast*, I gave up on them.

Boats, reefs and various small islands dot the turquoise, light blue and dark blue water below.

I bought wire for the air conditioner, screws, nuts, bolts, lock washers, and various other odds and ends needed while at West Marine. I had to get a soccer ball inflation needle to stick in the new fender so it would deflate and not blow up on the plane. I opened the Hookah box, took out the hose and used the space to pack other stuff like auto wax, books, DVDs etc. At Mom's I bought another LARGE duffle bag.

We left Mom's in Clearwater yesterday, with the air conditioner unit in the passenger front seat, the dog carrier in the back passenger seat, two 38-inch duffle bags and our two backpacks in the trunk, Mary in the seat behind me while I drove. Five hours and 300 miles later, we arrived at RPM Diesel in Ft. Lauderdale around 3:00 PM to buy oil filters for JD, the last of our purchases. Fortunately, we also found a pet friendly motel right across the street and checked in for the night.

At 05:00 AM we got up, showered and loaded up. By 06:00 we were on our way to Miami International and there thirty minutes later. Then I drove around in a maze of roads to find a gas station, paid $3.80 a gallon to tank it up, and then worked my way back to the departure gate. There I unloaded onto two carts and left Mary and Nicholas while I drove the car back to the rental return. With the rental car dropped off, I returned by the bus to rendezvous with Mary and start to check in.

We checked in the two boxes and two giant duffle bags (one marked HEAVY) and the only question about the boxes was whether they contained any flammable liquids. NOT. Since the air conditioner weighed in at 95 lbs, we paid an extra $100 for freight and $100 for Nicholas. The was a two check-ins per person limit, so I carried the antenna. Otherwise, it would have cost another $100 just to check it in. Then we took all our bags and boxes to TSA, they took them and they disappeared. TSA did not call us so I assume they are onboard. So far so good!

We kept Nicholas with us for another two hours so he would be out of his box as long as possible. Then we returned to TSA and checked him in. With Nicholas we were worried that we had all the right paperwork and that the temperature in El Salvador airport would be below 85 degrees Fahrenheit so that they would allow him to fly. They took him away. TSA did not call us, so we assume he is onboard too. The antenna cleared TSA, so all is good so far. Whew!

The water below is now cloudier and too deep to see bottom. It looks like there are whitecaps. Mary is filling out our Immigration and Customs forms. Next stop, El Salvador!

Friday, May 02, 2008 2:57:30 PM

Location: Barillas Marina

Well, we all made it back ok and with all our goods duty free! Here's the story. On the customs card for El Salvador the second or third question is how many baggage items you have. Near the bottom, it asks if you have any merchandise other than your baggage that you are bringing into the country. According to this, anything in your "bags" is not merchandise and is not subject to duties. At least this gives you and excuse for saying that you are not bringing anything in. We had two boxes (about $3,000 there) plus a bunch of stuff in our large duffle bags. Our plan was to declare the antenna only, and hope to get a green light at the Aduana checkpoint.

We picked up our bags, boxes and Nicholas at the baggage claim and headed over to the Aduana line. As soon as we got in line, an officer came over from the other side of the room and asked us to go over to his desk. Apparently, he manages pets coming into the country and did not speak a word of English. After a while, we understood that he wanted to place Nicholas in thirty days of quarantine. Mary went ballistic. Meanwhile I found the health certificate that we got from the veterinarian in Usulután; explained that we had arrived by boat a month ago, and had taken Nicholas from El Salvador to the US and back. A second officer came over and joined the discussion. They huddled and a third officer came over who did speak a fair amount of English. After about twenty minutes, the fact that we had the El Salvador certificate of health, combined with us having a yacht in Barillas (impression of wealth and power) made them very friendly. They did have a fourth officer check Nicholas out and I figured out they were looking for drugs in his belly.

Well, once Nicholas passed inspection they just said we could go. We looked over at the Aduana line, back at them and then to the beckoning doors. We decided to make a beeline for the doors! No lights, no Aduana. Thank you Nicholas!!!

It is in the high 80's and low 90's here now and has not rained since we left two weeks ago. Getting the air conditioner installed is top priority. I spent most of the day unpacking and completing small projects now that we had the parts. I replaced the old Sony stereo in the pilothouse with the new one I bought duty free at the El Salvador airport on the way out. Yup, duty free out to the States, and back again. Then I studied the installation instructions and planned the installation of the air conditioner. It will be a chore, but doable in about four or five days.

Thursday, May 08, 2008 1:00:54 PM

Location: Barillas Marina

Well, after working like a dog in the heat and humidity, we have 16K BTUs of air conditioning! We luxuriated in cool dry air last night, running it until we went to bed. With *Jenny* closed up, and the lower outside temperatures at night, we were very comfortable all night. Nice. The installation was straightforward but a lot of work. The system is water cooled, so there is an inlet side that brings seawater to a new 120-volt water pump that pumps it to the unit and then to an outlet side that dumps the hot water overboard. There also is a condensation drain the runs from the unit to the bilge. Then there is the control panel and its wiring, the water pump and its wiring and the 120-volt power supply wiring.

After much thinking and planning, I decided to take out *Jenny's* ULine icemaker and put the air conditioner in its spot. I had determined that making ice consumed too much energy to be practical. We had not used it since entering Mexico. Instead we have been buying bags of ice and storing them in the freezer. It became a useless piece of equipment and its location turned out to be ideal for the air conditioner to cool the staterooms. I did not even have to run any ducting and we did not lose any closet space. The cold air blows directly into the master stateroom, directed right at the door to the forward stateroom. With the door between the master stateroom and the salon closed, both staterooms get cold. The air conditioner then pulls the return air up the stairs from the forward stateroom to the pilothouse, then back down into the galley. If we close the door between the staterooms and open the door between the salon and the master, then the cold air is pulled into the salon and back to the galley, cooling the salon. Pretty cool...

However, *Jenny* really needs two of these 16K units to be properly cooled. This unit does pretty well for two rooms, but the other two remain warm. Ideally, I should install the second unit to blow cold air into the pilothouse with the return down in the salon somewhere. However, that is a project for another day. I also got a new control unit for the furnace and plugged that in so we have reliable hot water again.

Our plan now is to clean up *Jenny* and head for Nicaragua Saturday morning, stopping first in the Bay of Foncesca. Marina Puesta del Sol in Nicaragua has slips, power and water, so we can run the AC full time and that will allow me to complete several other projects out of the heat. We will also be able to really clean *Jenny* and wax her. We will stay there until *Jenny* is back to 100%. I hope also to go inland and see an active volcano!

Passage: Barillas to Isla Meanquera

Departed Saturday, May 10, 2008 at 1:57 PM local time from Barillas Marina. The departure location was latitude 13 degrees 7.713 minutes north, longitude 88 degrees 23.773 minutes west.

Arrived Saturday, May 10, 2008 at 3:20 PM local time at southeast side of Meanquera at anchor. The arrival location was latitude 13 degrees 10.977 minutes north, longitude 87 degrees 41.541 minutes west. The customs check in was none. The trip covered 54.75 nautical miles in 0d 9h 10m with an average speed of 6.00 knots and a maximum speed of 7.40 knots.

Saturday, May 10, 2008 6:10:01 PM

Location: Isla Meanguera
Latitude is 13 degrees 10.979 minutes north.
Longitude is 87 degrees 41.559 minutes west.

Dealing with officialdom is often a crapshoot. Yesterday afternoon I went through the process of checking out of El Salvador, which consists of getting official stamps on our Zarpe, crew list and passports. All was going fine until I went to Immigration and the official got confused. I thought it was because we left El Salvador and returned by plane, going through immigration a second time at the airport. He asked for yet another $10 per person and put yet another set of stamps in our passports. I left for the restaurant to have a couple of drinks with folks we met and would be leaving behind. After a few minutes, the immigration official showed up, gave me back the $20 bucks, and explained that a mistake had been made. He then took our passports again to "fix" the problem. Wow. Great service and a conscientious official. Outstanding.

I then went to Heriberto, the marina manager and asked what was going on. It turned out that the official thought we were one of the two boats that had just arrived and had stamped our books with yet another arrival. After a while, he reappeared and gave us our passports back with exit stamps. Hmmm... What is that fragment of paper stuck to the page! The officer had pealed the new entry stamp off the pages! I am hoping nobody will notice...

Jenny dropped her Barillas mooring at 06:00 AM. She was happy to have just Mary and me onboard. Her trip down the estuary and getting beyond the bar was a two hour, twelve-mile trip. For thirty minutes, she ran between the beach and the bar and we watched the ocean waves breaking over the bar. This coupled with the tidal current created a chop mostly on her beam. It is ugly and uncomfortable, but not very dangerous. Once she emerged from behind the bar, the sea was wonderfully calm. Our trip to Isla Meanguera was nice and uneventful. *Jenny* anchored off a small town on the southwest side, and is well protected from the swell coming out of the south. However, the wind is gusting above twenty knots.

I am now trying to figure out if we should leave for Puesta del Sol tomorrow, or take a day to visit the town and go to a restaurant with *Tropical Dance*, a sailboat that left Barillas with us this morning. The catch is the tide. Ideally, we should enter Puesta del Sol on slack high tide. Well, tomorrow it occurs at about 7:00 PM. We will have to enter on the last of the flood. Monday, it will occur about 7:50, and so on. We would be going in on a faster current. The consensus right now is to leave in the morning.

Sunday, May 11, 2008 6:50:42 AM

Location: Isla Meanguera
Latitude is 13 degrees 10.856 minutes north.
Longitude is 87 degrees 41.566 minutes west.

Last night was eventful. *Jenny* was enduring gusts of wind up to twenty knots, and in unexpected currents. After a while, *Jenny* was sideways to the wind, sometimes an indication that she is dragging. *Tropical Dance* was too. After *Tropical Dance* re-anchored, I figured we were dragging too. I hauled *Jenny's* anchor in the dark and changed our location. Then, I discovered we were in only eighteen feet of water and too near a couple of pangas. I hauled again and anchored her about where she was the first time. UGH.

There was a thunderstorm over the mainland that gradually worked its way out to sea. We had our first tropical Boomer and it was a good one! Better than fireworks on the forth. It cooled everything down nicely and rinsed *Jenny* off well.

We are heading for Puesta del Sol today. The tides dictate it unfortunately as this is a lovely spot and worth exploring.

Passage: Isla Meanguera to Puesta del Sol

Departed Sunday, May 11, 2008 at 7:25 PM local time from Isla Meanguera. The departure location was latitude 12 degrees 46.487 minutes north, longitude 87 degrees 37.877 minutes west.

Sunday, May 11, 2008 1:45:34 PM
Location: Unrecorded
Latitude is 12 degrees 45.205 minutes north.
Longitude is 87 degrees 36.304 minutes west.

This weather observation was taken on Sunday, May 11, 2008 6:36:29 AM local time.
Observation location: Isla Meanguera.
Latitude is 13 degrees 10.857 minutes north.
Longitude is 87 degrees 41.567 minutes west.
The air temperature is 82, and water temperature is 80 degrees Fahrenheit.
The forecast is Sunny.
The current weather is dry.
The sky is overcast (more than 90% clouds).
The wind is 1 knots from the north.
The visibility is 10 nautical miles.
The wave height is 0 feet with 0 foot swells.
The barometer is 1009 millibar and rising.

Sunday, May 11, 2008 1:58:38 PM

Location: At Sea
Latitude is 12 degrees 45.205 minutes north.
Longitude is 87 degrees 36.304 minutes west.

This weather observation was taken on Sunday, May 11, 2008 6:36:29 AM local time.
Observation location: Isla Meanguera.
Latitude is 13 degrees 10.857 minutes north.
Longitude is 87 degrees 41.567 minutes west.
The air temperature is 82, and water temperature is 80 degrees Fahrenheit.
The forecast is Sunny.
The current weather is dry.
The sky is overcast (more than 90% clouds).
The wind is 1 knots from the north.
The visibility is 10 nautical miles.
The wave height is 0 feet with 0 foot swells.
The barometer is 1009 millibar and rising.

It is nice not being on a schedule. I guess if you get past the six-month mark, you get into a different groove, a different understanding of cruising. At this point, *Jenny* has become a home instead of a vehicle. You keep your home in a place for as long as you want / can afford to and enjoy being there. Then, you can move your home to a new place and be there for a while. It is very different from thinking about where you are going. It is more about being in different places. On the other hand, keeping a boat in top working condition is a constant challenge. Below is my list of things to do while we are in Puesta del Sol.

* install new gaskets on JD's exhaust
* install a new water temperature sensor on JD
* add a water pump to the Tecma toilet
* install a new VHF antenna on the dinghy
* do the regular maintenance list items
* install new stabilizer up-haul rigging
* install new boom rigging
* install a new magnetron on the open array Furuno
* replace the deck light bulb
* install new navigation running boards and lights
* clean the keel coolers and propeller
* find out why the refrigerator is not getting enough current in DC mode and fix

That's all. Many of these items have been accumulating over the past six months, waiting for the arrival of parts. Now that the parts are onboard, the work begins.

Puesta del Sol is only about 100 miles north of the southern edge of the hurricane zone and is the last inexpensive marina before going through the canal. It is a good place to leave *Jenny* for inland excursions, which shamefully we have not done to date. I hope to stay there at least a month. Then we will move southeast again, see what Costa Rica is all about in June and July and then explore Pacific Panama in July and August. Life is good.

Arrived Sunday, May 11, 2008 at 5:12 PM local time at Marina Puesta del Sol. The arrival location was latitude 12 degrees 37.559 minutes north, longitude 87 degrees 20.487 minutes west. The customs check in was Nicaragua. The trip covered 50.48 nautical miles in 0d 8h 1m with an average speed of 6.30 knots and a maximum speed of 7.90 knots.

Wednesday, May 14, 2008 6:06:57 PM

Location: Puesta del Sol, Nicaragua

I am sitting at the desk in the master cabin with the generator and air conditioner running, eating the last of the Pepperidge Farm Brussels cookies. I deserve it after a long sweaty day in the office (engine room) replacing the gaskets on the three engine exhaust flanges. The generator is on because the shore power is turned off, but more on that later.

After taking the insulation off the exhaust pipe from the header up to the point where it goes up the stack, it was apparent that all three gaskets were gone. They must have been made of some kind of ceramic, but all were completely fractured with pieces missing. To make things worse, the nut on one of the ½ inch by three-inch bolts on the first flange was stripped and I had to cut it out with a hacksaw. UGH. The rest came out easily. I worked from about 07:00 AM until about 3:00 PM taking out the connecting pipe, cleaning the flange surfaces, cutting new gaskets and getting them installed. I will post more details to the Nordhavn 46 group along with pictures. I still have the one gasket to install, but need the bolt I had to cut. Our friend Mark on *Wahoo* at the dock has a car and he is going to town tomorrow and will try to get one. Fingers are crossed. In any case, I ran out of energy and quit for the day. The shower felt wonderful, as does the air conditioning.

Looking back on El Salvador and comparing it Nicaragua, El Salvador is a very nice country with an upbeat personality. I think they are going to do very well. I talked to a native who went to the same prep school in Tampa as my son Terry. He is a landowner and I just happened to bring back an article regarding a plant that Florida is experimenting with to produce bio diesel and replace citrus crops. They hope to get 1,000 gallons of fuel per 1,000 acres. That would make a huge difference for the US and if it was successful in El Salvador it could easily make them energy independent in a decade. Well, this guy knew about the plant, and in fact is in Florida this week trying to get grant money to try it out down here.

While the people outside the capital of San Salvador are poor, there are many trucks on the road and commerce is bustling. People are smiling and kidding around all the time. If you are interested in ocean front property, a cruiser I met decided to make El Salvador home, and purchased an oceanfront home, complete with pool and compound for $70,000. Yup! He has a full time house cleaner and a grounds keeper / guard on duty and the windows have bars, but I will bet the need will gradually go away over the next decade. This is something to think about!

Back to Nicaragua. We took a ride into town yesterday on the marina van. Subsistence farming homesteads lined the dirt road between the resort and the paved highway. Some appeared to have electricity, but most had none and only well water. The homes were inferior to the quality in El Salvador, with some being only thatched roof huts. Each homestead looked like it was an extended family surviving as best they could. They used horses and mules to carry loads, with some dragging wooden carts running on old automobile wheels and tires. A few people had small motorcycles. The schools we saw were open-air, and seemed to be over by noon. The paved road to town looked new and filled with bicycles, horses, and horse drawn carts but very few cars or trucks. The public transportation buses were parked along the road because they could no longer afford the fuel to run them. The rolling blackouts that hit the marina are because the country cannot afford the fuel to keep the power up. The town was larger than Usulután in El Salvador, and seemed more modern and prosperous with all the roads paved. But the people here are just not joyful like in El Salvador and some are angry. One of our fellow cruisers said Nicaragua is the poorest country in Latin America after Haiti. What is obvious is that any country can be successful and prosperous if it has an intelligent, caring and durable government.

We are going to stay here a while longer to get our projects done, then head south. There really is not much to see and do here.

Sunday, May 18, 2008 8:54:58 PM

Location: Puesta del Sol

After making progress on our waxing the superstructure and completing some small projects, Dee Dee and Larry Biggs with their daughter Isabella from *Nexus* came over to visit. We spent a very nice few hours with them. They of course loved *Jenny* and had many favorable things to say about 46's in general. Their Nordhavn 47 is quite nice too and at 85,000 pounds a lot bigger than *Jenny*. Dee Dee and Larry are east coast people, and after spending the year up in Alaska and down the west coast, were very ready to get back to the Caribbean with its wonderful islands, warm water and European flavor. They made us feel that the best is yet to come.

We also chatted about politics, healthcare, business opportunities, east coast boating, and the transition of *Nexus* from being a vehicle to being a movable home. We have quite a lot in common with them and will probably hook up with them again in Panama.

There are about seven cruising boats here that are continuing south. The big debate is whether to leave here tomorrow for Costa Rica or Tuesday. After looking at the weather forecasts, Mary and I chose to go on Tuesday and avoid some heaver winds that will blow across from the Caribbean Monday night. We will also get another chance to grocery shop before being on the hook for a few weeks. Everyone is looking forward to clear water and nice beaches. The water here is warm, but still not clear. Larry uses Caribbean standards (100 ft visibility) and needless to say is disappointed in the west coast even Panama. Right now I'd settle for thirty feet and be happy!

I woke up at 02:00 AM this morning to significant commotion outside and met some new buddies. When I got to *Jenny's* starboard pilothouse door, I could see the action. I opened it up and stepped outside for a bird's eye view. Mike from Walrus was floundering around in the water in the slip next to us with his dinghy upside down. Dan on *Spirit* and Timo on *Pipe Dream* were on the slip trying to rescue him. They had been over at the surfing camp all evening drinking and were thoroughly plastered. It was in celebration of Mike's birthday. Well, Mike weighs in at about 250 pounds and as he stepped on the side of his dingy, it flipped up on him and down he went. They were so stupid drunk that they were laughing themselves silly trying to haul his butt back into the dingy. Mary came up to watch the action and we laughed ourselves silly as the show went on for about 20 minutes. They eventually pulled Mike back into the dinghy and motored off into the darkness.

P.S. Did I say the air conditioner is very nice?

Passage: Puesta del Sol to Bahía Santa Elena

Departed Tuesday, May 20, 2008 at 5:40 PM local time from Puesta del Sol Marina. The departure location was latitude 12 degrees 35.263 minutes north, longitude 87 degrees 21.627 minutes west.

Wednesday, May 21, 2008 6:11:01 AM
Location: At Sea
Latitude is 11 degrees 26.179 minutes north.
Longitude is 86 degrees 13.607 minutes west.

This weather observation was taken on Wednesday, May 21, 2008 5:58:21 AM local time.
Observation location: At Sea.
Latitude is 11 degrees 26.282 minutes north.
Longitude is 86 degrees 13.764 minutes west.
The air temperature is 80, and water temperature is 80 degrees Fahrenheit.

The forecast is rain.
The current weather is dry.
The sky is overcast (more than 90% clouds).
The wind is 3 knots from the northeast.
The visibility is 10 nautical miles.
The wave height is 2 feet with 2 foot swells.
The barometer is 1007 millibar and rising.

Five vessels left Puesta del Sol Nicaragua two days ago to go Bahia Santa Elena in Costa Rica and are presumably already there. Five more left yesterday, us included. We released *Jenny's* tethers and left around 10:30 AM local time. The rest went later. The forecast was for light and variable winds all the way down. Well, I guess the weather model does not consider local weather phenomenon. *Jenny* had a good fifteen knots of wind onshore all day and I put her birds down around 5:00 in the evening. Then it quieted down around 8:00 PM and thunderstorms grew up on shore. They were fun to watch for a while until they started moving toward us. By 9:00 PM Mary and I were in the middle of our first boomer while underway. It rained, boomed and flashed for the next three hours. Fortunately, the wind stayed low most of the time. It was quite the experience since neither of us knew quite what to expect. The rain was so intense it blocked out the radar and our GPS. We had zero visibility and our compass was our only working navigation instrument.

I stashed all the backup electronics in the oven in case we were hit. A lightning strike that takes out all our electronics is my biggest fear. *Jenny* also bucked a good 1.5 knot current until about 05:00 AM so she was only making about five knots most of the way. She is now making 5.7 and is avoiding some of the adverse current by hugging the shore as it turns from southeast to northwest making a shallow bay.

The sea turned clear and blue and came alive again a few hours south of Puesta del Sol. It was the best we have seen since Huatulco. *Jenny* was joined by a school of over fifty bridled dolphin (have the book now) that came over and kept us company for about an hour. Nicholas really enjoys watching them. They have been keeping *Jenny* company all morning. For some reason, the coasts of El Salvador and Nicaragua have cloudy water and apparently little marine life. The book says we will see clear turquoise water in Costa Rica. I am looking forward to it!

The sky is still overcast with cumulus clouds dumping rain in various spots over land and on the water. This area is notorious for Papagayo winds that blow through from the Caribbean so hugging the coast has additional benefits. I will turn west when we get close to the bend in the land, and then duck into Bahia Santa Elena. A nicely protected little bay should have about ten boats in it soon.

Our cheap $40 West Marine binoculars hit the floor last night and broke into two large pieces. I was not vigilant enough to have properly stowed them. This is the reason you only buy cheap binoculars. It is inevitable that they will be thrown to the ground and break. In this case, I screwed the pieces back together and they are functional once again.

07:30 AM - It's a comfortable 78 degrees F out and we are actually running in a rain shower for the first time since we were in the Pacific Northwest four years ago. It is a real nice change. Van Morrison is playing on the stereo. We are cruising again...

Arrived Wednesday, May 21, 2008 at 1:02 PM local time at Bahia Santa Elena. The arrival location was latitude 10 degrees 55.322 minutes north, longitude 85 degrees 48.879 minutes west. The customs check in was None. The trip covered 142.03 nautical miles in 1d 1h 21m with an average speed of 5.60 knots and a maximum speed of 7.10 knots.

Thursday, May 22, 2008 7:39:04 AM

Location: Bahia Santa Elena
Latitude is 10 degrees 55.342 minutes north.
Longitude is 85 degrees 48.902 minutes west.

Sunset in Costa Rica

Well, it rained the rest of the day yesterday, but this morning dawned bright and blue. Last night was nice and cool so we did not need the air conditioner at all. The anchorage here is beautiful and the water is clear to thirty feet. I caught a Dorado on the way in yesterday and had a few pieces for dinner. Yummy!

Later today I will break out the new Hookah unit and do some diving. There are four other vessels here and I suspect we will be doing some snorkeling.

I will continue doing some projects here like cleaning the bottom and finishing the waxing. We will also take the dinghy in and do some exploring on shore. This is a national park, and looks quite interesting.

Friday, May 23, 2008 6:43:40 AM

Location: Bahia Santa Elena

Yesterday was another busy day. We woke up to a bright blue sunny sky. The weather is one of alternating sun and downpours. As yet, there has not been any thunder and lightning within the bay. *Jenny's* water catching is working, but not quite keeping up with our consumption. It is nice to have sun and rain, creating a nice variety through the day that we missed in California and Mexico. We can hear howler monkeys on shore as well as wild parrots.

I broke out the Hookah yesterday and used it to begin cleaning the bottom. The last time I did this was in Acapulco. I had thought that the month in Barillas would have kept most of the growth down to nothing. It did for the most part, however, it left a brown growth on the hull that requires strong brushing to get off. The barnacle growth was minimal except on the propeller. It was covered with barnacles that contributed to *Jenny's* slow speeds since then. I will have to dive on her bottom again today and maybe a little more tomorrow to get it clean and her propeller polished.

The Hookah is a wonderful tool. Except for the noise from the pump pulses going down the air hose, it is completely unobtrusive, unlike Scuba. With Scuba, you are carrying up to 100 lbs of gear that is clumsy and tiring. With the Hookah, the gear is no more than the addition of the regulator. Nothing else intrudes. Without the Hookah, I can now see that it would be impossible to keep up with bottom maintenance, thus resulting in slower passages and additional fuel consumption. Combined with the cost of having someone else clean the bottom when they are available, the cost of the Hookah easily pays for itself.

I have also been tuning up on my weather data gathering while remote and without Internet access. Weather Buoy is our primary tool now. But it does not give us the big picture through our email requests. I spent a few hours yesterday setting up frequencies and schedules to receive the weather faxes for this area. It takes some work to fine tune the schedule as the broadcast times and content change over time. I need to verify and finish that work today too.

I want to say here until I finish our spring waxing, bottom cleaning, and some projects. It is beautiful and many say the best of Costa Rica. The beach is also very nice and good for exploring and swimming. Mary is bored, and will not go swimming or walking on the beach.

Saturday, May 24, 2008 6:50:54 AM

Location: Bahia Santa Elena

Well, *Jenny*'s bottom is now clean as a baby's butt. Today I will finish working on the propeller and the superstructure waxing. Then we will be ready to go again. I also replaced the magnetron in the large open array radar and it's working like new again.

When we wake up, the temperature is around 75 degrees and very comfortable. Nicholas and I take a trip into the beach where there are loads of shells. Hermit crabs inhabited many of them. *Jenny* is the only boat in the bay now and walking along the beach is like being on a deserted island. It is very quiet and peaceful.

Monday, May 26, 2008 7:54:12 AM

Location: Bahia Santa Elena
Latitude is 10 degrees 55.332 minutes north.
Longitude is 85 degrees 48.913 minutes west.

The weather has closed in with a tropical depression sitting just off the coast. We are still in Costa Rica, but have not checked in yet. We have had sunny mornings and rainy afternoons consistently. But, today we woke up to an overcast sky and light rain. Later in the week, the weather is supposed to turn nasty with winds up to thirty knots and twenty-two foot seas out of the southwest. Since this bay is well protected from that direction, I plan to say here until the system passes. The three other vessels with us sailed down to Playa de Coco, the port of entry, yesterday and plan to clear in today. However, that bay is open to the southwest as are many along this coast. They might be coming back up here later today or tomorrow.

I have been gathering water while here and while it has not kept up with our consumption, it has helped quite a bit. What I really need is a downpour or two.

Passage: Bahia Santa Elena to Playa de Panama

Departed Monday, May 26, 2008 at 8:55 PM local time from Bahia Santa Elena anchor. The departure location was latitude 10 degrees 35.477 minutes north, longitude 85 degrees 39.583 minutes west.

Arrived Monday, May 26, 2008 at 2:56 PM local time at Playa de Panama. The arrival location was latitude 10 degrees 35.477 minutes north, longitude 85 degrees 39.585 minutes west. The customs check in was Coco Capitan del Puerto. The trip covered 40.96 nautical miles in 0d 6h 48m with an average speed of 6.00 knots and a maximum speed of 7.60 knots.

Monday, May 26, 2008 7:23:06 PM

Location: Playa de Panama Costa Rica
Latitude is 10 degrees 35.489 minutes north.
Longitude is 85 degrees 39.609 minutes west.

Jenny had a bumpy ride down here today. We rounded two points of land and a bunch of islands that tore up the water. So, her birds went in. On the weather front there are now two new pieces of information. First, the word from a boat coming north is that the Poterio bay does not offer much of any protection. Second, the big wind and waves have been removed from the forecast, but a nasty eight-second chop is forecast for Wednesday through Saturday. We have our Barillas boating friends around us now, and the consensus is to say put until this weather resolves itself. One of the vessels heading for Ecuador has a crew and thus has a schedule. They are staying but not happy. Having crew is definitely a two edged sword.

This is a big bay and very pretty. The hills are being terraced for homes and development is evident. Tomorrow we will go to shore, take a taxi into the port captain's office to check in and do some shopping. We will probably head south when the rest of the vessels do. There is a big bay (Nicoya) about 200 miles from here where we want to stop and spend some time. But, in the meantime...

Wednesday, May 28, 2008 8:20:07 AM

Location: Playa Panama
Latitude is 10 degrees 35.495 minutes north.
Longitude is 85 degrees 39.622 minutes west.

It continues to amaze me how comfortable the temperature is here all day long. We wake up to the lower 70's and it seems to peak in the lower 80's. We have not run the air conditioner since leaving Nicaragua. A frontal system stalled off Panama is causing the overcast sky and steady drizzle, and has me wondering if it is the cause of these fine temperatures. We are enjoying them anyway.

We took a taxi into the small town of Playa de Coco to check in. It is a nice town, but I was expecting to see better infrastructure. This area is under heavy development with condominium's and timeshares going up all over the hills. Sea view lots seem to be going for about $120,000; condominiums for about $200,000. There is a big condominium development going up in Playa de Coco and a new supermarket. In spite of that, the native buildings, roads, etc. are at pre-affluence levels. Maybe that will change as people buy and move in.

I noticed something odd about the taxi service. Each driver gave us his business card with his phone number on it. At first, I thought this was just a custom and a way to tie in repeat business. Later I found out there was much more to it.

Crime against vessels seems to be higher here than anywhere before. *Catching Up*, a sailboat with three boys onboard had thieves sneak on deck and steal their dinghy and dinghy motor while they slept. It is the first incidence of such a thing on a vessel we know since leaving the US. Costa Ricans are supposed to be more affluent and worldly than their neighbors to the north, but it seems to be at a price. Also, there are very few firearms being carried in the open here unlike the countries to the north. Maybe that is a mistake.

Playa de Coco has nice tourist shops and restaurants and a very nice grocery store. The grocery store is heavily oriented to North American shoppers and has all the American brands. Mary had a good experience! However, you have to walk in the street since sidewalks are rare. Watch out for the mud puddles and passing cars, trucks and motorcycles. It is all a very odd mixture of foreign wealth and local poverty. There is a lot of private money pouring into the area for the real estate, but none of seems to be trickling down to the locals and their local government. This could easily be one reason why the people seem unhappy and unfriendly toward us gringos.

Another item of interest is that all the license plates since Mexico have the name of the country across the top and "Central America" across the bottom. There seems to be a political consciousness and affiliation that extends beyond national borders. I noticed that some of the political parties cross national boarders too.

While in town, we saw white squirrels with a black Mohawk running down their heads to their tails. We saw a few new and exotic birds and a lemur that apparently lives in one of the back yards in town. It was ambling around the yard and then climbed up one of the big trees. We need to go into town one more time to get a National Zarpe to move to the next port and I will bring the camera in. There is also an internet cafe, so we will get caught up on our regular email and web activities.

The main part of town is a broken down street with open-faced bars and restaurants. The bars are open 24 x 7 and the patrons start appearing around 10:00 AM. You can find a Canadian in one who was once a heart surgeon, author, fighter pilot, corporate lawyer, etc. He knows everything about everything. And for a drink he would tell you all about it. The places seemed harmless enough in the half-light of the drizzling rain forest.

We plan a quiet day today making spaghetti sauce, cleaning *Jenny*, cleaning Nicholas' teeth, etc. I hope we will get some heavy rain for *Jenny's* tanks.

Wednesday, May 28, 2008 11:35:25 AM

Location: Playa Panama
Latitude is 10 degrees 35.495 minutes north.
Longitude is 85 degrees 39.629 minutes west.

At first light (05:00 AM) thousands of fish jumping and splashing boil the water under *Jenny*. At first, I thought it was pesky pelicans diving on the usual bubble fish that always take up residence there. This morning Mary and I got up to investigate. The pandemonium was being provoked by a school of large predator fish running under *Jenny* and coming up under the shoal of baitfish that hide under her. The predators come flying out of the water as well as a couple hundred minnow sized baitfish each run and was the cause of the racket right outside *Jenny's* portholes.

In spite of the rain, this fishing opportunity was too tempting. First, I rigged the fresh water rod and reel (twelve-pound test) with a small hook. I learned from the fishermen in La Cruz that you can jig a hook through a shoal of baitfish and snag them. It worked. I jerked the hook through the shoal that took up residence on the starboard side. Then I left the baitfish on the hook to see what would happen. It swam to the middle of the shoal trying to be inconspicuous with the hook hanging out of it. The next time the predator fish came through, wham it took the baitfish, and snap, broke off the rig. Hmmmm... I re-rigged the line and tried again. Bam, it struck pulled the baitfish off and left a bare hook. Now it was getting exciting!

I tried to use my larger saltwater rig, but could not gig a baitfish on. I went back to the fresh water rig. I was jigging for another baitfish when the team of predator fish came through the shoal. Wham! One took the bare hook and was off. It was BIG. Much too big for the rig, but with the drag set right, nothing broke.

An hour later I was still fighting it and it was hard to tell if I had gained any ground at all. After another twenty minutes I caught sight of it, a beautiful young yellow fin tuna, about twenty to twenty-five pounds. Over the next hour I slowly fought it to *Jenny's* side, had the gaff in hand and the fish right at the surface in reach. When I touched the gaff to the fish, it exploded. The next thing I knew the rod was straight, the line somewhere in the air and the fish gone. When I recovered from the shock, I found the line up in *Jenny's* stabilizer rigging. The hook was still there. Apparently, the hook was too small and only caught bone. When twisted in the right position, it just let go. Lucky fish...

My arms felt like waste material, burning from the constant effort. This was the best fish fight I have ever had.

Friday, May 30, 2008 7:15:48 AM

Location: Playa Panama
Latitude is 10 degrees 35.558 minutes north.
Longitude is 85 degrees 39.573 minutes west.

Yesterday morning the trimaran *Stravaig* called Mayday on the Pan Pacific Net. Jeff and Jose Allen, a British couple from Inverness Scotland had been up for fifty hours, struggling to keep their boat afloat after being caught in the tropical storm Alma. They reported peak winds over eighty knots and steady winds of over fifty-five knots. The thirty-five foot seas had been breaking over the boat and had reduced their rigging to a tangle. Water had entered the main hull and the engine room. The engine would not run. Their position was 11 degrees 02 minutes north, 86 degrees 47 minutes west. They were off the coast of Costa Rica. The vessels here were the closest to them, about seventy miles southeast. Jeff and Jose were below, exhausted and *Stravaig* was drifting with the seas.

The net reached out to the Maritime Mobile Service Net, the Costa Rican coast guard, etc. and alerted them to the emergency. There was significant confusion regarding their responses except for the US Coast Guard rerouting a C130 airplane due to arrive in four hours. There was a report of the Costa Rican navy sending a frigate, but never verified. *Stravaig* did not have a life raft, they believed waves had damaged their dinghy, and had an old EPIRB that came with the boat. They were reluctant to activate their EPIRB. After about an hour, they signed off and would come back on in two hours while they worked on their vessel.

When they came back on at 10:20 AM Costa Rica time, they were in the eye of the storm. They reported a position of 11 degrees 06 minutes north, 86 degrees 44 minutes west. *Stravaig* was drifting in the waves and wind toward the Nicaragua coast. They were told that US Coast Guard C130 was on its way and that a Costa Rica Navy frigate was on its way with an ETA in ten hours. Jose was very concerned about their chances for survival. When Jeff took the mike, he was concerned that the rescuers would force them to abandon their vessel. He repeatedly asked the intension of the rescue teams and believed that they were not in immediate danger. The rescue teams assured them they would not be required to abandon *Stravaig*.

They checked in again at 2:00 PM Costa Rica time and reported a position of 11 degrees 14 minutes north, 86 degrees 37 minutes West, on a steady course for landfall. They were twenty-seven miles from a dangerous shore. They had their engine running but did not have *Stravaig* under control. The best they could do against the wind and current was ¼ knot. They also had very little diesel fuel. Due to sleep deprivation, their ability to communicate clearly was diminishing. Also, the closer they were getting to land, the more they were getting wave reflections, causing the sea to be wild, making everything on the vessel more difficult. The C130 was overhead and asked them to turn on their EPIRB. Jeff refused, believing that would signal they were willing to abandon their vessel. The C130 asked them if they would like a de-watering pump, food or other supplies dropped. Jeff refused. The USCG C130 stayed overhead until their fuel ran low and left. The C130 declared them to be in an emergency and dispatched a USCG Cutter to the scene with an ETA in fourteen hours.

They checked in again at 4:00 PM. They were at 11 degrees 20 minutes north, 86 degrees 31 minutes west still on a steady course to the breakers now just 19 miles away. Earlier, the rescue teams wanted them to go to San Juan del Sur forty miles southeast of their current position. However, San Juan del Sur was reporting breaking twenty-five to fifty foot waves at the entrance even if they could have regained control over *Stravaig's* course. They still had no control over her drift. The US Coast Guard Cutter was reportedly getting within radio range, but other than that they were alone. There was no indication that Costa Rica or Nicaragua had any boats underway or anywhere near them.

I advised Jeff of his position, course and closeness to land. Jeff was aware of the danger from the nearing lee shore and their plan was to use the engine as a last resort to keep them off the beach. *Wahoo*, a forty-foot sport fishing boat in our anchorage was the local controlling contact with Stravaig. They set a new check in time of 7:00 PM, which was after dark but did not change the sideband frequency to one that would work after dark. I was talking with the Marine Maritime Service Net when that occurred. That was the last contact we had with them. Needless to say, this brings home our vulnerabilities and the folks in our anchorage have been very subdued throughout the day. You could have heard a pin drop that night.

At 09:00 AM the next morning *Stravaig* came on the net!!! They did rendezvous with the USCG Cutter sometime last night. The Cutter put divers in the water and gave them a lee. They delivered diesel to *Stravaig* just in time to keep them off the beach and then escorted them to Bahia Santa Elena. They are now sleeping.

We checked into Costa Rica when we were in Playa Panama. The port captain's office was down the bay a bit in Playa de Coco, so we took a taxi to that town. When I checked in, I found out that you need a national Zarpe to move from port to port. This afternoon Mark from *Wahoo* and I went into Coco to get our

National Zarpe's to move south. The port captain said he would be on duty but was not there when we arrived around 4:00 PM. We hung around. As the sun set, the place became more spooky by the minute. The rain was still dripping off the trees, keeping the mud puddles filled. Exotic creatures came out in the canapé and in the bars. Prostitutes and drug dealers lined the shadows and there was no Law in sight. The port captain finally returned to his office down by the waterfront and we cleared out. Then he immediately cleared out of town. Outside again on foot, we realized there was not a single taxi in sight and we had been strongly warned about getting into any car that did not have a taxi license stamped on it.

Then Mark and I remembered the business cards. We found a phone in one of the safer looking establishments and called one of the cabs we had used. We were still unmolested when it arrived. The driver explained that the card meant that he had determined we were safe to pick up at night. Otherwise, no cab picks anyone up after dark. The place was right out of the darkest Humphrey Bogart movie.

Passage: Playa Panama to Potrero

Departed Saturday, May 31, 2008 at 6:21 PM local time from Playa Panama. The departure location was latitude 10 degrees 26.860 minutes north, longitude 85 degrees 47.749 minutes west.

Arrived Saturday, May 31, 2008 at 12:22 PM local time at Bahia Potrero. The arrival location was latitude 10 degrees 26.859 minutes north, longitude 85 degrees 47.747 minutes west. The customs check in was none. The trip covered 20.09 nautical miles in 0d 3h 17m with an average speed of 6.10 knots and a maximum speed of 8.40 knots.

Sunday, June 01, 2008 7:36:13 AM

Location: Bahia Potrero
Latitude is 10 degrees 26.605 minutes north.
Longitude is 85 degrees 47.109 minutes west.

Jenny carried us eighteen miles down the coast to Bahia Potrero and continued our journey south. The trip was short and the bay is ok for a road stop, but not completely protected. There are several resorts and hotels lining the beach and many local boats on mooring balls. We came down with *Wahoo*, but they left this morning for the next stop leaving us as the only active cruising boat here.

Mary is going to the beach this morning after we listen to the SSB nets to check out the resorts and town if there is one. She needs some land time. Tomorrow we will continue down the coast toward the Gulf of Nicoya, a large gulf with several islands, bays and towns.

Passage: Potrero to Carrillo

Departed Monday, June 02, 2008 at 12:04 PM local time from Bahia Potrero. The departure location was latitude 10 degrees 27.532 minutes north, longitude 85 degrees 48.379 minutes west.

Monday, June 02, 2008 9:32:45 AM
Location: At Sea
Latitude is 10 degrees 6.801 minutes north.
Longitude is 85 degrees 51.682 minutes west.

This weather observation was taken on Monday, June 02, 2008 9:19:42 AM local time.
Observation location: At Sea.
Latitude is 10 degrees 6.973 minutes north.
Longitude is 85 degrees 51.807 minutes west.
The air temperature is 81, and water temperature is 82 degrees Fahrenheit.
The forecast is Sunny, Thunderstorms.
The current weather is dry.
The sky is clear or a few clouds.
The wind is 4 knots from the east.
The visibility is 20 nautical miles.
The wave height is 1 feet with 3 foot swells.
The barometer is 1010 millibar and rising.

Jenny is on her way from Bahia Potrero to Carrillo and it is a beautiful day. The seas are glassy smooth with a gentle swell out of the south. I expect the wind to turn onshore soon as the land heats up. Looking at the weather charts, it is clear that wind moves into the Costa Rican, Panama peninsula from both sides and converges in the middle, forming thunderstorms. This seems to happen most every day.

We had a nice night last night in Potrero and collected a bunch of water as the cumulus clouds dumped their load. The water catch is keeping up with our usage nicely now and the last water we loaded was in Nicaragua. We have full tanks and it looks like the daily rain will keep them that way. The water maker has been pickled since arriving in Barillas over a month ago.

Jenny will be staying in a roadstead called Carrillo tonight and *Wahoo* who stayed there last night said it rolled them a lot, but better than doing an overnight. I hope these seas will make a better night for us tonight. In any case, I will probably have her birds down as roll dampers.

Arrived Monday, June 02, 2008 at 2:09 PM local time at Carrillo Cove. The arrival location was latitude 9 degrees 51.967 minutes north, longitude 85 degrees 29.358 minutes west. The customs check in was none. The trip covered 55.20 nautical miles in 0d 8h 26m with an average speed of 6.50 knots and a maximum speed of 7.80 knots.

Passage: Carrillo to Ballena Bay

Departed Tuesday, June 03, 2008 at 5:52 AM local time from Carrillo anchorage. The departure location was latitude 9 degrees 51.199 minutes north, longitude 85 degrees 29.221 minutes west.

Arrived Tuesday, June 03, 2008 at 1:01 PM local time at Bahia Ballena. The arrival location was latitude 9 degrees 43.036 minutes north, longitude 85 degrees 0.604 minutes west. The customs check in was none. The trip covered 46.26 nautical miles in 0d 7h 7m with an average speed of 6.50 knots and a maximum speed of 7.70 knots.

Passage: Ballena Bay to Naranjo

Departed Wednesday, June 04, 2008 at 2:22 PM local time from Ballena Bay anchorage. The departure location was latitude 9 degrees 43.134 minutes north, longitude 84 degrees 59.904 minutes west.

Arrived Wednesday, June 04, 2008 at 12:29 PM local time at Naranjo, Oasis del Pacifico Resort. The arrival location was latitude 9 degrees 56.524 minutes north, longitude 84 degrees 57.833 minutes west. The trip covered 27.76 nautical miles in 0d 4h 6m with an average speed of 6.80 knots and a maximum speed of 9.40 knots.

Thursday, June 05, 2008 11:30:29 AM

Location: Gulf of Nicoya, Oasis del Pacifico Resort
Latitude is 9 degrees 56.516 minutes north.
Longitude is 84 degrees 57.841 minutes west.

I think I found a good spot for us. The usual stop is across the bay at Puntarenas. But, with a six foot draft and a ten foot tide the channel is only navigable at high tide and the vessels sit in the mud at low tide. The moorings are up a mangrove estuary with the usual no-see-ums and mosquitoes. That is where the yacht club is. I decided not to go there. Instead I chose a spot across the bay. There is a resort here, nice to yachters. We still have the ten foot tides, but we are away from a regular shore so do not have the bugs. The resort is on a cove with a very nice beach. Our entire stay looks like it will cost us $10.00 for the use of the beach and take in trash. It also seems very safe here.

We had a three-hour downpour last night that nearly filled our water tanks again. Today we are doing laundry. Our little machine did a full set of queen size sheets! We are hanging the laundry to dry on the upper deck. Not very elegant, but it gets the job done with the intense sun and light breezes. Tomorrow, we will even try to do a few towels!

We walked into "town" this morning with Nicholas to discover it consists of a nice cafe and the ferry dock. Along the way, you notice the monkeys in the trees and groves of teak. We stopped at the cafe, chatted with the locals, and had breakfast. The breakfast for two cost all of $8.00. The hotel is in caretaker mode since this is the off-season and the woman in charge is very nice. We are meeting her at 3:30 PM to walk to a restaurant the other way down the road. We found out more about a town where the Super Mercado is and the bus. The town is about twenty kilometers from here and the bus stops at 07:30 AM and 11:00 AM. It returns at 4:00 PM and maybe sometime earlier. No one seemed to know. The woman at the hotel is taking the bus tomorrow morning and we are going to go with her. If that does not have the shopping we are looking for, then we will take the ferry to Puntarenas. Given what is within walking distance, easy bus or ferry rides, this is turning out to be a very nice spot.

Thursday, June 05, 2008 5:39:12 PM

Location: Oasis del Pacifico
Latitude is 9 degrees 56.519 minutes north.
Longitude is 84 degrees 57.839 minutes west.

This place has an appropriate name. The dinghy dock is serviceable in the top half of the ten foot tide and is the first dinghy dock that has been usable since Acapulco. We checked out the restaurant this evening. It's a ½ mile walk from the resort and has a limited but ok menu. It was a good break from dinner on *Jenny*.

Tomorrow we will take the 07:30 bus to Jicaral where the shopping is supposed to be and the day after we will go into photojournalist mode. This place is teaming with life. It is amazing. There are groves of teak trees, howler monkeys, skinks and small lizards, birds, and insects galore. There are two high volume streams coming down from the hills and the Puntarenas ferry *San Lucas* is passing buy on its last trip for the day. Shania Twain is playing on the USB drive. It looks like there will not be rain tonight. Life is good.

P.S. We might be able to get Wi-Fi tomorrow in Jicaral.

Passage: Playa Naranjo to Los Sueños

Departed Sunday, June 08, 2008 at 1:09 PM local time from Playa Naranjo anchorage. The departure location was latitude 9 degrees 57.041 minutes north, longitude 84 degrees 57.109 minutes west.

Arrived Sunday, June 08, 2008 at 11:08 AM local time at Bahia Herradura. The arrival location was latitude 9 degrees 38.619 minutes north, longitude 84 degrees 39.570 minutes west. The customs check in was none. The trip covered 29.10 nautical miles in 0d 3h 58m with an average speed of 6.70 knots and a maximum speed of 8.90 knots.

Passage: Los Suenos to Quepos

Departed Monday, June 09, 2008 at 1:22 PM local time from Bahia Herradura anchorage. The departure location was latitude 9 degrees 38.731 minutes north, longitude 84 degrees 39.914 minutes west.

Monday, June 09, 2008 10:18:25 AM

Location: At Sea
Latitude is 9 degrees 28.834 minutes north.
Longitude is 84 degrees 30.288 minutes west.

This weather observation was taken on Monday, June 09, 2008 9:57:32 AM local time.
Observation location: At Sea.
Latitude is 9 degrees 28.859 minutes north.
Longitude is 84 degrees 30.456 minutes west.
The air temperature is 82, and water temperature is 82 degrees Fahrenheit.
The forecast is Sunny, thunderstorms.
The current weather is dry.
The sky is broken clouds (60 - 90% clouds).

The wind is 3 knots from the southwest.
The visibility is 12 nautical miles.
The wave height is 1 feet with 4 foot swells.
The barometer is 1010 millibar and steady.

Jenny is now working her way down the Costa Rican coast to Gulfito. Playa Naranjo was a very nice place to stay. The bus ride ($1.40) to Jicaral was very native and interesting. We went through the countryside on a small country road that picked up folks all along the way going to town. We were the only non-locals. The little town of Jicaral was also very native. It had an internet "library" where people could use the computers and internet connection. School kids were the visible users. We plugged in and sent off some photos, checked in with our bank, etc. I called the Port Networks serviceman and he confirmed that the radio in the box had become "desensitized" whatever that means. Probably from being blasted by the SSB. We had to be sent back for exchange. I may be able to do this in Gulfito, but otherwise it is likely to be in Panama.

We did some shopping and had lunch in a local cafe. The cafe's here have no menu. The locals know what they want and the kitchen just cooks it. Figuring out what to order is a challenge. In Jicaral I had breakfast and Mary had lunch. Both were good. We took an unofficial cab back to Oasis del Pacifico for $16 since the bus was not scheduled to be there for another two hours.

The next day we went on a photo excursion and got some pictures of the local flora and fauna, including a chestnut colored squirrel with a black Mohawk, a blue skink, flowers, and butterflies. I also got a shot of the national bird of Costa Rica, an eagle. This eagle is supposed to be the largest bird of prey in the world. Ours was regular eagle size, but the big ones have a six-foot wingspan and prey on monkeys, etc. Good thing Nicholas was on *Jenny* at the time. We also came across a lime tree and harvested some. They were delicious!

We are still hungering for civilization, so decided to continue south. Last night we stayed at Bahia Herradura where Marina Los Suenos is. The marina charges $3.00 per foot per day so no one we know actually stayed there. The bay had rolling waves and the water was too murky to dive on *Jenny*'s bottom, so today she is going to Quepos, the next stop on the way to Gulfito. The sea is glassy smooth so the trip is very nice in spite of an adverse current. *Jenny* should arrive by 1:30 PM local time. We have not had any decent rain for several days now so are hoping we get some tonight. The temperatures continue to amaze me. Last night got down to about 70 degrees F and it is only 82 now!

Arrived Monday, June 09, 2008 at 1:08 PM local time at Quepos. The arrival location was latitude 9 degrees 25.794 minutes north, longitude 84 degrees 10.328 minutes west. The customs check in was none. The trip covered 35.85 nautical miles in 0d 5h 45m with an average speed of 6.20 knots and a maximum speed of 7.40 knots.

Passage: Quepos to Drake Bay

Departed Wednesday, June 11, 2008 at 12:34 PM local time from Quepos anchorage. The departure location was latitude 9 degrees 25.337 minutes north, longitude 84 degrees 10.921 minutes west.

Wednesday, June 11, 2008 10:48:05 AM
Location: At Sea
Latitude is 9 degrees 4.427 minutes north.
Longitude is 83 degrees 57.212 minutes west.

This weather observation was taken on Wednesday, June 11, 2008 10:36:04 AM local time.
Observation location: At Sea.
Latitude is 9 degrees 4.549 minutes north.
Longitude is 83 degrees 57.311 minutes west.
The air temperature is 82, and water temperature is 82 degrees Fahrenheit.
The forecast is Overcast, thunderstorms.
The current weather is dry.
The sky is overcast (more than 90% clouds).
The wind is 2 knots from the southwest.
The visibility is 20 nautical miles.
The wave height is 0 feet with 3 foot swells.
The barometer is 1009 millibar and steady.

We stayed a day in Quepos trying to find a way to visit the town. As with too many anchorages on this coast, there was no way to get to shore. There was a floating dock that we could drop off and pick up from, but not leave the dinghy. It was two miles from town so Mary did not want to take the hike alone. This morning we left disappointed and are heading now for Drake bay.

Jenny picked up a squad of Boobies during the first couple of hours. They see her and think she is a fishing boat. Then they flock over and make low passes to see if there are any fish scraps they can steal off of her deck. They are persistent. I had the meat hook out and one of them found it. The Booby somehow got tangled in the line but not hooked. Then another Booby, thinking this one had a meal, landed on it and did some waterskiing using the first Booby as the board. The first Booby was desperately trying to keep its head above the water and remain alive. The top one was trying to drown the first one and get the prize. I slowed *Jenny* down to idle and started pulling them in. Eventually the top Booby decided things were getting out of control and flew off. That left the first one on the surface. Then his pals started to dive bomb him. It was a very unlucky bird, taking hit after hit. But you never know who your friends really are since one of them eventually knocked it loose of the lure. Then pandemonium broke out as all the remaining Boobies went for the now free lure. I was hauling it in as fast as I could so I would not have to unhook an angry Booby. I got it in without an attached Booby and I kept it in until they tired of harassing us.

Nicholas knows these birds are no good and starts growling and barking when he sees them! Good dog!!

We are going to Drake Bay today. It is an open bay on the north side inside a national park. We are hoping we can get to shore easily since the books say this is the spot to go hiking and observe the Costa Rican wildlife. The park gets over 200 inches of rain a year making it the wettest place in the country. As we approach the shore, it is covered in rain clouds, looking like an island out of a Jules Verne book or something.

Arrived Wednesday, June 11, 2008 at 3:02 PM local time at Bahia Drake. The arrival location was latitude 8 degrees 41.809 minutes north, longitude 83 degrees 40.046 minutes west. The customs check in was none. The trip covered 54.44 nautical miles in 0d 8h 27m with an average speed of 6.40 knots and a maximum speed of 7.50 knots.

Passage: Drake Bay to Gulfito

Departed Friday, June 13, 2008 at 11:48 AM local time from Drake Bay Anchorage. The departure location was latitude 8 degrees 42.157 minutes north, longitude 83 degrees 40.260 minutes west.

Friday, June 13, 2008 11:24:58 AM
Location: At Sea
Latitude is 8 degrees 23.056 minutes north.
Longitude is 83 degrees 25.269 minutes west.

This weather observation was taken on Friday, June 13, 2008 10:58:00 AM local time.
Observation location: At Sea.
Latitude is 8 degrees 23.082 minutes north.
Longitude is 83 degrees 25.429 minutes west.
The air temperature is 85, and water temperature is 82 degrees Fahrenheit.
The forecast is Sunny, rain.
The current weather is dry.
The sky is scattered clouds (10 - 50% clouds).
The wind is 4 knots from the south.
The visibility is 20 nautical miles.
The wave height is 0 feet with 3 foot swells.
The barometer is 1008 millibar and rising.

Drake Bay town

Drake Bay was a nice stop, although with rolling waves in the anchorage. There are several nature lodges, camps, etc. here associated with the park. If you want to get back to nature, this is your spot. It rained every day and night to various degrees. Yesterday we took the dinghy up a small stream and tied it to a tree at the base of one of the lodges. Creeks and rivers are about the only way we can get to shore with *The Beast*. We then made a lunch reservation with the lodge and went on a hike back toward "town". The wildlife was everywhere and I got some photos of some of it. There were lots of exotic birds, flowers, etc. Unfortunately I still do not have any photos of the monkeys, and have yet to see a sloth. We did see two wild scarlet macaws, an iguana that must have been three feet long, and a lizard that definitely looked prehistoric. Someone will have to identify it when I send out the photos. (It was a Basilisk lizard.)

There was an overgrown eighteen-inch wide ancient cement stairway into the rain forest up along the edge of one of the steep hills. The hillside it was cut into was filled with fist size holes that were just about chest high and only a few inches away as you climbed up. I wondered what lived in them as I inched by... Laura later said they were Tarantula nests. Mary waited below. At the top there was a landing with a fence. My bet is this was Dracula's home at one time... Might still be...

When we got back to *Jenny*, the water was barely clear enough to dive on the bottom, but I did. There weren't any barnacles since Bahia Elena, and the prop and coolers were in good shape. It only took an hour to brush the growth off the bottom, polish the prop and the cooler.

This morning we pulled anchor at 06:30 AM for our 66 mile trip down to Gulfito. I discovered we had an eight-inch flying fish on *Jenny's* front deck. It must have been flying five to six feet above the water in order to get there. The book says they just glide. Garbage! These things fly. I also think it used the rainstorm last night to get some extra lift. In any case, it was fully airborne. I put it on a hook for later...

A flying fish

Later the flying fish caught a two foot long Hogfish; a big funny looking fellow. I do not believe they are very good to eat, so it went free. (Turns out Hogfish are delicious. UGH) Unfortunately suffered it some damage. I then dropped the feather lure that looks like a small flying fish. In a few minutes I had a Bonito on the hook. They are not good to eat either, so it went back. About an hour later I caught a small one foot long something that I figured would be better used as bate than food. It went back out, but I think it got free on the way. Then about an hour after that I hooked a thirty pound tuna. Now THAT is food... It made about ten good steaks and we will have tuna for dinner tonight! The meat hook is again stored for another day.

Gulfito is *Jenny's* last stop in Costa Rica. It has a couple of small marinas, stores, etc. We will need to heavily provision here because Panama is wilderness until we get to Panama City at the canal. Then it will be supermarkets, movie theaters, malls, and civilization again. Yummy.

Arrived Friday, June 13, 2008 at 3:13 PM local time at Gulfito Mooring. The arrival location was latitude 8 degrees 37.215 minutes north, longitude 83 degrees 9.206 minutes west. The customs check in was none. The trip covered 62.59 nautical miles in 0d 9h 24m with an average speed of 6.60 knots and a maximum speed of 7.70 knots.

Tuesday, June 17, 2008 6:56:49 AM

Gulfito Anchorage with Wahoo in the middle.

Location: Gulfito Costa Rica

I am lucky to be using this laptop this morning. At 01:00 AM today, I caught a thief. I had felt an unusual motion that reduced the depth of my sleep a little, then heard a noise that was also unusual. I climbed up to do a normal boat check, which I do as a matter of course every night. I do this quietly in the dark. When I reached the pilothouse, I noticed that *Jenny's* port side door was partially open. I went to it, opened it and discovered a thief climbing over *Jenny's* side into his panga with our laptop, power supply and mouse. I saw he was not armed. So I grabbed his arm, and started yelling at him in English as if that would do any good. He was small and very compliant, handing back the laptop and pleading "no problem". I demanded the rest of our stuff, let him go into the panga and he produced the power cords, pleading that was all. He had the mouse too, but I was too rattled to remember.

By this time Mary was up. I asked her to watch him as I went to get the camera. He started untying his panga from *Jenny* and made his escape. Unfortunately, by the time I remembered it was in one of our backpacks and dug it out he had paddled out of range of the flash. I flashed at him anyway. I called the Port Captain on the radio but got no reply.

He was obviously a career thief. He had padded his panga so it would not make noise against *Jenny's* hull and had used bungee cords to keep them from knocking together. He picked a night that was very calm. While he attempted to take *Jenny's* navigation computer, he gave up when he found it was bolted down. He was also interested in our stereo radio, but that too was difficult to remove.

I will talk to the Marina owner this morning to see what, if anything, I should do in terms of reporting. I had the dinghy raised so it would have been very difficult to steal. But, it also made it difficult to quickly give chase. I will be locking our doors at night now.

Wednesday, June 18, 2008 6:48:56 AM

Location: Gulfito Costa Rica

I met with Tim, the owner of the marina, yesterday to report the attempted theft. He wished that I had called him on the VHF radio. If I had, he would have zoomed out and taken control of the situation. He stated that the police here do nothing about thieves. The matter is usually resolved personally. His solution is to sink the thief's boat and let him swim for shore. I knew he had a VHF radio at the "club house" but did not know he had one at his house that he monitors 24 x 7.

I guess I have learned the following from this. First, while you tend to believe a boat invasion cannot happen to you, it can. When you feel a bump or hear a noise, go on your investigation properly armed. I prefer not to announce myself, and go with the lights off, quietly. That way I preserve my night vision and have the element of surprise. A heavy flashlight and / or a long knife make good weapons in close quarters. On the other hand, it is probable that an escalation is the very last thing the thief wants. In this case, he was very contrite.

You have to think very carefully about the use of force, making split second decisions. You do not know whether you are dealing with the son of the local police chief or drug lord. So, you want to use the minimum force necessary. Photos are your best weapon. The invader knows you have evidence and that you can marshal many people to look for him. He also knows he cannot return and do you harm without being the primary suspect. Have a camera easily accessible. Take pictures. The flash will also blind him. You may not ever use them, but it is proof you can give to the police if they care.

Next, if you want to detain the person, have some heavy wire ties readily accessible for hand and foot cuffs. If the person is on the boat, then you are the law and have the right to detain the person. On the other hand, you will probably be ignorant of the local laws and customs and formal prosecution takes time. If you hand the criminal over to the cops, you may need to show up for trial sometime in the distant future. Jim the marina owner here has been the only foreign national EVER to prosecute a theft to conclusion and that was in 1987.

As long as we are ok and our goods are intact, a very good scare put into the mind of the thief is what I think is sufficient to prevent a repeat visit. Have your handheld VHF by your bedside so you can call for help and respond to calls for help easily if you are trapped below. Put its charger there.

Moving on, I changed both of JD's thermostats yesterday. I tested the old ones and they were opening ok, but they looked original. I changed them out anyway. Both were 82 degree centigrade. The new ones seem to support a higher flow rate. I will see if they make any difference in keeping the temperature at 82 degrees. I also hooked up *Jenny*'s port side pilothouse gutter to the water catch system. Yesterday's rain nearly filled the front tank and today's should do it!

Today we are going to visit the duty free shop, wash out the engine room, transfer some fuel and begin to wax the hull.

Monday, June 23, 2008 11:47:08 AM

Location: Gulfito Costa Rica

Today I finished the last of the major upgrade projects. The original navigation lights had decayed over time and no longer displayed true red and green colors. They also bled light all over the foredeck because of their mounting position, significantly reducing our night vision forward. I installed new ones properly on light boards. I used two of the teak stair treads from the rear ladder that I removed as bases for the light boards. In Barillas I used one of the resident cruiser's table saw to bevel the bottoms so that the slant of the pilothouse roof was compensated for. I mounted these teak bases on the pilothouse roof, near the edge. While we were still in San Francisco, I had a plastics shop create the light boards themselves out of black opaque plastic. These I mounted to the teak baseboards. I ordered new lights earlier in the year and picked them up on our trip back to the States from Barillas. I had the whole kit when we arrived in Gulfito. Since *Jenny* will be entering heavy ship traffic when we get down by the Canal, I figured now was the time to get her lights working properly.

Jenny's front awning combined with her rear roof extension and screens are very nice to have this far south. When the sun is out it is brutal. Not only is it hard on the horizontal surfaces, but it also needs to be kept out of the pilothouse and salon without closing off indirect light. And when it rains it is very nice to have the front hatch and back door open. We are very lucky to have them.

With all these projects now done, I am back to regular maintenance and cosmetic improvements. I start waxing the hull tomorrow. The pilothouse windows need new varnish so the next relatively large item on the list, but it might wait until we are settled in Cartagena for a while.

Usually it rains from 3:00 to 5:00 in the afternoon, but today it started around 11:00 this morning and looks like it will go all day. It might be a movie and popcorn day...

Tuesday, July 01, 2008 12:30:37 PM

Location: Gulfito Costa Rica

Well it is about time to say goodbye to Costa Rica. *Moody Blues* and *Encore* came in last night and we had pizza at the clubhouse with them. Another couple of vessels including *Spirit*, *Pipe Dream*, and *Gallivant* may be coming in today. They are planning to spend the 4th of July here, but I intend to pull *Jenny's* anchor around 04:00 AM on the 3rd to catch good weather and tidal currents out. I hope we will hook up with a couple of our other friends down at Isla Partida in Panama, our first stop. It is an 84 mile trip so departing early is necessary to get us there before sunset.

Costa Rica has been a nice adventure, but it is a very conflicted country. On one hand, the tourism industry is very effective at selling the pure nature of the country and brings in a fair income. On the other, the natives are no different than, and perhaps worse than other Central Americans in taking care of their environment. For example, the next time you are in Central America enjoying the pure nature of the place, ask where the town or city's sewage treatment plant is. They will answer, "What is that?" According to Tim, the owner of the marina we are staying at, all money going to nature preservation is coming in from outside the country. The natives do not care. The bay here sees diesel slicks at least once a week. We hope Panama is better.

On the project front, I covered and finished the holes left by the old running lights, and got *Jenny's* anemometer running again after taking down the sensor from the masthead and cleaning it. Knock on wood, but everything on her is now running well! I got her hull waxed too. I only need to replace one set of lines on her stabilizers and all the upgrade projects are DONE. *Jenny* will be in tiptop condition to take on the Caribbean.

It looks like we will be two weeks getting to Panama City. We will stay there a couple of weeks and then go through the canal. I hope we will hook up with *Wandering Star* and *Nexus* to see Portabella and the San Blas Islands. Then we will head over to Cartagena for a month or so. I found a report on how to dayhop around the coast of Colombia to the ABC islands and into Venezuela. We will stay there through the winter and leave *Jenny* there to visit home for the Thanksgiving and Christmas holidays.

Our long-term plans are to cruise up the Windward Islands next spring to Florida and Georgia. Then we will make our way up the east coast and winter over somewhere in the northeast, maybe in the Chesapeake Bay. Then the spring of 2010 head up the coast to Maine and the Canadian Maritime provinces. We might winter over again somewhere in the Northeast. And, that's about as far as we can see now.

Life is good and *Jenny* is the ultimate cruising vessel!

Tuesday, July 04, 2008 9:30:01 PM

Location: Gulfito Costa Rica

We stayed and joined the expats here for a Fourth of July celebration. *Spirit*, *Encore*, *Pipe Dream*, and *Astor* are here among others. As usual it was raining all day and evening. We missed *Catching Up* and *Wahoo* who already moved down the coast to Panama. It felt strange being in this remote outpost of Costa Rica and celebrating the birth of the United States of America. We had fun but I am sure we all wished we were home with our families.

Spirit (Erin), *Gallivant* (Maureen and Bruce), *Encore* (Buzz and Maureen)

Passage: Gulfito to Isla Partida

Departed Monday, July 07, 2008 at 5:01 AM local time from Gulfito Mooring. The departure location was latitude 8 degrees 37.213 minutes north, longitude 83 degrees 9.209 minutes west.

Arrived Monday, July 07, 2008 at 5:15 PM local time at Isla Gamaz, Panama. The arrival location was latitude 8 degrees 8.029 minutes north, longitude 82 degrees 19.004 minutes west. The customs check in was None. The trip covered 82.63 nautical miles in 0d 12h 14m with an average speed of 6.70 knots and a maximum speed of 8.20 knots.

Passage: Isla Parida to Bahia Honda

Departed Tuesday, July 08, 2008 at 8:52 AM local time from Isla Parida Anchor. The departure location was latitude 8 degrees 5.423 minutes north, longitude 82 degrees 5.152 minutes west.

Arrived Tuesday, July 08, 2008 at 3:57 PM local time at Bahia Honda. The arrival location was latitude 7 degrees 45.208 minutes north, longitude 81 degrees 32.762 minutes west. The customs check in was none. The trip covered 56.44 nautical miles in 0d 9h 17m with an average speed of 6.10 knots and a maximum speed of 7.20 knots.

Tuesday, July 08, 2008 7:28:58 PM

Location: Bahia Honda, Panama
Latitude is 7 degrees 45.21 minutes north.
Longitude is 81 degrees 32.761 minutes west.

Jenny is now in the last country she will visit on the Pacific Ocean. She went from Gulfito, Costa Rica to Isla Parida Panama yesterday, and then went on to Bahia Honda today for a total of 140 nautical miles mostly east. I do not mention the Bridal dolphins that come and go all the time now because they are part of our daily lives. But, they are always there along with all the other creatures we now take for granted.

I dragged the meat hook today, caught two large jacks within an hour and threw them both back. Then I waited until after lunch to put the hook back over and within twenty minutes I hooked a three-foot Dorado! Here we are in the wilderness of Panama in the pouring rain having a yummy salad, fresh Mahi Mahi and baked potatoes for dinner. And this side of Panama IS wilderness! The islands remind me of the Pacific Northwest, offering great protection from wind and waves, plenty of anchorages and islands for exploring, and a break from civilization. If you want the Pacific Northwest but with water you can swim and dive in, plus fish that you can easily catch and enjoy eating, this is the better place. Keep your boat in Gulfito for less cost, and make a day run into

Panama for a couple of weeks cruising in the islands. Better climate, water and fishing than Mexico. But there is no civilization.

Jenny's tanks are full of rainwater and all is good. We are sooooo fortunate. We have been underway for nine months now and we have encountered several "normal" years of incredible experiences. We have had years of memories in a very short time and all of it with a view of the sun and stars. It puts to shame normal living.

Rain is still falling, but has moderated from the Florida style downpour we have been getting. Bahia Honda is lovely with Pacific clear water and complete protection from the wind and waves. As we arrived, six dugout canoes paddled by children converged on *Jenny* wanting to see her and see if we had any goodies to offer. It was pouring, so unfortunately they left with only an unopened bag of cookies. Next an old guy in a dugout showed up and we arranged to see him in the morning for a market. He offered fresh fruit for gasoline. Next, his son showed up and we chatted only to find out they were all one family. His wife will show up tomorrow at 09:00 also to trade goods. Since there is no road within forty miles of here, everything is barter. The locals live in a small settlement on an island in the middle of the bay. They love visiting yatistas.

What can I say? *Jenny* is only two days away from the Panama Canal and is itchy to go through, get to the turquoise waters of the Caribbean and back to civilization. The end of one part of her adventure is drawing to a close with the climax and associated anxiety of the canal. Once through, a whole new adventure begins. Wow.

Passage: Bahia Honda to Isla Catalina

Departed Thursday, July 10, 2008 at 7:16 AM local time from Bahia Honda Anchor. The departure location was latitude 7 degrees 44.979 minutes north, longitude 81 degrees 32.073 minutes west.

Arrived Thursday, July 10, 2008 at 10:53 AM local time at Santa Catalina Island. The arrival location was latitude 7 degrees 37.575 minutes north, longitude 81 degrees 16.453 minutes west. The customs check in was none. The trip covered 22.36 nautical miles in 0d 4h 9m with an average speed of 5.40 knots and a maximum speed of 7.30 knots.

Thursday, July 10, 2008 1:34:35 PM

Location: Isla Santa Catalina, Panama
Latitude is 7 degrees 37.577 minutes north.
Longitude is 81 degrees 16.459 minutes west.

Below is an email I just received from Jeff, the captain of *Stravaig* describing their storm experience.

"Thoughts about our voyage: Sea of Cortez to Costa Rica aboard *Stravaig*:

We left La Paz on April 16th stopped overnight at Muertos to gather our wits and get a decent sleep and then the next day headed south.

Our immediate goal was to make a fairly quick passage down to northern Costa Rica, the idea being to try and arrive there by about the last week in May. Traditionally the hurricane season in the northern hemisphere begins on June 1st, however, of equal importance to us, we had learned that "tropical lows" often form in the Gulf of Tehuantepec as early as the third week in May so really we had no time to spare.

The weather was very pleasant and the winds were favorable and we made a good run down towards Isla Isabella where I hoped to stop for a few hours, weather and time of day permitting. The island visit idea was soon abandoned however when both the above criteria looked dubious. I altered course for Cabo Corrientes. Just after dusk we were making a steady five knots in a light following wind and sea when the boat shuddered and stopped dead in the water the sudden stop being accompanied by a loud crashing/cracking sound. It so happened that at that very moment I was looking forward on the port side and saw the cause of the impact. We had hit a large whale! At the moment of impact, he sounded and simultaneously he smacked us on the bow of the port ama, giving me a glimpse of his great fluke as he did so.[2]

Frankly I was just plain shocked by this sudden impact and it took me a few moments before I realized that poor Jose was most likely thinking that we had gone aground! I shouted out to her that "all is O.K. we just hit a whale" but all the time wondering if he was gathering himself for another attack! He must have been of a forgiving nature, for a second impact never came! As best we could we surveyed the damage and found where he had gouged out a small piece of the cut-water, cracking a part of the stem in the process. He had also broken the lashing used to secure the stainless steel cable that supports the leading edge of the bow net. Boy had we got off lightly!

Despite all, we arrived at Bahia Chamela on April 23rd, rested for one night and then hopped down to Tenacatita where the swell was less and we managed to do

---

[2] The term ama is a word in the Polynesian and Micronesian languages to describe the outrigger part of a canoe to provide stability. In a trimaran, they are the outside hulls.

a quick and dirty repair to the whale-damaged bow using some glass scraps and epoxy resin. Some bent fittings proved easy to be straightened and soon the starboard bow net was re-strung and returned to its former glory. Whilst congratulating ourselves on work well done, I was becoming aware that time was slipping past but I still decided to have some R and R in Las Hadas and then on to Zihuatanejo and Acapulco where we stopped for fuel before pressing on to Huatulco.

On the 11th of May we finally got through the almost-closed-out entrance to Chahué Marina. What a lovely and beguiling spot, we stayed too long really but set off to cross the dreaded Tehuantepec with a good forecast leaving Chahué on the 20th May (my birthday). We kept a conservative (and as it happened an un-necessary) 'one foot on the beach'. Our next port was to be Bahia del Coco, the port of entry for the northern part of Costa Rica.

There was almost no wind in Gulf of Tehuantepec, so we kept the engine on and motored out of this potentially difficult area before our luck had time to change. After two days we were in Guatemalan waters and we started to sail as much as possible to conserve fuel. Progress became painfully slow as we battled endless squalls and up to four knots of current, all from the east. On the nose!!

By the 25th May at mid-day we were abeam of the Gulf of Fonseca and were trying every tactic I could think of to make our way south-eastward down the Nicaraguan coast. Three grueling days later we had reached a position about ninety miles off the coast almost at the latitude of the Costa Rican border. By three in the afternoon woke me to the news that yet another huge squall was forming ahead of us, and prior to then she had been beating into a southeaster but had won some hard miles, on course!

We bashed on until dark, by which time we had a good increase in wind up to forty-five knots but it had shifted direction and I figured that if we were to set the staysail on the port tack with just enough rudder to head us up to windward, we might even keep our position or at least minimize our leeway. By morning, remaining hove-to ceased to be an option as the seas were threatening to roll us over. Despite the loss of the hard-won miles, I settled for as slow a downwind course as we could manage. Within an hour we had reduced sail to bare outriggers and this kept our speed to about eight knots.

The wind continued to rise; now fifty-five knots seemed to be the sustained wind strength with the occasional gust to sixty! About this time the penny dropped. I knew we were in a rapidly developing and un-forecasted tropical storm! The second realization followed almost immediately on the heels of the first. We were sailing downwind heading for the eye!

Any off-shore navigator knows that the quickest and surest way to get yourself into the worst part of the storm is to take the path of least resistance and run downwind! I quietly cursed myself for being such a fool! Adding even more damage to my self-esteem was the realization that the previous night I had kept us hove-to on a PORT TACK! How much more stupid could I get? To avoid an *approaching tropical storm, using the heave-to tactic in the northern hemisphere, any sensible man would heave-to on the starboard tack, for this at least might help to edge him away from the highest winds encountered near the eye!*

As the wind was building, we had to resort to hand steering if we were to avoid the ever increasing possibility of a broach and all its associated dangers. In order to maintain a modicum of control as we negotiated each wave, I was able to improve the rate at which the boat responded to the helm by forcing water past the rudder by keeping he engine in gear, taking care to use its power during turns only and to throttle back immediately the boat had adopted an attitude that would bring the next wave about five to ten degrees off dead astern on our starboard quarter.

Interestingly, in the darkness the bio-luminescence made the seas all around us somewhat visible. They appeared as huge whitish-green glowing lumps, all partially hidden by the blowing spindrift. As the night wore on, the wind continued to increase until seventy knots became the average speed with gusts to seventy-nine and perhaps a little more. All during this night our angle of heel on the larger seas was becoming alarmingly close to the point where capsizing was a very real possibility. So precipitous were the seas, that in order to make it possible for me to keep steering and at the same time able to operate the engine controls, Jose braced herself against me, and somehow managed to keep us both from being thrown across the cockpit. As dawn came, it brought with it a slight improvement to the visibility and I was able to make a rough guess at the wave height. To my horror, I could not even conservatively bring my estimate to a figure any less than forty feet!

Quite suddenly the wind dropped to about sixteen knots, the seas remained large and chaotic but the respite from the ocean's onslaught seemed like a gift from the Gods. Of course it was to be short-lived; we were in the eye of the storm. I knew that the worst was yet to come, but none the less I marveled at the sight of the wall-clouds on the radar. In about ten minutes the full fury of the storm returned. The wind speeds went howling up to a mean of eighty knots and gusting. The highest gusts I noted were eighty-eight and by now seas were above the height of our fifty-foot mast! About this time, we lost the use of the engine. We thought that we had taken enough 'green water' into the cockpit that the motor may well have drowned. Certainly the engine room bilge pump was working hard.

Regrettably, too much was going on to be able to pay much attention to the engine. No matter what I tried to do, I could no longer control the boats speed or course and in fact found that any attempt I made to steer only seemed to increase the number of near-capsize events. In fear and trepidation I reluctantly took my hands off the wheel and just stood and watched. The boat was doing better without my interference! Things were not, however, improving. In one of the first eighty knot gusts, the Achilles ten-foot rib inflatable, which had been tied down on the aft cabin top, albeit rather carelessly, was swept of its perch by wind and wave and crashed into the life-lines. The boat lurched and swung around bringing the wind and sea on the starboard beam, which caused the rib to crash against the canvas cockpit closure. If the canvas had ripped, the rib would have crushed us both!

After innumerable near capsizes and noting that conditions were still not abating, I asked Jose to call a May-Day on the V.H.F. radio, channel sixteen. After a couple of calls, somebody who sounded drunk came on and muttered for a while in a mixture of Spanish and gibberish. It soon became obvious that this strange signal was some radio anomaly and was not intended as an offer of help! We decided to carry on and tough it out a little longer, for after all, the boat had already survived through the highest gusts that I had noted so far.

Meanwhile, we could hear the constant crashing and banging as the mainsail and other gear flogged mercilessly on the cockpit hard-top. The boat and the two of us could still so easily be lost. Leaving Jose in the cockpit I went below and called May-Day on the morning Panama-Pacific Net on 8143 KHz, using our S.S.B. transceiver. By the time I had finished on the radio, the net had alerted various agencies as to our plight and arrangements were made for future radio check-ins.

(The details of the incredible efforts made on our behalf by so many caring people, I shall attempt to work out later. At this moment, I am finding the establishment of a time-line upon which to hang the events, particularly troublesome. Slowly but surely, however, I hope to collect and collate as much information as I can, so as to better understand and appreciate the help we got.)

Returning to the tumult in the cockpit, I quickly explained to Jose that even if the worst happened, people would at least know where to look for what was left of us. As I spoke, I had a strange sense of a weight being lifted from me, was I imagining things or had conditions marginally improved whilst I had been below? Just wishful thinking I told myself but, after staring suspiciously at the dial of the anemometer for about another hour, I finally became convinced that the abatement was indeed a reality. Now, if the boat could only stay on her feet for a little longer... we might yet survive!

Evidence that help was at hand soon appeared overhead, a U.S. Coast Guard spotter plane, making many low and close passes over us whilst chatting happily with us on V.H.F. The wind and seas were still enormous, so fearing for our safety, the pilot chose to stay with us until his fuel was getting low. He left us at dusk but not until he had assured us that a U.S. Coast Guard cutter would be with us by eleven o'clock that evening. By now, the principle danger was that we were being propelled rapidly towards the Nicaraguan coast, and more importantly, we still had virtually no means with which to fight our way off this rocky and fast approaching lee-shore.

I should mention that as the spotter plane departed; we acquired three additional crew members, two exhausted booby birds, who took up residence within the confines of the bow-pulpit and one storm petrel in a state of collapse! The petrel fluttered into the cockpit and immediately went below in search of creature comforts! Jose found a warm plastic box for him but despite all her best efforts, she could not find anything on board that he would eat. His chances of survival looked slim. Late the next morning, when they judged conditions to be more to their liking, the booby birds flew off.

By the time the Coasties arrived and sent over a boarding party to check us out, the conditions had become more manageable and we had been out on deck assessing damage. Some of our sails were damaged but in a pinch could be serviceable. The crew was in far worse shape, an incredible lethargy was setting in but we had lots more yet to do if we were to get ourselves to a safe harbor. Just before the Coasties had arrived, I had got the engine running. It must have sucked air when the boat had been heeling so radically, so after a few kind words and bleeding out a few air bubbles from the fuel-line, it fired up just fine.

Our remaining problem was lack of fuel and we gratefully accepted ten gallons of diesel fuel from our visitors. We still were facing another exhausting night in high seas and strong winds but nothing compared to what had gone before. At two o'clock the next afternoon we finally and with a huge sense of relief, arrived in Bahia de Salinas and got the hook down. Wow! Safe at last! Just before dark, we remembered the little petrel. What a state he was in! We dragged the poor creature out on to the deck where he tried to hide under one of the dinghies. We chased him out knowing that if he would not use his remaining energy to quest for food, he would have no chance. He fell overboard but before he hit the water, his flight instincts took over and the last we saw of him, he was flitting between the waves most surely on the hunt! We wished him all the luck in the world and fell into our bed!"

Below is Jose's account of the story.

"The time between us leaving Huatulco and arriving in Costa Rica was interesting to say the least! The weather window we took advantage of as we crossed the gulf of Tehuantepec turned out to be well chosen and we had no unpleasant Tehuantepecer winds to content with. We continued down the coast, past the Mexico-El Salvador border and eventually we began to make our way down the Niguaraguan coast.

We encountered huge squalls with strong winds on the nose and two to four knots of adverse current. We were not making good progress at all despite our attempts to motor sail. In order to be able to switch off the engine, having already used a lot of precious diesel fuel getting nowhere, we headed out to sea, cutting across the wind and current until it seemed there was a better possibility of tacking to lay a course for Costa Rica.

A low-pressure cell was reported on the Panama Pacific radio net in the morning of the 28th of May. We duly plotted its position on our chart, added some wind arrows and figured that it could well produce more favorable winds as the day went on. The squalls got even bigger and as night came on we decided to heave to under a staysail alone as the wind had picked up to forty knots. We found that being hove to on the port tack allowed us to work our way to windward on a course for Costa Rica.

By about midnight our situation of being hove to was untenable and we took down the staysail and let the boat run before the building wind and seas under bare outriggers. Two or three hours later we realized that we were headed towards the eye of something far more violent than the unnamed low we had been expecting! By 03.00 we registered gusts in the seventy knot range, the average wind at that time being sixty-five knots. Suddenly the wind died away to a mere sixteen knots, we were in the eye!

As the storm moved over us, the winds came back and gusts up to eight-eight knots became frequent. During this time the dinghies broke lose, the smaller Sabot managing to snare its painter under the edge of a ventilation hatch of the main cabin. The hatch was ripped out and the waves sweeping the decks poured in through the opening. The inflatable rib crashed into the side of the cockpit and by sheer good luck it did not crush us where we stood trying to steer the boat. The engine by this time had died and where it had been a useful aid to steering by pushing water passed the rudder we now had lost all control of the boat. The submersible pump in the engine room was running and we assumed that the engine had aspirated water.

We decided that I would call a Mayday on the VHF, but we had no response. Fearing capsize was imminent with seas in access of fifty foot and winds of eighty knots, Jeff went below at 08.00 and called a Mayday on the Pan Pacific Maritime Mobile Radio Net. The purpose of the Mayday was not a forlorn hope of being rescued, it was to inform people where to look for us should the worst happen. By the time Jeff got back to the cockpit the winds were down to seventy-three knots average and Stravaig was still on her feet despite the conditions. As the day progressed news came that a USA Coast Guard airplane would soon be overhead and indeed they arrived in the afternoon and kept us company for about four hours. Before leaving they had calculated our drift and were concerned that we were headed towards the rocky coast of Nicaragua.

Without the engine and insufficient fuel anyway, we were a pretty lame duck. We had learned that the US Coastguard Cutter Chase was heading to our assistance and we could expect their arrival by about 22.00. By the time they had got to us the seas were down to fifteen feet and the winds in the thirty knot range. Just after dark we had got the engine going again; it had not been inundated with water after all. At 02:00 the US Coastguard Watch Keepers came aboard, making the dangerous jump between the two vessels to bring us ten gallons of diesel fuel and to assess our situation. They examined the boat and talked to both of us separately and together to decide if we were fit enough to go on to the first anchorage in Costa Rica by ourselves, which was another fourteen hours away. One of the men gave us his cap, as a memento, they wished us well and continued with their other missions.

As you know we did finally make it to Costa Rica and after sixty plus hours of constantly struggling with Mother Nature, it was wonderful to be able to anchor and get some sleep! We found later that the storm had been given the name Alma and that NOAA had briefly raised its classification of Tropical Storm to Hurricane, just before it had reached the Nicaraguan coast. Alma was the first tropical storm in 125 years of record keeping in this area! Cruising sailors have always trusted that these tropical disturbances do not occur in northern Costa Rica. When we encountered Alma, our latitude was approx. that of the Costa Rican border. Times have changed! We have omitted here to give any of the details of the wonderful help and support we got from the yachting community and the various radio nets that provided the links to the US Coast Guard initially and gave us so much comfort and good advice. We are completing a full report, which when finished we hope to publish.

So, that was all the technical part of things, the emotional one is more difficult. We just are so happy that we came through this in one piece. We had quite some time where neither of us thought we were going to get out of this safely; we were ready to abandon the boat if help had been able to get to us in the worst part of the storm. We talked about what we needed to do if the boat were to capsize, what would be the best way to stay with the boat etc. I was very scared, Jeff less so, but I think we kept each other going by talking about what was happening and what we could do to improve our situation, which was not a lot! I thought a house somewhere in the country started to look very nice! I had managed to get some things like our papers together in case we did abandon the boat, so we would at least have some identification and credit cards with us.

Later, when it all got slightly better and we could not physically steer the boat anymore because the engine had stopped, I decided to keep sane I would start cleaning things up a bit! Really, you do strange things when you are in such a situation. It was incredibly comforting to see that US Coastguard plane for the first time and talk to the guys; they kept passing over us and talking to us for hours, when they left we knew it was only a few more hours before their cutter would be with us to give us some diesel. We were extremely tired and had to keep each other awake and alert. After the cutter left, we had another fourteen hours or so to get to the closest anchorage and we took turns to have short naps to try and feel a little bit better. Anyway, after about twenty hours sleep, we left for the next anchorage where we needed to check in. We got so much help and support from all the cruising boats that were there, really wonderful, we do not know how to say thank you to everybody. Now we are in a safe place, waiting for our parts to arrive, we are doing some jobs on the boat and relax, will go south to Golfito maybe end this week and from there we will have to see, no real plans yet. We will let you all know what's going to be next when we have figured it out ourselves!!"

Passage: Isla Santa Catalina to Bahía Naranjo

Departed Friday, July 11, 2008 at 7:04 AM local time from Isla Santa Catalina Anchor. The departure location was latitude 7 degrees 37.737 minutes north, longitude 81 degrees 16.923 minutes west.

Arrived Friday, July 11, 2008 at 1:03 PM local time at Naranjo Cove. The arrival location was latitude 7 degrees 16.568 minutes north, longitude 80 degrees 55.597 minutes west. The customs check in was none. The trip covered 35.70 nautical miles in 0d 5h 57m with an average speed of 5.60 knots and a maximum speed of 6.90 knots.

Friday, July 11, 2008 6:05:14 PM

Location: Naranjo Cove, Panama
Latitude is 7 degrees 16.559 minutes north.
Longitude is 80 degrees 55.593 minutes west.

JD is beating a reassuring rhythm below and driving *Jenny* steadily east. She stayed at anchor behind Santa Catalina island last night, then came thirty-five miles over here today to get set up to go around the big bend into the Canal Zone. The peninsula we go around is the large one that juts south out of the middle of the country and has the infamous Punta Mala. I have been paying close attention to the weather, and it looks like the next few days will be good for a rounding. We have the option to stop halfway around at Boneo Cove but it is open to the south where the swell and wind are coming from. Also, I am not sure how strong or what direction the currents are going to be. If we stop, the second leg is a very long 90 miles and if the current is against us, we will not make our next anchorage until after dark. I will make a call when we get there. If we do not stop and go through the night, we will continue all the way to Marina Fuerte Amador (Flamenco) anchorage at Panama City. Also, I think it would be awesome seeing all the ship traffic at night.

There you have it.

Passage: Naranjo Cove to Flamenco Amador Anchorage

Departed Saturday, July 12, 2008 at 10:59 AM local time from Naranjo Cove anchor. The departure location was latitude 7 degrees 10.560 minutes north, longitude 80 degrees 41.355 minutes west.

Saturday, July 12, 2008 8:29:44 PM

Location: Punta Mala, Panama
Latitude is 7 degrees 14.338 minutes north.
Longitude is 80 degrees 22.16 minutes west.

This weather observation was taken on Sunday, July 13, 2008 1:28:42 PM local time.
Observation location: Marina Fuerte Amador Anchorage.
Latitude is 8 degrees 55.274 minutes north.
Longitude is 79 degrees 31.551 minutes west.
The air temperature is 86, and water temperature is 82 degrees Fahrenheit.
The forecast is Thunderstorms.
The current weather is dry.
The sky is broken clouds (60 - 90% clouds).
The wind is 2 knots from the south.
The visibility is fifteen nautical miles.
The wave height is 0 feet with 0 foot swells.
The barometer is 1010 millibar and falling.

Jenny had an interesting passage around Punta Mala. She released her claws from the seabed of Naranjo in an overcast sky that turned into some kind of storm over the peninsula. I dropped her birds in the water around 10:00 AM and have had them down since. She was steaming along in fifteen to twenty-five knot winds and four to five-foot wind waves with rain the whole way around. The good news is that we were warm and dry in her embrace and the wind and waves were on her aft quarter or stern the whole way. *Jenny* was smoking along at 7.5 knots for several hours even with her birds down. I was planning to give her a break at Beneo Cove for the night but by the time we got there the wind was blowing white capping waves right down its throat creating havoc inside. I easily decided to skip it and do the overnight.

By the time *Jenny* reached Punta Mala, all of the rain had ended and most of the storm effect was over so she rounded gently about 6:00 PM. She steamed on through the night to get to the Flamenco anchorage in the morning. As darkness fell, the sky cleared up enough to give her the moon to shine light on the water.

Now it is blowing about eleven knots on *Jenny's* port side and building up another set of wind waves. I am hoping this is just some of the cape effect and it will die as we get further offshore. This chop is thrusting *Jenny* sideways as the wind waves slap *Jenny's* port side. This is not good for sleeping. I am glad I kept her birds in the water.

I think *Jenny* had good current until Boneo, but unsure since she had such a good winds and waves behind her. However, the weather quieted down between there and Punta Mala and *Jenny* slowed down to 4.9 knots. Yup, 4.9 and she never saw better than 5.9 all the rest of the way. Here are two items of interest. First, the current up to and around Punta Mala is dead against you, and because of that, you will need an overnight to get from Boneo to Flamenco anyway!

And, the GRIB files and BuoyWeather showed absolutely nothing of the sort of weather we had!

We have only seen a few ships so far, and *Jenny's* AIS has helped a great deal by assuring us that we are outside of the shipping channel. Both radars are also going and we have good visibility, seeing boat and ship lights where they should be. There seems to be a thunderstorm to the south of us (starboard beam) as I can see the sky light up now and again. There is some lightening ahead too, but not for a couple of hours. I checked into the Marine Mobile Service Net just so someone knew where we were.

This whole trip would have been a blast in a sailboat. One would have beaten us here for sure. In any case, it was routine until we got to Isla Bona. *Jenny* went on the north side of it, away from the shipping lanes. Between there and Isla Taboga we ran into a fleet of panga fishermen. At first there were so many lights we thought they must be shore lights. But they weren't and they did not show up on the radar. As we got closer, even more flashlights were turned on! There also were some fishing net flags with small red blinkers that we could not see until within 100 ft of them. We made it through, but it took both of us on full alert for about an hour.

All the way in the seas were choppy, much to our surprise. As *Jenny* got to Isla Taboga she converged with the shipping traffic which piled up as day broke. She needed to get across to the other side of the shipping lane, with mammoth freighters and tankers charging along at seventeen knots. I called Flamenco Station on VHF channel 12 and told them our intention was to cross the channel to get to the Perico Island north anchorage. They thanked us for the information, and asked us to call again as we neared the outer marker.

I called again when *Jenny* was just off Isla Taboguella, two miles due south of the outer marker. With no less than six ships approaching from the south I thought traffic control would give us some directions about how to proceed. However, they just said to proceed to our destination. OK! All six ships steaming full bore down on us had closest points of approach (CPA) of less than two miles. Thank God for AIS. I took the wheel and gave *Jenny* a hard starboard turn. She started her run across the traffic just after a big car carrier passed. One tanker had her in her sights with a CPA of less than a mile. I revved JD up and we watched as it bore down on us. It is a very disturbing sight to have a tanker going sixteen knots coming right at you with its big white bow wave making it look like a huge wild beast foaming at the mouth. *Jenny* made it through and we sighed with relief.

There must be twenty ships anchored here waiting for the canal or various other things. *Jenny* had to weave among them to get to her anchorage and that was cool. It is a good thing she had all her San Francisco Bay experience. Thank God for her AIS as there were so many radar targets it was useless. The AIS gave us CPA distance and timing against all the moving targets.

Jenny found the anchorage and a nice spot to settle in. She dug her anchor into the seabed and stretched out 200 feet of chain to give it scope. After a brief cleanup, Mary and I crashed.

Arrived Sunday, July 13, 2008 at 11:13 AM local time at Flamenco Anchorage north of Perico. The arrival location was latitude 8 degrees 55.264 minutes north, longitude 79 degrees 31.561 minutes west. The customs check in was done at the Flamenco Marina. The trip covered 164.51 nautical miles in 1d 3h 30m with an average speed of 5.80 knots and a maximum speed of 7.90 knots.

Sunday, July 13, 2008 1:41:55 PM

Location: Marina Fuerte Amador Anchorage
Latitude is 8 degrees 55.273 minutes north.
Longitude is 79 degrees 31.552 minutes west.

When we woke up we were looking at the Panama City skyline from *Jenny*. The spot is beautiful. The city is magnificent with new skyscrapers going up. We will check into Panama tomorrow and get our bearings. Then to the City!!! I spotted *Walrus*, a sailboat we know already here, so we will call Mike later today and get the scoop.

Thursday, July 17, 2008 4:00:52 PM

Location: Flamenco Anchorage

We have been shopping! Tuesday we went to the Albrook mall. It may be the biggest I have ever been in. Many of the stores are what you find in US malls. I bought a couple pair of Columbia nylon pants to replace the cotton ones I have. One was a pair of shorts and the other was a shorts/pants coverable set. These lightweight nylon pants are exactly what the doctor ordered for the tropics. In Panama, as in most of Central America, men do not wear shorts regardless of the heat. In Panama, the dress tends to be even more formal, so long pants are necessary. These are so light that they are cool, and dry very quickly after it rains, which is just about every third hour. Mary bought some shirts and stuff. There was a very nice large food store there too, so we stocked up on some supplies on our way out. The cab ride was only $5 each way.

I began shopping for marine supplies on Wednesday. I bought some large shackles and small stuff at the local marine stores, but none of these stores stock stuff for cruising boats, especially sailboats. I needed electronic charts for Colombia and Venezuela, some double braid line, a block, etc. After a few dead ends, I ended up at the Marine Warehouse talking to Arturo. The Marine Warehouse is just an office. Nothing is there. However, it is all available! Arturo went through the West Marine and Bluewater Charts and Books catalogs with me. Then we got on Windows Live Messenger with his counterpart in Miami and voila, I had ordered all the stuff I needed. The cost of shipping by FedEx was $67, which was exorbitant. However, he had a shipment leaving Miami on Friday. He charged me $40 for the shipping, only a little more than shipping within the US. Customs was 1%; less than any US sales tax. I actually paid less than what I would have paid in the US!!! Awesome!

Last night, the wind shifted to the Southeast, something it is not supposed to do here at this time of year so *Jenny* rolled like a rubber ducky all night giving us an uncomfortable sleep. Neither of us actually got much. This morning we moved *Jenny* to a new spot, a little bit better, but not much.

We settled in, listened to and contributed to the nets, and had Beno, the owner of the Diesel Duck named *Diesel Duck* stop by. He dropped off some catalogs, and I gave him some flags for Ecuador, Peru, Chile, and Argentina that we were not going to use. Having sailed the east coast (starting in Toronto) and the Caribbean for several years, they are on their way around South America counterclockwise. Theirs is the second boat built to the Bueller design, and they managed the build themselves. It is forty-one feet long, 35,000 lbs. and beautiful. Beno being German, everything is very well done, neat and clean. The story is that the guy who started Diesel Ducks saw their boat and decided to manufacture them. He also stole the name of their boat for his company and the boat brand. They have sails, a 67 hp 4-cylinder Westerbrook diesel with a variable pitch prop. Their range is awesome.

This afternoon I went looking for motor oil (Delo 400 15/40). The last I got was in La Paz Mexico and it has not been available since. I arrived here with insufficient oil to do a change. The hunt was on. Arturo gave me the name and address of a place he thought had it, but I thought I would hunt around here first. After a couple of hours, I ended up in an upstairs office at the Flamenco Boat Yard buying two five-gallon cans. They cost $77 for five gallons; a little more than what I paid in SFO ($75 for six gallons). That was a find. I have only a few more items to get before we are ready to go for another nine months.

Tonight we are having the family from *Lauren Grace* (a catamaran) over for cocktails and to pick their brain about cruising Venezuela, Colombia and the San Blas islands. It should be fun.

Tuesday, July 22, 2008 8:50:23 AM

Location: Flamenco Anchorage, Balboa

Yesterday I hired a cab for a few hours to drive us around to the specialized stores I needed to get to. I paid $10 / hour and it was a bargain. Our first stop was half way across the country to get to the Northern Lights dealer/importer. I needed a couple of spare water pump belts and oil filters for the genset. Getting there and back to the next store took about 1.5 hours. Next, I tried to get dinghy glue for gluing down pieces of *The Beast's* skin that have come loose. We got to the store, but they were out. Then we went to a store to stock up on diesel additives. They did not carry Stanadyne which I prefer, but did have Racor. Since Racor has a good name, I got enough to treat another 1200 gallons. Then we went to a bookstore downtown where they had a nice selection of books in English and we loaded up.

By the way, our driver, a young strong Panamanian asked us how we liked Costa Rica. We told him we did not very much and he concurred. He went up for a week, was verbally assaulted at one of the clubs for dancing with a Costa Rican girl, decided to leave the next day and was robbed before he got to the airport. Our opinion continues to be that Costa Rica is dangerous and should be avoided.

Our friends on *Tropical Dance* started the process for going through the canal yesterday and we had a nice dinner with them at one of the local restaurants. I will be going as one of their line handlers to get the experience of going through and have been keeping track of how they are doing it. I made up a canal transit process in Word that they are using and validating. I should have a good set of instructions when I am done.

Today I have been working on the BoatExec software and will be putting together some photo emails for transmission later today. We have finished most of our exotic shopping now are on to the small and mundane stuff. We need to load 500 gallons of diesel that should get us all the way to Venezuela and asked the net where the best fuel is. After asking many questions, it turns out that the Flamenco Marina has the best diesel (no dirt, water, goo) around. I need to get that done sometime this week. Then the only remaining item is our parts shipment from the States due in on the 31st. We may go out to the Las Perlas islands in the meantime to get to some clean water, swim and fish.

Except for the long and often wet dinghy ride into the marina, we are having a good time here and getting a lot done. There are nice restaurants and stores within walking distance and the cabs are not too expensive. The malls are expansive and we have been able to get everything we need so far. The canal traffic has picked up and we watch ships coming and going regularly now. It still is a bit of a thrill just being here.

Wednesday, July 23, 2008 3:59:35 PM

Location: Flamenco Anchorage, Balboa

We made *Jenny* ready for sea again this morning and went over to the fuel dock in the marina. *Jenny's* last fuel stop was Acapulco, so fortunately I can be pretty choosey about where I load. However, the fuel in Acapulco was $2.50 a gallon and this was $4.70! How rude.

I used the fuel transfer pump to move all the fuel out of the two forward tanks to get them ready for the new fuel. In Acapulco, I loaded about 100 gallons less than I expected. Here I expected to put 500 gallons in the front two tanks, but was again surprised only to get 390 in. I was paying attention this time and discovered the port forward tank only held 220 gallons while I was assuming that it held 320 gallons. The bad news is that my total capacity is around 900 gallons instead of the published 1000 gallons. The good news is that I have been using less fuel than I thought. *Jenny* now has about 700 gallons on board which is plenty for reaching Venezuela where the price of diesel is $.14! I will tank up there for our trip up the Windward's to the States.

Our friends on *Tropical Dance* got their date for their canal transit. They are going through on Saturday so I will go over Sunday PM for the 3:00 AM start. Tomorrow we are all going up to the Miraflores locks to see them and go to the museum.

Life is good.

Monday, July 28, 2008 3:20:20 PM

Location: Flamenco Anchorage

The day before yesterday I went through the canal on *Tropical Dance* as a line handler to get a firsthand understanding of how it works and any challenges we might have. It was a great experience and pretty cool. Because it is well orchestrated by the canal authority with an advisor onboard and line handlers on the locks, locking was actually easier than docking into a slip. Crossing the continental divide to the east coast is quite a thrill. At the divide, the ATON buoys switch sides, putting green to starboard for the rest of the trip. Our advisor was Edgar, who was a very nice guy, knew the ropes. He does this as a side job, is well educated and musically talented. I hope we have him on our trip.

Catching Up, *Delfin Solo*, and *Spirit* came around Punta Mala in a local gale and got beat up. *Ketching Up* said they experienced winds at fifty-five knots for several hours and the waves built to eight feet. They broke their propeller shaft somehow. Once the gale ended they had very light winds and could not make headway against the current under sail. *Delfin Solo*, a sailboat from Turkey, was with them and helped tow them from island to island through the Las Perlas. It was a very nice thing to do considering they were smaller than *Ketching Up* and at times motored all night just to hold them in place against the current.

Wahoo, a twin motored sport fishing boat from CA suited up and towed them the rest of the way in on Saturday when I was crossing the canal with *Tropical Dance*. All *Jenny's* friends have nested here now. *Catching Up* anchored next to us is working on getting the logistics and services they need to get her fixed. This kind of failure both stops you immediately and the cost of repair can significantly reduce your cruising budget. I suspect their motor mounts wore out and the bad weather they went through getting around the Punta Mala caused the shaft to snap.

Mary, Ashley (*Ketching Up*) and Patricia (*Rhapsody*) went grocery shopping today and came back with wheelbarrows full of food. Patrick (*Rhapsody*) and I hit the marine stores. The towing experience with *Ketching Up* showed that *Jenny* had 200 feet of good towing line but did not have big enough shackles to put a towing rig together. *Wahoo* managed because we combined our inventory of line and shackles. I also dropped off our empty propane tanks for a refill. I found swim booties for Mary so I have now outfitted her for snorkeling when we get to the Caribbean. We are planning to go out to an Italian restaurant tonight to celebrate her birthday.

Tomorrow I will wrap up our west coast routes and tracks for Mexico and the West Coast of Central America and put them up on our web site at

http://www.boatexec.com/Jenny.htm

I will also start to put together our routes for the canal and the east coast of Panama.

Tuesday, July 29, 2008 7:15:14 AM

Location: Flamenco Anchorage

The *Ketching Up* saga continues. First I should explain the Noel and Ashley have their three boys with them on their journey that started in Coos Bay Oregon. They are going back home to the Carolinas. Well, Noel was out looking for a yard to replace his broken propeller shaft with Ragna and Tashan from the Turkish boat *Delfin Solo*. They got to a nearby yard and the security guard asked them for their "permission to enter" information. The taxi driver explained that they had talked to the yard manager on the phone and were here to secure services. Well, the situation escalated and the taxi driver somehow got in touch with the guard's manager and suggested that the guard was looking for a bribe (mordida). The manager talked to the guard and they got in. While inside, the guard was obviously steaming. On the way out the guard asked for Noel, Ragna and Tashan to produce their papers. The taxi driver went nuts and the whole thing escalated again. The guard called the cops. No joke! No one had his or her papers.

The first I knew of the situation, Noel was next door on *Delfin Solo* getting their documents. Ragna and Tashan were in the clink. Noel asked us to find Ashley and let her know what was going on. As it turned out, the situation escalated to the commandant of the area. However, the police were very polite and professional and while obligated to make sure they were who they said, felt this incident was low priority. When Noel got back to the police station, Ragna and Tashan were comfortably seated in a lounge watching TV. Noel produced their passports and boat documentation and they were free. The police never even looked at the documents. After four hours of adventure, they came back with yet another interesting story.

Passage: Towing *Ketching Up* to Balboa

Departed Thursday, July 31, 2008 at 10:11 AM local time from Flamenco Anchorage. The departure location was latitude 8 degrees 55.334 minutes north, longitude 79 degrees 31.819 minutes west.

Ketching Up in tow to the Balboa Yacht Club

Noel decided to haul *Ketching Up* on the rail at the Balboa Yacht Club. It was the least expensive place and allowed him to do the work. We rigged a towing line to *Jenny* and off we went. *Jenny* was very gentle with *Catching Up* as she took the load. She rounded the Amador peninsula with her friend in tow without even breaking a sweat. I called Flamenco control and let them know we were transiting down the Canal channel to the Balboa Yacht Club and got clearance. As we got to the yacht club a launch came out and put *Catching Up* on a mooring ball. *Jenny* turned around and headed back to her spot in the anchorage.

Arrived Thursday, July 31, 2008 at 10:12 AM local time at Flamenco Anchorage. The arrival location was latitude 8 degrees 55.337 minutes north, longitude 79 degrees 31.826 minutes west. The trip covered 10.47 nautical miles in 0d 2h 11m with an average speed of 4.80 knots and a maximum speed of 6.90 knots.

Sunday, August 03, 2008 8:55:57 AM

Location: Flamenco Anchorage

Well, we are in our third week at the anchorage here. On Monday, we are starting the paperwork to cross over the great divide. We have a group of six vessels here that have been together off and on for the past several months and we are having fun with them. We all went out for drinks and dinner on Mary's birthday and had a good time. So far, *Tropical Dance* and *Wahoo* have passed over to the other side. *Ketching Up* is on the hard in the Balboa YC replacing her propeller shaft. She is hoping to go through on Friday with *Jenny*.

I went down to help Noel get *Catching Up* on the rail. This rail is very old and rickety. I was afraid it would collapse under her weight. A launch came out and released her from her mooring, then towed her into the cradle now mostly under water at the end of the rail. There was a current and *Ketching Up* had no propulsion because the propeller shaft was broken. As much as we tried, *Ketching Up* went into the end of one of the cradle's iron I-beams and gouged a nice furrow in her gel coat. OCHE! The Yacht Club paid to have her mended at no cost but she will still carry a scar.

Our line handlers are going to be Dan and Erin from *Spirit*, Timo from *Pipe Dream*, and Ragna and Tashan from *Delfin Solo*. Tashan went on *Wahoo* as a line handler yesterday, so he will be experienced. We should be getting the tires we lent to *Tropical Dance* back today from *S/V Lotus* that came this way yesterday. We should not need anything except four 125-foot lines. I am meeting with Tony the Taxi Driver tomorrow to start the paperwork process, hope to have the admeasurements done on Tuesday, and be scheduled to go on Thursday or Friday.

We are doing some heavy provisioning and picking up some groceries for *Monju*. We plan to spend a month or two in the San Blas Islands and they are pretty much wilderness. The Kuna Indians control the province and are like the Mennonites of Pennsylvania, adhering to their traditional lifestyle. They do provide some fruits and vegetables, but little else. Therefore, we need to bring everything we need for an extended stay.

I have been suspicious about the state of *Jenny's* batteries for a while. I knew they were old, but had not really tested them or determined their true age until yesterday. I replaced the two 4D batteries in the front cabin last year when they shorted out and boiled over. Yesterday, I tested a couple of the 8D's and found them in poor condition. I then looked up the prior owner's maintenance notes and found out they were bought in May, 1998. They are now over ten years old, which is end of life. I am now shopping for seven new batteries. I am hoping the Free Zone in Colon will have them at a good price. Since they weigh about 200 lbs each, getting the old ones out and new ones in will be a serious effort. We will be staying at the Shelter Bay marina in Colon, so at least we can offload and load them at the dock.

Everything else is good. Mary is really enjoying the company of the other boats and the city. I am really hoping she will like the San Blas.

Thursday, August 07, 2008 8:42:32 AM

Location: Flamenco Anchorage

We moved into the Flamenco Marina on Tuesday so the ACP can measure us for the canal transit. This is the first step in the process since they price the transit based upon the boat's length. We measured out at 47.65 feet, just under the fifty-foot maximum length for small boats. The next step was to take the measurement document to Citibank and pay for the transit. The cost was $609. They also put a buffer charge of $891 on our card in case they need to tow us or provide some other service on the way. Once done, we were in the pipeline.

Meanwhile, Mary was off doing some serious provisioning. We need to provision for a month or two in the San Blas Islands, which only has fruits and vegetables available. We are also getting Coke, Beer and Vodka for *S/V Monju* already there. She went out for the first run in the morning, and we trucked that on board, and then went out again in the afternoon. We went with *Ketching Up* to Price Smart in the afternoon in Toni's van. Between the two of us, we completely filled it with groceries. We had to take a separate cab back. We took advantage of being at the dock to load the goods.

I needed to create a new place to store the cases of Coke, Beer, Soda, Milk, etc. I put stainless loops into the wall at each end of the guest cabin settee. They serve to anchor a canvas lee cloth when necessary. However, we need to get one made first. I turned the cushion on its side and formed a storage area. We filled it to the brim. The good news is that *Jenny* trimmed out level with all the new weight on the starboard side!

Wednesday morning we moved back out to the anchorage with full water tanks and a clean boat. I called the ACP and found out that they scheduled *Jenny* to go through the canal on Saturday morning. We will not know the pickup time until Friday evening. They have a web cam set up for the locks at

http://www.pancanal.com

I will call Laura when we are approaching the lock and ask her to send out an email if you want to watch us go through. I do not know if you can capture the web cam output though.

We are all excited to get into the Caribbean and start a new phase of our adventure!

Friday, August 08, 2008 5:12:07 PM

Location: Flamenco Anchorage

The night before Transit and all through the boat not a creature was at rest, not even Nicholas. Today I picked up *Jenny's* 2008 USCG boat documentation. The old one expired in June, and fortunately no one seems to have noticed. FedEx could not figure out how to deliver it to one of only three marina's in the area and the only one on the island. I had to take a taxi to the airport for a 90 minute ride to pick it up.

I was going to check out with our friends on *Catching Up*, but when the time came to leave in the taxi, they could not find any of their papers, including their passports. Visions of returning to the local jail danced in Ashley's mind. She was frantic and close to a meltdown. While I drove to get my new boat documentation certificate, they hunted for their papers. After backtracking day by day, they determined that they last had them on Monday at a 7/11 kind of store near the marina. Noel went in and asked the attendant if anyone had seen a notebook of papers and passports. She turned around and pulled the notebook out from behind the counter!!! They were incredibly lucky. They had left it outside on the sidewalk against the wall. Whew!

We were both finally ready to go through the paper shuffle. Tony, the expert taxi driver for all this took us through the various stops to clear out. I cleared *Jenny* out all the way to Cartagena, via the San Blas islands. In theory, we will not have to do any more paper dancing in Panama. We will see.

We are supposed to pick up our transit advisor (pilot) tomorrow morning around 08:00 so I will get my crew on board around 06:30, lash *The Beast* onto *Jenny's* back and turn her loose.

Passage: Panama Canal Transit

Departed Saturday, August 09, 2008 at 7:32 AM local time from Flamenco Marina. The departure location was latitude 8 degrees 54.312 minutes north, longitude 79 degrees 30.873 minutes west.

Arrived Saturday, August 09, 2008 at 9:09 PM local time at Shelter Bay. The arrival location was latitude 9 degrees 22.050 minutes north, longitude 79 degrees 57.044 minutes west. The trip covered 45.14 nautical miles in 0d 13h 37m with an average speed of 3.30 knots and a maximum speed of 7.80 knots.

Monday, August 11, 2008 1:22:02 PM

Location: Shelter Bay Marina
Latitude is 9 degrees 22.077 minutes north.
Longitude is 79 degrees 57.058 minutes west.

We had a pick up time for our advisor for 08:00 AM off the Flamenco Signal Station and he showed up at 09:30 AM. Our schedule was to be at the first locks at 11:00 AM. We did not really need to wake up at 05:30 and get the crew on board at 06:00 AM. However, it gave us extra time to finish getting *Jenny* ready and having a good breakfast that Mary made.

Our advisor was Jorge. I was hoping for Edgar who is the best of the three advisors I have now seen. Around 10:00, *Jenny* started moving toward the Miraflores Locks with her friend *Ketching Up*. The ACP asked *Jenny* and *Ketching Up* to go through rafted together. As *Jenny* got to the first locks, I moved her fenders to her starboard side and they moved hers to their port side. Then we tied them together. Since *Jenny* is the bigger more powerful vessel, she became the tug. While our friends relaxed and enjoyed the ride, we worked like devils maneuvering them and making sure they were safely locked.

We had our friends Dan, Timo and Erin on board as line handlers. Mary was the fourth. But by rafting with *Ketching Up*, we really only needed to worry about *Jenny's* port lines and had Dan and Timo to take care of them. Erin helped with the stern line since we had to catch the messenger line from the top deck and then run the one-inch line out from below where the cleat was. During my transit with *Tropical Dance* as a line handler, I learned the value of using the anchor windlass to tighten up the bowlines when necessary. We had it powered on and the clutch slipped out so we could use it when needed it.

The mass of both vessels was about 100,000 lbs. This was quite a load to get positioned and tied down safely. To compound the problem, the line handlers on the sides of the canal were not very attentive this time. In the first lock they were late getting *Jenny's* lines over the wall cleats and we got a little sideways. With no place to go forward, we had to use the lines to center us. Timo on

Jenny's bow was having difficulty using the windlass, but got it going and we centered.

Unfortunately, after the water started pouring in, he was pulling up on the port side line and pulled it off the top of the windlass. I was going out to tell him not to pull up when it came off. Both boats started moving rapidly toward the starboard side wall. These cement walls are the originals, with decades of scars from ship encounters. Erin sprung to action and Junior, a line handler from *Ketching Up* leapt over the rails and got us stabilized. We then used the windlass to re-center our vessels again and I made a personnel change on the foredeck. Dan later explained that Timo was at a disadvantage since we had not given him his morning beer. What did we expect?

Miraflores Locks looking at Pedro Miguel Locks

We motored as a raft the mile between the first and second up-side locks. When we arrived at the second lock, Jorge informed me we would side tie to the tug on *Jenny's* port side. First of all, the tug was brand new and I had been watching it collide with the wall several times. It had swivel propeller pods controlled by a joystick and appeared totally out of control most of the time. I figured the captain was new to the vessel and its steering and was not about to tie to it. Also, we had all *Jenny's* fenders on her starboard side between her and *Ketching Up*. I told Jorge no, we would not tie up to the tug. He argued a little, but finally realized I was not going to change my mind. He then called the lock and told them we would center tie again.

After that, things went smoothly. I was still sweating bullets driving the raft while *Ketching Up* was having a party. As soon as we got through the up locks and into the lake, we separated the boats. Mary served a nice lunch and Jorge fell asleep. He slept all the way across the lake.

Passing a freighter in the Canal

Meanwhile, the advisor on *Ketching Up* found out that we needed to be at the Gatun locks at 5:30 PM, not the 7:30 PM time Jorge said. While Jorge slept I sped up to make the schedule and decided to go through the Banana Channel that saved a couple of miles. When Jorge woke up, I informed him of the changes. He did not believe me and said I did not need to go through the Banana Channel. I asked him to call the other advisor, and told him I was going through the channel anyway. He only called the other advisor when I called Noel on *Ketching Up* to get an update. When we got to the turn off for the channel, which is hidden until you get right to it, Jorge disappeared. I think he figured I would not see the channel and blow on by it.

Jenny got to the Gatun locks on time but the ship we were to go in front of was delayed. We waited. Just before going into the locks, we lashed *Jenny* up to *Ketching Up* again and took our position in front of the ship. All went well until the last chamber when the line handler on *Jenny's* port bow decided it was more important to get his messenger line untied from *Jenny's* one inch line than cleat her to the wall. We could not stop *Jenny's* drift toward the starboard wall. Finally, the advisor on *Ketching Up* yelled at the guy and he dropped the one inch line over the cleat. We used *Jenny's* windlass again to bring the boats back into position. If you are going through the canal and have a windlass, make it ready to use on the lines!!!

Ship behind *Jenny* in Gatun Locks

The last chamber doors opened and we were in the Caribbean!!! Wahooo! We untied the vessels and headed to the buoy where our advisor got off. He did not get a big hug from us. Then we went over to the Shelter Bay marina in the dark. Thankfully, I had the course plotted. There are so many lights, boats and ships that it would be very difficult to make the three-mile segment otherwise. Just as we got to the Marina, the heavens opened and it poured. We groped our way into the marina basin using radar primarily and went all the way to the second pier where they wanted us. You could not see more than twenty feet through the downpour. The first slip we came to was a port side tie and about fifteen feet too short for us, but I had no way to see what the situation was. I went in. Crew from other boats at the dock came out in the pouring rain and helped us in. Whew!

Dan and Timo climbed over the bow with our rented lines and returned them to Tony the taxi driver. We were done. We showered, had snacks, drank Jose Quervo shots and beer and celebrated until about 03:00 AM.

The next morning Dan, Timo and Erin helped tidy up *Jenny* and move her to a much better slip next to *Wandering Star*. Then they took a taxi to the bus station to catch an express back to their boats in Panama City. Mary and I continued to tidy up a bit and then crashed. Last night we watched Boston Legal episodes until we could not keep our eyes open and crashed again. I slept like a log until this morning.

The marina here is very nice with a big screen TV in the bar and small restaurant. It is on the Fort Sherman property and is across the canal from Colon. It is also where the US Navy Seals hold exercises and a crew of them are here now. The Colon crime we hear of is far away and this makes for worry free nights. I am talking with Bruce, the manager of the Boat Yard here about getting *Jenny's* batteries and bottom paint. He has a connection with Marine Warehouse, the same folks I used in Panama City to import *Jenny's* charts, lines and blocks. He's working out a price.

Bruce is an American that came to rest on his catamaran with his wife and two daughters. They are very nice folks and have a pet baby three-toed sloth, the only one we have seen so far. Every morning I take Nicholas for a walk up one of the roads that led to the officer's homes. There is nothing left of them now except the foundations, but we have seen monkeys and a pack of lemurs running wild. Lemurs are not native to the Americas so they must have escaped from some zoo or private collection along the way.

Three toed sloth named Pippen

We are having cocktails with *Wandering Star* tonight and should also get *Jenny's* new Port Networks Wi-Fi box from *Ketching Up*'s guests who are flying in from the States tonight. All is really, very good. Big smiles all around.

Wednesday, August 13, 2008 8:50:07 PM

Location: Shelter Bay Marina

It is our anniversary. Twenty years! And, here we are in Panama. This journey really began five years ago in Juneau Alaska. We were at the tail end of a fantastic vacation and had committed to looking at trawler yachts as a possibility for retirement. It was raining, and rather cold, but the future was looking bright and sunny.

Here we are in Panama. Who would have guessed it would have progressed this far and in a flash. Mary would have been the least likely to have guessed. She still struggles with this lifestyle. Perhaps she will like Caribbean cruising better. Perhaps she will pack up and leave soon. It is hard to tell. She does not say anything. She still is more of a passenger on the journey than a participant or driver. I do not know how much I contribute to this problem. I just do not know because she does not communicate. It is a shame she cannot revel in the journey we are taking and a loss for me that I do not have an engaged partner.

We are so fortunate to be able to be on this journey in style and time we have. Others have chosen the journey at a far less comfortable level, but have chosen it none the less. We see the sun, moon and stars most every day. This for me is real life compared to the corporate office I lived for so many years. Tonight I walked by a couple of sportfishing boats with underwater lights on and marveled at the jellyfish zooming about eating the plankton attracted by the light. On the other hand, vessels and friends we know have all departed for other places today, and the other vessels we know have yet to come across from the other side. We celebrated our anniversary alone as we did in Juneau.

We have been watching season two of Boston Legal and have really liked the show. I sympathize with Allen Shore, a brilliant person who strives for perfection and struggles to be good. His self-image and brilliance leads him down a lonely path. Most people are constrained by not having the choices. Some fortunate few have both the choices and the awareness to understand how precious few achieve bliss. I sometimes wonder about the college choice decision that determined my future. What different path my life might have taken if I had pursued Marine Biology at the University of Florida instead of Physics at Rutgers University?

BOOK 5: ROMANTIC PANAMA AND COLOMBIA

You're nobody 'til somebody loves you.
You're nobody 'til somebody cares.
You may be king, you may possess the world and it's gold,
But gold will not bring you happiness when you're growing old.
The world still is the same, you never change it,
As sure as the stars shine above;
You're nobody 'til somebody loves you,
So find yourself somebody to love.

The world still is the same, you never change it,
As sure as the stars shine above;
You're nobody 'til somebody loves you,
So find yourself somebody, find yourself somebody,
Find yourself somebody to love.

Russ Morgan, Larry Stock, and James Cavanaugh 1944.
Recorded by Dean Martin

Passage: Shelter Bay to Chagres River

Departed Sunday, August 17, 2008 at 12:19 PM local time from Shelter Bay Marina. The departure location was latitude 9 degrees 18.290 minutes north, longitude 79 degrees 59.509 minutes west.

Arrived Sunday, August 17, 2008 at 12:20 PM local time at Chagres River at Anchor. The arrival location was latitude 9 degrees 18.290 minutes north, longitude 79 degrees 59.508 minutes west. The trip covered 11.90 nautical miles in 0d 1h 59m with an average speed of 5.00 knots and a maximum speed of 7.60 knots.

Sunday, August 17, 2008 1:20:18 PM

Location: Chagres River, Panama
Latitude is 9 degrees 18.29 minutes north.
Longitude is 79 degrees 59.506 minutes west.

Today *Jenny* took her first baby step passage in the Caribbean. It was a total of twelve miles from the Shelter Bay Marina to this river, but the difference is extraordinary. The river snakes through a tropical rain forest, teaming with life. In the first hour, we saw a pack of howler monkeys make their way, tree to tree up the river. It is raining now and the forest is quiet. I expect it to come alive again this evening and night should be a hoot!

The Caribbean treated *Jenny* nicely her first time out. She has to become familiar with this new body of water. The oceans and seas are all very different and have their own personalities. I discovered this as *Jenny* carried us down the west coast. We had slowly absorbed the sea changes as *Jenny* slowly worked her way. The canal crossing was an abrupt discontinuity in our experience. Suddenly we were in the Atlantic Ocean basin and the Caribbean Sea within. The water is dramatically different. Looking at the weather reports, GRIB files, Buoy Weather, etc. must be seen in light of the personality of this water. It is time to learn again with baby steps. So far so good!

This morning Nicholas and I were on a walk and saw one of the small rodent creatures about the size and shape of a football scamper into the woods. I think it was an agouti. We have yet to see a three-toe sloth in the wild, but given their stealthiness, we are not likely to. Ah well, so far the Caribbean is a treat.

Monday, August 18, 2008 11:17:27 AM

Location: Chagres River

It is very nice to have coffee and tea in *Jenny's* cockpit while listening to the jungle that surrounds us. I spotted a very large reptile up in one of the trees, sunning to warm up. Its head was gray and dry so I think it was some kind of lizard. However, it was big enough to be a very large snake too. Once it got warm, it disappeared.

Then we spotted a troupe of black howler monkeys further up the river, also out sunning themselves in a tree. Just now we spotted a troupe of white faced howlers in a big tree just across from us. I have tried to take pictures of all of this to no avail. I only have a 250mm lens and it just is not enough. I have nice pictures of trees, but you cannot discern the lizard or the monkeys. I guess you have to be here with some serious camera equipment. If you are purchasing a camera, a super-fast lens is the most important feature since quite a bit of the action occurs at dawn and dusk. Then a very long lens, perhaps 600mm also fast since even in the river, *Jenny* is always moving.

We are in the company of a French vessel behind us yesterday and today just passed us, slowly moving up the river. The current is much faster than I thought it would be since the dam is only six miles up. I guess the daily rainfall is enough to drive it. My guess is two knots.

Nicholas is curled up on top of the pilothouse closet to see the action, when he is awake that is. Mary is cooing over all the monkeys and reading about the San Blas. We will probably head there tomorrow. After we get *Jenny's* batteries back at Shelter Bay, we will probably head here again. It is a very nice spot.

Passage: Chagres River to Portobello

Departed Tuesday, August 19, 2008 at 8:12 AM local time from Chagres River Anchor. The departure location was latitude 9 degrees 20.893 minutes north, longitude 80 degrees 0.284 minutes west.

Arrived Tuesday, August 19, 2008 at 12:00 PM local time at Portobello. The arrival location was latitude 9 degrees 33.310 minutes north, longitude 79 degrees 39.723 minutes west. The trip covered 27.55 nautical miles in 0d 4h 27m with an average speed of 6.20 knots and a maximum speed of 7.20 knots.

Tuesday, August 19, 2008 12:19:08 PM

Location: Portobello Anchorage
Latitude is 9 degrees 33.3 minutes north.
Longitude is 79 degrees 39.721 minutes west.

The Caribbean was good to *Jenny* again today. Her twenty-six-mile journey from the Chagres River to the town of Portobello was like crossing a lake except for the ships we had to dodge around the canal entrance. The Spanish founded the town in 1597 as their port for exporting gold and silver to Spain. There are many very old ruins here we plan to visit.

We saw a glimpse of turquoise water as we entered the small bay, but the anchorage has cloudy water from the river. The islands are beckoning nearby, but we need to wait for *Jenny's* batteries to arrive back at Shelter Bay before we go any further. I had to run the genset this morning to get enough power to start JD! I guess it is time...

I will send some emails to our friends around both sides of the canal and let them know we will be here for a week or so. *Monju* is supposed to be just on the other side of the peninsula here and we have some groceries for them. They might come around for a pickup.

Tuesday, August 19, 2008 10:05:19 PM

Location: Portobello, Panama

We went out to dinner with the *Ketching Up* crowd this evening. She now has six children and four adults onboard now and just came back from the San Blas islands. This is payback to Noel and Ashley for asking their friends to manage their mail and finances while away. Needing desperately to get off their boat, we marched to the only "restaurant" in town for dinner. Chaos! What were they thinking? Noel has gone mystic on us and moved into a Zen state for relief. Ashley is just numb and zombie like. They head back to the marina tomorrow and the beginning of downsizing. They are not sure of their plans, but I think we will see them again in Cartagena.

Tonight the stars are out, Milky Way bright and full until the nearly full moon rose over *Jenny*'s bow, obliterating the more subtle and meaningful light show. I like the Caribbean. I feel more at home here. The few worms in the sky are heading to Florida instead of LA. You can feel some Rasta and Jamaican influence in the fabric of this place.

The weather is entirely different on this side of the canal. Here, vertical weather and trade winds rule. The other side is confused about its physics. Should it be windy or not? Should it rain or not? From what direction should the wind blow? Each day is a mystery. Not so here. The wind blows from the northeast or east. The clouds form all day and dump buckets around 3:00 PM. No problem man. We filled out tanks in an hour of downpour. No need to do it again for another week or two. The sky supplies this basic need.

Tropical Storm Fay skipped Jacksonville, as usual. These storms can beat up most of Florida and the Carolina's, but Jacksonville is a walled city to them, nice and safe. We might summer there in 2009. I am beginning to become more and more convinced that moving about in *Jenny* is my only future. I am finding it harder and harder to relate to the anxieties and strivings of the first world and the ineptitude of the third.

I think it is about time to begin writing my SiFi novel.

Passage: Portobello to Isla Grande

Departed Friday, August 22, 2008 at 1:04 PM local time from Portobello Anchor. The departure location was latitude 9 degrees 37.623 minutes north, longitude 79 degrees 33.924 minutes west.

Arrived Friday, August 22, 2008 at 1:05 PM local time at Isla Grande Anchor. The arrival location was latitude 9 degrees 37.621 minutes north, longitude 79 degrees 33.924 minutes west. The trip covered 10.21 nautical miles in 0d 1h 48m with an average speed of 5.70 knots and a maximum speed of 8.40 knots.

Friday, August 22, 2008 3:34:02 PM

Location: Isla Grande, Panama
Latitude is 9 degrees 37.623 minutes north.
Longitude is 79 degrees 33.924 minutes west.

Jenny left Portobello this morning with *Monju* and headed out to our first Caribbean island. It has been a very long time since Portobello was belle. Aside from the 16th century fort remains, it is a very poor and rundown neighborhood. In fact, a sailboat within 200 yards of us had their dinghy stolen last night. *Monju* said the motor was a new four stroke fifteen HP Yamaha. Just what the local population would lust for. They did not raise the dinghy and big surprise, it was gone this morning. The captain is a local and should have known better. There is more to this story...

Yesterday an Australian kid walked up to us at the local restaurant near the dinghy dock. He and his girlfriend had paid for a ride to Cartagena on the sailboat that subsequently lost the dinghy. The kid was alarmed because the owner of the boat had a fight with the captain, and both had disappeared. The kids were left on the boat all by themselves and now did not even have a dinghy to get to shore with. Eventually the captain showed up and we searched for the dinghy without luck. They were still there when we left.

This lead to a story that Carl on *Monju* told us about the sailboat passenger trade going on between Portobello, which has no government presence, and Cartagena. This couple were the typical young backpackers who could have flown between Panama City and Cartagena for about $350 each, or for about $300 total, they could take a sailboat on a five day cruise to the San Blas and then over to Cartagena. Well, they chose the latter.

The anchorage at Isla Grande is very nice. There are a number of nice homes, restaurants, beaches, etc. nearby and the water is clear when the sea currents push the river water aside. People come over from Panama City on the weekends and for vacation here, so there is a reasonable economy. We plan to hang out here until *Jenny's* batteries come in instead of Portobello. I will dive on the bottom and take Nicholas and Mary to the beach for some fun. I know Mary is still not happy and want to expose her to the islands here as much as possible in the hope that she likes them.

We are having *Monju* over tonight for movies. They are very nice folks and we share many thoughts about cruising at this point in our journey. They are heading down the San Blas tomorrow, and then are turning back west to go up the Central American route back to the States. We are going to take the South

America, Caribbean Islands route. We might just meet up in Chesapeake Bay the winter of 2009-2010. Funny world this is.

Sunday, August 24, 2008 8:45:35 AM

Location: Isla Grande, Panama

Jenny has been anchored in the pass between Isla Grande and the mainland for a couple of days now. This is a nice spot, used by the locals as a weekend and vacation spot. It has a good restaurant, trinkets economy with plenty of dinghy docks. A couple of new homes / vacation cabins are being built and there are a couple of large homes are up on the hills.

We have had a couple of days of rain, but today has dawned bright, sunny and hot. Off to *Jenny's* side is *Monju*, and we have been enjoying the company of Carl and Mei. Last night we played Hearts and had a blast. Today, we are going to take a dinghy tour of the neighboring Isla Linton and some coral reefs and tonight I think we are going to dinghy into a restaurant.

The water here is crystal clear to twenty feet and we can see the bottom easily. Occasionally I watch a ray swim under us. We have white sandy beaches, warm clear water, coconut palms and Pina Colotas! We have made it. If it remains sunny, we will jump in the water this afternoon to swim, and clean *Jenny's* hull a little. I have been doing small projects in the mornings while it is cool and / or sunny and am making good progress.

We heard bad news from *Spirit* today. Lightening is one of the acts of nature that you really have no control over. A strike on a vessel can sink her or at least take out a bunch of her electronics. Here is Dan's account of the strike they took while in the Flamenco Anchorage.

"We just got the engine fixed and were planning on sailing to the Las Perlas Islands for a few days to test out the work. The day before we left, we had a severe lightning storm. Erin was in town shopping and I was on Spirit. The lightning strikes were so loud and close I was literally ducking every time it cracked. I had everything unplugged and all the circuit breakers turned off. I also had all portable electronics stowed in the oven. They say this is the thing to do because the metal box of the oven acts as a Farad box. But I believe that if you get a direct hit, it doesn't matter where you put the stuff.

Anyway, one bolt hit nearby and scared the crap out of me. Afterwards, I could hear the electricity in the air by the electronics. The radio was making a light humming noise. After the storm and a few choice words, I began testing the systems. The only thing I could find was that I could not transmit on the VHF. Not a big problem as I have two other VHF radios on board.

We woke up the next morning and were just about the haul anchor when I turned on the auto-pilot. Guess what else is on the same breaker as the VHF....the autopilot and radar. Both are currently out. I have power to the auto pilot but it's giving me an error message. The radar is completely dead. All this happened just one week before my parents arrive and ten days before our scheduled canal transit. We have the names of two marine electronics experts that should be able to help us and will be seeing them first thing tomorrow morning. I can do without the radar for now but I need the auto pilot. No way I am hand-steering to Colombia!"

I believe there is no way to protect against or avoid lightning. One school of thought is to run a grounding system of heavy gauge wire from the mast to a big copper plate in the water. If you then get struck by lightning, the theory is that the electricity will flow down these wires to the saltwater and the boat will be ok. Unfortunately, these same wires allow electricity to run up to the top of the mast and attract lightning strikes. I have seen a few photographs of boats being struck and have seen one such strike myself. Many photographs show small sailboats in the middle of much larger sailboats being hit. Now why would that happen? In the one case I witnessed, the small boat was running a grounding wire and no other boat was.

Tuesday, August 26, 2008 11:18:26 AM

Location: Isla Grande, Panama

I dove on *Jenny*'s bottom twice yesterday and again this morning. The water was clear and warm, and she needed a good going over. Yesterday I brushed off the algae and slime and knocked off some barnacles. Her propeller was in good condition with hardly any barnacles, just a bit of algae and slime. Some sort of a thin layer of calcium forms that has a wave like pattern in it. I suspect it is the beginnings of coral. I have to scrape it off with my dive knife. I hesitate to call it a knife though, because it is very dull and is more of a scraper than anything else. It is a good tool though, and I have had it since I started diving in Florida in the 1980's.

Today is picture perfect. The sun is out and the thermometer says it is 95 in the sun, but we have a good breeze and it feels more like 80. A French sailboat showed up next to us this morning. It is an old design and looks like a wooden boat about thirty-five feet long. We will have to go over and say Hi to the crew of four or five people.

This morning I dove on *Jenny*'s bottom again to polish up the hull and stuff, but mainly to tackle her bow thruster. I gave up on it long ago, and it had turned into its own ecosystem, completely eliminating any functional value. I figured if I left it long enough, I would have my own living reef with us and I could spear fish any time. But, my work ethic took over and I took a long screwdriver to it.

The Remora fish that has been keeping company with *Jenny* came over and snacked on the busted up barnacles and small oysters. It even came over to my hand and nudged it to say thanks. After a couple of hours pounding on the growth, the propellers emerged along with the gear housing. And, you could see through from one side to the other. Imagine that! Now I have done it. It will probably work now and I will have to keep up on the maintenance.

Once done my work, I dove down to *Jenny's* anchor to see how it set and for the first time just dove for fun. It was nice. The Hookah has sixty feet of hose on it so I could easily swim around at twenty feet. The school of bait fish that has been hiding in the shade of *Jenny*'s bottom came over and swam around me, checking me out. They looked like flying fish, but I could not see their long wing fins. Perhaps they were invisible folded against their sides. They do come to the surface now and again and fly off in various directions, probably when under attack.

When in Panama City I bought Mary the rest of her snorkeling equipment and maybe I will get her in the water this afternoon. Keep your cards and letters coming. It is a tough assignment down here, but remember, someone's got to do it!

Friday, August 29, 2008 12:00:43 PM

Location: Isla Grande, Panama

We went snorkeling on one of the coral reefs near the boats. Mary put on her mask and fins for the first time and we paddled out from the beach to the coral heads. There weren't any big fish, rays, etc. on this reef, but it was alive and full of aquarium fish. The fish were everything from pastels to bright reds, blues, yellows, etc. One little fish was solid black with diode bright blue lights on its side. They probably were just catching and reflection light from above, but were so bright they appeared to be internally lit.

After a little while, Mary headed back to the beach and I stayed out to watch the ecosystem on the reef. It was nice to be on a coral beach again and be able to snorkel on a reef. We hooked up with Caroline and Edward on *Pendragon*, a sailboat from Salam, Massachusetts. We have been enjoying the evenings with them. They are on a hiatus from work and are trying to figure out how to keep it going as long as possible. They might also end up in the Chesapeake Bay when we are there the winter of 2009-2010.

It has not rained here in any serious amount for the past several days and I am hoping we will get some to fill the tanks before we head out to the San Blas. They get less rain there, being off the coast several miles. Right now, I think we will go out to the first islands for a week before heading back to Shelter Bay on the sixth. Mary wants to spend more time here, and we can when we come back out from picking up the batteries. We wanted to spend the month of September in the islands, but it now looks like we will not have *Jenny's* batteries loaded until around the tenth or eleventh. We have to start toward Venezuela on November 1, so we are starting to eat into our Cartagena time. UGH.

Sunday, August 31, 2008 10:14:08 AM

Location: Isla Grande, Panama

Last night we went bar hopping with Caroline and Edward from *Pendragon* and had fun. The island population blossomed with the weekend crowd, with Panamanians, Germans, French, Americans, etc. Helicopters flew in the wealthy. Pangas ferried in the masses. We left *The Beast* at our favorite restaurant and walked the strip. We then returned for fish, shrimp, and lobster dinners.

This morning we took *The Beast* and circumnavigated Isla Grande. It turns out there is a very upscale resort on the north side. It looked nice with separate cabanas for guests, a nice beach, kayaks and snorkeling. When we return here in a couple of weeks I am going to take it over to the north side and snorkel the massive coral heads. The coral is the biggest and healthiest I have seen with intriguing canyons to explore. I did not see any large fish, but I will bring the spear gun anyway...

Due to Hurricane Gustave we have not had rain in about a week. We are becoming more conservative with our water usage. I hope we will get a good downpour soon. I am monitoring the SSB stations regarding Gustave and pity New Orleans. It now looks like they are in for another category five hit.

Passage: Isla Grande to Chichime Cay

Departed Monday, September 01, 2008 at 7:23 AM local time from Isla Grande anchor. The departure location was latitude 9 degrees 38.691 minutes north, longitude 79 degrees 31.945 minutes west.

Arrived Monday, September 01, 2008 at 1:32 PM local time at Chichime Cays. The arrival location was latitude 9 degrees 35.256 minutes north, longitude 78 degrees 52.893 minutes west. The trip covered 41.67 nautical miles in 0d 6h 27m with an average speed of 6.50 knots and a maximum speed of 7.30 knots.

Monday, September 01, 2008 5:00:54 PM

Location: Chichime Cays
Latitude is 9 degrees 35.266 minutes north.
Longitude is 78 degrees 52.878 minutes west.

Jenny steamed 42 miles east today to get to our first San Blas islands. The water was deep blue and flat calm all the way. I dragged the meat hook but without results, supporting my belief that this area is pretty much fished out.

Coral islands and reefs are new to us and even though I have spent a lot of time in Florida and sometime in the keys, navigation among the reefs and channels to anchorage is something we are learning. We followed the charts in the Bauhaus guide and made an easy entry here, noting the difference in water color and surface patterns as we came in. There were seven boats already here in this small anchorage, but a good space was still available. *Jenny* got a good hookup on the bottom and ran out 200 feet of chain to secure her in place. This is important since reefs surround her. Coral walls rise abruptly from about thirty feet, most times stopping just a foot or so below low tide levels, and occasionally breaking the surface. You need to be careful.

If you have a stereotype of what a tropical island is, this place would fit the image. It is stunning. We have two, palm forested small islands on both sides of us. They have coral sand beaches and coral reefs extending from them. Kuna families occupy a couple of thatched huts on each of the islands. The water is teal and clear to thirty feet. Once anchored we set up the lawn chairs on the upper deck, jumped in the water and then kicked back with a couple of Cerveza. Life is good...

Beautiful Chichime in San Blas Islands

Tuesday, September Cays02, 2008 1:03:04 PM

Location: Chichime Cays

Late yesterday afternoon the wind picked up and we saw fifteen knots from the south and southwest. It really cooled things down, and blew away all bugs that were here. It settled down to five to ten knots all night that gave us a wonderful breeze to sleep in. I set up an anchor alarm on the GPS and set the display to watch our position. I needed to be sure *Jenny* is not dragging into the reef walls around us. A periodic check through the night showed all was well. I should rest even better tonight.

This morning several boats here checked out and a couple came in. There was a charter sailboat here with the captain, his wife and two pairs of guests. They arrived late last night and headed over to PourVenir this morning to check in. I think they sailed over from Cartagena.

Nicholas and I took a stroll around the smaller of the two islands this morning. It looks like there are two families living here on opposite sides of the island. These are Kuna Indians and their life is easy, if Spartan. They are friendly, and sell seafood and fruits to cruisers. I found a shell from a blue crab and showed it to one of them to find out the name. They call them something like conguero. I then ordered four or five large ones for this evening. They said they get them and bring them to *Jenny*. I also bought some limes yesterday so I could make Mojitos! I got fifteen limes for a buck. Not bad. I soon need some more. No, no, I used them for Ice Tea and lemonade.

Nicholas and I then took *The Beast* over to the charter boat to chat. They had a dog on board, something like a Chesapeake Bay retriever, but lighter color and build. I then picked up Mary and headed over to the tiny island here. I am sure it has been used for commercials that depict a guy shipwrecked on a tiny island with his babe, a case of cold Corona's. All is well. In any case, Mary and Nicholas cavorted on the island while I snorkeled the coral reef. The reef was not as robust as the one at Isla Grande due to an abundance of starfish. There were lots of pipefish, damselfish, and other exotics, but no big fish. I know they are around here somewhere because a Kuna dugout came by around noon with a three foot Barracuda and, more importantly, a ten-pound red snapper. They also had some spider crabs, and a spiny lobster. If I hadn't already ordered blue point crabs for dinner, I would have bought the snapper.

There are plenty of downpours going on the mainland, but nothing here. It would be nice to get a good wash down and load some rainwater. But, other than that, life is pretty good.

Thursday, September 04, 2008 12:16:52 PM

Location: Chichime Cays

Fifteen to twenty-five knot wind pounded *Jenny* for the past 48 hours. The system on both sides of Panama and is causing most, if not all boats to remain at anchor. *Jenny* is in eleven meters of water with 200 feet of chain out and holding steady. I should have moved further into the cut here when there was room, but did not. While some of the vessels are pretty well protected by the big island here (about 600 yards long), *Jenny* is pretty much out in the open. There is a reef to windward of us, so we are only getting one-foot wind waves. Even so, I took down *Jenny's* awning to keep it from been beaten up. I am hoping it dies down tonight so we can have an easy trip back to Isla Grande.

The islands here are small and manicured like parks. There is little if any undergrowth and the Kuna sweep the sand using palm tree fronds. These islands sit about four feet above water level, and are perfectly flat. There is no source of fresh water as far as I can tell, no sanitary system, no electricity. The people just walk out into the water to relieve themselves.

Last night we had Carl and Mei from *Monju* and Caroline and Andrew from *Pendragon* over for potluck dinner and storytelling. *Pendragon* came down through Bocas del Toro and Carl and Mei have been thinking about going up there, but are not sure and got some information. It was a lot of fun. Gatherings like this seem to be a cornerstone of what is different and good about cruising. No TV, just good folks exchanging information and entertaining each other.

This morning I went out snorkeling off the calm side of the big island with Carl, Mei, Caroline and Andrew. We found a lot of coral, but not much diversity. Carl and Mei say diving is much better on the outer islands. We will have to visit them after we pick up *Jenny's* batteries.

Passage: Chichime Cays to Isla Grande

Departed Friday, September 05, 2008 at 7:12 AM local time from Chichime Anchor. The departure location was latitude 9 degrees 35.092 minutes north, longitude 78 degrees 54.058 minutes west.

Arrived Friday, September 05, 2008 at 1:19 PM local time at Isla Grande. The arrival location was latitude 9 degrees 37.611 minutes north, longitude 79 degrees 33.841 minutes west. The trip covered 41.60 nautical miles in 0d 6h 5m with an average speed of 6.60 knots and a maximum speed of 7.20 knots.

Saturday, September 06, 2008 1:50:53 PM

Location: Isla Grande

The wind finally died down and yesterday morning *Jenny* released her grip on the bottom at Chichime Cay in ten knots. During her ride back to Isla Grande, the wind died further so she had a very smooth ride in deep blue seas. Dolphins were playing and several groups came over to see her. Nicholas enjoyed seeing them too. I dragged a meat hook and caught a small barracuda. I released it even though I have heard the small ones are good to eat.

Jenny arrived back in Isla Grande around 2:00 PM and dropped her hook over twenty feet of sand. It is nice here. We had to switch over to *Jenny's* aft water tank though since we still have not had any rain in over two weeks. UGH.

Spirit (Dan and Erin)

Our friends Dan and Erin came in around 17:30 yesterday afternoon and dropped their hook next to us. Dan is hosting his parents for the next five days, taking them out to the San Blas. This morning we all went snorkeling on the reef here and had a good time. I saw a couple of baby barracuda, and Erin spotted three small squid. There were about six inches long and were the first squid I have ever seen swimming in the wild. Too cool! We are going into one of the restaurants this afternoon and then they are heading east to the islands, while we will head west, back to Shelter Bay. *Jenny's* batteries are in!

Passage: Isla Grande to Shelter Bay Marina

Departed Monday, September 08, 2008 at 6:51 AM local time from Isla Grande anchor. The departure location was latitude 9 degrees 37.516 minutes north, longitude 79 degrees 34.083 minutes west.

Arrived Monday, September 08, 2008 at 12:13 PM local time at Shelter Bay Marina. The arrival location was latitude 9 degrees 22.076 minutes north, longitude 79 degrees 57.065 minutes west. The customs check in was normal check in. The trip covered 29.17 nautical miles in 0d 5h 23m with an average speed of 5.40 knots and a maximum speed of 7.00 knots.

Thursday, September 11, 2008 8:23:53 PM

Location: Shelter Bay Marina

We are back in Shelter Bay Marina and are making some significant changes in our lives. Mary is leaving Nicholas and me and heading back to the states. We lived in Orlando Florida before moving to California for my job at Kaiser Permanente. I went out first, but Mary did not want to go. She had a job she liked and a lot of friends there. It wasn't until we sold the house that she finally decided to join me. We were working out there when we bought Jenny.

I do not know exactly the underlying reason is for leaving. We are not communicating. Maybe it is me, maybe it is the life, and maybe it is her need to be part of civilization. Maybe she wants to return to her life in Orlando. Nevertheless, she is going.

It took her less than twenty-four hours after we had an internet connection to get a contract job. Looking back, that was probably in the works for some time. She packed all her stuff into the two huge duffle bags we used to bring in all the boat supplies into Barillas plus a couple of smaller ones. It does not look like she intends to return. On September 19th she took a taxi to the airport. She will be spending some time with my mother and my kids, and then on to Orlando where her friends are.

I am not ready to stop cruising and exploring and will see what it is like going solo for a while. I will be flying back to Florida for Christmas and might find that she is ready to come back to us. Who knows? In the meantime, I will take *Jenny* over to Cartagena and experience that city. Carl and Mei warned her not to leave me alone there. I might stay there through Christmas, and then continue to the ABC (Aruba, Curacao, Bonaire) islands, and on up the chain to Florida. I do not know.

Passage: Shelter Bay to Isla Grande

Departed Saturday, September 20, 2008 at 6:52 AM local time from Shelter Bay Marina. The departure location was latitude 9 degrees 23.933 minutes north, longitude 79 degrees 54.511 minutes west.

Arrived Saturday, September 20, 2008 at 11:04 AM local time at Isla Grande. The arrival location was latitude 9 degrees 37.591 minutes north, longitude 79 degrees 33.913 minutes west. The trip covered 29.26 nautical miles in 0d 4h 50m with an average speed of 6.00 knots and a maximum speed of 7.30 knots.

Saturday, September 20, 2008 1:24:59 PM

Location: Isla Grande
Latitude is 9 degrees 37.591 minutes north.
Longitude is 79 degrees 33.917 minutes west.

Mary made it back to the States ok and is staying with my mother for a few days. Nicholas and I are back at Isla Grande. Tomorrow Nicholas and I will head back to Chichime and start searching for *Spirit*. Erin is also returning to the States so Dan will be single handling *Spirit* again. We are going to buddy boat down through the Panama islands, then over to the Colombian islands and on up to Cartagena. I am looking forward to being in a medium sized city and being able to walk in town and see the sights. Everyone I have talked to says this is an awesome town, so I will probably stay there a while. There is a large cruiser population there and Nicholas and I will need the company of people in the city instead of the isolation of the islands.

Jenny has her new batteries and is in tiptop condition. She is wearing a big smile. I replaced the last of the wire running rigging on the dinghy boom with rope, so all rigging is now new. I also discovered *Jenny* had running backstays! I have been staring at these two lines that run from her masthead for years, wondering what they were for. I also had been staring at two deck plates with rings in them for about just as long. The light bulb went on in the middle of the night a couple of days ago. When I put the outriggers out today, I hooked the lines up to the plates to provide extra support for the top of the mast. It will not be until I actually run her birds in a good sea that I will find out if they change anything. But *Jenny* revealed yet another of her secrets!

Carl and Mei on *Monju* gave me dinner and a farewell party last night. We drank too much, and philosophized about the cruising life. With the market where it is, they will probably have to go back to work and they are thinking about where and how to set it up so they can live on *Monju*. Many cruisers are having the same discussion and I am very lucky to have our finances set up so I think I am not at risk through this.

Passage: Isla Grande to Chichime

Departed Sunday, September 21, 2008 at 7:06 AM local time from Isla Grande Anchor. The departure location was latitude 9 degrees 38.691 minutes north, longitude 79 degrees 31.982 minutes west.

Arrived Sunday, September 21, 2008 at 2:02 PM local time at Isla Grande Anchor. The arrival location was latitude 9 degrees 35.216 minutes north, longitude 78 degrees 52.953 minutes west. The trip covered 41.70 nautical miles in 0d 7h 17m with an average speed of 5.70 knots and a maximum speed of 6.90 knots.

Sunday, September 21, 2008 7:15:14 PM

Location: Chichime Anchorage
Latitude is 9 degrees 35.222 minutes north.
Longitude is 78 degrees 52.942 minutes west.

Jenny carried Nicholas and me out of Isla Grande around 06:30 this morning. Since it gets very hot in the afternoon now, the mornings are the best time to get things done. I worked up the courage to put a new trip line on *Jenny's* anchor. I hope she is willing to give this rig a chance and I wanted to see how it worked. I learned this setup from a Mexican Navy boat a long time ago, but did not put it together until last week in Shelter Bay.

The trip line attaches to the anchor in a place that allows you to back it out if it becomes stuck on a reef, underwater cable, or other hazards on the seabed. I had been using a forty-foot trip line with a buoy on the surface until a panga snagged it in Mexico. Back then I could see exactly where *Jenny's* anchor was and pull it out of a snare easily if necessary. As you know, *Jenny* did not tolerate it and forced me to abandon that setup.

You want to be able to pull the anchor up easily on a trip line if you have to. A surface line is the easiest since you just need to get it on deck and wrap it around the windlass. No line means you need to dive all the way down to the seabed; find the anchor and then attach a line directly to the anchor using a shackle. That is not easy or may be impossible if the water is deep and you do not have scuba or a Hookah. While the probability of needing to trip the anchor is low, it does happen and consequences are large. Noel on *Catching Up* had to free dive thirty feet to attach a trip line to his anchor and bled from his ears for a two days.

The Mexican Navy goes part way, playing the odds and reducing the problem. I saw that they used a ten to fifteen-foot line attached to the trip point of their anchor and put a light fishing buoy on the end. Yes, the buoy is pulling on the trip point of the anchor, but it is an insignificant pull. The buoy puts the tail of the trip line straight up off the anchor. The attachment point for tripping the anchor is now ten to fifteen feet above the bottom. I spliced a loop on the tail so that I could easily pass a longer line through it when I need to. That is much easier than attaching a shackle to the anchor. My line is about ten feet long, so it always rides below outboard motor depth and is below *Jenny's* bottom. She cannot play her games with it. In clear water, the buoy makes it very easy to spot the anchor. The setup works great and is now standard equipment!

Jenny did not complain as she released her grip on the Isla Grande seabed in a dead calm and had easy seas all the way over to the Chichime islands. I caught a fish but do not know what it is. It is in the refrigerator for tomorrow night on the grille to share with my friends on *Spirit*. It looks like a small (sixteen inch) tuna, jack, or mackerel. Horizontal steel blue lines along the top, silver sides, white bottom. I don't know.

The Panama Guardia Coasta visited *Jenny* on her way over to the islands early in the morning. They came up in a big panga with a Ma Duce dumped in the bottom of the boat, M-16s on their shoulders and asked to board. I thought it would be a good idea to comply. They gave me time to slow to idle and put out fenders. Then they came up and tied alongside. *Jenny* had the helm and they left one (of four) soldiers at the panga's helm to keep her even with *Jenny*. They were very courteous and careful. Only one spoke English, but the Lieutenant and the guy who spoke English were very nice. It was a routine check and after going through our papers, getting some cokes and tea, they passed me with flying colors. They had been up all night and I think they were really just looking for some Java! They really liked *Jenny* too. Interestingly, my Zarpe included Mary on the crew list. She was not on board, but it did not seem to mean anything to them. One purpose of the Zarpe is to make sure everyone who leaves on a vessel also arrives safely. Hmmmm…

When I arrived at Chichime I was again surrounded by canoes with Kuna Indians peddling Molas. I explained that there was no mujer (woman) on board this time and that drove them off. They did however remember Nicholas from our last visit and asked to see him.

I made radio contact with *Spirit* on the way in today and will rendezvous with Dan and Erin tomorrow morning. They are only eighteen miles away. Erin is flying home the day after tomorrow.

Listening to NPR, it seems like the US financial system is falling apart.

Passage: Chichime to Coco Bandero

Departed Monday, September 22, 2008 at 6:52 AM local time from Chichime Anchor.

Arrived Monday, September 22, 2008 at 10:42 AM local time at Coco Bandero Cays, Orduptarboat Island. The arrival location was latitude 9 degrees 30.873 minutes north, longitude 78 degrees 38.839 minutes west. The trip covered 18.70 nautical miles in 0d 3h 49m with an average speed of 4.90 knots and a maximum speed of 6.80 knots.

Monday, September 22, 2008 6:22:49 PM

Location: Coco Bandero Anchorage
Latitude is 9 degrees 30.88 minutes north.
Longitude is 78 degrees 38.822 minutes west.

Jenny steamed the eighteen miles over to Coco Bandero to meet up with *Spirit*. The water here is awesome, clear to thirty plus feet. She had to anchor in fifty feet in order to get good holding. At thirty feet her anchor just slid over a hard coral bottom. Dan and Erin came over for snacks and beer before heading over to the small town on the mainland. Erin's flight is at 06:00 tomorrow, so they are going to anchor over at town, and have a farewell dinner.

Dan is having refrigeration problems, probably a leak and seems interested in getting to Cartagena quickly. *Scott Free* just went this morning and I just talked to them on the SSB. They are in hardly any wind and have flat seas. I will have to get the weather faxes tomorrow and see how long this good weather is supposed to last. If I can dive on the bottom tomorrow and get a good night's sleep, then we might kick off the next day. I would have preferred staying here a while though and done some more snorkeling and enjoying these islands. Dan and I will have to talk some more tomorrow.

Tuesday, September 23, 2008 11:47:55 AM

Location: Coco Bandera Anchorage 2
Latitude is 9 degrees 30.784 minutes north.
Longitude is 78 degrees 36.902 minutes west.

Jenny moved over to the islands at Coco Bandera yesterday to meet up with *Spirit*. *Spirit* was inside a small cluster of islands with another vessel but it was just too small and shallow for *Jenny* to feel safe. She stayed overnight on the outside in fifty feet of water with some wind waves pushing her around. It was ok but too far away from her friends, the islands and coral. This morning she eased her anchor out of the sand and headed over to the islands on the eastern end. This set of four islands provides good shelter and offers several good anchoring spots. After navigating through the reefs around the entrance, she found a good spot next to the big ketch she met in Shelter Bay with Derek and Caroline on board. The boat was recently built in Maine using cold molded wood and is stunning. *Jenny* likes to snuggle up with beautiful vessels.

I unstrapped *The Beast* and lowered it over *Jenny's* side. Nicholas and I explored two of the islands. They are so small it only takes about twenty minutes to walk completely around their circumference. There is more sea life here than the other San Blas islands. I saw a couple of rays, and a squid from the beach. Nicholas was really glad to get on land and had a good run! He's pooped now.

I got out my snorkeling gear to check out *Jenny's* anchor setting and the nearby reefs. It's cool to jump off *Jenny* and be able to swim to a reef full of fish. I always worry about wind changes and whether she will swing too far and end up on one. You always feel that the anchor could be placed just a little better than it is. UGH. But this is nice and calm and well protected, so I should have no worries.

Pendragon is in the same town as *Spirit* and are heading out this way this morning. It will be good to see them again. I have been trying to raise Dan to tell him I moved. I need to spend the afternoon with him talking about sailing plans. I got an email from *Ketching Up* this morning saying they hope to be down here in a couple of weeks. It would be nice to just sit here for a while and then go over to Colombia with them. However, I do not know if *Spirit* wants to wait that long.

Thursday, September 25, 2008 9:42:36 AM

Spirit in Coco Bandero island group

Location: Coco Bandero Anchorage

This is our third day in this idyllic anchorage. *Jenny* is between two small islands and well protected from waves. Every evening, a good breeze comes off the mainland and cools her down nicely. The sky has been clear and the stars sparkle brightly. As the sun sets, swallows come to *Jenny* and fly inside seeking a place to roost for the night. Nicholas is cool with their visits and I gently escort them back outside. Sometimes they are persistent and do a few laps around the pilothouse. They are almost unafraid of humans, so you have to get within a foot or two before they get nervous.

Dan bought some lobster in town yesterday before returning to the *Spirit*. I also bought some from a couple of Kuna in their ulu (canoe). In the morning I asked for a couple of grande padre's. I have made it a point to let them know I would not buy madres or niños to try to get them to practice some sort of wildlife management. They generally just do not get it, and keep everything that they catch regardless of size or gender. Well, it paid off. They arrived in the afternoon with several very nice sized male spiny lobsters. Last night Dan and I had a couple of Cerveza and lobster. Yummy!

Dan has a couple of more things to take care of on *Spirit*, and wants to make another trip to town for internet access. It looks like we will leave here in a couple of days for Isla Fuerte on the Colombian coast. *Pendragon* left this morning for the same. Today and tomorrow are forecast to be absolutely flat calm, so it would have been a good window for me. But Dan wants some help from the wind to conserve fuel and I cannot blame him. I will continue to monitor the weather for a shot that I hope includes some wind out of the west. *Jenny*'s all ready to go.

This laptop is becoming more and more cranky about starting. It took nearly an hour of turning it on and off to get the screen to work right. It looks like I will need to get a new one for Christmas. I have been just leaving it on all the time now, but now and again forget to plug it back in after using the SSB and it runs out of power. UGH.

Hope all is well with everyone back in the States. I get NPR on the SSB and it sounds bad.

Friday, September 26, 2008 9:29:04 PM

Location: Coco Bandero Anchorage

Today was fun. Yesterday Dan and I met a Frenchman who sailed from France with his wife and two children. He is a charming guy and their children are adorable. Well, he is an expert spear fisher and asked if we wanted to join him this morning on his hunt. He did not have to ask twice! We headed out to the outer reef at 08:00 and found a good spot. The reef was excellent with a nice forty-foot drop and lots of coral canyons and ledges. It was a great spot for fish. Unfortunately, the Kuna also hunted this ground so the fish were sparse and wary. In spite of that, Dan got a nice small grouper and the Frenchman got a nice snapper. I got nothing.

I did see a nice sized eagle ray and a couple of large sharks. These were the first sharks I have ever seen while in the water. It was right at the end of the dive and I was tired. When they came by a second time, I thought maybe they were getting too interested in a tired swimmer and launched myself into *The Beast*! I cooked Dan's grouper whole on *Jenny's* Weber tonight and we had yet another feast. Tomorrow we are going back for another round.

A couple of the sport fishing boats from Shelter Bay pulled into our anchorage this afternoon and the families were playing on the beach. Each is spotless with at least two crew in attendance and all the necessary toys.

It now looks like we will be pulling anchor on the 30th and arriving at Isla Fuerte, Colombia on October 1st. The waves will be in the one to two foot range with some wind out of the southwest. It should be a very easy passage. Life is good.

Sunday, September 28, 2008 1:27:29 PM

Location: Coco Bandero Anchorage

There is a Kuna town on the mainland about seven miles away that Dan has been visiting to do email and dine at the local restaurant. This morning he and I went over in *The Beast* to do the same. This was the first good use of this rather heavy and odd dinghy. Here in flat water and dinghy docks it does much better. We got up on plane and it took us about twenty minutes to get there in a flat sea. We motored in under their footbridge that connects the mainland part of the town with the other part on the barrier island, and tied up at the dinghy dock. No beach landings here!

Kuna Children, Mei from Monju in the hat.

The town is Kuna, but apparently this is a breakaway group. Some wore the traditional Kuna dress, but most were in western cloths, playing volleyball, basketball and baseball. Dan, being the ladies' man, had already checked out that non-Kuna could marry a Kuna and that divorce was a $75 dollar expense.

I had hoped to get cell phone coverage here, but to no avail. I did get an internet connection, but it was too slow for Skype. There was not much on the email either, so after checking the weather I packed up and hit the tiendas. I needed more limes, my favorite fruit now, and got two dozen for $2.00. Dan needed some other stuff, too, including junk food. They knew him since he and Erin made several trips, and rolled out the chips and cookies as he approached.

Lunch was scrumptious. We each had lobster cooked in spices and veggies, tomato and cucumber salad, and French fries. They cooked it to perfection, as good as you would find in any high-end San Francisco restaurant. Throw in two Pepsi's each and the total bill was $12.80. Yup!

Tomorrow *Jenny* will have the wind on her tail with one to two foot seas forecast. She's pulling anchor and heading over to Isla Fuerte, the closest of the Colombian islands in the morning. It will take about twenty-five to thirty hours depending on the currents. This will be my first solo overnight passage. *Jenny* is all ready to carry us over with her usual casual competence, so no worries. *Pendragon* is already there and says it is nice and that the Colombian coast guard will meet and greet us, which is good.

Passage: Coco Bandero to Isla Fuerte, Colombia

Departed Monday, September 29, 2008 at 8:05 AM local time from Coco Bandero Anchorage. The departure location was latitude 9 degrees 30.796 minutes north, longitude 78 degrees 36.940 minutes west.

Monday, September 29, 2008 12:26:33 PM

Location: At Sea
Latitude is 9 degrees 30.911 minutes north.
Longitude is 78 degrees 11.812 minutes west.

This weather observation was taken on Tuesday, September 30, 2008 11:11:36 AM local time.
Observation location: Islas Bandero, Colombia.
Latitude is 9 degrees 47.102 minutes north.
Longitude is 75 degrees 50.837 minutes west.
The air temperature is 84, and water temperature is 82 degrees Fahrenheit.
The forecast is Sunny, Rain Showers.
The current weather is dry.
The sky is broken clouds (60 - 90% clouds).
The wind is 6 knots from the southwest.
The visibility is fifteen nautical miles.
The wave height is 1 feet with 0 foot swells.
The barometer is 1012 millibar and steady.

Jenny released her grip in the sand and as soon as we were beyond the coral channel took the wheel out of my hands. She carried Nicholas and me out to sea and is four hours out of Coco Bandero and on her way to Isla Fuerte, Colombia now. The sea is a lovely royal blue as clear as air. Spirit left at 06:00 this morning and is about nine miles ahead of us. *Jenny's* running about a knot faster, so we should cross paths at about nine tonight. We are using ITU channel 6D on the SSB to maintain radio contact since his VHF is still very limited after his lightning strike. We just chatted at noon and since then a school of dolphins came up to play on *Jenny's* bow wave. Nicholas and I really enjoyed seeing them! I think they were grey bottlenose dolphins this time. Because the water is so clear, I could see them diving down fifty feet or more and then surfacing to jump in the air. It was quite a show. I have never seen water this clear!

I have the meat hook in the water and have had three bites. I hooked two but they both got off as I pulled them in. I think I have been using the same lure since Huatulco, so the hook might just be a little dull. I also think the bungee I was using was a little too soft. I replaced the bungee with a stronger one. If I lose another fish on the way in I will break out a new lure and retire this old soldier.

The sea is just a little lumpy but otherwise benign. As long as *Jenny* does not run into *Spirit* or anything else tonight I should have a good crossing over to Colombia.

Arrived Tuesday, September 30, 2008 at 10:43 AM local time at Islas San Bernardo. The arrival location was latitude 9 degrees 47.099 minutes north, longitude 75 degrees 50.848 minutes west. The customs check in was None. The trip covered 180.21 nautical miles in 1d 2h 36m with an average speed of 6.80 knots and a maximum speed of 8.00 knots.

Tuesday, September 30, 2008 11:25:52 AM

Location: Islas Bandero, Colombia
Latitude is 9 degrees 47.104 minutes north.
Longitude is 75 degrees 50.843 minutes west.

Jenny carried us through our first man / dog solo overnight passage safely and comfortably. I am tired, but not overly. Nicholas was on dolphin duty all night. Whenever he heard their squeaks, he started growling to let me know they were around. The perfectly clear water became the stage for a magic show put on by the dolphins. They created wonderful trails of bioluminescent light as they flew through the water at incredible speeds and glowed as they jumped in *Jenny's* bow wave. They created braids of intertwining bubble and light trails down fifty feet as they dove, swirled, and danced together in twos and threes. It was nature's own Circ de Soleil. The stars were out in force and I saw a meteor come in. It was heading north and turned into a giant green ball of light as it augured in. Under the canopy of stars, I saw thunderstorms over land to our south and water to our north. *Jenny* delightfully squeezed between them. It was quite a light show. Unforgettable.

The sea was calm all night and the adverse current turned around about sunset and then gradually increased to 1.2 knots through the night. At midnight *Jenny's* navigation computer estimated we would arrive at Isla Fuerte at 06:00 AM, which was too early. This was due to the wonderful current pushing her along. Dan and I called an audible and changed course to the Islas Bandero, the next in the set of islands towards Cartagena. *Jenny* was flying almost eight knots over ground in the morning and she arrived at about 11:00.

These islands do not compare to the San Blas though. They are big, filled with homes, resorts and restaurants. This anchorage is huge like the Flamenco anchorage in Panama and quite exposed to the south and west. It has sand / coral shoals about twenty feet deep among channels that are sixty feet deep. *Jenny* did a few laps around what looked like a good spot, one of the twenty-foot deep areas. She dropped her hook and 200 feet of chain. As she backed down and tried to dig it into the seafloor, it skipped over hard coral a few times and then grabbed. She let another 100 feet of chain out just to be sure she would give me a sound night's sleep. Someone on the net this morning advised that the winds can get high here.

Very soon after *Jenny* arrived a panga came out. It was the Colombian Department of Agriculture. I am not sure what they really had in mind, but they liked *Jenny* and asked about the stabilizers. They said I picked a good spot to anchor, fish and swim. Then they spotted my lure with its triple hook and asked if I had another. I have several so I gave them a couple. That made them happy and they left.

Tomorrow *Jenny* and *Spirit* will go up to the Rosario Islands that are twenty-five miles away and seek a more comfortable anchorage. All is well.

Passage: Isla Bandalero to Islas Rosarios

Departed Wednesday, October 01, 2008 at 8:04 AM local time from Isla Bandalero anchorage. The departure location was latitude 9 degrees 47.084 minutes north, longitude 75 degrees 50.731 minutes west.

Arrived Wednesday, October 01, 2008 at 4:23 PM local time at Cartagena, Colombia. The arrival location was latitude 10 degrees 24.490 minutes north, longitude 75 degrees 32.561 minutes west. The customs check in was Colombia. The trip covered 48.32 nautical miles in 0d 8h 29m with an average speed of 5.70 knots and a maximum speed of 7.80 knots.

Thursday, October 02, 2008 7:22:20 AM

Location: Cartagena, Colombia
Latitude is 10 degrees 24.491 minutes north.
Longitude is 75 degrees 32.575 minutes west.

Spirit and *Jenny* left the Islas Bandalero yesterday morning and planned to stop at the Islas Rosarios. When we got there and studied the charts, it turned out that the anchorages are tricky and small. After a lot of chart studying and watching the ferryboats and panga traffic we finally decided at noon to go the remaining twenty-two miles into Cartagena. *Jenny* arrived there around 15:30 and took up residence near Club Náutico. *Scott Free* was just pulling her hook and heading for Five Bays the first stop on the way to the ABC islands. Club Náutico held a happy hour at 5:00 this evening so we went in and discovered *Pendragon* had arrived yesterday. Then around 03:00 AM *Astor* pulled in and anchored right between *Spirit* and *Jenny*. It is like old home week again. I am feeling a lot less lonely.

I walked to a Mexican restaurant with Andrew and Caroline and had dinner, then crashed. This morning I have to connect with an agent and the marina to check into Colombia, take laundry in, figure out how to get water, etc. I am going to check out the other marina too. This one seems full, and has a twenty-five ton limit, which is less than *Jenny*'s Net tonnage. Nicholas will go in with us this morning and set paw in yet another country.

It is beautiful here. The city is very modern like Panama City, only closer. There are several new high-rise condominiums being built. I will send photos when I get a Wi-Fi connection.

Astor in Cartagena

Saturday, October 04, 2008 1:10:44 PM

Location: Cartagena

Astor, *Spirit* and I decided to take a cab out to a Costco like warehouse store called Makro to pick up soda and booze. It was quite a drive, but cost only $3.50 for the four of us. The cabs here are cheap. Makro gave us free membership based upon our foreign passports, and once checked in I headed for the soda and booze. A girl named Carolina was there, supporting a promotion for the local Colombian rum. I asked about prices, and the location of vodka, gin, etc. Well, in Colombia, there aren't any large bottles of anything, and everything is very expensive, compared to Panama and on up the coast.

We chatted a bit, I picked up a couple of liters of the local rum and I promised to fill out her prize form for a motor scooter once I had my receipt. Later Lani came over and had some more questions and I scouted out Carolina to help again. She was delightful help. I complemented her English I found out she is an English major in college here. I went about my shopping and a while later checked out with Dan, Lani and Richard. Carolina happened to be in the parking lot, and I remembered my receipt. I gave it to her and she took my contact information and found out that I was on *Jenny*, here at the marina. She told me she helped a local Christian organization and let me know she was a good girl. She commented that she needed to practice here English and I replied that I needed to practice my Spanish. We thought it was a good idea for us to help each other and she gave me her phone number!

I called her this morning to arrange for us to meet and have lunch somewhere and asked her to help me explore some of Cartagena in the afternoon. She agreed. I will be calling her this evening to set up the details. Dan and the crew on *Astor* are going to old town this evening to scope out the party scene, and I will join them, at least for a while.

Sunday, October 05, 2008 8:30:05 PM

Location: Cartagena

It has been a very long time since I have been on the dating scene and desires turn quickly to fantasy. Dan and I met Carolina and her friend Natalia this morning to walk the huge old fortress and walled city today. Natalia is also a professional tour guide for Cartagena. They were an hour late, and that gave Dan time to get coffee and try to come out of his hangover from his 03:00 bar binge last night. Dan expected Carolina's friend to be a dog. "All tour guides are." We were pleasantly surprised when she turned out to be quite pretty. As the day went on, we went to the old town and had lunch, walked some more and then ice cream. Natalia knew where the good spots were. She also turned out to be very intelligent, spoke English very well after her two years in the States, and we gradually gravitated to each other sharing similar interests in travel, art, music, beer, etc. Carolina was dull, and spent all of lunch and ice cream time on the phone. She was really disconnected and rude. However, Natalia captivated both of us with her smile, wit and mind.

She gave me her phone number and let me know she would be interested in another encounter. This is only the first week in Cartagena. Is there someone more ideal just around the corner? Dan is pressing for perfection and I am sure when he finds it he will just raise the bar for the next contestant. I think I open my heart too easily and too quickly. Maybe it is the years of gradual isolation and loss of warmth with Mary that fuels my need. I will call Natalia tomorrow night. Is she just another fantasy?

Old walled city, Cartagena

Thursday, October 09, 2008 5:46:39 PM

Location: Cartagena

Well, it has been busy here! I signed up to run the net on Thursday mornings. *Jenny's* VHF radios seem to be running ok now, but I worry they will disrupt my net because sometimes they change channels in the middle of a transmission. I ran the net this morning and started using *Jenny's* ICOM IC-M127. I had both radios on and was ready to switch from one to the other if necessary. As feared, I was mid-sentence when it switched the channel. UGH! I turned it off and went over to her new IC-M422. It is on *Jenny's* port side and I pick the mike up with my left hand. Folks on the net said they could barely hear me. I made it through the net, but I decided I needed to fix my VHF radios.

After the net, I unloaded *Jenny's* birds and anchor chain onto a panga to have them re-galvanized. I had noticed for several months that there was rust on the chain that I was putting in the water. As we unloaded it, there were sections of rust all along it even though the bitter end never went in the water. I do not believe the rust is sufficient to impair the strength, but nonetheless I had to stop and fix it. The cost of new chain is $6.00 per ft and I have 600 feet of it! This is an item that you cannot ignore. The cost to get the birds and the chain galvanized is 6,000 pesos per kilogram. For me that works out to about $1,400 which is considerably less expensive than new chain. *Jenny* is anchored on her secondary rode and her chain will be ready the day after tomorrow.

I am going over to the home depot tomorrow to by some paint to mark the chain in 100-foot increments and the workers here are going to lay it out and paint it before loading it back into *Jenny*.

Nicholas and I go for walks at sunrise and see all the walkers out for their morning exercise and the legions of dogs that are out. Nicholas is nose bound and would stay in just one spot for an hour sniffing if I let him. We also went out to happy hour at the marina last night. He is quite the party dog and very happy with all the attention he gets.

Cartagena is quite the spot and the winter is the time to be here. Dan was trying to talk me into going up to Jamaica with him in November, but there is just too much to do here. The parties apparently start on Halloween, then November 11th is their independence day, then there is some other holiday, then Christmas, and then New Year. Staying at anchor cost about $20 per week for dinghy and internet fees. I am settling in. I love this place.

I have been waxing the white superstructure when it is cool out and only have the bow yet to do! Then I think I will hire one of the general workers to do the hull when I get some more wax. So far the bottom appears to be clean. I got detailed charts of the Rosarios and recommendations on a spot to anchor. After I get the chain back I am going to get another boat or two to go out and I will dive on the bottom to do a scrubbing. Once I finish, I will start refinishing the windowsills in the pilothouse. It is nice to sit still for a while, really enjoy a place and catch up on the maintenance.

Jenny is at anchor. As usual the water in the basin is too dirty to run the water maker and there is no rain. I bought three seven-gallon water jugs to ferry water out to *Jenny*. It took about ten runs to top off. The trick was to set up a system to lift the heavy jugs and load the water into *Jenny*. First, I found out that if I ran the dinghy boom all the way down straight off *Jenny's* stern, I could raise The Beast against *Jenny's* hull at night. It had about six inches between it and her hull when in the water. And, because her hull goes out as it raises above the water, *The Beast* snugs up against her as it is raised. I put a flat fender between the two to prevent rubbing when *Jenny* rolls. I should use two but only have one. This is a satisfactory solution for easily raising it every night and it keeps *Jenny* from listing from the weight of *The Beast* if I raised it on one side or the other. The main challenge now is keeping *The Beast* from hitting and scraping *Jenny's* hull with its hard surfaces when I raise or lower it.

With that done, *Jenny's* boom was out over her stern. To load water I hook the heavy jugs to the winch line and raise them up to the boom. Then I just run a hose from the jug to the water pipe in the bow and let gravity do the work! There is always a system for avoiding work! Now I just need to see how much water I use in a week or two, and set up a schedule for refilling. I am thinking I only need to break out the jugs every two weeks, but I will see.

Wednesday, October 15, 2008 6:50:05 PM

Location: Cartagena

I am sitting on the top deck with Nicholas looking at Cartagena's new city skyline and watching *Ketching Up* motor on out. *Spirit* left an hour ago. They are on their way to the ABC islands hoping to catch favorable winds off the backside of hurricane Omar north of Bonaire and heading north. *Spirit* figures they have about sixty hours of good wind and then the trade winds will come back and be on their nose for the last twelve hours of their trip.

I spent the morning on projects. I first looked into the new IC-M422 and called Walter on *China Clipper* with it. He said he could hear me just fine. How strange. *Jenny* was protecting her secret. I then switched to her IC-M127. Walter said the transmission was about the same. As I was talking to him though, it switched itself to another channel. Hmmm...

Later I was in the Club talking to Walter about it with some other guys. One mentioned that he thought this radio had a return-to-16 circuit. The circuit automatically switches the radio back to channel 16 when you hang up the microphone. Hmmm...

I downloaded the service manual for *Jenny's* ICOM IC-M127. Sure enough, it has a return-to-16 circuit. The User Manual does not mentioned it at all. But, although I have had the radio out several times, I had not seen any wires running from the back of the radio up to the microphone holder. I pulled it out one more time and sure enough, two wires came out of the back as part of a cluster and ran up to the microphone hanger. I had it! Apparently, vibration or some other spurious short was causing the circuit to trigger and drive the radio to change channels! I clipped the wires! Yes.

Jenny's re-galvanized chain did not arrive until about 16:00 today so I did not receive it or pay the second half of the fee. It is at the marina now and looks good. Tomorrow I will see the folks at 08:00 and take possession. Then I will stretch it out and paint marks at 100-foot increments. I will let it dry a bit and then bring it out to *Jenny* to load it. If it is calm, I might re-anchor, but then again I might wait to put the anchor back on the chain until Friday. I am thinking about taking a trip out to the Rosario's to check the islands out, and dive on the bottom. If I do that, then I switch back to the anchor on the way out.

I am using *Jenny's* navigation computer for my working computer now because the other one finally died. It had a creeping crud in the video board somewhere. At first the screen would boot up correctly once out of every four or so times it was started. Gradually that decreased to one out of every forty or so tries. This week, after three days of trying to get the screen to come up correctly, I gave up. It is a known problem with this PC and the only known solution is to buy a new motherboard that cost more than a new laptop. *Jenny* is down to only one computer and I do not feel very secure going to sea without a backup.

The evenings here are very nice and it is a comfortable 75 degrees on deck. It would be better however if the two tugboats hadn't decided to anchor next door. When I anchor here the next time, I will move a little further in. Life is good and it will be fun getting to know this place and the people here.

Thursday, October 16, 2008 9:30:55 AM

Location: Cartagena

This morning I ran the net again. I started using the IC-M127 thinking I had found *Jenny's* secret. But, soon after starting the net it switched to channel 16 again. UGH!!! I picked up the IC-M422 microphone and continued the net. I have figured out the problem I have with this radio is holding the microphone in my left hand. Yup. The actual micro-microphone is not located in the middle of the grate, it is located off to one side, just where my left thumb rests. That is why people could not hear me. I completed the net holding the microphone in my right hand and then went after the IC-M127.

This time I noticed something when the IC-M127 switched to channel 16. I noticed that it switched when I touched *Jenny's* steering wheel. Pretty strange huh. After the net, I looked at the service manual again. Sure enough, two more wires go from the circuit board to the microphone with one attached to the metal button on the back. I turned on the radio and set it to channel 68. Then I held the microphone so I was touching the metal button and then touched *Jenny's* steering wheel. Voila! My body carried enough current to trigger the circuit and the radio homed to channel 16! I had uncovered yet another of *Jenny's* secrets. She hid this one very well! I took the microphone apart and clipped the wires. It has worked perfectly ever since.

Saturday, October 18, 2008 6:50:05 PM

Location: Cartagena

I had dinner with Natalia last night and it was almost comical. She let me know she had a bad experience in the States with a Jewish guy she wanted to marry and convert. She spent money following him from Michigan to Florida and he dumped her saying she was only interested in US Citizenship. She continued by relating how her mom had been dumped by her husband and following boyfriends. Her only focus now was to achieve financial independence and relationships were out of the question. Oh by the way, was I interested in some property in Old Town! That was the last time I saw her.

Wednesday, October 15, 2008 7:02:12 PM

I have been working on making contact with some of the other local people here. So far I have met a nice lady, Jacqueline who manages one of the emerald stores in the old walled city. She is probably around fifty with two kids. Her husband was kidnapped several years ago and killed. In spite of that tragedy, she displays joie de vivre that warms everyone around her. I also met Armando, a former marine from NYC who has been down here a decade and is a professor at one of the universities. I asked him over for a beer tonight and he said he would call after his last class.

Old walled city, Cartagena

As the vessels I know blow through here, I hope to be establishing new friendships with the people of Cartagena and getting to know them and their country. I am beginning to think it is easier to do this as an individual than as a couple. Even *Monju* seems to have difficulty with this and they are probably the crew that has the most interest in doing so. There are many couple dynamics that seem to get in the way. The other thing that hinders the full enjoyment of cruising is the "got to make the next passage" mentality. *Ketching Up* and *Spirit* both said the same thing on their way out of here. "Well, if you do not make this window, then you'll be stuck here for a year." Well, how many people can to vacation for a year in another country in a wonderful location? I cannot think of anything better.

Wednesday, October 22, 2008 9:30:55 PM

Location: Cartagena

Felix Malo is the local computer guru. He has a very small shop in Centro and hangs around the marina on occasion to advertise for work. I have given up on *Jenny's* backup tablet PC. I cannot get it to fire up any more without the video going nuts. I have searched the internet and this is a known problem with no known fix other than changing out the motherboard. HP says that is what you have to do and the tablet PC owners' forum says the same. And, these guys are the geek gurus.

I took my broken tablet to Felix and said "I do not have any hope that this will ever work again. But if you want to give it a shot it is your call. I will not pay you for trying, but will pay you if you fix it." I told him about what I found on the Internet and we arranged to meet at his place in the morning.

The next morning I walked it over to Centro. Centro is a Spanish style covered mall that is one-step up from a covered flea market in the States. His business consisted of a stall about the size of a walk-in closet. The front is open to passing pedestrians. The walls have shelves loaded with dated desktop machines, display monitors, wires, piles of circuit boards, more wires, keyboards, bits and pieces of long dead machines. A tabletop juts out of the wall forming the boundary between employees-only space and customers' space in the walkway. More machines and the guts of others litter its top. One floor machine was actually running. His chair faced an old monitor and the machine was his internet connection to the world.

In a typically Colombian way, we exchanged pleasantries limited only by our mutual ignorance of the other's tongue. Then he went to work. Within minutes he had found and downloaded the tablet PC shop manual from somewhere on the net. In an hour, he had it apart down to the motherboard. In another thirty minutes, he had isolated the problem to the NAVIDA chip. In another ten minutes, he determined that the chip solder joints had broken from the motherboard and that was the problem. Bada bing... Bada boom...

"I cannot fix this," he said. He did not have the microscoped soldering tools necessary for the job. But he knew who did. "I will bring it to you at the marina around noon tomorrow." The folks down here are very good at fixing things. Felix showed up with the tablet PC at 1:00 PM and fired it up for me. It has worked ever since. The charge was $80.00 and I gave him an extra $10. He was my hero.

It's Wednesday night and I just took my second Salsa lesson! I signed up for three lessons a week for a month. They are given in a building half a block from the marina set up for dance, karate, yoga, etc. I love it! So far, there have only been two students in the class, so it is semi private lessons and it is sort of like Dancing with the Stars. I do not know if the instructor is pulling my chain, but asked if I had taken lessons before. Big smile! I feel like I have two left feet though and my feet move so slowly compared to hers. The other student has been a different woman, Monday and today, but fortunately they speak English and help translate what the instructor is saying. It is a lot of fun and work for an hour. I feel alive.

I moved *Jenny* three times today. Last night another big tugboat anchored within spitting distance of her and that was enough. These big tug boats just cannot resist a beautiful gal like *Jenny* and she does nothing to discourage it. I had to exercise some parental control. She is closer to the Marina now and nestled among the sailboats. I am waiting to see if the tugboats come after her here! It also makes for quicker, more fuel saving dinghy rides into the dinghy dock.

The trawlers *Wandering Star*, *Voyager* and *Dreamweaver* are leaving in the morning for Aruba. It is strange that while they all say they love it here, they are bailing out after only a couple of weeks. Ah well. I did meet Jim and his wife this evening at the happy hour (before class, Pepsi only) and they are also staying through Christmas. Jim walked over to the studio with me to see where it was and they probably will join me for lessons. I should have kept my mouth shut...

I started my pilothouse varnish project today. The original is all yellow. Unfortunately, I think it is epoxy based and even with eighty-grit paper it is like sanding metal. Ugh. I might hire one of the day workers here to help with the sanding. All the window and doorframes need to be taken down to the wood and refinished.

Nicholas had his spa treatment today with a haircut, manicure and shampoo. I trimmed his ears back so more air gets inside. He was breeding some nasty crud and I was slack in catching it. His ear wash seems to have done the trick though. Nicholas is now well known at the marina and up and down the park we walk. He seems to be quite happy except for the heat and is pure love.

As you travel, you will recognize the types of places that are simpatico with your soul. There are not many. When you find them, stop a while and savor them. For me, Cartagena is a necessary stop in the western hemisphere.

I really need to start my sci-fi book. But every minute of every day is consumed somehow. I just learned that a manager of mine and friend at Kaiser is down with stage four cancer. It is never too early to bail out of the US and start enjoying life on the hook. I had a discussion with a few boats, good people with kids. We talked about how special our experiences are and how unfortunate it is that our families' careers keep them from visiting and enjoying what we are experiencing. Our unanimous hope is that at least their children will be able to visit us during summer breaks while we are still doing this.

Saturday, October 25, 2008 5:04:43 PM

Location: Cartagena

Well, Jacqueline called Wednesday evening and hit me up for $20. I was surprised. As it turns out, I guess I am just another Gringo mark for her. The women here seem only to be interested in Gringo money. I got a call on Friday from Yuliana, pleading to spend time with me. She is young and beautiful. She was supposed to visit me on *Jenny* last night, but I called her and pleaded sick. Yup. I swear to God.

Well, I actually only postponed the encounter and only in the hope for a better relationship. I met Katarina at the mall sports bar last weekend. Ok, I know it sounds a bit cliché, but you should see her. She is petite, athletic, and very gorgeous. She looks like a lighter complexion Janet Jackson. Yesterday was her birthday, and I am guessing in her twenties. I cannot help thinking about waking up next to her. More to my theme that chemical life is far superior in many ways to electronic life. Maybe this is all part of my book research! In any case, I am captured.

On the other side of the coin, I am getting more and more depressed about ever finding the perfect match. Yuliana speaks some English, but not much. Katarina is does not understand any English. How can I have a meaningful relationship with someone I cannot even talk to? Mary and I were not really communicating long before she left *Jenny*, so this can be more than a language issue! In any case I guess it is up to me to learn Spanish really well.

The women here are interested in American men regardless of age. Maybe age is actually an asset. I was buying an ice-cream cone at the mall and I notice that one of the schoolgirls in a trio spoke some English. I commented and we exchanged a few words. She was very pretty and very eager to talk. Really! I am in shock. She did not ignore me. She did not think I was a dangerous kidnapper. She did not think I was a pervert. How refreshing.

Then depression sets in. Very bright people tend to be lonely because they have no one with whom to communicate. When I was in first and second grade, I played alone in the school stairwells at lunch and recess. I could not understand other children. They did not think like I did. Today I would probably been diagnosed as autistic to some degree. I know I am going to go out the same way; all alone. The probability of finding an athletic intellect that will join me in this adventure is so small as to cause despair. All I can hope for now is to find either an adventurous outdoorswoman who wants to share the adventure or find a woman who will at least love me deeply and care for me. Maybe the Latin culture allows a woman feel at home taking care of her man. I may be lonely on an intellectual plane, but I hope not on the emotional one.

Thursday, October 30, 2008 9:19:30 PM

Location: Cartagena

The night before last I was with Yualana. She turned out as I suspected; a prostitute and one without any personality. Imagine that. It was $100 for about a two-hour experience. She was showered and dressed before I got started. Ah well. What can you expect? I felt embarrassed and ashamed for letting this happen. I learned the Yualana is providing for herself and her twelve-year-old sister. She could earn a living other ways, but this is the one she chose.

Fortunately, I went to my Salsa lessons last night and had fun. The people here are so much fun. The instructor and two other women students, all more my age than not, loved the CD's I bought and the instructor was overjoyed when she learned that I was giving them to her. She teaches the ballet and modern dance lessons, but seems to be too poor to buy any music. That is just wrong and to see her light up when I gave her the CDs was priceless. I am really trying to make some difference in the lives of the ordinary people here. It does my heart good.

I went over to the sports bar this evening with only moderate expectations of seeing Katarina. She was there. She speaks no English and I was relying on Tammy, another host to help me let Katarina know I was interested. Fat chance! Katarina appears to be quite nice and smart. I was going to the mall to get some auto wax, some fish and chips at the sports bar, and a movie afterward if all hopes died. Well, both Tammy and Katarina were there and Katarina was interested in getting to know me better. I know I am in for serious trouble here.

We talked a little as if we were deaf mutes, using a notepad since I can read Spanish much better than hearing it. She learned that I am living on *Jenny* and will be here for about another five months. I learned she has no interest in leaving Cartagena. I have never lived day by day on an emotional basis.

Everything has been according to a planned outcome. This might be new for me.

Friday, October 31, 2008 10:35:35 PM

Location: Cartagena

Cartagena; town of the heart? I just had a wonderful dinner with Katarina. She is incredibly beautiful outside and in. She speaks no English and my Spanish is pathetic. Never the less, we got to know each other a little on a notepad. Frustrating but with heart and we both persisted. After a while I asked her what she wanted to be. She could not even understand the question. People here do not get to choose. The concept is foreign. In another world she could be so much. Here, she did not know how the fates were going to deal her life. Katarina Endive Blanco I will remember for a long time. We parted after dinner and that was the last date we had.

Saturday, November 01, 2008 5:04:35 PM

Location: Cartagena

Mary and I have agreed to lead separate lives for a while. Although it is not the optimum solution for us, we are both pursuing the needs that drive us. We have agreed to let this play out and see what happens. Nicholas will stay with me on *Jenny*. He is now conditioned to have companionship all day and lots of interaction with people. Mary is looking for an apartment or condominium to rent in Orlando and then will get our remaining stuff out of storage and set up home. She might get a kitten.

I am considering leaving here in the spring for Europe although I might wait until the hurricanes start up again before heading over to Trinidad or Grenada. The passage east is considerably nicer when a hurricane is sitting on Cuba and reversing the trade winds. That would mean heading over in 2010 instead of 2009. I would go back to the San Blas for a spell if that were the case.

I am actively looking for a cruising partner to share my adventures with. I need a woman who speaks English, is intelligent and athletically fit for active cruising. I seriously doubt I will find this person in Latin America. The women here tend to be soft. Only a few are trim and fit and even fewer have any concept of life beyond life's daily struggle. None seem to dream of world travel. It seems that only North American and European people have developed a worldview with some women having dreams of venturing beyond their shores.

Friday, November 07, 2008 10:27:21 AM

Location: Cartagena

I am still busy! I am in the process of refinishing all the window and doorframes that I did not do in La Paz. It seems that year-end is the time to do varnish work. It also requires that you are not going to move *Jenny* anytime soon. It is hard work, but the results are really rewarding. Instead of dull yellow looking teak, you get a high gloss finish over a rich brown and auburn color.

David in the La Popa Monastery, Cartagena

The vanity table in the master cabin never had a bench seat. I have been using a fold up camping chair and it just does not work. Consequently the vanity desk does not get used. I went looking for a small teak bench that would fit and be the right height. I stopped in one furniture store and met Juan Carlos. He is an

American, married to a Colombian and owned the store. He had some folding teak chairs but nothing close to what I needed. Instead of showing me the door, he walked me down a couple of streets and orchestrated a deal with the local furniture maker. I drew the design and Juan Carlos helped negotiate the price.

The furniture maker has a small garage like building next to a small lumber garage. He had no fancy wood working machines like those that you would find in the basement of a hobbyist in the States. Just hand tools. With Juan Carlos translating and me drawing he understood the design and dimensions. He had to order the teak and said to come back in two weeks. I gave him half the payment so he could buy the wood.

I have been making progress on my salsa lessons and am now learning some choreography. Dancing with the Stars here I come! It is a lot of fun and a good workout three times a week. I am also meeting many local people who are not associated with the marina or boating. It is great to meet these nice people. One guy I met is Rubino. He is in the Department of Justice police department and is quite a character. The police down here are in a constant state of war with the drug industry and FARC. They are quite brave and I have a lot of respect for them. I had him and his girlfriend Gina over on *Jenny* last night. His girlfriend's sister Lisa also came along. I wish I could speak better Spanish. I am getting better but it still severely limits how well we can communicate.

I also met Julio who is a silver artesian and living in one of the condos along the harbor. He speaks English quite well and is dreaming about getting a boat. I invited him out to *Jenny*. He invited me up to his condominium overlooking the anchorage and we shared tea and coffee. He lamented that while he worked hard all his life, he had very little to leave for his son. His son did not have silver in his soul and he could not pass on his trade. He showed me some of his beautiful work.

Most of the cruisers here limit themselves to our own community. They do not reach out and are amazed with the contacts I have made, and how busy I am doing things with the local people beyond the marina. I found a computer program that is very good for translating English to Spanish and back. I hope to use it as an aid to communicate with these folks when I have the computer at hand. I also hope it helps me learn the language better, but I fear it will become a crutch.

Next week is Independence Day for Colombia and the whole week is a holiday. This should be fun to watch!

Sunday, November 09, 2008 11:34:44 PM

Location: Cartagena

I have been going to Mr. Babillas Salsa Disco on Saturday nights. Sometimes I go with other cruisers and sometimes on my own. It is wild. Last evening I was going with Rubino, Gina and Lisa. It was a bust. First, Mr. Babillas was closed to the public for a private party probably associated with the Miss Colombia beauty pageant. Also, Lisa sprained her ankle and could not have danced anyway. We sat at an outdoor cafe and had a couple of Cerveza instead. Lisa is a very nice young woman who expressed an interest in crewing onboard *Jenny*. She has never been on a yacht and does not speak a word of English so this is a challenge. But, I will see.

Living in a world where skin color is only a cosmetic attribute is wonderful. People are a continuous spectrum of shades of black, brown, cinnamon, and white. When talking to local guys about girls they talk about skin color as easily as talking about eye color. Girls will ask if you like their skin color as easily as ask if you like the color of their hair. It has no more significance than that. While the US has made huge strides in overcoming discrimination based upon skin color, for the most part we still associate a world of thoughts about a person with their skin color. In this country the concept of associating other concepts to skin color does not make any sense and as far as I can tell does not happen. I am afraid we still have a very long way to go in this regard. However it is completely refreshing to live it here.

I have asked Rubino, Gina and Lisa to come to *Jenny* again on Tuesday, the Colombian day of independence, along with some cruiser friends from *Pendragon* and *Delfin Solo* for a little party and salsa. It should be fun.

Sunday, November 09, 2008 11:49:54 PM

Location: Cartagena

After drinks at the café yesterday afternoon, Lisa surprised me by asking to go to *Jenny* unescorted. She met Nicholas for the first time and was a delight to have onboard. This was the third day from our first meeting and she is stealing my heart. All I compare this to is the scene from Harry Potter where the dementors are sucking the soul from an unfortunate. She took a taxi home at 02:30.

We are following some kind of formal choreography for dating. She did not allow any serious contact. Also, she said that she needed her mother's permission before she could stay over on *Jenny* and staying over meant separate bedrooms. I like this. It shows class and tradition still live. She is Catholic and goes to church with her family every Sunday. She does not like coffee, but likes tea instead. She does not drink or smoke. Her 28 year life has been completely limited to her barrio and Cartagena.

Today she came over to help me get *Jenny* clean after all the sanding dust from the varnish work I have been doing. I took her over to *Astor* to introduce her to them and she passed inspection. She is very shy and was terrified. I asked Caroline (who speaks Spanish) and Andrew from *Pendragon* over for drinks and a movie. Lisa was supposed to stay for the movie, but had to go home at 20:30. It is some kind of curfew I think.

I do not know where all this is going or will end up, but I am going to let it go on. I am happier than I have been in a long time. She is coming over at 10:00 tomorrow.

Monday, November 10, 2008 8:44:53 PM

Location: Cartagena

Lisa came to *Jenny* at 10:00 this morning and spent the day. We did a little cleaning up from the party last night and then we had lunch and we studied English and Spanish. We are helping each other so we can better communicate. She remains a pure soul. I have no idea why she seems to care about an old guy like me. She is picture perfect beautiful and could not be nicer. When we were walking with her sister Gina, Gina called me Jefe that means boss or executive. Perhaps it has something to do with the attraction of power and it being associated with older people. In any case, it does baffle me. I feel a deep sense of responsibility for the lives under my care. I still have deep feelings for Mary and do not want to hurt her. On the other hand, she has not brought much joy to my life in quite a while. She claims she wants us to reunite, but I think only her loneliness talking.

It looks like Lisa and I will be going to the Rosarios with *Pendragon* when they complete their projects and are ready to go. It will be her first time underway. So far motion on *Jenny* has not bothered her. *Pendragon* will probably leave from the Rosario's to their next destination and not return to Cartagena. *Astor* said they will be leaving next week and *Delfin Solo* will probably leave too. I will be the only west coast boat left. However, *Rhapsody* is still in the San Blas and may arrive here sometime.

So far I have not mixed much with the people at the club. I have been too busy and not very interested. It may be that Lisa and I will begin spending more time with her friends and family. I will see.

Saturday, November 15, 2008 3:39:38 PM

Location: Cartagena

I have been skipping the cruisers happy hour and dominos games. Women here are expected to live with their family until they are married. In many if not most family units, the man is not married to the woman. He might be married to some earlier love though and not divorced because of the church. I met two nice young women so far. Both said they wanted to go cruising. Both were not telling the truth. Lisa was part of my life for two weeks. I was foolish to think she could leave Colombia with me. But I did and she took a chunk out of my heart. We had a discussion today that started with a timeline for leaving. That was the catalyst for a real discussion about our mutual expectations. I had suspected that the family was pressuring her about money. The truth was that she expected me to support her parents and even her sister Gina and remain in Colombia. Her family was first in her mind and she had absorbed total responsibility for them. Her sister had a son and was pregnant again. She had no husband and apparently was ok with placing the financial burden on Lisa. Lisa was prostituting herself for the family, only in a different way than the prostitutes on the street.

I thought about this for a long time and this is what I see. If any children are educated, it is the boy. When boys become men and marry, they abandon their mother, permanently. By so doing, they also abandon their sisters. Then often they abandon their wife and children. If the mother loses her husband for any reason, she is destitute except for what she can earn and what her daughters can earn. The husband of the youngest daughter must assume the financial responsibility for the mother. Therefore, the last daughter is rarely married. They become completely dependent on menial jobs and men. Men love this arrangement and perpetuate the economic slavery. The mom sees a daughter sleeping with a wealthy man to bring home money as just part of their normal lives. An exclusive relationship with a family benefactor is not prostitution it is patronage. They bring their daughters up to think this way and these young women completely accept it. It is an honorable outcome for them.

There is a reason why western culture places the burden on the men to provide for the family and that a woman leaves her old family behind when she joins his. It removes this sort of terrible exploitation of women.

Friday, November 21, 2008 6:50:44 PM

Location: Cartagena

I went to see my furniture maker again today. When I went on the 15th he had completed the bench and was proud of it. It had all the right curves and was a nice piece of work. But something was wrong. At first I could not figure it out, but I knew it was too big in some way to fit under the vanity. I asked to see the drawings again. Hmmm... He had determined that a bench made to the drawing design would not be stable, especially on a boat. So he turned the legs sideways, perpendicular to the seat. This made them stick out in the front and the back. It would not fit the space. I pointed this out to him, praising him for his work and his considerate thinking. He understood. He agreed to use the remaining teak and rebuild the whole thing. No extra charge.

Today I picked the chair up and it was perfect. I stopped by Juan Carlos' shop and invited him, his wife and daughter for an evening on *Jenny*. He was thrilled.

A couple of days ago I met Li Chu Yuan along the path that I walk Nicholas and she runs. She is an exchange student from Beijing, PRC. She is tall, thin and attractive. Since then we have spent some hours talking about China, Colombia and America. She is here to learn Spanish and the Colombian culture. Like for us Americans, the Colombian culture is very different from hers. Family, time and work have different meanings here and schedules do not exist.

On the other hand, her life has been very different from what most Americans experience. She is an only child because of the law. She lived with her grandfather in the western part of China until she was nine and he allowed her to become a free spirit. Then her parents moved to the city opposite Hong Kong and she moved with them. Her father left her mother two years later. Then, when she entered high school, she lived away at school and was only home for the weekends. For college she went to Beijing and was there full time. She has had virtually no family life since she was nine. Consequently she has no domestic skills and no idea how she would raise a child. I suspect this is true of millions of Chinese women.

Her life has been shaped mostly by her Granddad. She has a strong blend of Buddhist religion mixed with Mao indoctrination, Chinese traditional folk lore and superstitions running around in her head. The system focused her education very narrowly. The education system is finely tuned to turn out people who can pass the state examinations for specific roles in their government and economy. For example, when I showed her a map of China it was the first time she had seen a map of the entire country. She was surprised to find Beijing so near Korea. She is studying to become part of the diplomatic corps in China and majored in Spanish. She can speak Spanish very well and learned English on her own from other students at her college in Beijing.

She is surprisingly open about the faults of their education system and the corruption in the government and Buddhist "church". Things we do not see, but are logical extensions in a society where the people do not have the capability to remove people or companies from power. We just vote them out or stop buying their goods or services. This is a huge difference. Her early years of relative freedom make her uncomfortable with the forces that rule her life now.

Lee Chu Yuan visiting a farm in Colombia

This is her first time out of the country and her life experiences have not prepared her well for dealing with a world with few rules and even less structure. I have been trying to be a sounding board and offer advice when I can.

Saturday, December 13, 2008 5:56:23 PM

Location: Cartagena

Well, it has been a while since I have reported. I guess I need to provide an update. There is not much exciting going on. I have been working on the varnish project and have nearly done the pieces I am going to do here. The doors and windows I have done have turned out well, but the temperature and humidity here are very high and the varnish sets too quickly for my taste. In any case, it is really rewarding to see the dark red-brown teak emerge with all its' splendor from beneath the yellow old varnish.

Juan Carlos and his family came over last night. We sat up on the back deck and had some coke and Cerveza. He also brought his wife's sister and her daughter, trying to introduce us. Such a nice guy... They really enjoyed watching the view of the harbor and sunset, but even in the calm evening waters, the children and women became seasick. We sat on *Jenny*'s top deck and talked about life as the sun set over Cartagena. It was very nice.

New city, Cartagena

They thanked me profusely as I shuttled them back to dry land on the dinghy! It was a good evening.

I am going to modify *Jenny's* stabilizer rigging again. Right now I have a dock snubber acting as a vibration damper for the wires. In an epiphany, I realized that very small tires would work much better. Today I found some and I will switch them out when I get to an anchorage that is flat calm. There is much too much boat action here to go up the outriggers and do the switch.

I have also learned that much of the culture that I have been describing about Colombia is really particular to Cartagena. You can think of this city as the Miami Beach of the US. It is the vacation spot for people from all over South America and is very tourist oriented. I understand that Bogota, up in the mountains is very different with a very different culture. I have only touched one part of the elephant.

Here, there is an ethnic mix of black and Indian that has been going on for 100's of years. There is an endless variation of skin color, most of which is a beautiful cinnamon and the features of the people are beautiful too. However, there are white people of Spanish decent in the country, mostly in Bogota the inland cities who are very prejudice and consider all these people to be Negro (their word). Such a shame! The white people here say all the Negros are lazy and do not want to work and why they are so poor. I did not experience this at all. It is obvious that the government could break the cycle of poverty here through better-funded education, but chooses not to.

This coming week Nicholas and I will fly back to Florida to spend Christmas with the family. It will be nice to see everyone and have some time off *Jenny* and in a cooler climate! When I get back in January, I will have *Jenny* hauled and the bottom painted. I expect three other boats that were on the West Coast to be here by then and look forward to seeing them again. February is relatively good weather for crossing the Caribbean Sea. It is never good though. So that's when I will be heading for the Dominican Republic.

Spirit and Ketching Up were right, if you don't catch a hurricane up around Cuba to back wind the trade winds, the Caribbean is a nasty piece of water to cross. So, September and October are the months to move from here. This is the reason why so many Spanish treasure ships got caught by hurricanes.

I also plotted out what it would take to go through the ABC's and found it would add 3,000 miles to my journey back to Florida. It was just too far to do my myself. Also, the Dominican Republic has a famous bay (Samana) where whales come to calve January through March and definitely on the list. I am tempted to cross over to Puerto Rico for a visit too. Then it will be up through the Bahamas and back to the States in May or June. I have not checked out the Florida laws regarding boat sales and use taxes. Until I figure that out, I dare not enter Florida waters without being at risk for paying them. So, I will probably touch down in Georgia.

Then, I might head on up to the Northeast for the summer, maybe as far as Maine. Who knows? I have made some progress on my Sci-Fi book, but it is just too hot here to really work on it. Maybe that will be next winter's project. I keep hoping the price of diesel will fall here, but so far, it has not. Maybe it will in January.

Being single handed on *Jenny* is a lot of work, and nowhere near as enjoyable as when you can share the experience with a soul mate. I continue to look for that someone.

Monday, January 12, 2009 11:45:56 PM

Location: Cartagena

Wow. It has been a month since my last entry! Well, here is the story. Nicholas and I flew back to Florida for the holidays. The trip was arduous with an overnight each way since there was not a direct flight from Cartagena to Tampa or Orlando when you are traveling with a pet. That meant a stop in Bogota. Bogota is the capital of Colombia and is up in the mountains. It sits in a high mountain valley with a year around climate much like San Francisco. The temperature is always in the fifty's and sixty's with lots of cloud cover. The people up there love it but it is not for me. I reunited with Mary in Tampa and had a wonderful holiday. Mary made a special effort to make it all good. All the kids were in town so we saw them a lot and many of the grandchildren too.

Heather, my daughter in law, is completing her residency at Vanderbilt University Medical School this spring and has gotten a great job at a hospital in Sarasota, so they will be moving down there soon. All the kids will be back in the Tampa area again. That makes seeing them easier. I just need to figure out how to avoid Florida tax laws regarding *Jenny* and I will be able to practically steam right up to their doors. That would be awesome.

We all had a good Christmas and had dinner together at Nancy's, my first wife and mother of my children. She has put on this spread for several years now and really goes out of her way. Thank you Nancy!

The kids are all growing and we did some outdoor activities that we all liked. We also went ice skating and had a ball. Mary even tried it, but after two laps hugging the rail, took over bench warming duty. After Christmas I went back to Mary's pad for a couple of days. She is a guest of her childhood girlfriend who lived next door in Rockville Center on Long Island. I thought she was suffering in some closet sized add-on apartment. But no, the girlfriend lives in a huge house and the guest apartment is bigger than *Jenny*, all modern, big screen TV, huge bathroom and shower. No, she's not suffering!

Her friends have a little boy and we stayed at their place for New Year's Eve and had a lot of fun. I think it was good for them too, since they had not been getting out much and maybe they will start to develop friends in the neighborhood. They have been living there for years, and yet no one in the neighborhood is friendly. Funny how some neighborhoods are like that.

Mary and I had a good time together and she says she wants to come back to us. I would welcome that and will try to mend what has been broken.

Nicholas and I headed back to Colombia on January 2nd. I stocked up on Marine goods as usual and had two big duffle bags. Unfortunately I put all the heavy stuff in the larger one and was forced to repack them while at the counter in the check in line in Tampa. My total weight was good at 100 pounds but each bag HAD to weigh no more than fifty pounds. I could feel the ugly thoughts of the people waiting behind me...

I think Nicholas is sensitized to air travel because he is really behaving badly, especially during takeoffs and landings. Fortunately, I had a whole row to myself on the long four-hour flight from Houston to Bogota and was able to put him on the seat. But he chewed through his soft bag during the flight from Bogota to Cartagena. I think that is all the flying Nicholas wants to do.

Cartagena is a beautiful place with lots to see and do, but it is time to move on. I have started final projects and preparation for the trip up to the Dominican Republic. I had the boom lengthened by thirty-five centimeters so I could better store *The Beast* at the back rail overnight, and fully raise and lower it over *Jenny's* stern. This will be very handy when in a slip. The people here did an excellent job and you cannot tell they worked on it. I also put stronger blocks on the boom lift and dinghy lift lines. I really like this change. *Jenny* does not list at night now with it hanging off her stern, so no more worries about marine growth above the bottom paint line. It also is very easy now to get *The Beast* out of the water. I also use it to lift my big water jugs for loading water. I have no idea why Nordhavn did not get the boom length right in the first place.

I have *Jenny* scheduled for a three day haul out on January 26th for bottom cleaning and painting. I have the paint. The haul out and labor should run about $1000 total. The Trinidad SR has held up very well and the guy who cleans the bottom every other week says it is the best he has seen. This water is virulent! On the 29th I will fuel up and then come back to the anchorage for provisioning. At least one sailboat is lined up to head out on February 1st. It should take us two to three weeks to do the passage, with overnight stops along the Colombian coast to the northern point. Then I will wait for a weather window before making the three-day passage across the Caribbean to Boca Chica, Dominican Republic. I will start making more entries now that I am on the move again!

Monday, January 19, 2009 6:16:30 PM

Location: Cartagena

I have had a wonderful time here; more wonderful than I could have possibly hoped for. I have met several young women who do not consider age to be a communicable disease as they do in the States. I will not forget any of them and if Cartagena is my last great adventure, then I am happy.

Monday, January 19, 2009 7:31:48 PM

Location: Cartagena

This weekend I went to La Havana, a salsa club, with some friends and had a wonderful time. It was a fitting end to a wonderful stay. Today I waxed the upper sides of *Jenny* getting her ready for putting the storm windows back up. I took the storm windows off the rail up top and got them unpacked. The starboard side went up very easily. I will get up early tomorrow and mount the port side ones from the dinghy before the boat traffic kicks up the water and before sunrise.

The upcoming passage has about 250 miles of open sea to cross, so the storm windows are necessary to assure safety. My friends on *Moody Blues* left yesterday and are on their way up to the Dominican Republic. They sent an email today and said they skipped the first anchorage because of the slow progress they were making. They lamented not getting their bottom cleaned before leaving. I advised them to stop and get it done before heading across. You want to scoot across that open sea passage quickly while you have a weather window.

The window they have is wide though with relatively good seas, five to six feet at ten seconds, through the next two days. Then the seas and wind will pick up a bit. By the weekend though, it will be bad again.

Just a few more things to do and *Jenny* will be ready to head out. I am ready.

Wednesday, January 21, 2009 4:04:03 PM

Location: Cartagena

God is smiling on me. Yesterday, by pure chance, I came across three young European travelers looking for a seagoing experience. The two guys are from England and the lass is from Ireland. They flew into Buenos Aries a couple of months ago and have been backpacking through South America since. They were going to hop a sailboat to Panama, but after a short discussion and seeing *Jenny*, they decided this was a good opportunity to spend some time at sea. They came on board last night and will again tonight to help me wax the superstructure. They are also paying for our provisioning.

Meanwhile I am in daily contact with *Moody Blues* about their passage. They are making slow progress in choppy water. It does not sound pretty. I have been feeding them weather information too. It is unclear right now whether going offshore further, or hugging the coast provides a better ride. They are going much more slowly than they expected and the weather window is closing. I fear for them.

Colombia celebrated Barak's inauguration (as did the British kids). This part of the world is embracing the change with tears of joy. One thing that Americans do not realize is that people in Panama, Colombia, Venezuela and maybe beyond are all family very similar to how families are spread across the United States. They travel easily among the countries and visit relatives all the time. They are not isolated countries as we would believe.

Jenny is ready to go. By next Wednesday she will be fueling up and provisioning.

Thursday, January 22, 2009 11:17:11 PM

Location: Cartagena

I got an update from *Moody Blues*. They chose not to hug the coast and consequently were caught in strong current that has been pushing them west. They are hoping now to make landfall in Haiti. Their wind and waves have been good so far and their window does not close until Monday. They should be ok. My plan is to head as far north as I can along the coast of Colombia and then jump to the Dominican Republic. Then if I get caught in strong trade winds and nasty (wave height > period) water, I can ease off to the west and make Jamaica.

My crew came onboard again last night and waxed the superstructure on the bow. They are nice kids and quite enthusiastic about the trip. We are going out to the salsa disco with *Hiatus* and another boat on Saturday for some fun. I have been gradually showing them the systems on *Jenny* and processes like anchoring, etc. It is nice to be able to introduce them to this world.

Tomorrow I will get up at 06:00 AM or so, take Nicholas in for his morning walk, check email, change the oil in the genset, get some more cash for the yard work next week, call the travel agency about my rebate, eat, take a nap, go to the mall to see Australia, get a burger and beer at the Sports Bar and call it a day. Oh, and pick up laundry (rags from the waxing) and drop off laundry. I probably forgot something...

That's my life.

Saturday, January 24, 2009 10:23:43 AM

Location: Cartagena

I am starting to get excited about traveling again. This morning my diver Alberto came to *Jenny* and did the bottom. He worked longer this time because it had been three weeks since the last cleaning instead of the usual two, and we are preparing for the haul out on Monday. There should be much less cleaning to do on the hard now, and we should be able to get a coat of paint on the first day. He also cleaned the chain and chain snubbers. The chain had less growth than he expected. I was hoping the growth would be light because of the new zinc from the recent galvanizing. I will pick up Alberto and Pedro at 06:00 AM on Monday and we will head over to the boatyard. Pedro and his pal will be doing the bottom work.

I called the boatyard this morning and Alberto talked to the yard manager to make sure they haul *Jenny* first, and do not delay us with other boats. The yard charges by the day, and if you haul at noon, then you still pay for the whole day.

Tomorrow I will wash down the hull and get it ready for a coat of wax. I will wax the hull at the yard in the evening.

I scheduled the crew to come on board on the 30th and after we provision and tank up with fuel and water, we will head out to our first anchorage. That should be an easy day's run and will get us out of this nasty toxic water. We will stick to my plan of hugging the coast and I hope catching counter currents up to Puerto Bolivar. *Moody Blues* did not take my advice and are having a very difficult time staying east enough to hit the Dominican Republic. Most likely they will land in Haiti.

Sunday, January 25, 2009 1:53:13 PM

Location: Cartagena

Last night I took Heather and Kent from *Hiatus* and my new crew to Mr. Babillas, the local salsa disco. We arrived around 11:00 PM and as usual, the place started hopping around 11:30 PM. It was the usual madness with the locals putting on an incredible display of dancing and fun. By 01:00 AM Kent was loosened up and dancing, so were Russell and Caroline. Ed was nowhere to be seen. I bailed and came back to *Jenny*.

This morning Nicholas and I slept in late (06:30) and the day began. I took Nicholas in for his morning walk before the sun gets going, and made two runs loading water. Then I washed down *Jenny's* hull. It was very dirty and I wanted to prepare it for waxing at the yard. I fired up JD for the first time this year and let it warm up. I will have two locals on board tomorrow to help me navigate to the yard and get in the slings. I probably will not have Internet for the next three days while I am there. All is on schedule for a February 1st departure. *Moody Blues* was only twenty miles off shore in their last report and was proceeding along the Dominican Republic coast to Boca Chica. They made it ok!

Next Nicholas gets a bath and then tonight I will head up to the sports bar to get my last good burger and fries for a while and say goodbye to the girls there. Then come back and crash.

Monday, January 26, 2009 8:06:35 PM

Location: FeroAlquiMar Cartagena

I took *Jenny* to the boatyard today and had her hauled. Her bottom was in good shape due to the biweekly cleaning and her good bottom paint. Surprisingly all the zincs still had zinc on them after 15 months. Today the team of two sanded the bottom. Tomorrow they will clean the keel coolers and the keel shoe under the propeller.

I am spraying the propeller and bow thruster with Petit Barnacle Buster. I heard about this stuff from *Miestra*. It is a spray about 80% zinc and it keeps growth off metal surfaces. I believe zinc is something that marine life has a tough time growing on. There never are any barnacles on the zinc anodes in the water. This is going to be an experiment, but should work. I have three cans of the stuff, so I can go wild.

Nicholas is such a good boy. This is the second time he has been onboard when *Jenny* has been hauled and is doing fine. When *Jenny* is out of the water, it is like being in a second floor apartment. He has to stay on *Jenny* alone while the lifting and moving takes place. I did not hear a single bark during the process. I guess he is fully comfortable with his moveable home, even when it moves on land. Papa is not so comfortable with *Jenny* being on land. It is an un-natural place for her and the sooner she is back in the water, the happier we all will be.

Tomorrow the first coat of new bottom paint goes on. All is well...

Tuesday, January 27, 2009 5:52:59 PM

Location: FerroAlquiMar Cartagena

Jenny, FerroAlquiMar, Cartagena

After a long hard day of work, we finished preparing *Jenny* for the bottom paint and got two coats on and another ½ coat on the high wear areas. It was a lot of work and I had as many as four men on the job. I also uncovered yet another of *Jenny's* secrets. *Jenny's* shoe is solid bronze and should not be painted.

The job so far is the best I have had. They applied the paint very nicely and *Jenny*'s bottom is smooth with no sags or runs. Tomorrow we finish cleaning the keel coolers and Pedro is going to wax the hull.

Wednesday, January 28, 2009 6:23:42 PM

Location: Club Nautico

Jenny is back at base. They said it could not be done, but I did it. Out-and-In in three days! Bottom cleaned, 2.5 coats antifouling, polished prop, Zinc spray on prop, shoe and bow thruster, new zincs on bottom, hull compounded where it needed it and waxed, and keel coolers cleaned. Wow. *Jenny* launched at 3:00 PM today. Nicholas did not eat until we were underway. Somehow he knows.

The secret here was to engage the locals at the club. Arturo set up the arrangement with the yard and saved me the daily charge. He introduced me to Pedro who marshaled the work at the yard and super cleaned the bottom before I hauled anchor to assure the cleaning in the yard would be completed the first day. That left day two to begin the work on cleaning the coolers and do the painting. Trinidad requires eight hours before launch, and recommends overnight. I had to get the painting done on day two and did.

Day three, we finished cleaning the coolers and propeller. I sprayed the prop with the zinc barrier. Pedro and his helper were up on a makeshift scaffold when it collapsed and damaged his hand. He brought in two other workers to do the waxing. There was some really ugly petroleum goo on the waterline and nothing would dissolve it. We had to compound it off. There were some other scuffs that got the treatment too.

We brought in the lift at 1:00 PM to remove the stands and paint under them. This paint got two coats, but was in the water in less than two hours. I do not know how to do it otherwise. We launched *Jenny* at 3:00 PM. She is now in just about the same condition as when she launched in KKMI in San Francisco. I think the bottom paint job is actually better and the coolers cleaner. The shoe is better off than it was. The propeller and thruster zincs are better secured. There are a couple of small dings on the hull from various unfortunate events, but nothing really noticeable.

The way out was blocked by a beached ship leaning over the launch area and very close to *Jenny*'s rigging. On the other side I had a tug parked in the way. I placed line handlers on the tug and carefully walked *Jenny* out. The ship cleared *Jenny's* rigging by less than a foot. UGH.

It was an uneventful trip back and *Jenny* is at anchor just about exactly where she was before. The spot was good until some wacko in a sailboat decided to park too close. UGH. Tonight I will lower *The Beast* when the water calms down and get ready for another busy day.

BOOK 7: CROSSING THE CARIBBEAN

Princess acted as if she knew what was best for both of us. The sea did not have the foggiest notion. The wind was raving like mad. She kept ducking around, trying to get me to go back. The wind put her up to it. It was no fun unless I could get my girl to let tomorrow take care of tomorrow. She was not too hard to handle. She responded as quickly to the touch of my hand on her tiller as she did to the force of the gale.

Joe Richards
Princess 1956

Passage: Cartagena to Punta Hermosa

Departed Sunday, February 01, 2009 at 2:58 AM local time from Club Nautico Anchorage. The departure location was latitude 10 degrees 24.207 minutes north, longitude 75 degrees 32.674 minutes west.

Arrived Sunday, February 01, 2009 at 2:56 PM local time at Punta Hermosa. The arrival location was latitude 10 degrees 56.717 minutes north, longitude 75 degrees 2.131 minutes west. The customs check in was none. The trip covered 56.11 nautical miles in 0d 12h 18m with an average speed of 4.60 knots and a maximum speed of 7.20 knots.

Sunday, February 01, 2009 6:22:09 PM

Location: Punta Hermosa
Latitude is 10 degrees 56.714 minutes north.
Longitude is 75 degrees 2.131 minutes west.

This was the first time I saw a wave break over *Jenny*'s bow.

I got up at 02:00 and roused the crew to get a good start on the limited window we had. *Jenny* released her hold on the harbor floor in the morning's darkness and headed down the channel to the sea. I expected and *Jenny* suffered six-foot waves at six seconds. What surprised and amazed me was that this dominate wave was only so marginally dominate. The sea was chaos incarnate. Ed and Russell were puking their guts out all day. Caroline was queasy, but did help on the watches.

Jenny was well clear of Cartagena and heading up the coast when all of a sudden this freak wave came together. I was the only one up to see it form and crest. I knew it would be a ride. With a wicked heart, it came upon *Jenny's* port forward quarter and lifted her up on its flank like a toy. When she was fully captured it broke over her bow and down her side ripping her port side life ring off and forcing its way through her port side pilothouse door. *Jenny* crested the beast, composed herself on its summit, threw its wild water back into the sea and went on. She is a natural at this.

She and JD worked hard bashing against wind, wave and current only claiming 4.6 knots against the sea. As the weather window started to close, we saw some seven and eight foot combers and the wind picked up to twenty-five knots.

I adjusted *Jenny's* route a little to drive us toward the shelter of land sooner and by about 1:30 PM we were out of the worst of it. *Jenny* is anchored in a large sand cove with good protection from the raging waves on the other side. She is hardly moving while the wind howls by. The kids are up now making dinner. They have plenty of energy after their 24-hour nap. *Jenny's* genset seems to be starved for fuel and will not run. I will have to look into that. We might set up the big screen and watch a movie tonight if I can get the genset running.

Monday, February 02, 2009 1:33:21 PM

Location: Punta Hermosa, Colombia
Latitude is 10 degrees 56.716 minutes north.
Longitude is 75 degrees 2.132 minutes west.

We had a good night's rest and all is good. The crew is smiling again and making good meals. This morning I fixed the genset by replacing the primary filter. The wicked water must have stirred up a bunch of gunk in the bottom of the tank it was using. I also fixed the forward head that had some mussel shells in the intake. This afternoon I will unpickle the water maker and get it ready for use when we get to clear water. The water here is silty from all the wind and wave action. I hope we will be able to make some water on our trip over to Rodereo Beach tomorrow.

I looked at the weather and unfortunately tomorrow is the best day all week to make the next hop. It looks about the same as we had coming here with only the possibility of some better protection offered by the next land we are headed for. The bay we cross cuts deeper south and could give us better protection. Like yesterday, I will probably make some course corrections as we go to make the best of it. I also hope we can catch some counter current this time to help us along. We did not get any yesterday.

Jenny is in good shape in spite of the beating she took yesterday and no worse for wear. JD's reported temperature still bothers me a great deal. My latest theory is the keel coolers get air trapped in their hull boxes and it considerably reduces their effectiveness. We ran a little hotter yesterday than I would have liked. Last night I also figured out that I have a relatively easy solution for *Jenny*. On *Jenny* I have another keel cooler on the starboard side for the genset. I checked out the plumbing today and with the right parts and hoses, I could easily plumb in the second keel cooler for use with the engine. I would put a couple of valves in place so I could cut it in and out, but I would not even have to take *Jenny* out of the water. The genset cooler only has two tubes, but it would still give me 50% more cooling. If I wanted to, the hull box is big enough to take a four tube cooler just like JD has now.

Tomorrow we head out into this angry sea again and it wants to do us harm. The passage after this one is easy and something to look forward to. It is only fifteen miles long. It goes to a nicely protected fjord and positions us nicely for taking advantage of weather openings for the crossing. The weather forecast says we will not get a window for crossing until next week. We will just hang out for a while on anchor.

Passage: Punta Hermosa to Rodadero

Departed Tuesday, February 03, 2009 at 4:53 AM local time from Punta Hermosa anchorage. The departure location was latitude 10 degrees 56.293 minutes north, longitude 75 degrees 2.455 minutes west.

Arrived Tuesday, February 03, 2009 at 4:06 PM local time at Rodadero Anchorage, Santa Marta, CO. The arrival location was latitude 11 degrees 12.103 minutes north, longitude 74 degrees 13.981 minutes west. The customs check in was None. The trip covered 58.08 nautical miles in 0d 11h 13m with an average speed of 5.20 knots and a maximum speed of 7.10 knots.

Tuesday, February 03, 2009 6:10:16 PM

Location: Rodadero Beach
Latitude is 11 degrees 12.105 minutes north.
Longitude is 74 degrees 13.983 minutes west.

I never thought I would see the wire holding one of *Jenny's* birds break. They have a breaking strength of about 1700 pounds. But one did today.

I had high hopes for an easier day today than the one to Punta Hermosa and for the most part we did. I got the crew up at 04:00 AM, did our departure tasks and had *Jenny* underway by 05:00 AM. The area we were in was sheltered and as usual, the wind in the morning is considerably nicer than the wind in the afternoon. We had a good run up to the Magdalena river mouth. This is a huge river running through most of eastern Colombia. It is bigger than I thought it would be. We got into the muddy river water around 08:00 and gradually worked our way across. The muddy water flowing north out of the river is grabbed from underneath by the sea and bent to its will, turning it west, creating a chaotic sea state. The river waves hit *Jenny* on her starboard side and the sea clubbed her nose. She was not happy with me. We met and talked to a sailboat from Austria that had crossed the Atlantic and headed to Panama. They were on a three-year journey to circumnavigate. We found out from them that we were only about a mile or two from the northeastern edge of this mess.

What I now know is that the strongest river currents are the last to give into the sea currents and the monumental struggle prosecuted under *Jenny* got more and more violent. One giant arm of the river thrust up about twelve feet and lifted *Jenny* from the port side with its steep fresh water face. *Jenny* tried to roll with the blow. It amazed me as I watched the 1700-pound wire snap. Boom! The bird was gone. *Jenny* rolled, unbalanced by the punch, then steadied, regained her balance and crested the wave. The kids came up to find out what had just happened.

Jenny was now without a bird on the port side, the one getting smashed with the waves. We pointed more into the waves and got out of the wrestling match to nice blue and relatively well-behaved seawater. It was still blowing stink, and the chop was a good five to six feet at six seconds. Nasty stuff! This is the second time I have had a bird snap off. The first was in Mexico when I think we hit something in the water. Fortunately, I did not lose either bird and the fix is simple. In the first case, I merely cut off the four inches of frayed end by the bird and put another end on it. In this case, the wire broke about twenty inches from the boom end and is frayed for another foot or two. I need to break out the spare wire and put it on tomorrow.

This wave caused a 1700-pound load to go against *Jenny's* rigging including her boom, its fittings, her mast, etc. I initially thought that I should increase the diameter of the wire to make it stronger now that I know that it can break just with a wave. But if I beef up the wire, what might be the next point of failure??? Hmmm.... I need a naval engineer to figure out these things.

In any case, I marshaled the crew to get *Jenny's* bird out of the water and back in its shoe to make sure we did not lose it. Fortunately, they had been vertical most of the day and only Ed had a twinge of seasickness. The three of us put on our life jackets, snapped onto the lifelines and went up top. Ed brought the bird in, Russell raised the outrigger and I put her bird back in its shoe. Then I tied her bird into the shoe to make sure it was not knocked out and we lowered the outrigger to brace the starboard side gear. We rolled on.

As we got nearer to the shelter of Rodadero Beach the seas quieted down and we have a nice anchorage about ½ miles offshore. The water is clear and we are making water, the only limited resource we have at the moment. Tomorrow we will stay here the day and get the stabilizer back in shape. Then we will move up around the bend on a thirteen-mile trip into Bahia Guayroca. It is a remote fjord that we will use to kill some time and have some fun fishing and diving while we wait for MUCH better weather before proceeding to the jump off point at Puerto Bolivar and head across.

Nicholas was sick and worried the whole day. Nicholas is a funny dog. He lays down in front of his food bowl for a minute, looking at before he starts to eat. It is as if he is saying a prayer of thanksgiving. He said an extra-long prayer tonight. Never a dull day.

Wednesday, February 04, 2009 11:47:01 AM

Location: Rodadero Beach
Latitude is 11 degrees 12.094 minutes north.
Longitude is 74 degrees 13.978 minutes west.

We had a busy morning catching up with all the minor maintenance that the rough weather and general use created. We replaced the wire on *Jenny's* port side bird. It turned out to be an easier job than I thought because I could climb up the boom and reach the coupling between the wire and the rope. Originally the rope was long enough to reach from the deck, which was the idea to allow the replacement from the deck. However, the rubber snubbers took up a bunch of line and now the coupling is several feet above the deck. It took less than an hour to do the job and the next time I work on the stabilizer rigging I will make sure that this coupling is lower. We could have done the job at sea, but it would have been very difficult to hold on and get it done. With the coupling lower, I could have done it at sea with minimal risk.

I also climbed up and replaced *Jenny's* anchor light bulb. I worked on her forward head and figured out the overboard discharge valve was closed and was causing all the current problems. I also discovered that *Jenny's* macerators will not run unless the 12 volt outlet circuit breaker is on. Who would have guessed?

The kids cleaned the forward head and the galley. The galley required special attention because a sugar bowl tipped over and sugar was everywhere.

The kids went swimming last night just before dusk and I am sure it will be on their list of activities for today. I have a general saltwater wash down on their list along with scrubbing the teak rails. It will be nice to see the tan of the teak again.

The crew: Caroline, Nicholas, Russell, Ed

We took a set of team photos today and will send them out when we get internet again. I also took some shots of the shore where there are a bunch of new condominiums and more going up. I tried to get on the internet here, but all the access points were locked down in one way or another.

Nicholas is a much happier dog today and is napping at my feet. He made the photos too.

Tomorrow we will move to the nice bay around the corner and stay there until the 9th. If I see a weather window opening we will move to the jump off point at Puerto Bolivar on the 9th and 10th. Then we will be only three days out from the Dominican Republic.

Passage: Rodadero to Bahia Guayraca

Departed Thursday, February 05, 2009 at 10:56 AM local time from Rodadero Beach Anchorage. The departure location was latitude 11 degrees 19.404 minutes north, longitude 74 degrees 6.465 minutes west.

Arrived Thursday, February 05, 2009 at 10:57 AM local time at Bahia Guayraca. The arrival location was latitude 11 degrees 19.416 minutes north, longitude 74 degrees 6.462 minutes west. The customs check in was none. The trip covered fifteen.81 nautical miles in 0d 3h 45m with an average speed of 4.20 knots and a maximum speed of 6.70 knots.

Thursday, February 05, 2009 12:08:36 PM

Location: Bahia Guayraca
Latitude is 11 degrees 19.446 minutes north.
Longitude is 74 degrees 6.431 minutes west.

Each passage seems to have its own surprise. Today we were stopped by the Colombian Navy.

Jenny weighed anchor at 08:00 and was underway in winds that varied between twenty-five and thirty-five knots. Fortunately, we were under the lee of the land for nearly the entire trip. This kept the seas in the two to three foot range. While she was making only about 4.5 to 5 knots against the wind, her motion was easy. We passed by several fishing boats (pangas) that were very curious as usual. Local folks think we are a commercial fishing boat when they see *Jenny's* stabilizers.

As we approached our midway point an outboard cigarette-style navy boat came up and ran its siren asking us to follow them back into a nearby "port". It was really just a roadstead. They too were curious about *Jenny's* stabilizers and my guess is that one of the fishing boats alerted them to us, claiming we were a foreign fishing boat in their waters. They came alongside, asked us to raise the birds, and after exchanging some information let us go on. The lieutenant spoke English very well. We got *Jenny's* birds back in the water and off we went.

Once we came around the point *Jenny* was again hit with six foot waves, this time at about seven or eight seconds. The wind gusted into the high thirties. This water is definitely not west coast stuff. *Jenny* worked her way to the bay and found the chart's small rock island was about ½ mile from where it was marked. I gave her some course adjustments and we got in.

At Rodadero Beach *Jenny* was on the west side of some hills and the land was dry like in California. However in this bay she is surrounded by green trees and has showers now and then giving her a nice fresh water bath. The temperature here is also about ten degrees cooler than Rodadero Beach. The wind comes from all directions because the hills are on all sides. Some might be coming down from the big mountains nearby that have snowcaps. *Jenny* is getting a little swell coming in but this little fjord is very nice.

Yesterday I dove on *Jenny's* bottom and it is sparkling clean. Her water maker has given us fifty gallons so we are ok there and the water here is nice and clean so we can make more.

I am going to make a batch of spaghetti tonight. When we are in calm water we set up the big screen and watch a movie at night. I am also listening to the 7th Harry Potter book that my son and daughter-in-law Derek and Heather gave me before leaving. Now we just need to wait here for good weather for the crossing.

Friday, February 06, 2009 10:23:50 AM

Location: Bahia Guayraca

Yesterday I made spaghetti sauce and we had a good dinner last night. This bay is quite nice. It has strong gusts of wind coming off the hills now and then that really move *Jenny* around, and today we have a gentle swell making its way down the fjord. Overall, it is a very nice respite. The temperature is very pleasant and most of the time we are in a breeze.

I still have no fix on a good weather window for crossing the sea. I am looking at using a small window on the 9th and 10th to get up to the jump off point at Puerto Bolivar. The kids are not anxious to start the crossing if the weather is even close to what we had the first day out of Cartagena. I am inclined to wait until we have a couple of days of ten second period waves. However, none is in sight.

We are making water so we are good there, but I think the kids underestimated the amount of food they eat. We may be down to biscuits in another week. Unlike normal shore life where the grocery store is just around the corner, situations like this are unforgiving. The kids are starting to come to that realization.

I will check the weather again today. There is nothing much else to report.

Saturday, February 07, 2009 7:31:34 AM

Location: Bahia Buayraca

Russell, Ed and Caroline went swimming yesterday and I worked some on my BoatExec software. There were some nagging small problems with it that I have been delaying working on. Sitting here has given me some quiet time to fix them and polish the code. The rolling waves here are too large to be able to set up the big screen. Last night I broke out the Season 1 Boston Legal DVDs that Mary gave me for Christmas and watched the first three episodes on the laptop screen. It did not disappoint me and remains the only TV series I find worth watching. The crew liked it too.

Today we will tackle the small leak in the forward cabin head and do a load or two of laundry. I will also do some more software work, and get weather reports. I am still planning on our first overnight trip on February 9th or 10th to get up to the jump point. The forecast is for mostly three to five foot seas with some periods of four to six foot seas. We will be hugging the coast the whole way. I have not seen a weather break for crossing the sea out through the 12th though.

Sunday, February 08, 2009 9:01:11 AM

Location: Bahia Guayraca

We are going to have a cleanup party this morning when the forward cabin decides to wake up and a discussion about keeping *Jenny* squeaky clean. It is beginning to look like a clothes hamper up there. This anchorage is probably the best protection along the entire Caribbean coast of Colombia and still we get gusts of wind from every direction running up to about thirty-five knots. The wind builds up behind the hills and then floods over and pounds the bay here. We moved *Jenny* yesterday to minimize the periodic pounding.

The weather still looks good for a departure tomorrow with the most challenging wind and waves at the start and gradual improvement all day. Below is the latest forecast from Buoy Weather at a point 1/3 along the way and the second at 2/3 along the way to Puerto Bolivar.

	WIND				SEAS		
Date	Hour	Dir	Deg	Range (kt)	Dir	Per (sec)	Range (ft)
First Waypoint							
2/9	01	ENE	104	12-16	NE	7	4-7
2/9	07	ENE	108	13-17	NE	7	4-7
2/9	13	ENE	77	11-15	NE	7	4-6
2/9	19	ENE	63	11-15	NE	7	3-6
Second Waypoint							

Date	Hour	Dir	Deg	Range (kt)	Dir	Per (sec)	Range (ft)
2/10	01	ENE	101	9-13	NE	6	3-5
2/10	07	ENE	109	10-13	NE	6	3-5
2/10	13	ENE	73	9-12	NE	6	2-4
2/10	19	ENE	69	12-17	NE	7	3-6

The best weather in the middle of the crossing to the Dominican Republic now is:

	WIND				SEAS		
Date	Hour	Dir	Deg	Range (kt)	Dir	Per (sec)	Range (ft)
2/14	01	E	86	17-23	E	8	9-14
2/14	07	E	82	17-23	E	8	9-14
2/14	13	E	93	15-21	E	8	9-14
2/14	19	ENE	78	14-20	E	8	8-12

Fourteen-foot chaotic seas at an eight-second period are very dangerous. This is far from good enough. I hope the trend to better conditions will continue and give us a break.

Thinking about this passage, I am convinced that the only good time to cross the Caribbean is during hurricane season. You have to catch the calm that a hurricane creates along 12 degrees north as it passes over Cuba. The problem is that if you want to experience Cartagena at its best you need to be there at Christmas. Otherwise it is too hot, wet and you do not have anywhere near the events you can enjoy over the Christmas period. If you are going to do Cartagena correctly, you will need to stay there until the hurricanes start up again. That is not until August at the earliest. Then your destination has to be Trinidad or Granada, because if you go north, you are exposed to the next hurricane going through. A Christmas in Cartagena costs a year in getting from there to the States. Otherwise, you are stuck fighting the trade winds in the Caribbean Sea as we now are.

Nicholas got his shampoo yesterday and is quite the dapper dog now.

Passage: Bahía Guayraca to Puerto Bolivar

Departed Monday, February 09, 2009 at 11:08 AM local time from Bahia Guayraca at anchor. The departure location was latitude 11 degrees 22.055 minutes north, longitude 73 degrees 46.120 minutes west.

Arrived Tuesday, February 10, 2009 at 12:04 PM local time at Puerto Bolivar. The arrival location was latitude 12 degrees fifteen.285 minutes north, longitude 71 degrees 57.222 minutes west. The trip covered 145.47 nautical miles in 1d 0h 55m with an average speed of 5.80 knots and a maximum speed of 6.40 knots.

Tuesday, February 10, 2009 8:05:04 PM

Location: Puerto Bolivar

While there were periods where the wind and waves were larger than forecast, on the whole, the average was pretty much on target. By last night at 10:00 the seas were in the two to four foot range and *Jenny* steamed through the night very comfortably. We had a full moon to light the way too. For down here, you could not ask for much better. We also made water all the way across and have *Jenny's* tanks filled. *Jenny's* water maker is down to four GPH, but it is keeping ahead of the needs of the four of us. I will have to get a new membrane before too much longer.

Jenny arrived at Puerto Bolivar around 10:00 AM and finally received permission to enter after several attempts to contact the port captain on channel sixteen. It was only after I announced that *M/V Jenny* was steaming down the channel that I got any response. For all they knew *Jenny* could have been a coal carrier and that got their attention since there is only space for one ship at a time in the port.

This is one of three spots to anchor around here. Unfortunately, it is a choice among three uncomfortable spots. The whole area is very flat and the wind is howling overhead. This is supposed to be the best of the three anchorages and *Jenny* is anchored off a turning basin for the coal carriers. The ship dock is the only thing here and ships are lined up outside waiting their turn to come in and load, one at a time. Three tugs turn them and our entertainment is watching the action.

Upwind of us are very shallow flats and beyond them is a huge bay that you cannot get into because it is so shallow. The area shallows gradually so you cannot get close enough to the weather shore to avoid the water having a nice fetch to build an annoying three foot chop. We will be glad to get out of here! *Jenny's* temperature gauge for JD continues to be a giant thorn in my nerves as you know by now. It is driving me absolutely crazy! In spite of giving her new gauge and JD a new matching sensor *Jenny* continues to lie to me! I cannot take it anymore. She consistently tells me JD is running a fever between 200 and 210 degrees when normal is supposed to be 180 to 190. I know she is lying because I have caught her at it. Every time I hook up the temperature sensor on my multimeter and tape it to JD right where the sensor is, the millimeter reads 170 degrees. I even put insulating tape over the sensor this time. It still read 170 degrees. I know *Jenny* is toying with me. The only thing left is her wiring.

By afternoon, I had worked myself into a frenzied state of desperation and pulled *Jenny's* instrument panel open. I was not messing around anymore and tore all the wiring for JD's instruments out. I went wild. The kids saw wire spaghetti being flung from the guts of *Jenny's* instruments and hid. I could hear Gaelic prayers wafting up from below.

A single power wire jumped from one instrument to the next. It jumped to the instrument; it jumped to the instrument light; it jumped to the sensor. It then jumped to the next instrument. One skinny gaily hopping red one and another skinny hopping black one hopped all around the back of the panel conspiring to strangle the life out of the gauges last in line by giving them hardly any current. The original wiring even used mounting brackets to connect the hopping wire mess! It was definitely not ABYC compliant.

I was on to something. I hear the gauges, sensors and lights all screaming for isolation and more power. JD's temperature gauge was wacky because it was starving for amps and volts. I started snipping wires, pulling wires, making up new wires. Fortunately, I had a spare buss bar and enough wire to provide each gauge with its own power leads.

Time passes...

I have recovered now. My wild energy turned to accomplishment. I hope I finally uncovered the secret of *Jenny's* gauges.

While I was flailing around with the wires, a mullet threw itself onboard. Yup. Ed and Russell had been dragging a lure the past 24 hours and got nothing. This mullet just gave itself to me. I heard it hit the salon window and went out to see it flapping on the deck. I called them up and asked them to pick it up and get ready for a meal. Well, to my surprise they were afraid to touch it. Really! Such a terrifying mullet it was. I told them to get the bucket and put the mullet in until I could attend to it. Both of these big strong Englishmen men brought the bucket over, turned it on its side and stared at the mullet, hoping it would flop in. REALLY!

I had not had lunch yet, was hungry after my wiring frenzy and decided they had no right to it. I cleaned it while the grill was warming up, put it on the Weber while the meat was still twitching and had it for lunch. Yum. Oh yes, we are down to veggies and potatoes for dinners now. Lord knows what we will be eating a week from now. Caroline expected to go shopping here. Yup! And on the subject of some choices have consequences... In spite of me saying repeatedly to Ed that he had better check out Puerto Bolivar via the net through family or friends, he was sure he could get off *Jenny* here. NOT. We are all checked out of Colombia and there is nothing here; certainly not immigration. The port captain would not let him off *Jenny*. Hmmm... Things are getting interesting...

It looks like there is a weather window showing up on the 16th and I hope lasting a couple of days. If it holds we will go. If it gets too bad, we will turn down wind, down current, down waves and surf to Jamaica maaaan. We should be either in Jamaica or the Dominican Republic by end-of-day on the 19th. I will get more forecasts tomorrow.

I have some other minor projects to do on board, but this place has nothing to offer. We will be going nuts by the 16th for sure. Time to sleep. Nicholas has already crashed.

Wednesday, February 11, 2009 7:02:57 PM

Location: Puerto Bolivar

The only good thing about this anchorage is that the waves outside are much larger than the four foot chop *Jenny* is anchored in. It is an awful anchorage. I originally planned to stay in Bahia Guayraca until just before a weather opening. But Ed was keen to be on his way here because he figured he could get off. To be fair, I also was anxious to be ready to jump as soon as an opening showed up. We left earlier than we should have. Puerto Bolivar is conditioning us for the journey ahead. We are eager to depart that is for sure!

I am looking hard at leaving at 04:00 AM on the 16th. We will have at least two solid days and probably three of wind in the teens and waves mostly less than six feet. I will keep monitoring the forecasts. I am also hoping to lose some of this chop as we pull away from the coast.

Today we did some maintenance on *Jenny's* stabilizers, I changed JD's primary fuel filter we used getting here. It was very dirty. I imagine the tank is clean with all this action! We now have two fresh filters for the crossing. We also did a major cleaning of the inside of *Jenny*, wiping down all the surfaces with fresh water. Other than that, we spent most of the day resting and reading. I made Chili for dinner. It is missing some of its usual ingredients, but I think it will be a hit anyway.

Thanks for all the emails. They help. It is nice to know we are still connected to the world.

Passage: Puerto Bolivar to Bahia Honda

Departed Thursday, February 12, 2009 at 10:26 AM local time from Puerto Bolivar at anchor. The departure location was latitude 12 degrees 19.188 minutes north, longitude 71 degrees 56.068 minutes west.

Arrived Thursday, February 12, 2009 at 1:19 PM local time at Bahia Honda. The arrival location was latitude 12 degrees 22.631 minutes north, longitude 71 degrees 45.911 minutes west. The trip covered 16.77 nautical miles in 0d 3h 47m with an average speed of 4.40 knots and a maximum speed of 6.90 knots.

Thursday, February 12, 2009 3:00:38 PM

Location: Bahia Honda
Latitude is 12 degrees 22.627 minutes north.
Longitude is 71 degrees 45.012 minutes west.

Jenny had enough of Puerto Bolivar and headed out this morning. She went fifteen miles further northeast to Bahia Honda. While this is still a wild and windy place with a lot of rolling waves it is noticeably better than Puerto Bolivar. So here we stay for a while.

The very good news on this small trip is that *Jenny's* gauges are all reading spot on now. JD's temperature hits 190 and stays there. Perfect. All *Jenny's* gauges for JD are right on their spec!!! After all this time, her wiring was again the problem. If you have some mysterious gauge issues, make sure each gauge is wired directly to a buss bar, not gauge to gauge! When I have time I will increase the gauge of the power supply wire to the buss bar.

In Puerto Bolivar I decided we needed to replace the shock absorber rubber in *Jenny's* stabilizers. I got her starboard side done ok yesterday, but this morning I could not get the old rubber on her port side untied. The knot was thoroughly jammed into the rubber. Again at 05:00 AM tomorrow when the wind and waves are least, I will go back out and try to get the whole rig down. This morning I went up with the pole vertical and could not reach the top where the shackle is. Tomorrow I will go up with the pole out using the boson's chair. I should be able to reach it.

The new rubber takes more line to tie, to the starboard bird flew three feet closer to the surface than it should. I will put an extension on that wire tomorrow and when I make up the new line, I will make it three feet longer. When I get to a slip, I will rebuild the other and get rid of the wire extension. The good news is that the new shock absorber worked great on the way up this morning.

The weather for the crossing is deteriorating slightly, but still doable. We might need to head down wind on the third day though.

		WIND			SEAS		
Date	Hour	Dir	Deg	Range (kt)	Dir	Per (sec)	Range (ft)
2/16	01	E	91	13-18	ENE	7	5-9
2/16	07	E	91	11-15	ENE	7	5-9
2/16	13	ENE	78	9-12	ENE	7	5-8
2/16	19	ENE	50	10-14	ENE	7	4-7
		ENE					
2/17	01	ENE	67	10-14	E	7	5-8
2/17	07	ENE	58	8-11	E	7	4-7
2/17	13	NE	43	9-12	E	7	4-6
2/17	19	NE	36	13-18	E	7	4-6
		NE					
2/18	01	NE	31	20-27	NNE	5	6-10
2/18	07	NE	35	18-25	NE	5	6-10

| 2/18 | 13 | NE | 45 | 16-22 | ENE | 5 | 6-9 |
| 2/18 | 19 | ENE | 54 | 15-20 | ENE | 5 | 5-8 |

Friday, February 13, 2009 12:52:34 PM

Location: Bahia Honda

We had a terrible night at anchor, reminiscent of Los Frailes. The wind was blowing out of the east at twenty knots, pointing *Jenny* east, and then a swell started coming in from the north hitting her side. No one got any sleep as we were tossed about. We cannot put her birds down because we are only in fifteen feet of water.

One of the nice things about how I re-rigged the outriggers is that you can unhook one end from the hull now and use it as a three-part block and tackle to raise things to the end of the boom. I got out *Jenny's* drogue, got the guys up and tied some dive weights to the bottom end. We then rigged the open end to the end of the boom. It helped a lot, working as a break on *Jenny's* rolling. At 07:00 AM we got up and re-anchored. I moved *Jenny* up more alongside of the bluffs here to block the east wind and we put a stern anchor out to keep her pointed into the swell. This is a good anchorage now and we are comfortable finally!!

After that I built a new line with a new shock absorber for the port side. We again used the boom down haul to raise the boson's chair lines to the end of the boom. The guys helped me get launched over the side and up to swap out the two lines. I was swinging around like a monkey on a trapeze. We are good now on both sides.

It now looks like we will leave here at 06:00 AM on the 15th and get into the Dominican Republic in the afternoon of the 19th. The weather has improved through the middle, so the only real bashing seems to be on the 16th and we are now pretty used to that. *Jenny* is all ready to go and so are we!

Sunday, February 15, 2009 8:05:03 AM

Location: Bahia Honda
Latitude is 12 degrees 22.77 minutes north.
Longitude is 71 degrees 45.884 minutes west.

All the systems on *Jenny* are in excellent condition and we are well rested. We will be making water as we cross and have enough food to make it. I have upgraded the shock absorbers on both stabilizers and they will be running deeper than they have been. Nicholas is getting bored with being on *Jenny* and keeps going into the cockpit to sniff the land. He knows we are close and is greatly disappointed that *The Beast* is not in the water.

To catch the best of the weather, we will begin to stow all the gear we have out around 04:00 PM. We need to pull in the drogue / flopper stopper and reattach the downhaul lines. It needs to be washed and stowed. Then we need to run a line from the bow back to the bitter end of the stern anchor line. I do not want to let go of the bow anchor until the stern anchor is up and stored. With the stern anchor line tied to the bow we will maneuver *Jenny* to loosen and then drop the stern anchor off the stern cleat. Then she will be anchored by the bow on both. By letting out 300 to 400 feet of anchor chain on the bow anchor we should be able to come up on the stern anchor and bring it over the bow. Then we need to disassemble that anchor (a Fortress that has worked perfectly) and get it stored. Then a final check and we are ready to raise the bow anchor.

		WIND			SEAS		
Date	Hour	Dir	Deg	Range (kt)	Dir	Per (sec)	Range (ft)
13 degrees north waypoint ETA at 13:00							
2/15	07	E	90	14-19	ENE	7	6-9
2/15	13	E	81	13-18	ENE	7	5-8
2/15	19	E	80	15-20	ENE	7	5-9
14 degrees north waypoint ETA at 17:00							
2/16	01	ENE	77	13-18	ENE	6	5-8
2/16	07	ENE	75	12-16	ENE	6	5-8
2/16	13	ENE	78	9-13	ENE	6	4-7
2/16	19	ENE	54	10-14	ENE	6	4-7
15 degrees north waypoint ETA at 02:00							
2/17	01	NE	45	10-14	E	6	4-6
2/17	07	ENE	61	8-11	E	6	3-6
2/17	13	NE	48	11-15	E	6	3-6
2/17	19	NE	43	13-18	E	6	3-6
16 degrees north waypoint ETA at 10:30							
2/17	01	ENE	64	7-11	E	6	3-6
2/17	07	ENE	57	8-11	E	6	3-6
2/17	13	ENE	43	11-15	E	6	3-5
2/17	19	ENE	42	11-fifteen	E	6	3-5
17 degrees north waypoint ETA at 19:00							
2/17	01	ENE	79	5-7	E	6	3-5
2/17	07	ENE	57	10-13	ESE	6	3-5
2/17	13	NE	34	10-13	ESE	6	3-5
2/17	19	NE	39	15-20	ESE	6	3-5
18 degrees north waypoint ETA at 08:00 (Boca Chica) on 2/18							

The weather forecasts have been all over the place. The latest looks very good. We may be able to beat *Jenny's* current ETA on the 19th. Now that the engine temperature gauge is telling the truth, I will not need to worry about burning JD up if I step up the beat. The worst weather is on the first day and is not much more than what we have already experienced.

Passage: Bahia Honda to Boca Chica DR

Departed Sunday, February 15, 2009 at 10:33 AM local time from Bahia Honda Anchorage. The departure location was latitude 12 degrees 23.050 minutes north, longitude 71 degrees 46.197 minutes west.

Monday, February 16, 2009 2:33:14 PM

Location: Caribbean Sea

Latitude is 14 degrees 6.567 minutes north.
Longitude is 70 degrees 0.801 minutes west.

This weather observation was taken on Monday, February 16, 2009 2:32:53 PM local time.
Observation location: Caribbean Sea.
Latitude is 14 degrees 6.378 minutes north.
Longitude is 70 degrees 0.881 minutes west.
The air temperature is 80, and water temperature is 0 degrees Fahrenheit.
The forecast is Sunny.
The current weather is dry.
The sky is scattered clouds (10 - 50% clouds).
The wind is 9 knots from the northeast.
The visibility is fifteen nautical miles.
The wave height is 3 feet with 4 foot swells.
The barometer is 1016 millibar and steady.

The good weather moved in a little and at 10:00 I decided to spring into action. *Jenny* was underway a couple of hours later. So far we have had the luck of very good weather, at least for the Caribbean Sea at this time of year. The first 24 hours started very nice with about a four foot chop out of the northeast, but built as expected through the evening into five to six foot wind waves at about five seconds by midnight. Then it started to come down again as forecast and became a four-foot chop at about five seconds mostly from the northeast, but some coming out of the north as well. There really is not a defined swell that you can see, just a lumpy sea. We have made two of our three turns north already and have gradually decreased how much *Jenny* is pounding into the waves. *Jenny's* birds are working their wonder, and we have no perceptible roll. While not lake-smooth, we are not uncomfortable.

It is a wonder to me how you can be in the middle of nowhere and have a committee meeting. Here we were in the middle of nowhere at 01:30 this morning we had four ships crossing our path from various directions. Two Princess cruise boats were coming from the Canal with one heading for Aruba. That one was going to pass within .04 miles of us. We slowed way down for about an hour and changed course to let it go by. Meanwhile I could hear the pilots on both boats yakking on VHF channel 69 about their jobs, never giving any indication that we were here.

This morning I found about eight large flying fish in the cockpit. I scooped them up and put them in a zip lock in the refrigerator for bate. But, with one on the meat hook so far all morning, I have not had a single strike. This is quite different from the Pacific where we would have had a strike within an hour. Nicholas is not happy with this continuous movement. I think this is only his second multi-night passage and he wants it to be over. He wants dry land. Poor pooch! I owe him big time. We are eating the dinners we froze on the way up the Colombian coast, and I made up Suddenly Salad with Tuna for my lunches. So, all is well on that front.

Just before leaving, I got an email that said something about *Catching Up* heading for the Dominican Republic so I will have to send them an email when we get in. We are about halfway across now and *Jenny* is purring along. What a magnificent vessel.

Tuesday, February 17, 2009 2:40:20 PM

Location: Caribbean Sea
Latitude is 16 degrees 32.723 minutes north.
Longitude is 69 degrees 41.133 minutes west.

This weather observation was taken on Tuesday, February 17, 2009 2:40:04 PM local time.
Observation location: Caribbean Sea.
Latitude is 16 degrees 32.454 minutes north.
Longitude is 69 degrees 41.142 minutes west.
The air temperature is 77, and water temperature is 0 degrees Fahrenheit.
The forecast is Sunny, Windy.
The current weather is dry.
The sky is clear or a few clouds.
The wind is 13 knots from the northeast.
The visibility is 12 nautical miles.
The wave height is 5 feet with 5 foot swells.
The barometer is 1018 millibar and steady.

Jenny had a very nice (for this sea) night last night and even had her birds up for a few hours to get some speed. She managed to get up close to seven knots for about five hours and is now showing us an arrival time around 08:00 tomorrow. Cheers!!! We put her birds back in the water around 20:00 because the seas were building and she is again plowing through a five-foot chop with about a three-second interval.

We had another bird wire break last night and that prompted taking both up. The 1/8 inch wire is just not strong enough for the kind of chop that exists here. It was another quick repair this morning thankfully. When I get to the Dominican Republic, the next person flying in from the States will be carrying replacement wire that will be 3/16 inch. The 1/8 is rated at 1750 lbs. breaking strength and 3/16 is rated at 3700 lbs. That should fix the breakage problem. The 5/8 inch nylon line is rated at 11,000 lbs. so the wire will break before the line does. And I hope, before anything else does.

I have been reporting *Jenny's* position and checking in daily with the HAM Marine Mobile Service net on 14,300 KHz USB. It is good to know that someone knows we are out here and where we are. Unfortunately I have not been able to get an email connection so I know you are all wondering if we are ok. I feel bad about that.

This has been the longest and certainly the most challenging voyage in my cruising experience. It has made me ready for some shore time for sure. I have begun looking at various options and timings. I plan to contact *Ketching Up* and finding out what their plans are for heading back to the States. I may hook up with them and head back earlier than I previously planned. I need to find a nice inexpensive marina to stay at though and am worried about the prices in the States. Maybe with this recession, some deals can be made?

The crew is doing wonders and I am glad to have them onboard. I know I would have been really struggling to get this done solo. They are turning into real sailors and are good to be with. Nicholas hangs out with them a lot now and a friendship has developed among them.

We made enough water to fill out tanks so no worries there and we have enough food to get us through the night. Tomorrow we will dine out and drink some Cerveza. Hope all is well with all of you.

Arrived Wednesday, February 18, 2009 at 2:06 PM local time at Boca Chica Dominican Republic. The arrival location was latitude 18 degrees 23.930 minutes north, longitude 69 degrees 36.671 minutes west. The customs check in was Dominican Republic. The trip covered 407.00 nautical miles in 3d 14h 09m with an average speed of 5.10 knots and a maximum speed of 7.10 knots.

Wednesday, February 18, 2009 5:57:59 PM

Location: Boca Chica, Dominican Republic
Latitude is 18 degrees 26.688 minutes north.
Longitude is 69 degrees 37.371 minutes west.

I definitely would not like to do that trip twice. Whew. I cannot complain about the weather though. It was exactly as Buoy Weather predicted except for the wind direction last night. Buoy Weather predicted three to six-foot waves with wind out of the east or east-southeast. Well, for someone used to the Pacific, three to six does not sound too bad. However, it is not the same here. The three to six refers to the peak waves in a continuous chop with washing machine action that would make a Maytag proud. AND, the wind came out of the NORTH, right in *Jenny's* face. We were slowed to 3.5 Knots for twelve hours, all night AND the wire on the starboard side bird snapped AGAIN. None of us got any sleep. Nicholas is totally crashed next to me now.

We effectively lost four hours of transit time during the night because we had to slow down to survive the waves without *Jenny's* starboard bird. Yesterday, all was looking beautiful and we predicted a 10:00 landfall. *Jenny* took her Boca Chica Marina Zar Par buoy at 14:00.

The Russell, Ed and Caroline became a crew during the journey. They really began to understand that this was not just your normal tourist adventure and was a true adventure with significant risk and lasting reward. I am glad they were aboard and would have struggled to make it solo. I am very proud of them and thankful we met. This was the most difficult set of passages I have yet made, and they were a significant factor in its success. I hope they stay in touch.

Damage Report
1. I need to re-rig *Jenny's* stabilizers with 3/16 wire. 1/8 does not do it.
2. *Jenny's* refrigerator stopped being effective during the thrash. I think it just needs coolant.
3. One of *Jenny's* two 4-D batteries for the bow thruster shorted out during the night. I think it got bounced one time to many.
4. *Jenny* lost her port side throw able life preserver and all the port side porthole screens at the river.
5. When I rewired *Jenny's* gauges I left some of the gauges without lights.

Boca Chica Marina Zar Par is too much of a yacht club for me. It is too far from food shopping, town action, etc. It also has music blasting from across the bay already. I am spoiled by Cartagena!!! I only paid for a week here. I will start to research where next to go. I am thinking of hooking up with *Ketching Up* on their way back to the States.

Nicholas and I are heading into the Yacht Club for dinner now. There is not a crumb of food left onboard!

Wednesday, February 18, 2009 7:42:20 PM

Location: Boca Chica, Dominican Republic

Do not get me wrong, being in this perfectly flat water, on a mooring, temperature in the 70's, able to see the bottom in 20 ft of water is very nice. Especially after a long passage. But. The marina does not have an ATM, you have to go to Boca Chica. I arranged to go to the small grill here for dinner and to pay in Pesos tomorrow. Nicholas and I got there at 18:30 and they were closing up. UGH. I was hungry. Back to *Jenny*. The kids ate the bottle of spaghetti sauce. So it was chicken noodle soup for dinner and some Jose Quervo 1800...

Tuesday, February 24, 2009 8:20:42 AM

Location: Boca Chica, Dominican Republic

Latitude is 18 degrees 26.688 minutes north.
Longitude is 69 degrees 37.374 minutes west.

Jenny is all cleaned up and refreshed now. Just a little more food shopping and we will be ready to go. Our next stop is Samana Bay on the eastern side of the Dominican Republic. A small town there is an eco-touring spot. There are supposed to be whales in the bay now so it might be exciting. Laura, my daughter is coming down for a week and we will do whale watching and rain forest hiking stuff. It will be nice to see her. I plan to leave Boca Chica Thursday morning and be there on Saturday with a couple of stops along the way.

If Samana is a nice place, Mary will rejoin *Jenny* there. Since Christmas, she has professed a change of heart. She says her place is here with Nicholas and me and vows to rededicate herself to us. I have offered that once we are back in the States we can just cruise the inter-coastal waterway, rivers and bays where the water is calm and will not cause her fear. We will still have a very large territory to cover without exposing her to big water. I want it to work for us.

If we like it in Samana Bay then we will stay a while. Otherwise we will head up to the Turks and Cacaos and on through the Bahamas. We have never been, so it should be interesting and a nice reintroduction for Mary.

We have made reservations at a marina in Brunswick GA. It is right in town within walking distance of shopping, etc. It is also a port of entry, so we will probably go there directly from the Bahamas. Being in the Jacksonville nook, I am comfortable that we can stay there through hurricane season safely. We might take a year off from active cruising and settle down there or in Fernandina Beach for a while. Then in the spring of 2010 work our way up to Maine.

Passage: Boca Chica to Samana DR

Departed Thursday, February 26, 2009 at 5:46 AM local time from ZarPar Marina Mooring. The departure location was latitude 18 degrees 25.869 minutes north, longitude 69 degrees 37.610 minutes west.

Thursday, February 26, 2009 7:09:37 AM

Location: Underway
Latitude is 18 degrees 23.577 minutes north.
Longitude is 69 degrees 29.509 minutes west.

This weather observation was taken on Thursday, February 26, 2009 2:48:15 PM local time.
Observation location: Isla Saona.
Latitude is 18 degrees 11.594 minutes north.
Longitude is 68 degrees 47.046 minutes west.
The air temperature is 84, and water temperature is 0 degrees Fahrenheit.
The forecast is Sunny.
The current weather is dry.
The sky is scattered clouds (10 - 50% clouds).
The wind is 10 knots from the east.
The visibility is 10 nautical miles.
The wave height is 1 feet with 0 foot swells.
The barometer is 1016 millibar and falling.

Jenny dropped her mooring at Marina Zarpar this morning and headed back out to sea. We are on a two-part voyage to Samana Bay. Today she is going to an anchorage at Isla Saona and will stay overnight. I will take another look at the weather in the Mona Passage and up the east coast of the Dominican Republic over the next few days. If it looks good, I will give *Jenny* the helm around 17:00 for an overnight run up to Samana.

I do not want to say I did not like Boca Chica, but I did not. It was a vacation town with only a very base culture focused on prostitutes, drinking and the beach. It had no soul and the only people you could interact with were either visitors indulging in the debauchery or the locals who provided it. There are other people here, the ones that own the sport fishing boats and are white descent. They live somewhere out of sight and do not show themselves in town. They show up on the weekends on their yachts, throwing parties while anchored near the marina. I am hoping Samana is different.

The sea is being nice today, and *Jenny's* route goes along the south coast that is pretty well protected from the trade winds and waves. She has her birds up for now and her ETA is around 13:00. I had my tea and two boiled eggs for breakfast. By the way, there are only "free range chickens" here. You see them in every back yard. *Jenny* has the helm and I am listening to NPR on the sideband radio while she just steams along. Life is good.

Arrived Thursday, February 26, 2009 at 2:23 PM local time at Isla Saona anchor. The arrival location was latitude 18 degrees 11.604 minutes north, longitude 68 degrees 47.035 minutes west. The customs check in was none. The trip covered 55.66 nautical miles in 0d 8h 50m with an average speed of 6.30 knots and a maximum speed of 7.30 knots.

Thursday, February 26, 2009 2:54:45 PM

Location: Isla Saona Anchor

Latitude is 18 degrees 11.597 minutes north.
Longitude is 68 degrees 47.043 minutes west.

Jenny is anchored in twenty-five feet of crystal clear water after a nice day's passage. This is the first passage since arriving in Cartagena where I did not think the sea was trying to hurt us. What a pleasure!

Nicholas and I will stay here overnight and through tomorrow until around 4:00 or 5:00 PM. Then we will start an overnight passage up to Samana Bay if the weather forecast holds. The deal in the trade winds area is to make passages at night even when you could make them in a single day. The Van Sant book "Passages South" explains it all and is required reading when cruising the islands. It is timeless in its discussion of the weather, waypoints and routes, and island hopping strategies. However, much of the rest of the book is dated, he is heavily biased to the Dominican Republic and especially Luperon where he owns property. The anchorage here at Isla Saona is pretty and calm. It should be a good night. The bottom is hard coral and sand and it took a bit of backing down before *Jenny* was really hooked up.

Passage: Isla Saona to Samana Bay

Departed Friday, February 27, 2009 at 4:10 PM local time from Isla Saona anchor. The departure location was latitude 18 degrees 11.648 minutes north, longitude 68 degrees 47.596 minutes west.

Arrived Saturday, February 28, 2009 at 1:53 PM local time at Samana Bay. The arrival location was latitude 19 degrees 11.884 minutes north, longitude 69 degrees 19.733 minutes west. The customs check in was a Dispatcho. The trip covered 131.29 nautical miles in 0d 21h 42m with an average speed of 6.00 knots and a maximum speed of 7.40 knots.

Saturday, February 28, 2009 5:59:34 PM

Location: Samana, Dominican Republic
Latitude is 19 degrees 11.884 minutes north.
Longitude is 69 degrees 19.733 minutes west.

The dreadnaught *M/V Jenny*, Nicholas and I went through the notorious Mona Passage without breathing hard. *Jenny* carried us out of the anchorage at Saona around 16:00 and I watched as the moon and Venus rose together and set together. It was beautiful in a clear sky. As it got dark, Nicholas and I got set up for a long night.

The Mona Passage has a reputation for being a vicious body of water. It is the passage between the Dominican Republic and Puerto Rico. Wind and currents churn up a soup of nasty steep chop. While I did not have to cross the passage, I did have to scoot along the Dominican Republic coast side to get up to Samana. I did my homework. The weather forecast was good for all the points around the corner, I went at night to catch the "night lee" and I hugged the Dominican Republic coast. The result was a passage with a lot of motion, but no whitecaps, little wind and no trauma. Two other boats were using the same night to cross. At daybreak, *Jenny* was beyond the passage and starting to make her turn down wind and down wave. Big smiles!

As we entered Samana Bay, I was not paying particular attention and *Jenny* snagged a crab pot. Oh my! I got her other bird up and was just about to work on her problem child when the pot fell off. Thank you! However, I noticed her bird was not running right and had to bring it up anyway to get it untwisted. I was on full alert after that.

There are whales here. I saw a lot of blows, breaches and backs, all at a distance though. Quite a few boats here take people out to chase them too.

Jenny delivered us to the anchorage around 14:00 and set her anchor into the mud floor on 300 feet of chain. I have read that there can be high winds here, so I positioned *Jenny* in the middle. Then the Navy came out and collected my Dispatcho, the Dominican Republic port-to-port clearance document. I cleaned *Jenny* up, showered, and fell into bed. Sometime later, another panga came up with the port captain agenda and his friend Chito. They wanted to collect the port fee and talk about their service. The port fee is $32 per month for *Jenny* ($.70 / ft / month). That gives you a dinghy dock, water, and trash. Basically the same as Club Nautico in Cartagena, at ¼ the cost! I am beginning to like this place. Tomorrow I am meeting Chito at 09:00 to have him give me a tour of the town. It looks nice from *Jenny*.

Then I crashed again and got up at 17:00. I wanted to see if I could grab a free Wi-Fi connection so set up the laptop. Boy was I surprised to find the telecom here provides free wireless!!! I am beginning to really like this place!!!

Tomorrow, Joe the port agent wants me to move to another spot. We will see. I will ignore him if I can. I will lower *The Beast* and go in with Nicholas. He is ready for dry land.

Tuesday, March 03, 2009 1:28:30 PM

Location: Samana, Dominican Republic
Latitude is 19 degrees 11.938 minutes north.
Longitude is 69 degrees 19.841 minutes west.

I explored the town a little more today, looking for the local restaurant that I want to try this afternoon, the pharmacy and the smaller grocery store. I found all easily. The smaller store actually looks like it caters more to visitors than the other does. I was able to buy a half chicken, Tostitos Nachos, Lays Potato Chips, hot dogs, and most importantly Oreos!!! Yea, I know, not a good diet. However, after weeks of healthy food, you do get cravings! They even have canned anchovies. I had dogs and potato chips for lunch. Yum. Tonight I will check out the restaurant.

I have been running the water maker a couple of hours every morning before the tourist boats stir up the water. The harbor here is open on two sides so gets plenty of flow through. The alternative is to go into the public dock and load water. It might be feasible before or after work hours, but not during the day. There just is too much tour boat traffic. I am trying to avoid it.

More boats came in today, one a Swiss boat. I think we need to start a net soon. There are five cruising boats here now, but no one is talking / socializing. We will see.

I spent the mid-morning and noon perusing the guidebooks and charts for going up to the Bahamas. The first passage is 180 NM and an overnight passage that needs careful weather planning. After that, it gets much easier except that Mary and I will have to become expert Bank navigators. There are several coral banks that we will have to transit on daylight passages where the depth is very marginal. I am talking eight feet with occasional coral heads peaking up. It is scary, but all part of the experience. Vessels do it every day. We should be able to master this. The next several passages are island hops in the twenty to forty mile range. Not bad. Then we face one ninety-mile passage up to Rum Cay that is fairly protected, but again will require a nice weather window.

The locals say we should stay here for the Easter festivities. That is April 12th, so we might begin going north right after that. We are supposed to get strong winds out of the north tonight and tomorrow and the boats just swung around to the north. It looks like the front is coming in.

I have been looking for a well-designed flopper stopper to stop *Jenny's* rolling at anchor. I found the design I want, but it is made in Australia and not available in the US. I sent an email out to two good boat yards I know to see if they would give me a price for making two of them. They are small sea anchors with a two-foot diameter stainless steel hoop at the open end. After using *Jenny's* drogue in Colombia, I am sure these will work well, in as little as eight feet of water and be easy to store.

Wednesday, March 04, 2009 6:00:46 PM

Location: Samana
Latitude is 19 degrees 11.909 minutes north.
Longitude is 69 degrees 19.85 minutes west.

Well, I am just not used to this. It was cloudy with showers all day, and now it is RAINING! Boy this sucks. In addition, its only 70 degrees out. Brrrrr. I just turned on *Jenny's* diesel furnace. Nicholas is trying to scare up a game with his Chipmunk toy and I am nuking some of my frozen chili. It is a chili kind of night.

I took Nicholas out for a walk this morning. The usual dock at the town was jammed with tour boats being cleaned since there were no customers. I took him over to the park island on the other side. I broke out my raincoat and we went. He came back soaked and happy. He ran around in the rain like a maniac. He does not get of the leash in town. However, he was also a mud pie. He got a shampoo when we got back to *Jenny*. Then he totally crashed.

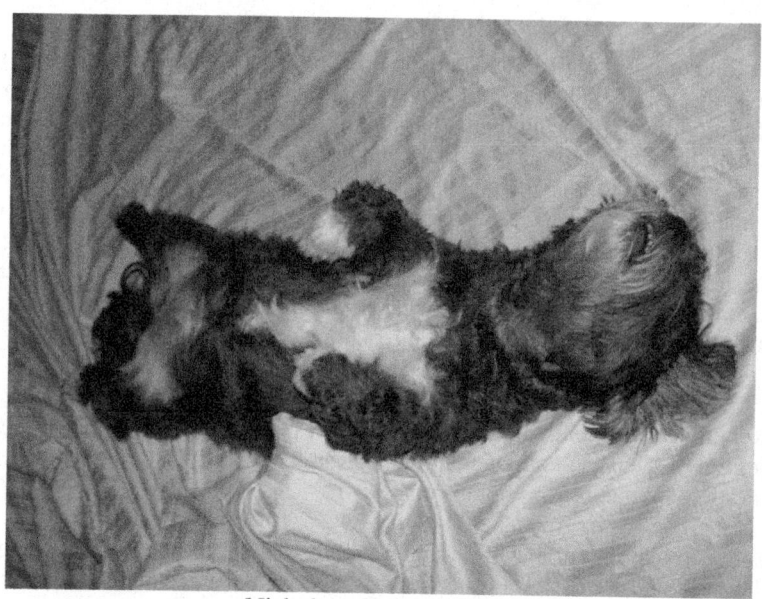

Nicholas after a hard day

Today was also a laundry kind of day, so I fired up a load while *Jenny's* genset and water maker were running. I did email, cleaned up *Jenny*, etc. kind of projects. Then I tackled an optional project.

I bought a 12db high gain Wi-Fi antenna for *Jenny* back in Mexico. I mounted it between *Jenny's* VHF antennas on her pilothouse roof and it worked wonders for our reception for a while. Then, suddenly the Port Networks box was dead. It could not see a single access point. I sent the box back to Port Networks and they replaced it without charge. The radio had been fried. I ran it again for a while and the same thing happened. Again, Port Networks replaced the box. I figured out that *Jenny's* SSB transmissions were sending too much energy down the 12db antenna and frying the box. So I disconnected it.

I just cannot leave something alone until it is "perfect". I want to hook up the 12db Wi-Fi antenna just to see what I am missing. I pulled out the SSB radio to get access to it and hooked up the box. *Jenny's* WiFi signal strength went from 41 on up to 56. That was good enough for me. However, when I tried to use the existing internet wire it did not work. After replacing the ends a few times (grrrrr), I ran a new wire. Voila, stronger internet. I can see maybe twenty access points now, where before I could only see about six. I could connect to the cruise ships out in the bay! The strongest one, free complements of Dominican Republic Telco, will do. Maybe now Skype will work a little better.

Now the challenge is how to keep the 12db antenna from frying *Jenny's* Port Networks box again when I use her SSB radio. One answer is to pull the SSB down and unhook the box whenever I make the transition from houseboat to trawler. That is a tiresome option. Another answer is to put a longer cable on the antenna and bring the box out of the overhead compartment. But, that means loss of signal strength and I cannot have that. It is less than perfection. My plan is to slip a metal tube over the antenna before using any of the radios. Tomorrow, I hope it will be dry enough to get to land. I will go to the local ferretería (hardware store) and find the piece of tubing. Then I will slip it over and see if all my signal strength goes to zero. If so, I think I am good to go.

No sign of the other boaters today. It is just too nasty out. I am so glad to be on *Jenny* instead in a sailboat. At least I have windows and some view on the world. Well, the timer on the microwave just dinged, calling me to action. When is summer up here???

Passage: Samana Bay to Las Haities Park

Departed Sunday, March 08, 2009 at 9:14 AM local time from Samana Anchorage. The departure location was latitude 19 degrees 11.434 minutes north, longitude 69 degrees 19.030 minutes west.

Arrived Sunday, March 08, 2009 at 11:33 AM local time at Las Haitises. The arrival location was latitude 19 degrees 5.009 minutes north, longitude 69 degrees 27.986 minutes west. The customs check in was none. The trip covered 14.20 nautical miles in 0d 2h 18m with an average speed of 6.20 knots and a maximum speed of 7.60 knots.

Sunday, March 08, 2009 3:33:14 PM

Location: Las Haitises National Park
Latitude is 19 degrees 5.01 minutes north.
Longitude is 69 degrees 27.984 minutes west.

My daughter Laura flew down yesterday for a short visit. We got up around 07:00 to start the day. Nicholas needed his walk of course. Then I started getting *Jenny* ready. I was not as ready as typical for a morning departure. We had to drop *Jenny's* front awning, raise her dinghy and pull in my makeshift flopper stopper. Speaking of which, I have given up on my idea of a drogue style flopper stopper after more experimentation here. It turns out that the recovery time is too long. That is, the time it takes for the device to be ready to block more water on the upswing is too long. Therefore, when you get into small, quick rolling, the drogue style device does not cycle quickly enough. I asked Mary to order and bring down a pair of Magma Rock N Roll dampers.

We got underway around 09:00 just as the wind was picking up. A cruise ship was outside the anchorage so we watched that beehive of activity as we went out. Then we turned southwest to get over to the National Park at Las Haitises. We did not see any whales on the way over, got the hook down around 11:00 and had lunch. Then we went into the ranger station to set up a hike for tomorrow. A boatload of people from the cruise ship was there and probably just had lunch. Nothing much was happening, so Laura and I went wandering. There are some limestone caves right where ranger station is and we went looking. They were interesting, but not very unique. We spent more time talking to the rangers. In the end we got one of the rangers to go in *The Beast* to the trailhead and take us a way up the trail and back.

It was 15:00 when we started and we needed to be back by 17:00. Off we went. We discovered the ranger station was a pathetic fraction of what the park is about. The ranger led us up a canyon of limestone cliffs, hanging trees, vines, mangroves, true jungle to a small dinghy dock. It looked right out of an Indiana Jones movie. That part was good enough, but then we started walking the trail and were immersed in a tropical jungle filled with caves, towers of limestone cliffs, insects, birds, etc. It was what we came here for. A very pretty hummingbird posed for us for minutes while we shot photos. Since this was spontaneous, I was in shorts and we did not have any repellent. As the sun started to go lower, the mosquitoes became the dominate life force. We were back at the dinghy by 16:30! The ranger was very knowledgeable but only spoke Spanish. Even so we got a lot of what he was saying. We gave him 400 pesos for his trouble. Tomorrow morning, we will take *The Beast* up some of the other grottos, exploring.

Jenny at National Park, Las Haitises

Passage: Whale Watching

Departed Monday, March 09, 2009 at 9:02 AM local time from Las Haitises Anchorage. The departure location was latitude 19 degrees 5.141 minutes north, longitude 69 degrees 27.885 minutes west.

Arrived Monday, March 09, 2009 at 12:41 PM local time at Samana Harbor. The arrival location was latitude 19 degrees 11.924 minutes north, longitude 69 degrees 19.844 minutes west. The customs check in was none. The trip covered 22.30 nautical miles in 0d 3h 39m with an average speed of 6.10 knots and a maximum speed of 7.20 knots.

Monday, March 09, 2009 6:54:35 PM

Location: Samana Anchorage
Latitude is 19 degrees 11.92 minutes north.
Longitude is 69 degrees 19.838 minutes west.

We are back in Samana now, having spent the day seeing the sights of Las Haitises and the bay. The anchorage down there is excellent with very good protection and no rolling. It was a quiet and peaceful night. We got up at the crack of dawn and got into *The Beast* to explore the grottos that line the southern shore of the small bay in Las Haitises. Nicholas came along and was a very happy dog having an extended dinghy ride!

The geology of the area is one of limestone hills, much like what you see in the limestone islands of Halong Vietnam. Where these hills meet the water, cliffs have formed where slices of the hills have broken away. The limestone also reforms into stalactites as water seeps through cracks and drips out through the fractured cliff faces. It is strange to see them hanging under the cliffs. Laura took photos that I will send off in a day or so. We saw a lot of birds and fauna, and pretty beaches. But there are few mammals here except rats. They need some cats going after the rats and then restore the original wildlife.

We got back to *Jenny* around 09:00 and the wind had not yet picked up. We raised *The Beast*, strapped it down like Frankenstein's Monster and went out to find whales. *Jenny* meandered about the bay while Laura and I looked for whales. Unfortunately, we saw no sign of them and *Jenny* headed back to her anchorage in Samana around 13:00. They are supposed to be here until mid-March, so there is a possibility that they have already left and are heading north. Tomorrow we will go to see the waterfalls and take a horseback ride. Then we will go on a tour of the town in the evening.

Wednesday, March 11, 2009 9:12:49 AM

Location: Samana Anchorage

Yesterday we took a tourist taxi to a set of waterfalls. The trip included going from the road stop to the falls on horseback. You could walk, but as it turned out, the horse option was the right choice. The trail was rocky, up and down some steep hills and often muddy including fording a stream. The horses were the usual tame follow-the-path variety and provided an uneventful ride. The falls were in the jungle and we arrived at its top. We had to climb down a rough trail to the bottom to see them. When we got that far, we discovered we also had to wade the small river flowing out from the falls. The crossing is right at the edge of the next 30-foot drop in the falls. The water is rushing pretty fast, is about a foot deep and really wants to take you with it. One slip and it would. A rope strung shoulder height from tree to tree above the stream is the only safety. This is not your typical US National Park experience! When you get across you see the full face of the falls and it is worth the risky crossing. Next, you can climb down another trail to get to the bottom of the second drop. There you had to wade the stream again to see the face. It was nice in that the people who made it to the falls were all rugged enough to handle the challenge.

David and Laura at the falls near Samana Bay

The cab charged us $60 for the trip and half day of his time. I thought it was a little high. I would recommend bidding $40 and going no higher than $50 for the trip. We headed back and stopped at the open market to pick up some vegetables. From there we walked back to *Jenny* and grabbed some lunch on the way. There is a small restaurant along the waterfront mostly local, but also has sandwiches and burgers. We went US. Then it was naptime back onboard. Nicholas loves his naps...

After our nap, we took Nicholas and went over to the small island the forms the southern wall of the anchorage. A huge cement walk bridge connects the island to the land. It seems as though it was someone's big idea to make a park of the island decades ago. Now the island is completely overgrown and the bridge and its patio areas are in disrepair. Nicholas liked going there again to run around and Laura went looking for sea life on the beach.

There are two professional dive boats here doing some treasure hunting. One is called Galleon Hunter and the other Dolphin. Both are rigged as professional treasure hunters. They are anchored off of this island and tied to it to form a small box that they are diving in. They have airlifts for removing sand and other material from the bottom and Dolphin has propeller wash diverters. We wondered what they were searching for...

Last night we went out to the Chinese restaurant at the top of the hill behind the town and had a good meal. The patio was perfect for looking over the bay. This morning we were up at 06:00 to get Laura to the airport. She is on her way now. It is overcast and cool now. A cruise ship is in. I believe the whales are gone.

We never saw a splash anywhere in the bay during the time we had views yesterday. Laura never got to see any. Time to clean up *Jenny* and begin another round of boat projects... Life is good.

Saturday, March 14, 2009 8:36:01 AM

Location: Samana Anchorage

Yesterday was busy. I invited *Emily Grace* (Tom Lawler's N46-20), *Pelican Bay* (Marty's Kaddy Krogen 42) and *Whiskers* a catamaran over for snacks and drinks that evening. My morning was spent cleaning up *Jenny*. It is nice to have a pleasurable event to drive you to do what needs to be done anyway. With *Jenny* all shiny, I went in to shore with *Emily Grace* and *Pelican Bay* to do some shopping and show them the town. They were pleasantly surprised having read Van Saints' decade old description. This town has a lot to offer.

Whiskers stopped by the pharmacy I pointed them to and thanked me profusely for doing so. The prices there are incredible, maybe 1/10 or 1/20 of what they are in the States and no prescriptions needed. They got three courses of Cipro for something like $2.00 and their heart medicine for next to nothing too. My Lisinopril cost about $1.80 per pill in Colombia and I got it here for $.30 per pill. I am going to stock up before I leave. However, the price is pharmacy specific. The other one I went to here was the same price as Colombia.

On my list was a new set of drinking glasses. Over the past eighteen months some disappeared, some were broken, some left on other boats. It was time for a new set since I no longer had enough for the company that evening. I found a nice set of six short glasses and a nice set of medium sized tall ones. Parting with old glasses is sad because of the memories they carry of sharing food and drink with good friends. It is also very nice to have new shiny ones. The short glasses worked great for rum and soda and the tall ones worked great for the Cerveza. I was worried about the tall ones being thrown about in the cabinet, but figured out they would be fine standing in a cup cake tin. I love it when I make these little discoveries.

The party was a lot of fun with good people and munchies. These boats are waiting here for weather before heading across the Mona Passage to Puerto Rico. They all are headed for Trinidad for the hurricane season. They will need to focus on moving to make it down there by June.

Nicholas thoroughly enjoyed the company. *Emily Grace* brought their daughter over and they had fun. Both *Emily Grace* and *Bay Pelican* have Magma or Magma copy flopper stoppers and they seem to work well. They only deploy on one side though due to their lack of stabilizer rigging. They both have hydraulic stabilizers. Tom has done an incredible amount of work on *Emily Grace*. He is inventive and an expert cabinetmaker from what I saw.

Monday, March 16, 2009 8:31:15 AM

Location: Santa Barbara de Samana

Nicholas was sick for the past 36 hours and refused to eat even grilled chicken. I was worrying like a mom, but late yesterday he came around and ate some of his chow. I took him for a walk on the park island and gave him some more food last night. *Emily Grace*, *Bay Pelican* and I went up to the Chinese restaurant for dinner, then to the Bon ice cream store for desert. Yummy.

This morning we woke up to a good rain shower. I scrambled to close *Jenny's* windows, turn on her furnace to get a little drying hot air going, turn on her water maker, and unplug *The Beast's* drain. Then I returned to the sack with Nicholas. Phew, he definitely gets a bath today...

The Internet just came up so time to check the email and watch two cruise ships get anchored.

Friday, March 20, 2009 7:20:10 AM

Location: Santa Barbara de Samana

A few more sailboats came in over the past two days on their way south. The weather window closed again so they will probably be here for a week. One of the boats has a young couple in a small, inexpensive boat. They are quite the adventurers and very nice. They bought a used outboard for their dinghy, but it died after a couple of weeks. Someone told them to run 100 to 1 oil mix and I suspect that is what did it in. I have been helping them get to shore and get their motor to a repair shop. Since this area has nothing but two stroke outboards and motor cycles, I suspect they will find an expert repair place.

Yesterday I dove on *Jenny's* bottom and cleaned the waterline and coolers. There was some slime on the bottom, but no barnacles. The prop was clean too with only a couple of baby barnacles that just brushed off. The Barnacle Buster spray that I applied seems to be doing a good job. It has worn off the edges of the prop as I expected. Also, the bottom paint that I applied to the bronze shoe is all gone. Next time I will spray it with the Barnacle Buster too.

Since the net is down for an unforeseeable time, I am going to try to buy a chip for the phone with a reasonable rate to the States. Mary, Laura and I had been using MSN Live Messenger, but it has been marginal. Sideband email is just not enough for extended periods. Also on today's task list is replacing the running light bulb in the dinghy and rewiring the SSB jacks properly. Oh yes, and a load of laundry is running.

Saturday, March 21, 2009 2:26:30 PM

Location: Santa Barbara de Samana

Its Miller time! Boy, this cruising life is hard work. Yesterday I was just going to fix the running light bulb on the dinghy. The wind was zero and the anchorage perfectly flat. I pulled the dinghy up to the back door and took the light apart. Just as I was looking for a new bulb, one of the big tourist boats decided to buzz the anchorage and caused the dinghy painter to get involved with what was left of the bow light, causing it to short out and burn up all the associated wiring. That took the rest of the morning to repair. I delivered the burned wires to the boat that buzzed us and thanked them for the trouble. They apologized, and they did not buzz *Jenny* this morning.

The least expensive way to have phone service in a foreign country is to buy a chip and plug into their network. Then, you have a local number, can make local calls, and calls to the states are really inexpensive. The trick is to have a phone that will work anywhere in the world. I did some research and found out that a 4-band (Quad-Band) GSM open phone is the answer. Being open means that it is not locked to a specific phone network. I found a NOKIA on the internet that fit the bill and bought it. It has been a great investment.

It took me two hours to find and visit the two cellular companies, compare prices, and get a chip and minutes for my phone. The best price was $.20 / minute. In Colombia, I had $.12 / minute. Oh well. Surprisingly, American area codes work here. You just dial as if you were in the States. The quad band Nokia has well paid for itself.

Nicholas is sick again today. He was fine for several days, and then this morning would not eat. He had a little diarrhea this morning too. I cannot figure out what he is getting into.

All the cruising boats left for Puerto Rico either last night or this morning. So far, all the boats are heading south to Trinidad for the hurricane season. None is heading north, but I think that may be because it is still early. I am hoping to see some boats heading north in April when we plan to go.

What do the boys do here on Saturday afternoon and after school every day? They are out at the park practicing baseball. Every US baseball team has at least a few players from the DR. This is exceptional considering the DR is about the size of Connecticut. You have to wonder what their training secret is. How to these poor DR boys end up beating US kids who have had the best equipment, the best facilities, the best coaches, the best summer programs, the best of everything?

First of all, they are motivated. Earning a place on a professional team is one of the extremely few ways a poor kid here can become wealthy. They are out on the field every day, not because their parents have signed them up for Little League, not because their parents are at every game cheering him on regardless of performance. Not because they go to baseball games and dream of the glory. But because it is a way out of poverty and they work hard to achieve it.

How do they do it without pitching machines, without manicured fields, without showers and lockers and scoreboards and coaches and bats and balls and gloves? They practice with sticks. Sticks that are about one-inch in diameter. Some are straight, and some are not. They practice with dark gray stones that are about 1 inch in diameter. Some are round, and some are not. They pitch small stones and hit them with small sticks. They catch them with bear hands. Their precision is honed to a fine edge. The best boys keep at it until they earn a cherished spot on one of the local teams and actually touch a regulation bat, ball, and glove. Their precision makes it easy to see a bright white regulation baseball, seam by seam at over 90 miles-per-hour. It makes it easy to hit this mammoth bright white ball with an equally mammoth bat. It also makes it easy to catch the mammoth bright white ball with an equally mammoth glove. There must be a lesson or two here for us.

Outside is glorious so, it is about time for Nicholas and me to take our evening walk. Hope all is well with you. The economic times are bad. I am fortunate to have a very low expense profile and ability to go where the living is cheap.

Wednesday, March 25, 2009 4:31:52 PM

Location: Santa Barbara de Samana

It has been raining just about every day and night now. Showers come through in waves, and then disappear. I have the front awning down for the sun. Otherwise it would be just to dark inside. It is kind of nice since all the salt is off *Jenny* and the rain is not hard enough to get you soaked. For the most part, it is just an occasional light rain.

Yesterday I had some guys out to work on the refrigerator. I noticed that the freezer was not staying frozen when *Jenny* was underway. And I noticed that the compressor was running longer and longer when at anchor. My local "agent" brought a couple of guys out yesterday. We discovered that the tubing was soldered closed from the factory. So, it never had Freon added. We guessed that a lack of Freon or fresh Freon was the problem. They added a fitting for the Freon gas apparatus. This let all the existing gas exit the system. Florocarbons escaping to the ozone layer... Nothing like modern technology! I put an ice cube tray in.

This morning there was no ice and I could hear the compressor running continuously. UGH. The guys came back out this afternoon. While my Spanish has improved considerably, these guys probably have difficulty being understood by their own families! We groped with words, they hooked up another can of Freon and looked serious. After an hour of words flying around with 10% comprehension at best on both sides, and Freon being let into and out of the system, the cooling coils finally got warm and the system began to cycle. Smiles were shared all around. They packed up and I took them back to the dock. They did not ask for any more money. I am ok with this. Now, the freezer is below freezing and I hope that all will be good by morning.

The young couple on the red twenty-six foot sailboat is back from their tour of the Dominican Republic by rental car. I think this is so cool. This couple is doing it. In the anchorage, their little boat is bobbing around like a cork. I found their v-berth foam floating by *Jenny* this morning, so I pulled some of it aboard the dinghy and lifted the soggy mass into their cockpit all smiles. These are mariner backpackers and while I fear for them, I think they are the purest form of cruiser. I go out of my way to help them. They are just coming back to their boat now, their dinghy motor running. Big smiles. They are coming over for some Cerveza in an hour.

Two more powerboats showed up today. I met one. It is a one-off Taiwan trawler about fifty feet long with towed passive stabilizers like *Jenny*. It has the Nordhavn style pilothouse windows. Otherwise, it looks very roomy but a little strange looking. They have their birds hung only from the ends of their outriggers and I noticed the lines were wrapped around the outriggers when they came in. When I drove the dinghy over, I noticed a number of deep chips out of their gel coat and they talked a little about the birds hitting their boat this morning. I invited them over to see *Jenny* mañana. I always look forward to showing *Jenny* off.

Another sailboat has just sailed into the anchorage and is dropping anchor.

Receiving internet on *Jenny* seems to be a past pleasure. I found a place on shore, just across from the best of the grocery stores that has good access for thirty pesos (about 90 cents) an hour.

Saturday, March 28, 2009 8:05:58 AM

Location: Santa Barbara de Samana

Last night I had dinner with the Nelsons on their seventy-foot custom trawler *Voyager*. Their homeport is Los Angles and they are working their way back that direction. The boat is long and narrow, with the extra length devoted to a very large living / dining room with all the feel of a condo. It is very nice and very spacious. However, they wish it were somewhere around fifty-five feet instead of seventy. Slip costs and availability are an issue for them. They have stabilizers like *Jenny* and on the way in a bird came out of the water and hit the boat. We discussed possible solutions. They find the birds are being towed way back, this causes the birds to fly nearer the surface then they would if they were flying up-and-down. They may have the chain attached too far back along the bird's fin. They were also interested in switching to wire to reduce the drag and get them to fly deeper. Another option would be to increase the weight of the birds. I run birds that are about forty pounds and theirs are only forty-five. The big seventy-foot sword fishing boats run 200-pound birds. Their speed and size might require them to run bigger birds, but that would require winches to get them in and out of the water.

Since the Nelsons have been through the Cacaos and Bahamas four times, I brought over *Jenny's* backup navigation computer and reviewed my planned routes with them. I am glad I did since they had several good suggestions for different route planning. They also provided a degree of assurance about being able to navigate the banks with *Jenny* since they have a seven-foot draft and they had no problems with the routes they recommended. In addition, the trip back sounds like it will be filled with nice stops.

Nicholas went over for dinner too and got lots of attention. Wendy was a vet so they are very dog friendly and knew all about the Havanese breed. She remarked that Nicholas was a little large for a Havanese. Yea... he is. We fed him too much as a puppy...

Mary is taking care of business back in Florida and getting set up for returning to *Jenny*. She's flying in on April 6th. Hurray... The Nelsons confirmed that there is very good weather in the Bahamas in May and June. We will wait here for a while before heading north. *Spirit* and *Catching Up* might come over and head north with us. That would be fun. The Nelsons also gave me some good ideas about how to see the east coast. Life is good.

Tuesday, March 31, 2009 12:37:07 PM

Location: Santa Barbara de Samana

All the boats heading south have left. I am hoping some more arrive today or tomorrow during this window. The windows seem to be getting more frequent and longer as we approach spring. I also talked some more with the cruisers here that have been through the Bahamas and got some more recommendations for routes and stops. I think Mary and I should leave no later than May 1st and head to the islands. The weather should be good and there seems to be plenty to see and do.

A few last comments on *Jenny's* tiresome refrigerator. It seems to work well on 120-volt current, but not on 12 volt. After fifteen years, I think the whole system is probably marginal and the 120-volt AC is supplying enough extra energy to overcome the overall set of problems. Either the 12-volt DC side does not have robust enough wiring, or the DC side of the circuit in the refrigerator is weak. The refrigerator is supposed to work on as little as ten volts DC and it is getting nothing less than twelve. I think the refrigerator components are the problem there. I started to run new wires, but found that I just do not have the stuff on board to do it and the effort would probably not produce any better results. The answer seems to be to run *Jenny's* inverter full time now until we get it replaced. It means an additional ten amps being consumed all the time, but I see no other option.

My project list for Brunswick GA is large now. I hope the West Marine store is not closed due to consolidations. I both want to work there to get a discount, and want to be able to walk to my parts store!

Life is good even without ice...

Thursday, April 02, 2009 1:04:17 PM

Location: Santa Barbara de Samana

A new sailboat came in yesterday morning from Puerto Rico. They are a nice French couple who sailed across from France to Granada. They worked their way up the islands to here and are heading up to the east coast of the US. She is the sailor and adventurer and he is the somewhat reluctant crew. It is nice to see a role flip-flop now and again. She wants to see New York City, then work their way back down the coast, head over to Jamaica, and then go to Guatemala. There they will leave the boat and backpack through Central America. Cool. She then wants to cross the Pacific, and he wants to head back to France. They still have a home there a little north of Niece. I had drinks on board their 35-foot Dufour and they are coming over for drinks this evening. She speaks English well and he only speaks French. I am trying to dust off my French, but Spanish words keep coming out.

I still have not gotten to the Pizza restaurant, but soon! And Mary arrives on Tuesday!

Thursday, April 09, 2009 5:22:16 PM

Location: Santa Barbara de Samana

Mary arrived on schedule. I took Alfredo's taxi over again and we went to the big American style grocery store in Santo Domingo before returning to Samana. Alfredo seems to have some government connection. He carries a Colt 45 ACP stuffed in his pants when we are out of the car! I am surprised that it is not noticeable under his Izod shirts, but you really cannot tell. Six hundred dollars later, we headed back to *Jenny*.

It is taking some time for both of us to get used to being together on *Jenny* again. I am finding it hard to open my heart again to Mary after the past years of threats of leaving. Nevertheless, I sincerely want to heal the wounds and bring us back together. Mary senses my shield though and that cannot be good. I guess it depends on how much she is willing to work on breaking it back down.

The temperatures here are now hot through the middle of the day, like in Cartagena. The evenings are nice and cool. Night temperatures come way down and make sleeping comfortable.

I have met many people in the town and we will hook up with some tonight. It takes about a month to establish friendships and really begin to share experiences with them. The folks here are good people. The town's economy is based upon tourism, but is very organic, very spontaneous, and very chaotic. Unlike most people in the States, people start each day with no idea just how they will earn enough money to put food on the evening table. They go out to the market or street and make it happen. Each day has a different outcome. It is an emotionally full life. I think few Americans can take the uncertainty of it all, especially if they are just arriving from the east coast. They have not adjusted. Life just is not orchestrated as it is in the States.

Mary brought down "flopper stoppers", new 3/16 wires and some other gear for *Jenny*. However, she did not bring much personal luggage.

The "flopper stoppers" hang ten feet underwater and keep *Jenny* from rolling around at anchor. We have them hooked up to the lines that secure the outriggers to the hull for *Jenny's* running stabilizers. They only weigh eighteen pounds, so are easy to drop in the water and pull out. We have had them on the deck until this evening when the roll picked up. I dropped them in and we are now much more comfortable.

On Monday, we will go into the fuel dock and pick up 200 gallons of diesel for the trip back to the States. We could probably make it easily on *Jenny's* remaining fuel load from Cartagena, but just in case, we will take on a little more. The bash up here chewed up a little more than I expected.

I plan to start looking at weather next week and catch the next very good weather up to the Turks and Caicos. Once there, the water seems a lot calmer and the passages short and protected. We will both like that.

Friday, April 17, 2009 11:15:56 AM

Location: Santa Barbara de Samana

You know how some days just turn bad and the bad days just keep on coming. Well, that has been this awful week.

Monday Mary and I were sitting on the patio of the nice Chinese restaurant looking over the harbor and waiting for our meal. We had a wonderful view of the boats and I asked her what she wanted to do this summer when we got back to the States. I was trying to find out how to meet her needs and offered that we could head up the Intercoastal Waterway to New York and go up the Hudson to visit here Dad and family. It would be a nice quiet ride with lots of interesting places to visit. We also could just stay in Florida and see the Keys and towns in the Southeast. I was willing to reduce the adventure to keep her engaged and happy with this life and was hoping for her to express a desire to do some east coast cruising or offer an alternative lifestyle for us. I asked her what she wanted to do a couple of times. I wanted to know what would make her happy. She did not respond. Finally, she said that she wanted to pursue separate lives and that I would be hearing from her lawyer. That evening she sat on the pilothouse roof and laughed with a friend on the cell phone. So, why did she make the trip?

Mary said she came down to rejoin Nicholas and me. However, thirty-six hours later she said that she just could not do it. She left yesterday almost as suddenly as she appeared. I feel betrayed and bewildered. I do not understand why this happened. Last night Nicholas waited in the cockpit for a couple of hours after I went to bed, waiting for her to return. I could not sleep either. She broke my heart.

Jenny's refrigerator is limping along too. I selected a replacement model and had it all planned to install it when I get to Georgia. Tuesday I got an email that the factory burned to the ground and no more were available. Ok. Deep breath.

Wednesday I talked to the dock master about loading 200 gallons of fuel and reminded him again last night that I would be coming to the dock at 08:00 Thursday morning. "No problem!" I was retrieving the anchor and washing the chain at about 06:30 AM when one of the commercial trawlers came in and took over the fuel dock. Ok. Deep breath.

Thursday at 08:00 *Jenny* was hovering just outside of the fuel dock when the trawler fired up and pulled out. Since one of *Jenny's* bow thruster batteries boiled itself to death on the way up from Colombia, she has no bow thruster. Fortunately, my pick of a windless day was on the money. I had to back *Jenny* into the dock to reach the fuel hose. However, *Jenny* just would not pirouette around for a starboard tie when she approached the high cement dock. She was unusually cantankerous this morning. My attempts at back and fill just did not get her butt around. Meanwhile she was closing on the cement pillar at the corner of the dock. The small wind and current was inching her closer and closer. *Jenny* was going to hit the cement corner broadside. At some point in an approach to land, your options expire. We were at that point. Anything I asked *Jenny* to do would make the situation worse. We slowly closed with the cement pillar with no headway. Fortunately, there were plenty of men on the dock who came to our rescue and we successfully fended *Jenny* off the cement, got her turned around and lashed down. Ok. Deep breath.

We started fueling. After fifty gallons, the pump sputtered to a halt, out of fuel. Hmmm... The dock master ordered up a pickup truck to bring the other 150 gallons. About forty-five minutes later, it arrived with one of those water tanks that you mount on the roof of a home to hold rainwater. In it was my 150 gallons of diesel. What else is in that thank? This was not exactly confidence inspiring. Deep breath!

We did get loaded with the fuel and topped up on our fresh water. The fuel was $3.05 / gallon plus some propina for all the extra help....

I am wiped out from all the stress. Ciao

Sunday, April 19, 2009 1:21:28 PM

Location: Santa Barbara de Samana

It is Sunday already, and the town is at rest. It is one of the few days I have seen it so quiet. All the spring break festivities are gone, the disco trucks and partygoers have gone. There are not any cruise ships here either. There is peace.

Nicholas has picked up a very big case of macho here. Before Cartagena he did not interact with other dogs. However, his daily walks there allowed him to observe and begin mimicking their macho behavior to a degree. You know; the growl, snarl, bark routine whenever confronted with another dog of any size delivered in the hope that nothing further develops. For Nicholas it was of course total bluff.

Well in the Dominican Republic, things got way out of hand. There are many free running dogs here scrounging for survival. Nicholas encountered them on every walk. But, at the slightest aggressive behavior by Nicholas, they scattered in the wind like leaves in a gale. This happened every walk. Nicholas now thinks he is some super dog, able to frighten every other dog regardless of size at the slightest glance. Oh boy.

It took me a while to figure out the dynamics. In the Dominican Republic the dogs that are fed and on a leash are all guard dogs. Mean to the bone. Whenever the free ranging dogs encounter a dog on a leash, they automatically assume it is deadly trouble and hence flee before the Hun.

Three new boats came in over the past couple of days. One is a nice sailboat from Rhode Island with a nice couple onboard. They are heading north too, so I am thinking we will probably go together. We had Pizza together last night.

One is a big DeFever now on a mooring behind *Jenny*. I briefly met them last night on our way to the Pizza place and they seem nice too. I will probably go over tonight for drinks. The last is from Holland and I have not met them yet. They are sleeping off their overnight passage.

When I connect with a new boat, I take them for a walk in town and show them where the stores and open market are. The people here are very friendly and open. For example, the second time I showed up at the vegetable stand in the open market, the woman behind the counter recognized me and greeted me with a big smile. Her face just lights up with a big smile as soon as she sees me whether I buy anything or not. We chat a bit in my awful Spanish and it is very nice. I always take new people to meet her.

I spent yesterday morning finishing up the sanding on the pilothouse table trim and got a sealing coat of varnish on. Then I broke out the Hookah and dove on *Jenny's* bottom again. My goodness, it was infested with baby barnacles. It took until I turned blue from the cold to do one side and her propeller area. I bought a three-millimeter shorty suit when in San Francisco and it is just too light. I should have bought a five-millimeter suit and a hood. I am surprised the water here is so cool. This morning I put another coat of varnish on the table and went diving again. I got *Jenny's* other side done and went after *The Beast*. Its bottom is just coming apart. It looks like a dead animal rotting in the water with all its skin is falling off. It was growing baby barnacles too. I think it is getting ready for a part in a horror flick.

Open market, Samana

Whenever I am scraping barnacles, a shoal of small fish comes to feed. Today the water was clear enough to see the second tier of larger fish swimming around and I even caught sight of something about three feet long. Probably a barracuda.

The weather is not cooperating with a departure this week, so it looks like I will be here yet another. No complaints though. It is a nice place to hang. I will change the oil in *Jenny's* genset and dive on her bottom again before leaving.

New plans and directions are kind of taking form in my mind about the near future. I found a small used motorcycle that weighs only 300 pounds and can be lifted up beside the dinghy and tied down. It is a road and dirt capable bike that I can use for basic transportation in the States and to visit the kids and family. But it is also capable of adventure touring on the less-than-perfect roads in Mexico and Central America. That would be fun. If I can get one, I might head down to Mexico's Isla Mujeres and tether *Jenny* there for a while I do some inland touring. Sounds like a nice adventure if I can pull it off.

For now, the plan is still to get to Brunswick GA and hang around that area until November. Then I will head down around the keys and up to the Sarasota and Tampa areas for Thanksgiving and Christmas to visit the kids and Mom. There are enough boat projects to keep me busy until then. Except for the refrigerator, they are not big and I just need a West Marine store handy.

Tuesday, April 21, 2009 3:37:40 PM

Location: Santa Barbara de Samana

As of yesterday, the weather did not look good for heading up to the Bahamas for several days. However, this morning it showed a nice three-day window. The scramble is on. Getting two things running at the same time here is often difficult. For a couple of days, the ATMs were down and I needed to fill the gas cans for the dinghy. Last night, I found an ATM that worked and got some money. This morning the electricity at the gas pump was out. I hailed a moto rickshaw and off I went. I had to do this anyway since I needed to pick up a couple of cases of Coke at the open market and they were too heavy to carry.

I got the gas and I got the Coke and some vegetables and headed back to *Jenny* with the first load. Then I went in to the grocery store and loaded up on chicken and burger. The burger here is pretty good; just a little more gamey than US beef. I picked up butter, milk, eggs, bread, lunchmeat, etc. and headed back to *Jenny* with another load. Then I printed off my crew list of one and some copies of *Jenny*'s documentation and headed to the Commandants office to get my Zarpe for the Bahamas and clear out.

The Zarpe was typed out by a woman who was clearly queen of the office. Her skills seemed limited to one finger typing. While periodically pecking away at my Zarpe, she entertained several military folks and one of her girlfriends with whom she shared the morning gossip, hand cream and the latest magazine. Yes, it all works very informally here. Eventually she finished pecking at the primitive one page form and collected my 700 pesos ($20). But the port captain who needed to sign it was behind a closed door. I had to wait. And I did. In just over an hour, I was done.

I bought a 2002 Kawasaki Super Sherpa motorcycle on eBay last night. It is all set up for adventure biking and is perfect for my needs. The guy is holding the bike in Michigan for me to pick it up in June. I will fly in and then drive it down to Derek's if they are still in Tennessee, then to my cousin Chris's in Atlanta and then to Laura's in Florida where I will get it registered. I will also get my Florida driver's license and claim Florida residency. Then I will be all set with transportation. The bike weighs 300 lbs. and will load onto *Jenny*'s roof easily from a dock.

I have told many people the story of Bruce Van Sant, a guy I worked with at IBM in Florida in the early 1980's. He had a nice sailboat and Swedish wife at the time who invited my wife and me out on a few times in the Gulf. He believed he was dying from Agent Orange exposure he got during the Vietnam War and worked on IBM to give him a medical discharge. His plan was to sail to the Dominican Republic, buy a brothel in Santo Domingo and live the good life. One day he disappeared and I never knew quite how the story worked out. While preparing for this trip, I came across a highly recommended cruising guide to the Caribbean written by Bruce Van Sant. Hmmmm... I could not verify whether it was him or not because there were no photos or email address. I just wondered.

Well, last night I had two couples over for drinks and one brought a second book by Bruce Van Sant. I told the story again and he said there was a photo in this second book. Well, son of a gun. It is him!!! My guest had met him and said he is living the good life over in Luperon with a lovely young wife and had been there for many years. Unfortunately his health is now failing, skin cancer and congestive heart failure. It seems like Agent Orange may indeed be killing him. I am sad to say that I will be skipping Luperon, as it would be fun to have some beers with him.

Nicholas and I are all packed and ready to go and *Jenny* is ready to take us. I will keep in touch via the SSB.

BOOK 8: HEADING HOME

"It has always seemed strange to me," said Doc. "The things we admire in men, kindness and generosity, openness, honesty, understanding and feeling are the concomitants of failure in our system. And those traits we detest, sharpness, greed, acquisitiveness, meanness, egotism and self-interest are the traits of success. And while men admire the quality of the first they love the produce of the second."

John Steinbeck
Cannery Row, 1945

Passage: Dominican Republic to Turks

Departed Wednesday, April 22, 2009 at 4:58 AM local time from Santa Barbara de Samana. The departure location was latitude 19 degrees 11.937 minutes north, longitude 69 degrees 19.803 minutes west.

Wednesday, April 22, 2009 6:00:04 PM
Location: At sea
Latitude is 20 degrees 3.76 minutes north.
Longitude is 70 degrees 1.926 minutes west.

This weather observation was taken on Thursday, April 23, 2009 5:53:38 AM local time.
Observation location: At Sea.
Latitude is 20 degrees 47.752 minutes north.
Longitude is 71 degrees 9.849 minutes west.
The air temperature is 77, and water temperature is 0 degrees Fahrenheit.
The forecast is Rain Showers.
The current weather is dry.

The sky is overcast (more than 90% clouds).
The wind is fifteen knots from the east.
The visibility is 5 nautical miles.
The wave height is 1 feet with 4 foot swells.
The barometer is 1022 millibar and falling.

The sun is setting now on a perfectly nice passage day. Nicholas and I got up at 05:00 to begin the day. It takes about an hour to wake *Jenny* up, get her ready and raise her anchor, especially when her chain is muddy. I put *The Beast* up last night strapped it down. This morning it still took an hour.

Jenny released her grip in the mud and left at daybreak in an utterly calm harbor filled with smoke from the garbage fires of the night. The sky was overcast and would soon deliver rain, washing the smoke into the sea. A cruise ship was coming in for a day of rest while its passengers were ferried to and from the local shops and attractions. *Jenny* had to go out and around the end of the peninsula and then northeast along it for a while. I could see a curtain of rain sitting there and so was the usual effect of the swell breaking on the shore and echoing back in unhappy discordant waves. It rained gently and nicely washed the salt from *Jenny's* decks.

Once free of land, *Jenny* claimed the helm took us out to sea. She is a natural in her element. The sea settled down to its forecast size and direction. My, it is nice to have the wind, the waves and the current behind us pushing us along. *Jenny* was seeing seven plus knots with JD beating at 1400 RPM. We are enjoying this. Nicholas was even frisky enough to scare up a couple of his favorite games with me.

About forty miles into the trip *Jenny* merged with two sailboats having the same idea. They started about the same time from Puerto Rico and we seem to be heading for the same island. Since the wind is pretty much right on our tails, they are jibing back and forth to keep wind on their sides a little. That is making *Jenny* a little faster toward the island and they are falling back now. I talked to one guy a little but he did not seem to be interested much in chatting.

Jenny's birds are down in beautiful cobalt blue water again. The rigging upgrades have worked fine and they are cutting a line of luminescence through the water. Occasionally a bird will hit a jellyfish and there will be an explosion of light. It is time to rig for night running and get some dinner. It is going to be Hormel Chili tonight.

Thursday, April 23, 2009 6:03:37 AM

Location: At Sea
Latitude is 20 degrees 47.817 minutes north.
Longitude is 71 degrees 10.05 minutes west.

This weather observation was taken on Thursday, April 23, 2009 5:53:38 AM local time.
Observation location: At Sea.
Latitude is 20 degrees 47.752 minutes north.
Longitude is 71 degrees 9.849 minutes west.
The air temperature is 77, and water temperature is 0 degrees Fahrenheit.
The forecast is Rain Showers.
The current weather is dry.
The sky is overcast (more than 90% clouds).
The wind is fifteen knots from the east.
The visibility is 5 nautical miles.
The wave height is 1 feet with 4 foot swells.
The barometer is 1022 millibar and falling.

Jenny carried Nicholas and me through another night at sea. With the wind and wave pushing us along we made good time and she was comfortable. I pulled out the pilot berth to make it wider and more comfortable since it was only Nicholas and me on the bridge. Then Nicholas wanted up. I tried it but he wanted to snuggle too much. He went down to the seat cushion.

Jenny's route has two possible stopping points. One is Big Sand Key, due south of the Caicos banks and the other further up the west side of the banks. At 04:00 I decided we had enough time to get into the second anchorage before dark and altered course. I also increased JD's beat by 100 RPM just to be sure. Now we are due to be at the final waypoint at 17:30. The west anchorage is also a better spot for the next couple of days since the wind will be backing around to the east-northeast and it is protected from all points east. The southern anchorage is not well protected from any action from the north.

A line of rain showers is coming at *Jenny* from about eight miles out. This will be her first Bahamas squall that the sailboats worry about. Sailboats worry about their sails being improperly set for the blasts of wind these squalls deliver and getting them torn up. They also worry about getting their caregivers soaked and cold in their cockpit as they manage the ever-changing situation. *Jenny* holds an impassive fascination for the fury, secure in her strength and knowledge that Nicholas and I are safe and dry inside.

Arrived Thursday, April 23, 2009 at 6:04 PM local time at French Cay. The arrival location was latitude 21 degrees 30.047 minutes north, longitude 72 degrees 12.128 minutes west. The customs check in was Boarded by Turks. The trip covered 240.40 nautical miles in 1d 13h 5m with an average speed of 6.50 knots and a maximum speed of 7.70 knots.

Passage: French Cay to Mayaguana

Departed Friday, April 24, 2009 at 5:29 AM local time from French Cay Anchor. The departure location was latitude 21 degrees 29.229 minutes north, longitude 72 degrees 13.347 minutes west.

Friday, April 24, 2009 7:33:13 AM
Location: At Sea
Latitude is 21 degrees 34.818 minutes north.
Longitude is 72 degrees 22.884 minutes west.

This weather observation was taken on Friday, April 24, 2009 6:15:43 PM local time.
Observation location: Mayaguana, Bahamas.
Latitude is 22 degrees 20.653 minutes north.
Longitude is 73 degrees 4.726 minutes west.
The air temperature is 73, and water temperature is 0 degrees Fahrenheit.
The forecast is Windy, squalls.
The current weather is dry.
The sky is scattered clouds (10 - 50% clouds).
The wind is 20 knots from the northeast.
The visibility is 10 nautical miles.
The wave height is 0 feet with 3 foot swells.
The barometer is 1024 millibar and rising.

The squall was powerful. *Jenny* saw wind up in the twenty-five to thirty knot range for about an hour and seas built to about five feet at five seconds. She handled it with the grace given to powerful athletes. I enjoyed the ride, safe in her arms. After that, *Jenny* was pretty much in the lee of the Caicos banks reef system and had only two to three foot wind waves pushing her along. We arrived at French Cay at 17:00 with plenty of time to get situated and anchored. At least I thought we did.

As I was getting *Jenny's* birds up I noticed an official looking PT type boat in the distance start heading my way. Oh boy. I was just about to unpin the anchor and get positioned to drop it when they got close enough to call. It was the usual stuff. "Where was your last port of call, where is your next port of call?" I told them and asked if I could anchor here for the night since French Cay is a bird sanctuary. They told me to go to channel fifteen and I did. Nothing heard. A few minutes later they cranked up their motors again and came closer indicating they wanted to talk on the radio. OK. I called them on fifteen and got no response. I went back to sixteen and apologized for being on fifteen as instructed.

They asked a second time, "Where was your last port of call, where is your next port of call?" I guess they had some kind of memory impairment. I told them again. They then asked what the rigging was. Oh boy. I explained that the rigging was for stabilization. They said: "Gee we thought you were a fishing boat. Is your boat a commercial boat or a pleasure boat?" Maybe they were having difficulty with English. I explained again that *Jenny* was a motor yacht, a pleasure boat. Then they asked a third time "where was your last port of call, where is your next?" Hmmmm....

After asking about guns, drugs, cargo, they decided they needed board us. So, here comes this PT boat with a nice heavy duty stainless steel anchor pulpit sticking a foot out its bow. It was all bent up, probably at the expense of other vessels they had boarded. They wanted me to raise *Jenny's* port outrigger so they could board. OK. I did. Then they came in, bow first at the stern having finally figured out they could not board on her port side since there is no walkway on that side. I could see these were real thinkers.

With four men working fenders and feet to keep the battering ram from hitting *Jenny*, two oversized military booted officers were safely onboard. They took copies of *Jenny's* documentation and my passport but had no interest in my Zarpe from the Dominican Republic. Then they wanted to search *Jenny*. I led them through and they peered in closets and the washer/dryer for whatever. As they were leaving, the guy in charge asked again about guns. I again said "none". Then he said I should have a gun onboard since it is dangerous here. Hmmmm. That was the first time any representative from any government suggested I should be carrying weapons. Nice place.

Then we did the battering ram dance again, this time bow to bow. Just as the "guy in charge" was leaving, he said he would be back in the morning to make sure I was gone. I said, "Tomorrow might be bad weather". He said, "Then you will have to come inside the reef and check in". Well, if the weather is bad for continuing up to Mayaguana Bahamas, then what makes him think I want to go over shallow banks for the first time in the same? As they pulled away, with the sun almost set, they suggested I go around to the west side of the island, "It's more protected." "It's shallow, but you can do it." Yea. Like I am going to go over unknown shallow reefs in the dark!

This was the most unwelcome reception I have received in this entire journey. These guys were clearly unfriendly and could not care less about my health and safety or impression of the Turks and Caicos that they represented. I am bypassing them this trip. They could have done much to make me want to stop next time instead of the opposite.

After that unwelcome visit, I got *Jenny's* anchor down, the birds nested and the flopper stoppers deployed. I made some soup for dinner and crashed around 20:00 after looking hard at the weather.

I am glad I jumped on the weather window made it all the way to French Cay over the past two days. The people who stayed in the Dominican Republic and Puerto Rico are stuck there for at least another week. And tonight we will be in the Bahamas!!!

I got up at 04:15 for an early start on a 73 mile trip up to Mayguana, the first of the Bahamas islands I will stop at. I expect *Jenny* to be slammed today. The wind and waves will be on her nose, plus squalls. However, the good news is that the slamming is less than it would be any time after today for at least a week. I will ask *Jenny* to take her licks today, get to a much better protected anchorage and stay there until the weather gets nice again.

Arrived Friday, April 24, 2009 at 5:24 PM local time at Mayaguana, Bahamas. The arrival location was latitude 22 degrees 20.645 minutes north, longitude 73 degrees 4.727 minutes west. The customs check in was None. The trip covered 71.50 nautical miles in 0d 11h 14m with an average speed of 6.40 knots and a maximum speed of 6.60 knots.

Friday, April 24, 2009 6:16:04 PM

Location: Mayaguana Island, Bahamas
Latitude is 22 degrees 20.651 minutes north.
Longitude is 73 degrees 4.725 minutes west.

I am always amazed that in a day or two I can have my home in a completely new country with completely different water, weather, people, language, customs, etc. It is kind of magical.

I was surprised by how easy today was. The wind and waves were much lower than forecast and they were from the east instead of northeast. *Jenny* had some beam and following seas and wind. None was very bad. Maybe four foot waves at best. There were rainsqualls here and there, but she went between all of them. It was a good choice to go. I did not see another boat and none are here to buddy up with *Jenny*. I wonder where all the cruisers are hiding.

The wind and waves are supposed to get very strong tonight and be so for several days. Just like this.

		WIND			SEAS		
Date	Hour	Dir	Deg	Range (kt)	Dir	Per	Range(ft)
4/25	01	ENE	77	16-22	ENE	6	6-10
4/25	07	ENE	69	16-22	ENE	6	6-10
4/25	13	ENE	71	19-26	ENE	6	7-11
4/25	19	ENE	70	20-27	ENE	7	8-13

We are well protected here from the north and east. *Jenny* is nicely anchored and will remain here for several days. It will be good to have a break.

All *Jenny's* gear is running great. I am finally completely satisfied with her stabilizer rigging. It does everything well. Mary brought down the final ingredients. I will update the web site with new photos when I get an internet connection again. I also really like the Magma flopper stoppers. I used them last night and was glad to have them.

Here, the wind is coming off the beach, but some residual swell is coming in around the corner and running down the beach. If *Jenny* was anchored normally, she would have this three foot swell directly on her beam, and her flopper stoppers would be overwhelmed. For the first time I rigged *Jenny* in a bridle. One chain hook runs to *Jenny's* port bow and the other runs to her port hawse by the pilothouse door. Each has the same amount of line. Her anchor is holding *Jenny* by the side and parallel to the beach. This is so effective that I have only one flopper stopper out now to take care of any small waves coming at her port side.

Considerations: I am close enough to the beach that there are no wind waves. The wind will be from the same direction for days and here, in the protection of the bay, will not get above ten knots. I feel comfortable about lying side to the wind.

Nicholas has been a good boy. He was somewhat less happy today than yesterday since *Jenny* was a little more active. Nevertheless, he still came over to play and snuggle. He will be happy to stop for a while, but unhappy about being on *Jenny* all day.

Sunday, April 26, 2009 7:14:53 AM

Location: Mayaguana, Bahamas

Sorry for all the technical stuff, but this is what it is like: a constant struggle against the elements. Nicholas and I had a good night sleep after another frantic beginning. I thought *Jenny's* port hawse by the pilothouse door did not have enough leverage to keep her bow into the waves. Yesterday morning I modified it by taking her port chain hook line back to the cockpit. That worked all day, *Jenny* was lying about 90 degrees to the wind with her bow into the swell, and it was very comfortable. The wind was gusting up to thirty knots and all was holding together. *Jenny* is sitting on a nice shelf of sand and coral about 300 yards wide and thirty feet deep. Off her port side is the beach and off her other is a cliff that drops to 600 plus feet. The water is crystal clear. Needless to say, I am monitoring the situation closely.

Last night the wind died down and shifted. I used JD to kick *Jenny's* stern further into the waves and all of a sudden she decided to turn through the wind. In a flash the wind was on the wrong side of *Jenny* and she was fully beam to the waves. JD pushed her forward just enough to tighten her bowline and that pulled her through the eye of the wind. It was getting dark of course. UGH

As I tried to recover, I lost her port side chain hook line over the side. I was furious at myself for not making sure one end was secure to *Jenny* and still am. I rigged the anchor with the remaining chain hook leading to the port hawse by *Jenny's* pilothouse and just used her anchor chain off the bow. This puts some side pressure on the bow roller, but most of the tension is on the chain hook line.

I also determined quickly that the Magma flopper stoppers are far too powerful to be run to the end of *Jenny's* outriggers. It is not the load itself, it is the shock load that happens when they open and stop the upward movement of the roll. The shock was hitting *Jenny's* mast and the rest of her rigging too hard. I took them in and used her birds again as flopper stoppers. Yesterday I figured out how to rig her flopper stoppers to run from the V joint on the boom closer to her sides. So, I did. But even though they are only about six feet out from her sides now, the shock load was still bending her outrigger too much. Finally, I took her running backstays and ran them to the same shackle that the Magma is attached to and pulled the line taught. That caused the shock load to be distributed up to the top of the mast and down the other side and is working better. They are not as powerful as they were at the end of *Jenny's* outriggers, but they are much more powerful than her birds.

So my day goes. I keep learning more and more. It looks like I will be here today and tomorrow before the weather gets better and I can move on. So far I cannot say the Caribbean or the Bahamas have been good.

Sunday, April 26, 2009 5:39:49 PM

Location: Mayaguana, Bahamas

Today went a little better. After breakfast and cleaning up *Jenny* inside and out, I figured there was a good chance of finding her missing chain hook and line. I broke out my snorkeling gear. The water here is crystal clear to forty feet with a white sand bottom and patches of coral. The line is black and had to be along the path of the anchor chain somewhere.

Nicholas gets extremely worried when I go in the water and leave him all alone on *Jenny*. I am not sure what goes on between them while I am gone. As soon as he saw what was happening he barked at me and had a fit. I tried to reassure him I would be ok. I checked for current and had the boarding ladder out. I also have the bosons chair rigged so I can use it to haul myself back in if I fall over. The wind and waves had calmed down to just about nothing. Over I went.

I had my meat hook fishing rig with me with a heavy fishing weight and treble hook on the end to snare the snubber line if I came across it. And in a matter of a few minutes I did. It was right where I expected it to be, just off of where the anchor chain lay. It was too deep to free dive on, so I lowered the hook and snagged it with ease. I hauled it up and threw it back in *Jenny*. That was good.

Then I went to see how *Jenny's* anchor was lying. It was not dug in. Apparently we are anchored by the chain snared in a coral head. It has held us in gusts to thirty knots so far, so I am going to leave it. There is plenty of sand around the anchor and I feel comfortable if we break free of the coral, it will dig in solid.

The rest of the day went quietly. As usual all the wind and weather change at sunset. We have been getting rain squalls around 17:00 and that kicks up the swell and changes the wind direction a little. The way I have the anchor bridle rigged I just use the anchor winch to fine tune *Jenny's* heading and keep her pointed into the swell as this all happens. By 19:00 all is quiet again.

The forecast is awful for the rest of the week, but getting slightly better on Friday and Saturday. The wind and waves also clock around from the northeast to east and then to east-southeast. This anchorage is not good for east-southeast weather. *Jenny* needs to move early Friday morning and head out into twenty knot winds and six foot chop for a forty mile passage to the next islands called the Plana Cays. There is an anchorage there good for east to southeast winds and waves. We will stay there overnight and then catch the east-southeast weather up to Rum Cay where there is a proper harbor and town.

For now, I am puttering about *Jenny*. Nicholas follows my every move. I finished one book today and will begin another tomorrow. Tonight is movie night, but it will be a repeat since I am out of fresh DVDs.

Monday, April 27, 2009 6:33:25 PM

Location: Mayaguana, Bahamas

A squall is running over *Jenny* now. The wind speed is in the high twenties and the water has kicked up a little. However, *Jenny* is snuggled close to the beach so it cannot kick up much of a fuss. I think the boats in nearby Abrahams Bay are faring worse since the wind gets to whip up the water for a mile or two before it gets to them and it is only six to twelve feet deep. It must be quite a scene.

I have one chain hook, fifty feet of line tied off the port pilothouse hawse, and it is taking almost all the load. I do not know if it was part of *Jenny's* design but that hawse is about where the center of drift is from wind. If just held by that point, *Jenny* will naturally be ninety degrees to the wind. This is very handy. I then use her windless to draw in or let out chain to point her bow into the swell that comes in around the bend in front of us. That keeps us relatively stabile and the flopper stoppers take care of any remaining roll. This configuration is working very well.

The day was pretty quiet with me thinking about the future, reading books, doing email and weather reports, and working on my software. I am tapping into the Microsoft Word spell checker for spell checking narratives. I am sure you have noticed a need!!!

Right now it looks like I will give *Jenny* her freedom early Thursday morning to head on an overnight directly to Georgetown. There seems to be a nice town there and good protection. I will untie and lower *The Beast*, check in and set up to stay a while.

Since diving on the bottom in Samana I have been battling a sinus infection sapping my energy. No doubt that came from the water there. But I think I have beaten it back and with all this rest I am healthy again. We are good to go. I had salad and chicken from the grill tonight and Nicholas got his. We are happy dogs. It is time to take a hot shower, shave and watch another movie.

Tuesday, April 28, 2009 7:08:16 PM

Location: Mayaguana, Bahamas

Nicholas and I are sitting here in the pilothouse with a rum and coke having just had dinner: couscous with curry and a Red Hind (a kind of grouper) that I caught today. A gentile rain is falling outside. We are about to resume watching Charlie's War. We are all alone on *Jenny* but there are other boats within VHF radio distance and we chatted with them a bit today. The sideband email gave us warmth through keeping in touch with friends and family.

I am not sure just how world events and my life will unfold, but I do know now that it is less about the adventure at sea than it is about staying in one place for a while and developing friendships with people who celebrate life together. I have seen many forms of this lifestyle in my travels and while they differ in style, there are places where it forms the center of society, not the edges. It will be interesting to return to the States now and stay in a small community for a while. I need to see if some kernels of this value system still exist there.

For most of us the force behind our departure was to exercise our self-assured superiority; to become brothers with those who preceded us to sea in small boats, and to be with contemporaries who possess the capability, courage, intellect and skills to thrive in the elemental sea. All those I met along the way did and are in that way great to be with.

Many of my cruising friends are at crossroads. Some are returning to the States to reenter the working world. Some are stopped at various places in space and life, trying to understand what essence of living gives them joy and how to move forward. For each now, come choices about the future. Is it to be more self-fulfillment? Is it time to bring joy to others and receive joy in so doing? Some combination of the above? If the latter, then who among all I have encountered should I spend at least some of the rest of my days with? *Astor* brings joy to all that see her and joy to Richard and Lani who are her caretakers. I do not know the secret of *Encore, Beverly S, Diesel Duck* or *Moody Blues*. They seem to have struck some balance.

Wednesday, April 29, 2009 1:03:32 PM

Location: Start Bay, Mayaguana

The activity is picking up here. Vessels are moving around in their stalls ready to be turned loose for the run up to Georgetown. Three came out of Abrahams Bay coral bank and are now anchored near *Jenny* for the early morning start. They are following *Jenny*'s example of using a swell bridle and after a few tries are settling in just fine. *Jenny* is champing in her bridle. The weather for the next two days looks like this:

Date	Hour	WIND Dir	Deg	Range (kt)	SEAS Dir	Per (sec)	Range (ft)
4/30	01	E	84	15-20	E	8	6-10
4/30	07	ENE	73	15-21	E	8	6-9
4/30	13	E	87	17-23	E	8	6-10
4/30	19	E	84	16-22	ENE	7	6-10
5/1	01	E	85	15-21	E	7	6-9
5/1	07	E	81	17-23	E	6	6-10
5/1	13	E	86	15-21	E	7	6-10
5/1	19	E	84	16-21	E	7	6-9

This is not the best weather but all the vessels are ready to leave and in going northeast we will have most of this at our backs. Fortunately the squalls seem to be dying out and more sun is shining. Saturday and Sunday are supposed to be better. If *Jenny* needs to rest along the way then she will still have a good window. It will also give me the ability to check into the Bahamas in Georgetown. Georgetown is the last major stop before Nassau so *Jenny* is getting close to home. I will stay there for a while to get a feeling for the Bahamas and life here. From there I will be able to dayhop in protected water up to Nassau.

My cousin Chris is interested in making the overnight passage from Nassau to Florida with his son. I hope we can coordinate the timing with his work schedule. That would be really great and would argue for doing an extra night to arrive directly into Brunswick. On that passage we will be catching the Gulf Stream and will have a mighty boost going north. It should be cool seeing the lights along the coast of Florida.

Passage: Mayaguana to Georgetown

Departed Thursday, April 30, 2009 at 5:06 AM local time from Start Bay. The departure location was latitude 22 degrees 20.638 minutes north, longitude 73 degrees 4.841 minutes west.

Arrived Friday, May 01, 2009 at 10:57 AM local time at Georgetown. The arrival location was latitude 23 degrees 30.479 minutes north, longitude 75 degrees 45.750 minutes west. The customs check in was Bahamas. The trip covered 180.43 nautical miles in 1d 5h 51m with an average speed of 6.00 knots and a maximum speed of 7.30 knots.

Friday, May 01, 2009 2:44:38 PM

Location: Georgetown, Bahamas
Latitude is 23 degrees 31.067 minutes north.
Longitude is 75 degrees 45.536 minutes west.

Three sailboats and *Jenny* released from the seabed and bolted out of Mayaguana at 05:00 AM yesterday, traveled together, came into Georgetown and set their anchors around noon. It was kind of a typical "good" Caribbean Sea as forecast. The good weather here is uncomfortable but safe. The chop sorely tests *Jenny's* stabilizer system though. The American sailboat in the group caught a Mahi Mahi just coming in and invited us all to dinner. In a little while I will get *The Beast* down.

It looks like the Bahamas in the pictures here. Turquoise water over white sand, a balmy breeze, and a zillion boats. It is very picturesque. Apparently a lot of boats spend the winter here and it is easy to see why. We are anchored by Stocking Island where there appears to be a beach restaurant and a nice beach to walk Nicholas in the morning. I am sure he will be thrilled to get on dry land again. He really gets upset by these passages and is so glad when they are over.

Stocking Island

I am going to try to find out the schedule for *Catching Up* and *Spirit* and see if I can meet them here before proceeding. Otherwise, I will stay here for a couple of weeks and then start working my way northeast again. From here you get in behind one of the continuous coral banks and kind of pick you way from anchorage to anchorage in day hops. It should be nice and easy right up until the last jump to the States.

There are several trawlers of all brands here and I picked a spot among them. It would be nice to meet them and hear their stories. I have to find out if there is Wi-Fi here. That would be nice. Tomorrow I will dinghy across the bay, check into the Bahamas, take in the laundry, and do a little exploring.

Saturday, May 02, 2009 12:20:33 PM

Location: Georgetown

Last night I had a gourmet dinner on board *Kyeta* with Ann and Dennis and the two other sailboats *Dubhe* and *Villomee*. One sailboat was from Spain and the other Quebec. *Kyeta* is from Michigan. Ann put on a full spread and I was ready after eating my own "cooking" for a long time.

I took Nicholas to the beach first thing this morning and he had a ball. He gets to run free and he loves it. I think it is his favorite activity by far. Of course, he gets covered in sand and saltwater, but he has so much fun I cannot stop him. I hose him down in the cockpit when we get back to *Jenny* before she gets upset with him.

Then, after the morning net and breakfast, I headed into town. While this is one of the biggest towns in the Bahamas, I would still classify it as a frontier town. There were a few natives about and the cruisers outnumbered them by about three to one. It was odd being in a grocery store stocked exclusively with US products, from Dole lettuce to Taco Bell salsa. It was very strange and a world apart from the open market in Samana. The people here are nice and it is a beautiful setting. Very much like a super-sized San Blas without any palm trees. But, for me, I could not see staying here for a season. This is only a North American culture transplanted by cruises. I wonder what Nassau is like?

That said; the place is set up very nicely for cruise boats and people. *Jenny* is resting on the east side of the bay under the shelter of Stocking Island. The beach is white sand with posts for tying your dinghy. It has a beach bar and volley ball courts. Further in there is supposed to be a nice restaurant and bar. I will explore that tomorrow. The town has a dinghy dock right behind the grocery store and offers free water. So far, the water has only developed about a one-foot wind chop and no swell. It is comfortable for sure.

This morning sixteen boats left, mostly toward the States. We have a nice wide weather window and tomorrow more are leaving. Two of the trawlers near me left this morning. In any case, Nicholas and I will hang around here for a week or two and then head up toward Nassau.

Thursday, May 07, 2009 10:06:26 AM

Location: Georgetown

This morning I dove on *Jenny's* bottom to get her ready for another move. It was nice and clean, with only a few barnacles that I had probably missed the last time. The propeller was smooth and the Barnacle Buster continues to do its job. However, it is wearing off along the edges.

The last few days have been a little rugged with the divorce sinking in. It is hard to have a bad day in Georgetown, Bahamas, but I am proof that you can. Yesterday was better and I may have bottomed out. I gave Nicholas a shorty haircut yesterday to keep him cool and manage the amount of sand he drags back to *Jenny*. He loves running on the beach, but is a sand magnet.

Tomorrow we have an excellent calm day and plan to go up to Staniel Cay. It is only about fifty-five miles away and we may not even need the birds in the water. There is supposed to be good snorkeling there and a famous blue hole used in the Bond movie Thunderball. I plan to stay there a week or two and really soak up the beauty of this place. I can see why people flock here from the northeast for the winter. As long as you do not need the stimulation of a real city, it is very comfortable and beautiful here.

My cousin Chris and his son Bennett are flying into Nassau on June 3rd to crew for the passage to Brunswick. If the weather that week is like it is this week, we will have a nice three day passage directly there. My friends in *Spirit* and *Catching Up* are still in St. Thomas, and plan to blow through the Bahamas on a direct run to Brunswick. They need to be there by May 22nd so they will be getting in before I do.

Once in Brunswick, I will need to arrange a flight to Detroit to pick up the motorcycle now named *Jasmine* and drive it back to Laura's in Florida. I am in the process of changing my residency to her home and will have the bike registered there. I will visit Chris on the way back and maybe my son Derek too, depending on their move status. They are moving from Nashville Tennessee to Sarasota Florida right around that time. All the kids will be on the west coast of Florida soon.

I have a good book to read and am chilling out. Nicholas is snoozing at my side. All is good.

Passage: Georgetown to Staniel Cay

Departed Friday, May 08, 2009 at 8:00 AM local time from Stocking Harbor, Georgetown. The departure location was latitude 23 degrees 31.908 minutes north, longitude 75 degrees 46.487 minutes west.

Arrived Friday, May 08, 2009 at 4:35 PM local time at Staniel Cay, Big Majors Anchorage. The arrival location was latitude 24 degrees 11.050 minutes north, longitude 76 degrees 27.725 minutes west. The customs check in was none. The trip covered 60.03 nautical miles in 0d 8h 46m with an average speed of 6.80 knots and a maximum speed of 9.60 knots.

Friday, May 08, 2009 5:40:17 PM

Location: Staniel Cay, Big Major Anchorage
Latitude is 24 degrees 11.047 minutes north.
Longitude is 76 degrees 27.731 minutes west.

Jenny took Nicholas and me on another magic carpet ride today. The wind was less than ten knots out of the southeast and the waves were only two to three feet and out of the southeast. She took the helm for the fifty-mile trip to the northwest and glided over deep blue water at seven knots and her birds up. It was beautiful.

At the beginning of the trip, *Jenny* had to negotiate a shallow channel from behind Stocking Island to the open water, and at the end, she made her first trip over the "banks". It was only about ten miles, but unnerving nonetheless. She saw as little as four feet under her keel and she was not happy about it. However, most of the trip was with about eight feet of crystal-clear water under her keel. Fortunately, the sea bottom is flat as a board and gradually rose and sank as we flew over it. There was about ten knots of wind, but the banks kept the waves to nothing. In addition, having good charts was comforting. The Explorer Charts are the bible here and Maptech incorporated all the routes and waypoints in their chart package. That took a lot of worry away.

I dragged a meat hook but only caught Sargasso weed. It builds on *Jenny's* birds too, but is a much better problem to have than kelp. Nicholas slept for almost the whole trip. I dozed and read my book.

This morning was some disturbing news on the VHF. Yesterday I heard a frantic Mayday call almost incomprehensible because the person was so frantic. I understood a few words about someone onboard in serious trouble. Later I overheard a few words about a shark bite. Well this morning I heard the scoop. A guy was snorkeling off one of the islands near Georgetown and a bull shark took his forearm. Nasty! The locals went shark hunting today.

There are two other Nordhavns here. One is Ralph Neeley's *Knot Yet II*, another Nordhavn 46 with San Francisco as their hailing port. The other is a 62 with their hailing port as Andover MA. I will check them out tomorrow.

The anchorage has a nice sand bluff on the north, east and southeast sides for protection from wind and waves. It is very quiet here. The temperature really gets nice here after the sun goes down and sleeping is very comfortable. There are no bugs. *Jenny* is anchored in twelve feet of clear water. Bob and Linda on *Villomee* are coming over in a few minutes. They have a Benetau 473 and are interested in St. Marys GA as a potential place to settle. He is a motorcycle rider so we will have plenty to talk about.

Passage: Staniel Cay to Highborne Cay

Departed Sunday, May 10, 2009 at 8:30 AM local time from Big Majors Anchorage. The departure location was latitude 24 degrees 11.033 minutes north, longitude 76 degrees 28.400 minutes west.

Arrived Sunday, May 10, 2009 at 2:48 PM local time at Highborne Cay. The arrival location was latitude 24 degrees 42.993 minutes north, longitude 76 degrees 49.905 minutes west. The customs check in was none. The trip covered

42.51 nautical miles in 0d 6h 16m with an average speed of 6.80 knots and a maximum speed of 7.20 knots.

Sunday, May 10, 2009 3:07:35 PM

Location: Highborne Cay
Latitude is 24 degrees 42.991 minutes north.
Longitude is 76 degrees 49.91 minutes west.

Nicholas and I decided we had enough of Staniel Cay and hauled anchor this morning. We went another forty-five miles northeast up to Highborne Cay to try to find a spot to settle in for a while. Cruising here is a breeze. We motored with ten feet of water under the keel almost the whole time and were surrounded by pleasure boats going north and south. There was a lot of VHF chatter on the radio and it felt like it was almost crowded. This is very different from the rest of *Jenny's* journey where we were all alone with no safety net. These vessels have it good.

We just arrived at Highborne Cay and found a real nice quiet spot off a nice big sandy beach. Nicholas will love it. The water was mostly emerald green the whole trip but the anchorage is kind of clear lime green. It is very pretty. There is a marina here and a general store around the corner. This might be where we hang out for a couple of weeks before heading back to the States. That said; Nicholas and I are getting anxious to get back and start some new adventures.

Monday, May 11, 2009 8:24:09 AM

Location: Highborne Cay

I had a nice time on *South by West*, the Nordhavn 55 anchored behind me. They are Americans of French origin. He was in Vietnam as a boy before Dien Bien Phu and she grew up in Algeria. They also have an American couple on board as guests. We had a couple of drinks and then a lively world political discussion. It was fun and great to get their insights and perspective. Their new 55 is a palace compared to *Jenny*. Weighing in at 115,000 pounds, it is enormous with a basement, two stories of indoor living and a fly bridge on the third. You can get a nosebleed on the fly bridge. I was fortunate to meet them and be invited over.

This is a nice anchorage. The water is clear and relatively deep close to the beach. You can snuggle up and have calm water. The beach is virgin and a great place for Nicholas to have his morning and evening runs. He is a happy boy.

It got a little crowded here in the last eighteen hours. First *South by West* pulled in behind us. Then a mega yacht *Elisa* anchored on *Jenny's* port side and this morning an even bigger mega yacht *Vava* anchored off *Jenny's* port stern. It must be 200 ft long. This seems to be the home of powerboats of all flavors.

The chart shows three rock patches in this area, two of which are clearly visible. The third is supposed to be behind me somewhere, but I could not find it with *The Beast*. I did spot what might be it right off the bow of *Elisa*, but it should be more like right under *Vava*. Maybe it is a chart error... I expect *Villomee* to arrive today too and there are a couple of other sailboats here. *Villomee* has a nice couple and good to chat with.

I think I will clean windows today and try to get rid of some rust spots. Then do some routine maintenance. Tomorrow I will break out the sandpaper and start on some more windows.

Tuesday, May 12, 2009 11:43:20 AM

Location: Highborne Cay

Well, here I am, all alone with Nicholas. I have not had an inbound email in days. I am beginning to understand how cruisers end up living their days out in some forgotten port where they manage to feel welcome and can contribute to the happiness of the local population even with meager means. Someplace where an extended family can be formed and age is honored instead of being considered a contagious disease. That is what I felt in Cartagena. As I left, the net announced that they would be many people missing me and that I had made a lot of friends and people happy. Maybe that is where I belong. I guess that is the question: Where do I belong? Where can I find joy and happiness and give the same?

Maybe the dull pain of loneliness is the loss of Mary. I am sure that is a big part of it, but she has been gone for over nine months now. I knew she would not be coming back when she left Nicholas and me in Panama. Maybe I am mourning the death of the twenty-year marriage. The isolation in the islands is not good for me just now. All I know is that this is not how I want to be spending these days of my life. Cruising is very isolating and most women do not like it. So, what does that mean?

I wonder what I will find upon my return beyond the pain of prosecuting the divorce. Maybe it is just a case of out-of-sight out-of-mind. Maybe the kids and grandchildren will in fact visit and enjoy time with me onboard *Jenny*. I do not know. However, based upon experience, it there may be a short burst of visiting and then the usual distance.

Maybe I should buy property in Panama or El Salvador and try to become an asset to some people there. I know I do not have enough resources to begin to affect the lives of even the poorest of Americans. However, for the price of a low-end laptop, you can change the lives of an entire family in Colombia. However, that would mean I would rarely if ever see the kids or grandchildren. Maybe that is my fate anyway even if I lived in a home in the Sarasota area.

Maybe I should go back to work and contribute there. Where do I belong? Where will I find and be able to give joy and happiness? I have to answer that question this year, for time is running short.

Passage: Highborne Cay to Nassau

Departed Thursday, May 14, 2009 at 9:25 AM local time from Highborne Cay Anchorage. The departure location was latitude 24 degrees 42.767 minutes north, longitude 76 degrees 50.395 minutes west.

Arrived Thursday, May 14, 2009 at 2:59 PM local time at Nassau Harbor, West Anchorage. The arrival location was latitude 25 degrees 4.837 minutes north, longitude 77 degrees 20.909 minutes west. The customs check in was none. The trip covered 38.08 nautical miles in 0d 5h 38m with an average speed of 6.70 knots and a maximum speed of 7.80 knots.

Thursday, May 14, 2009 6:28:57 PM

Location: Nassau Yacht Anchorage
Latitude is 25 degrees 4.826 minutes north.
Longitude is 77 degrees 20.793 minutes west.

I made a snap decision this morning after looking at the BuoyWeather forecast. It called for winds steadily rising over the next few days to the high twenties and a shift from the east to the south. The Highborne Cay anchorage is well protected from the east and some degrees north or south of east, but not from the southeast through the south. One way or another, I had to move. I consulted with my friends on *Dubhe* and said either we would have to move to the anchorage at the north end of Highborne Cay, or make a break for it. It was too late in the day (08:45 for them to cover the distance. They are in a thirty-five foot sailboat.

Jenny released her grip in the sand and jumped out of the gate in record time. By 09:30 she was underway. This included taking a flopper stopper up, putting it away, and raising *The Beast*. What a team! In the rush, I forgot to close the portholes in her master cabin and head. I would not find out about that until later.

The wind and waves were out of the east with the waves building from two feet into a five-foot wind chop as we glided across the banks. The trip included crossing the Yellow Banks where the usual twenty foot depth dropped to only nine under *Jenny's* keel. She could not use her birds because the water was too shallow, so she really rocked and rolled all the way. She was a mess inside with stuff flying all over the galley.

Nicholas is full share crew now. Once we got into deep (twenty feet) water, I headed to the galley to scramble up some eggs. Suddenly, he came down the stairs and looked at me. He cannot talk, but when he wants something, he stares at either what he wants, or me. I knew he was trying to tell me something. I went up to the wheelhouse and sure enough, *Jenny's* navigation computer alarm was going off. We were back in water less than twenty feet deep. What a team!

As we approached the east end of Nassau, *Jenny's* navigation computer alarm was constantly sounding as we went above and below twenty feet where the alarm is set. Then her CO alarm in the master cabin went off. UGH. That is when I found out about her portholes. Yup, her alarm got wet with saltwater and was going nuts. Water had splashed in all over the master bed. It never fails. One stressor leads to another.

Jenny was following the Explorer Charts route and only had to dodge an obvious coral head once. The route kept at least eighteen feet under *Jenny's* keel until we got close to the Nassau entrance channel. Then according to the chart, it went directly over zero foot coral heads. Which was correct, the route or the chart? It had my complete attention. As it turned out the chart was more accurate than the route at the entrance to the channel. Who knew?

We made it into the channel, called the Nassau Port Control to ask permission to enter and proceed to the anchorage. No problem. We went by some boats anchored at the east end, some in the middle and got to the official Yacht anchorage. No one was there. It is right behind the big cruise boat piers and so has good protection from the east winds. I dropped *Jenny's* hook and kept her instruments on as I went around and cleaned her up. I had to change the master bedding since it got saltwater wet. Nasty! I cleaned up the galley, noted my position on the shore and headed down for a nap.

Well, a peak or two at *Jenny's* overhead depth gauge told me we were dragging and now only had two feet under the keel. It was time to move. I hauled anchor and went back to the middle anchorage. I found out that even though there were not many boats there, the bottom was mottled with shallow areas and the resident boats occupied all the holes. I went back to the Yacht anchorage. This time I dropped *Jenny's* anchor in the ship's turning basin in thirty-five feet of water and backed into the designated area outside the buoys. We have a red buoy off *Jenny's* port stern about 200 ft. This time she is stuck, at least according to my eyeballing the shore, the depth gauge and the GPS. It will still be a restless night.

The weather I ran from has arrived. *Jenny* is just in a better anchorage and a few miles closer to the States. According to the latest Buoy Weather, it will be a week before good wind and waves return. Unfortunately, I have no place to land *The Beast* here. Nicholas and I are stuck onboard. At least I think so. I see one dinghy tied to the big concrete dock ahead. Maybe there is some hope.

The wind is now over twenty knots. I am glad we moved.

Passage: Nassau to Chub Cay

Departed Friday, May 15, 2009 at 10:16 AM local time from Nassau west anchorage. The departure location was latitude 25 degrees 5.938 minutes north, longitude 77 degrees 21.562 minutes west.

Arrived Friday, May 15, 2009 at 3:41 PM local time at Chub Cay. The arrival location was latitude 25 degrees 23.934 minutes north, longitude 77 degrees 50.118 minutes west. The trip covered 33.71 nautical miles in 0d 5h 38m with an average speed of 6.00 knots and a maximum speed of 7.10 knots.

Friday, May 15, 2009 6:02:39 PM

Location: Chub Cay Anchorage
Latitude is 25 degrees 23.937 minutes north.
Longitude is 77 degrees 50.115 minutes west.

I thought we were set this morning. *Jenny's* Rocna anchor held through the night and she had about fifteen feet of water under her. In spite of the wind, we had no waves at all. Cool. I got up casually and was trying to get a free internet connection when the harbor police pulled up for an inspection. Their first words, "You cannot anchor here, this is a turning basin for the ships." I informed them that I was outside of the nearby red buoy and that the chart designated the spot I was in as a Yacht anchorage. "This is not a matter for discussion, you have to move." in a Darth Vader voice. I asked where to? He pointed to the area I first dropped the hook, which was too shallow and another area that had even less water. I explained that to him without effect. Then he and his buddy checked our paperwork and the big guy went through *Jenny* to find whatever he was afraid I was carrying.

After he left, I looked again at the weather and decided *Jenny* could make a run up here to Chub Cay without much trauma, so we did.

The anchorage here at Chub Cay is nowhere near as nice as we had in Nassau. It is a wilderness anchorage and the bottom is too shallow to snuggle up to the beach. *Jenny* sits about ½ miles off the beach with some small wind chop moving us around. I rigged shock absorbers for her flopper stoppers out of bungee cords and have them out. They are back on the ends of her outriggers and are working great. While not perfectly calm, we are comfortable.

The weather calls for wind in the high twenties for several more days. From here, *Jenny* needs to cross the Great Bahamas Bank, sixty miles of shallow water that she must cross with her birds up. I am waiting for a period of two to three days of calm weather. If I get good calm weather, then I will run the sixty miles up to the northwest end of the banks and anchor *Jenny* on them. The anchorage will be wide open to the water from all sides, but on the banks so the waves cannot get too bad. Then Brunswick will be within thirty-six hours and I will weigh anchor in the morning. At least that is my current thinking. Nicholas has his doubts.

Passage: Chub Cay to St Marys

Departed Saturday, May 16, 2009 at 6:57 AM local time from Chub Cay. The departure location was latitude 25 degrees 23.476 minutes north, longitude 77 degrees 53.169 minutes west.

Friday night was tiresome because *Jenny's* anchorage was not well protected and the wind was howling. As I tossed and turned, I thought I would check out the weather report for the banks and Port Canaveral first thing in the morning. This morning I was up at 05:00 and turned around three Buoy Weather reports. SSB email is so important. They were for Great Issac at the west end of the Great Bahamas Bank, Port Canaveral and St. Augustine. They showed reasonable weather through end of day Sunday. However, Monday showed bad weather moving in from the north. I figured I could at least get to Port Canaveral. I woke *Jenny* up. She shook off her hold on the seabed, turned around and headed for the Bahamas Bank. I turned her loose at the helm.

It was down wind and wave from Chub Cay to the beginning channel across the bank. I was hoping we could do this twelve-mile leg with the birds up and was pleasantly surprised when *Jenny* did it in comfort! I saw a sailboat about six miles ahead and made contact with *Excalibur 12*. They were heading across the bank too, only they planned to stop at Biminis for the night. So, off we went on slightly different headings.

The bank was blowing around twenty knots, but because it is only fifteen feet deep most of the time, the waves do not build much. Nicholas and I were comfortable with *Jenny's* birds up for the sixty-mile leg across the bank. *Excalibur 12* called and said they caught a mackerel and a snapper. I threw the meat hook over the side. *Jenny* was doing about 7.5 knots so I did not think we would have much of a chance. But, I was wrong. I landed a three-foot barracuda and got him back in the water without either of us sustaining wounds. I quit fishing.

Jenny on the banks heading home

Going over the reef with ten feet of crystal clear water under the keel is awesome. It is like flying low on a magic carpet. You can see the coral go by in waves of dark and light aqua colors. After a while, you begin to trust the route and stop worrying about ramming into a coral head and sinking.

Sunday, May 17, 2009 12:41:58 PM
Location: At sea off of Port Canaveral
Latitude is 28 degrees 40.889 minutes north.
Longitude is 80 degrees 5.689 minutes west.

Jenny was not about to stop and anchor out here by Great Isaac on the Great Bahamas Bank for the night. She just kept on going. By 18:00 Saturday she was at the Great Isaac lighthouse and I had to get her birds down while she was in the protection of the bank. As soon as she was in thirty feet of water, I dropped them in without a hitch. Then I worried about what kind of seas we were going to experience. *Jenny* had to turn north and cross the end of the Northwest Providence Channel to head up the Gulfstream and get to Canaveral. The first couple of hours were moderately rough as we crossed the Channel but then it settled down and *Jenny* became comfortable being on an ocean again. As she approached her first waypoint off Vero Beach, she started picking up the Gulfstream and speed. Nicholas and I fastened our seatbelts as she gradually accelerated to a consistent ten knots.

The weather and the forecast are good for the next thirty hours. Then a bad weather system is supposed to drop down the coast from the north. *Jenny* is off Port Canaveral now and the weather is so good I have decided to let her keep going. As fate would have it our combination of speed, timing and weather now makes St. Marys our best destination. *Jenny's* navigation computer is saying her current ETA is around 10:00 on Monday. It will be great if we can get there before this storm drops in. My fingers are crossed. All is well onboard. *Jenny* is back in an OCEAN. Yes!!! Nice big rollers, no whitecaps, beautiful weather. I will take an ocean over a sea any day. I am sure she feels the same!

Last night I discovered *Jenny's* starboard navigation light was burned out and replaced the bulb this morning. I also pulled down her Bahamas courtesy flag. I then discovered *Jenny's* primary navigation computer was missing a bunch of charts including the details of St. Marys. I had to copy them across from her secondary.

Jenny is all alone out here except for a couple of sport fishing boats. I saw a few ships, but none nearby. I could have put into Port Canaveral this afternoon, but that would mean a week or two of working our way up the Intercoastal Waterway or going back offshore for another overnight or two. The seas are very nice now, so I calculated routes for St. Augustine and St. Marys. At *Jenny's* current speed she would have to enter St. Augustine in the dark and the entry is a little tricky. I calculate that she can get to the St Marys channel at 08:00 Monday morning if her speed holds. I hoped that would be early enough to avoid the storm coming in. I got another weather report and all is good until sometime Monday morning. Then all hell breaks loose.

Arrived Monday, May 18, 2009 at 11:24 AM local time at St. Marys, GA, USA. The arrival location was latitude 28 degrees 49.406 minutes north, longitude 80 degrees 9.866 minutes west. The customs check in was none yet. The trip covered 258.36 nautical miles in 2d 4h 47m with an average speed of 8.32 knots and a maximum speed of 11.48 knots.

Monday, May 18, 2009 5:36:09 PM

Location: St Marys
Latitude is thirty degrees 43.046 minutes north.
Longitude is 81 degrees 33.083 minutes west.

What a grand finally to this journey!!! The past fifty-two hours (260 miles) were like the last five minutes of a Fourth of July fireworks show. We had everything.

Sunday was a perfect day on the ocean. *Jenny* had deep blue water and a small swell with a long period. As good as it gets. As she steamed north I needed to constantly revise her course because of the pending storm. With all this heads down work and anxiety I got seasick after breakfast. UGH. The motion on *Jenny* was not even uncomfortable! I was mortified. Later in the morning, Nickolas got sick too. I think he was getting really frightened because I was so nervous trying to figure all this out. I felt very bad about having him in this.

The night was good to. At around 04:00 *Jenny* was off Jacksonville and I had to ask two freighters to acknowledge they saw her. They both were very nice and altered course to make sure she had a couple of miles between them.

Then the trouble began. *Jenny's* radar showed a large squall (thunderstorm) building off the coast ahead of her. By 06:00 she was in it and seeing twenty-five knot winds with the seas beginning to build. Then I heard my friend Noel on *Ketching Up* call the Coast Guard to find out about the conditions in the St. Marys channel! It turned out he was only about four miles behind me. How strange to be hooking up with him again after not seeing *Ketching Up* since Cartagena.

The squall kept building and *Jenny's* instruments showed winds just over thirty-five knots. *Ketching Up* reported winds over forty knots. The seas built into fifteen-foot combers running every direction, breaking over *Jenny's* side, and throwing water through window and door cracks. It was uncomfortable. However, *Jenny* had been in this kind of stuff before and I knew nothing bad was going to happen. She is so solid she just shrugged off the punishment and plowed on. She was still at the helm as we approached the long channel leading into St. Marys.

This channel is wide and deep. With forty-five foot depth all the way in, I could keep *Jenny's* birds in the water all the way. Thank you God! It was obvious that I now had to hand steer down the channel and took the wheel from *Jenny*. It was a wild ride. The wind was pushing us south and waves were bashing us on the beam and stern. The water got wild with anger as the seabed crept toward the surface forcing it up into the air. Nicholas puked again.

I lost contact with *Ketching Up* and *Jenny* battled her way down the channel. The wind, rain and spray were so fierce that visibility rapidly dropped to a couple of hundred yards. I was having difficulty seeing the next set of channel buoys. As I went past one set of markers, I could just barely make out the next. The breakwater boulders on the south side of the channel kept closing in on us as they narrowed to the channel's width. My eyes started to fixate on them. The wind and waves wanted to drive *Jenny* onto them and she was in my hands now. It seemed like we were in this for an hour. We finally got inside the breakwaters and into reasonably calm water. Wow!

Now I had to get *Jenny's* birds up before she got into shallow water. I got that done and decided to go up the St Marys River to the town to anchor. It is well sheltered and Nicholas and I could go to town after the storm blew through. I guided *Jenny* up the twisting river, got her anchor dug into good holding with twenty feet under her keel. The wind is howling, but there are no waves or swell. I could play pool on the galley table. After tidying *Jenny* up a little, Nicholas and I crashed. It is only supposed to be fifty-five degrees here tonight! I got up and broke out a blanket. More sleep.

A little later, I heard Ashley, Noel's wife calling him on the radio. When he did not reply I did. She drove down from South Carolina to meet her husband and sent a boat from the marina out to get him. That was nice.

Nicholas and I are going to have a quiet evening, and maybe watch a movie. The weather is supposed to be bad all week, so we will stay here at least until Friday. I think they have a nice Memorial Day celebration here, so we may stay through May 30th. I can take *Jenny* up the Intercoastal to Brunswick from here.

Wednesday, May 20, 2009 11:37:43 AM

Location: St. Marys, GA

Below is the account from Noel on *Ketching Up* about his trip back to the States.

"Hello All. This is the long lost captain Noel. I am alive and well after a good night's sleep in St Mary's, Georgia. It was an exciting final eighteen hours to an otherwise great ten day sail. The weather for the first eight days was perfect, sunny warm and breezy. The seas were behind me at six to eight feet the wind fifteen to twenty-five knots off the starboard quarter. I was sailing under Genoa, reefed main and full mizzen. I really did not even need to touch the sails for the first three days. Perfect! I made great time and entered the Gulf Stream through the Northwest Providence Channel on Saturday morning.

The only real adventure in the first seven days was when Genoa head blew out in twenty-five knots of wind. I was able to get it down and lash it to the deck without any real difficulty, but was now without a headsail. When I called Ashley from about ten miles off West Palm Beach on Saturday morning, things could not have been better. The winds were ten to fifteen knots out of the southeast and the Gulfstream was running at 3.5 knots. As soon as I hung up with Ashley I headed straight back out to about fifteen miles off shore and was making about ten knots over ground. The way the east coast curves and the gulf stream runs, the rhomb line from West Palm Beach to Charleston where I intended to check back into the US, takes you about 120 miles offshore.

It should have taken me about three days to sail to Charleston, check in and then sail the last night up to Little River; everything going according to plan. On Sunday morning at about 04:30 I was about eighty miles offshore and winds had dropped to less than five knots. The sails were slating back and forth making an ungodly amount of noise. I got up and pulled down the sails and raised the spinnaker. I sailed all day Sunday without ever touching the spinnaker. Ketching Up was only making about three knots through the water but with the current were averaging about 6.5 knots over ground; nothing to complain about. Being a sailor, I was having my evening Rum and Coke and trying to decide whether to bring the spinnaker down. So I turned on NOAA radio to listen to evening forecast. I was surprised when I heard that there was a gale warning issued, that seas were building to more than twenty feet. I had been listening to the forecast a couple of times a day, but the reports are local, not the full coast. So I had no warning this was coming. The reception was poor that far offshore, I was not able to hear it clearly and had no idea how far north or east the weather would reach. I was now about 100 miles offshore and needed to get out of the way of the weather, but was not sure which direction to head. It did not take long to determine the best course was to duck and run for cover.

I dropped the spinnaker, and fired up the engine for the first time in over a thousand miles. Ketching Up ran at full speed for St Marys Georgia. By 01:00 we were out of the Gulfstream and the worst of the potential risk. The weather was fine during the night but by 04:00 was blowing forty knots from the Northeast. Luckily I was out of the Gulfstream where seas were likely already twelve feet and very steep. It took sixteen hours to reach the harbor entrance the last four hours were very rough, not dangerous, but no fun. Waves were washing over the deck from the side. "Black Max" our on deck generator was ripped free from its tie down, breaking the hatch glass over the aft stateroom. Waves in the channel entrance were coming into the cockpit soaking everything.

We made it into the harbor around 11:00 and immediately everything settled down. Ketching Up is anchored off the town of St. Marys with M/V Jenny. I have a days' worth of repair work to do once the weather clears. When the forecast is good all the way up to Little River, we will head out and finish the trip. I hope we will be in our slip by Tuesday next week. Thanks for all you interest in my little adventure!"

Noel

Wednesday, May 20, 2009 11:51:43 AM

Location: St. Marys, GA

Nicholas and I have been sleeping well and staying on board while the gale, now in its third day, blows itself out. Fortunately, the anchorage here is very good. I have a good free internet connection on *Jenny* through *Jenny's* Port Networks box and high gain antenna. So, I have been taking care of a bunch of tasks necessary to get re-established in the States. I am set to fly up to Detroit on the tenth to pick up the motorcycle *Jasmine* and start driving her back to Florida where I will register her. I hope to stop at son Derek's and cousin Chris's on the way back. I will stay at Laura's while in FL and get my residence change completed. I will also go over, visit mom, and see how she is doing.

I do not have a cell phone yet. The nearest cell store is over in Fernandina so I will need some wheels to get there. I might have a ride from a fellow boater who lives over there and has been following *Jenny's* journey. I hope that this weather will begin to clear tonight and let us get *The Beast* down and to shore. It really is not supposed to be nice until Monday though. I talked on the radio with the folks on the next boat over. They are locals and related that this is very unusual weather. They are on a mooring and came to *Jenny* to make sure we were OK through all this. They also warned against going on the ICW over Memorial weekend because of all the drunken crazies that will be out. They are heading up to the Chesapeake for the summer, but not until after the Memorial Weekend is over.

Meanwhile, I shut down the water maker and pickled it. I need some fresh DVDs though. The onboard TV is worthless because of the digital conversion that happened over the years I was out of country. I have seen all the DVDs onboard a hundred times! Oh well.

I want to thank all the people who have written and welcomed Nicholas and me back to the States. It is very nice to know you are all out there and care.

Dan on *Spirit* left St. Thomas with *Catching Up*. He had one crew on board to help with the multi-day passage back to the States. While *Catching Up* and *Jenny* were now safely anchored, *Spirit* was still slugging it out in this gale. Here is his account of his trip back to the States.

"We had a great sail the first two days, flying the spinnaker and making anywhere between seven and nine knots over ground. As we went around the top of the Bahamas, the weather changed rather abruptly and the seas began to build. Within minutes, it was blowing thirty knots with twenty-foot seas. Not too bad but rather just wet and cold. During the night we had gusts probably hitting forty knots. At this point we were talking to the Coast Guard and asking for weather updates. Over the course of three days of complete hell, for lack of better words, they repeatedly told us that the gale would pass in about eight to twelve hours. When we got this first update, we decided to keep going. We had two options; stop in the Bahamas, or head for Florida. Both options were at least eight to ten hours away so we decided to stay out in the gale.

If we knew at that time that the gale would last three days, we definitely would have popped in somewhere and anchored. But like I said, every time we spoke to our Coast Guard friends, they told us eight more hours. Let's just hope they can sail boats and fly choppers better than they can read weather!

About four hours after the Coast Guard told us the weather was going to die down, we had sixty-five knots in the middle of the night! We got pooped three times over about fifteen hours. Pooped is when a wave breaks into your cockpit. It filled the cockpit up to the top, once causing three cushions to float overboard. I quickly found out that teak floor grates float as well. I was out there in sixty-five knot winds in waste deep water trying to keep the cushions and floor grates onboard. It took a very long ten minutes for the cockpit to drain each time.

The following morning, I had about a two-foot tear in the mainsail at the batten pocket. Also, the UV cover on the jib started to tear and fray simply from the wind and rain hitting it. Since the sail is old anyway, I plan on pealing the UV cover off the jib and fixing the main. New sails will be on order as soon as I get some funds. Arun at my old place of work in St Thomas said he'd give me a deal. Anyway, after the weather passed, we had a great final day as we approached Brunswick Georgia.

We reached the Brunswick channel markers at 03:00. I wanted to stay out until morning but Sean my crew wanted to go in. I thought about it and decided that I was ok with heading in as the channel is very well marked. Right about then an alarm went off and said that our batteries were low. I quickly looked down and noticed that although the engine was running, the tachometer was not which usually meant we had no alternator. This happened before and I simply turned off the engine, fired it back up and the alternator worked. Well, I killed the engine and tried to restart but remembered the low batteries too late! Oops. We thought about sailing in but then the wind died of course. Now we were true sailors with no wind and no motor. We sailed for about ½ hour and went approximately 300 yards. Once we cleared the channel, we dropped the anchor manually since we had no power for the windlass. The plan was turn everything off and wait for the sun to come up. The solar panels would charge the batteries and we could then fire up the engine.

Finally, something went right and the sun broke at 06:00 and at 09:00 we turned the engine over and were on our way in. About ½ the way in the engine started to sputter. I quickly switched over to the backup Racor and she settle down. About an hour later, in the middle of the channel, it sputtered again. I had Sean aim for the beach to get us out of the channel. As soon as got clear of the channel and had about thirty' of water, I dropped the anchor. As the anchor was paying out the engine died! Can you say perfect timing! Once again, we had no engine and no wind. I went down below and started the process of changing filters and bleeding the engine. About forty-five minutes later she fired up and we were once again underway. The marina at this point was laughing at us. It took us about eighteen hours to cover the last four miles of the trip.

Anyway, we finally got in, tied up and proceeded to drink, a lot. Sean flew home today (5/29) and I am back to the regular routine and going to the club house to search for some jobs online. This is a safe spot to leave Spirit so if I can find anything, I will simply leave her here and go work. Otherwise, I may head up to Wilmington next month."

Dan Kinkead

Thursday, May 21, 2009 11:26:29 AM

Location: St. Marys GA

The sun peaked through the clouds for a few minutes today and the wind died. I untied *The Beast* and put it in the water. Nicholas and I went for a long walk on shore. It was GOOD. We both needed it badly. Walking along lanes with regular grass, deciduous trees, familiar weeds, and American style homes was a real treat. It gave me a boost and Nicholas was really smiling.

Joe who lives nearby in Fernandina Beach and following *Jenny's* Journey has been great. He contacted me via email as soon as I arrived and is picking me up at noon to go shopping. It is a very nice offer as he is coming from Fernandina Beach and we have to go all the way back there to get to the AT&T cell store. We are also stopping at Publix to pick up some box-o-meals, dairy products, beer etc. On the way, I will ask him to pull over at the first Burger King so I can indulge in some junk food. Yum...

I realized yesterday that this weekend is Memorial Day weekend, and the weather looks like it will be at least reasonable. That will be nice. Then I plan to stay through the next week. There is a ferry from here to Fernandina Beach. It has not been running because of the weather, but I think I will take it over next week. I believe the Publix is in walking distance from the ferry dock and I will pick up more stuff if I need to.

The workboat tending the crab pots just made its round. They caught a couple in the one I saw come up. This is a nice boat and cruiser friendly place. I like it here.

Wednesday, May 27, 2009 9:33:02 AM

Location: St. Marys, GA

This is a nice quiet little town to stop and stay in for a while. It has been a nice break to unwind and get some initial things done to re-enter the US. My plan is to move *Jenny* down the river to Cumberland Island Friday afternoon, catching the flood tide turn. The ebb current is too strong to ride out, so we will catch the last of the flood and the beginning of the ebb tide.

Then, because I want to ride the tide into Brunswick, I will anchor overnight by Cumberland Island and head out the next day. The weather is supposed to be perfect with one-foot waves and no wind. That will be nice. I discovered the need to add tidal planning to all the other considerations for making a passage along here. It is easy, but just another step.

I have many unknowns in my life right now and many choices to make. Loosing Mary has been a painful experience. This journey has otherwise been incredible. I would not hesitate to make the same choices again to step beyond the rim of my old life. I hope to be back on track with a new set of life goals by the end of the year. Perhaps with a new life partner I will be stepping beyond the rim again into some new adventure. Life is too short and precious to do otherwise.

Cruise Totals

Total recorded distance is 8123.68 nautical miles. Time underway was 90 days, 13 hours, 25 minutes. The average speed was 3.7 nautical miles / hour. Total fuel used during this period was 2887 gallons. The total fuel efficiency during this period was 1.33 gallons / hour, 2.81 nautical miles / gallon.

I budgeted $20,000 per year for daily living expenses and $10,000 for *Jenny's* needs. I easily stayed within this budget by remaining at anchor almost 100% of the time. Jenny's condition improved throughout the journey and also remained within the budget by doing all the maintenance work myself.

Please communicate with David using the following Email address.
David@BoatExec.com

Made in the USA
Middletown, DE
14 March 2024

50913252R00215